ADVICE FOR ADVISERS

Advice for Advisers (THIRD EDITION)

Empowering Your Residence Hall Association

NORBERT W. DUNKEL
and CINDY L. SPENCER

Association of College and University Housing Officers - International (ACUHO-I) • Columbus, OH

Association of College and University Housing Officers - International (ACUHO-I)
941 Chatham Lane, Suite 318
Columbus, Ohio 43221 USA

Additional copies of *Advice for Advisers* or other ACUHO-I titles can be ordered directly from the association Web site at www.acuho-i.org.

Publishers Cataloging-in-Publishing Data
Dunkel, Norbert W. 1956–
Spencer, Cindy L. 1959–
    Advice for Advisers: Empowering Your Residence Hall Association (3rd edition)
        p. cm.
    Includes bibliographical references
ISBN-10: 0-945109-10-5 (pbk.)
1. Student affairs services—United States—Administration. 2. Student Activities—United States. 3. Student Housing—United States. I. Title.
    LB2342.9 A38 2006
    378.1 983

Cover design by James A. Baumann.
Text design and typesetting by Jennifer Shoffey Forsythe.
Cover photo of University of Oregon students by Tenaya Meaux.

The paper used in this publication meets the minimum requirements of the American National Standard for Information Sciences—Permanence of Paper for Printed Library Materials. ANSI Z39.48–1992.

9 8 7 6 5 4 3 2 1

Contents

Acknowledgements

We would like to thank all of the housing professionals who serve as advisers. Whether you advise a hall government, a campus programming board, a Residence Hall Association, or an NRHH Chapter, you are giving your time and talent to student leaders providing them an opportunity to learn and grow.

We want to thank the chapter authors. By providing your time commitment, expertise, and experiences, others will have the use of these tremendous resources. We also want to thank James Baumann, ACUHO-I Director of Communications and Marketing, for designing the cover and coordinating the copy-editing and printing of this book.

Norb wishes to thank his wife, Kim, and son, Nicholas, for their continued support of his writing and traveling. I would also like to thank the University of Florida Inter-Residence Hall Association, Mayor's Council, National Residence Hall Honorary, and the National Information Center hosted at the University of Florida for six years. These student organizations have provided me through the student involvement the motivation, energy, and excitement to continue to strive to provide better services and programs. I also thank Mr. Jim Grimm the former Director of Housing at the University of Florida - I will miss our great lunch conversations, but your spirit of student involvement remains.

Cindy wishes to thank her colleagues and friends, at the University of North Dakota, and past institutions where she has worked, for their continued support, encouragement and guidance. It is because of the support and autonomy she has been given by current and past supervisors that has allowed her to grow as an adviser. She appreciates the support she has received to work with NACURH, Inc. and the time to travel to present workshops on advising. She wants to thank Renee Hauschulz for her assistance and support with this project, and her ongoing support of the student leaders at the University of North Dakota. Finally she would like to thank the students she has worked with on the various campuses, especially the Association of Residence Hall at UND and within NACURH for challenging her, and helping her to continue to grow as an adviser.

Preface

Advising is one of the most truly rewarding experiences for residence life staff. Interacting with students, watching them develop, and witnessing the camaraderie of the residence hall association provides benefits that go far beyond a paycheck. However, with those rewards comes a unique set of challenges.

Most advisers remember their days in college when they were the advisee. But what can be done to help them best transition into their new role as the adviser? What type of formal training is provided for them as they begin work with a new generation of students and a new set of issues? While residence life staff members are taught student development theory, learning theory, program development, higher education management, communication, and ethics in their graduate programs, little formal classroom instruction exists for advising. As a result most training for advisers has occurred in the form of hands-on experience or on-the-job training.

In recent years, though, more formalized training opportunities have developed for student advisers. One specific and widely popular program is the Adviser Recognition and Training Institute (ART) and the Master ARTist curriculum. The opportunity to have a standardized curriculum provided at conferences and on campuses has assisted the formalization of adviser training.

This third edition of *Advice for Advisers: Empowering Your Residence Hall Association* is intended to be another resource and training manual for residence life staff. This edition presents updates on core topics that were discussed in earlier editions while also addressing new topics that have become more prevalent.

• • •

In creating this book we looked to arrange information in a clear and logical manner so that each chapter builds upon the previous one. When complete, the reader has a total picture of the different facets of a residence hall association. To that end, we start with some simple definitions and roles that advisers play in successfully serving student groups while also maintaining a personal/professional balance. Next, authors identify and discuss the key issues and responsibilities of successful advising. Using national survey results, they compare adviser responsibilities as identified by advisers and RHA presidents. Departmental expectations, plus the importance of balancing training to address different skills and needs, is discussed, as well as the ART and Master ARTist curricula.

Later in the book, the authors begin to offer more specific advice for advisers. We begin to answer the question, "Can you describe your individual advising style?" and learn that advising is situational and requires the ability to adapt their style and focus on different aspects based on an understanding of group dynamics and individual needs. Additional chapters explore the link between residence hall government and organizational effectiveness, traditional and alternative organizational models of RHAs, and the need for different approaches when working with residence hall associations housed in residential learning communities affiliated with academic programs or other campus departments or organizations.

• • •

To truly understand the residence hall association, one must understand the students that make them up. For that reason, authors examine how to better motivate and recognize student leaders while also identifying the motives of students who become involved in residence hall organizations. We look to understand the characteristics of today's students beyond their mere demographics. We study the issues that currently face students (including alcohol and drug abuse, sexual misconduct, and higher education funding among others) and hold them up against a brief history of previous issues. This provides the opportunity to explore how higher education administrators handled student behaviors in the past. Also included in this chapter is a list of topics with which to involve students. These include hall policies, dining and menu options. After reading these sections of the book, would-be advisers will have a deeper understanding of the diverse issues students face and, hopefully, a feeling of optimism about how they will meet these challenges.

Along with understanding the students as individuals, the book also offers information about the benefits and challenges of working with groups. Understanding the benefits and challenges prepares students and full-time professionals for the realities and rewards of being group advisers. Learn the fundamental issues related to defining groups, group dynamics, and stages of group development.

• • •

In the later half of this book, the discussion turns to more nuts-and-bolts matters of advising a residence hall association. There is the important subject of money management, developing budgets identifying funding sources, and following solid business practices. Additional discussion looks at the selling of merchandise as a fund-raising device while also providing guidelines on the contemporary use of corporations, how to identify companies to work with, how to develop bids, the adviser's role in contracts, and types of products and services.

An entire chapter is dedicated to addressing legal issues – one of the most requested topics by advisers. It is written to help RHA advisers understand some of the many legal issues they might face, ranging from campus policies to federal laws.

Other topics of discussion include transportation and travel issues, advising conference delegations, programming, managing executive board officers, and assessment of the association itself. Authors also examine how residence hall associations develop relationships with various other campus organizations and why the development of these relationships is vital to organizational growth. Then there is the question of the use of technology when managing a residence hall association. Since the last edition of this book series, no area has developed more quickly than technology. Here you will find detailed information and definitions for technological terms that students frequently use but advisers may not understand. Suggestions are also provided for how RHAs can benefit from engaging technology as a regular aspect of organizations in daily and monthly functions.

Finally, information on professional development for advisers is presented. The role of the adviser is an integral element in the success of student organizations. With the help of this book, advisers can perform critical self assessments and then explore the numerous options for professional development that exist for new, as well as seasoned advisers.

Readers of this book will also note that several chapters include case studies, exercises, and additional materials that supplement the learning process. If you are using this book as part of a training class, please be sure to take advantage of these.

• • •

This book is a valuable tool and resource for all levels of staff members who advise residence hall organizations. It provides readers with a variety of research, theory, and hands on exercises to advance the knowledge and skills of RHA advisers. There are few roles more rewarding than serving as advisers to residence hall organizations. Always remember, "to advise is to touch a life forevermore."

January 2006

Norbert W. Dunkel   Cindy L. Spencer
University of Florida   University of North Dakota
Gainesville, Florida   Grand Forks, North Dakota

Foreward: Lessons Learned

Bob Tattershall

It was spring of 1981 when the residence hall students at the University of Wisconsin - Whitewater asked me for advice about bidding for the next year's National Association of College and University Residence Halls (NACURH) conference. I was a hall director then, and the students knew I had been the midwest regional director the previous year. My few bits of advice were helpful, and as the bid progressed, the students asked me to serve as the conference adviser if they received the bid. I said yes, and they won the bid.

The NACURH conference was not my first advising experience, but it was definitely my largest. Advising this event was a tremendous learning experience, as was being involved with NACURH. This book addresses many of the issues that I, or any adviser, must address.

Since I was a hall director, the university administration asked the central office program planner to co-advise the event with me. Although he knew very little about NACURH, his purpose was to make sure the housing operation was prepared to host the 1,000 delegates soon to arrive on campus. Being inexperienced, I assumed that my passion for residence hall government was all that was necessary to advise student groups and that I was the "real" adviser. But when the dining staff was reluctant to change a conference dining location and the athletic department was reluctant to allow the conference to use desirable facilities, I found out how important it was to have a "secondary" co-adviser. I was fortunate my colleagues were both forgiving despite my egotistical presumptions.

Later, after the seemingly normal turnover in student leaders, the programming chair for the event found herself virtually alone in scheduling conference sessions and audio-visual equipment prior to the conference program printing deadline. She alternately cried and hyperventilated over the impossible task facing her. I offered to help.

Scheduling conference sessions was more difficult than it sounds today as 1981 preceded the widespread use of personal computers. On a wall-sized piece of butcher-block paper we wrote room numbers, session titles, and audio visual needs from early one evening through 6 A.M. the next morning. I am not sure in which advising quadrant I was working that night (read chapter 4), nor am I sure that what I did that night fits any description of what advisers do. What I did know was that failure was not an option because the consequences were too drastic. I also knew that someone needed me, and I had absolutely nothing more important to do than help her succeed. I consider myself lucky that such a meaningful lesson in active advising occurred so early in my career.

The next month brought another learning experience when the conference chair delivered a rant at a staff meeting, the likes of which I had never witnessed previously or since. I had no inkling he thought he was the only person on staff who ever did anything. The statement was not true and it was not helpful, although he certainly was the glue holding everything together. He stormed out of the meeting after 15 minutes and I was left with a stunned group of people with only a few weeks until the conference. Directing the resulting conversation toward a recommitment on the part of everyone to host a successful conference was probably one of my finest hours as an adviser. I suppose all I did was let others say what they needed to say. I asked them to think about why they had become involved initially and how they wanted to remember the conference. That night, the UW-Whitewater students had it in their hearts to succeed. The lesson I learned was that if I asked questions that directed students back to a beginning, back to core beliefs and purposes, they would respond with strength and vision. I was fortunate to be thrust into a position where I had to find my own strength and vision, or I might never have known I had it in me.

Several years later, in 1988 while I was serving as NACURH Conference Resource Consultant (CRC), the National Board of Directors was considering a proposal to eliminate alcohol use at all NACURH conferences. As CRC, one of my primary concerns was to ensure that a sufficient number of institutions bid for the next conference. In my opinion, creating a rule that some institutions would not be willing to enforce might reduce the number of institutions interested in bidding. Of course, I was on the wrong side of history. Fortunately

I was not alone in advising the National Board of Directors.

Dr. Ken Stoner, NACURH adviser at that time, focused on the bigger picture: Alcohol was not necessary at student conference. This was an example when student leaders should be left to their own devices. I was ready to offer my "wisdom" on the topic, but fortunately someone wiser was around to teach me once again when to be quiet. Even after years of advising experience, I was about to make the mistake of speaking when I should have been listening. The potential to learn from someone older and wiser always exists.

In retrospect, I view my years as an adviser as ones filled with incredible triumphs and miserable failures. My ability to predict which moments would be successes and which would be failures was less than perfect. However, most of life's important moments occur without a plan or without awareness of the importance of the moment until the moment has long passed. I seldom have had more powerful learning opportunities as when I was assisting student leaders through organizational and personal problems. Nothing is as instrumental in understanding personal reality as having to get all messy in someone else's.

Good advising skills come through observing those who are successful advisers. I was fortunate to have learned advising by observing great advisers. Most housing administrators will be advisers because the role is listed as a responsibility on position descriptions in housing and residence life. The advising role comes almost as an aside to the "real" job. Uninitiated supervisors often assume that anyone can advise, and so they enlist the newest staff members to the task. Many serve as advisers even though they are overworked, underpaid, and do not welcome the "opportunity." My advising roles were extra tasks that came at a time when I was so busy that working only 40 hours a week seemed like vacation. The times I served as an adviser were the most thrilling moments of my career. My volunteer time paid me in ways that can't be measured by dollars and cents.

Readers of this book are lucky in ways that I was not. There were no books on advising in 1981, and a search of literature about advising then and now does not result in as much information on this subject as can be found in this book. The third edition of *Advice for Advisers* serves as the distilled wisdom of many current and former advisers. Wisdom and energy do not always occur at the same time in a career. Readers of this book have the opportunity to learn from advisers who have the wisdom— and from many who still have the energy! These veteran advisers have had great successes and made plenty of mistakes. From their successes and mistakes comes the great wisdom. Readers of this book skipped the first mistake. They did not go it alone; they invited a number of wise veterans along for the ride. At some point, professionals "earn" enough respect so that those around them do not seem to notice they are making just as many mistakes as they once did. Hang in there. Your turn to be a wise old fool will come. Enjoy, and never stop learning.

Bob Tattershall is director of housing and conference services at Washington State University. He served NACURH as regional director, national conference adviser, conference resource consultant, and national adviser.

1

First-Year Advising Challenges

Kevin "KD" Linkous

Advising residence hall student groups is unlike other areas of concentration in the residence life and student affairs professions. Very few graduate assistantships or classroom experiences focus solely on advising in a college residence hall environment. Nor do most campuses have staff positions that are strictly devoted to advising; instead, advising is tacked on as a job duty or is relegated to a committee. Most professionals who are thrust into the adviser role for the first time have only their own student leadership experiences to guide them. This chapter offers baseline roles and standards for advising and provides helpful hints and important suggestions.

What Is an Adviser?

Over the years, first-time residence hall advisers have asked the question, "What exactly is an adviser, and what does one do?" There is limited research and literature on advising, so the question is not easy to answer. *The American Heritage® Dictionary of the English Language, Fourth Edition* (Costello, 2000), defines an adviser as "a person or firm that offers official or professional advice to clients" or "an educator who advises students in academic and personal matters." This definition is too broad to hint at what the role of residence hall adviser involves or how complicated and stressful it can be for professionals tackling it for the first time.

Baseline Skills for New Advisers

Schuh (1984) states that the roles of advisers are rooted in building good working relationships with student groups based on mutual respect and genuine concern. The following skills are key to successfully serving student groups and mentoring student leaders.

Accessibility

Beyond making students active parts of the system and giving occasional inspirational support, often the most advisers can offer is simply to be available at crucial junctures. This is especially true in developmental stages when the availability and visibility of advisers are crucial to the initial success of groups. Early hands-on involvement builds foundations and boundaries for everyone (including advisers) and sets expectations regarding adviser involvement throughout the year. Students begin to gain confidence and quickly learn to take appropriate risks when they know advisers are readily available to support their decisions. Successful advisers make work schedules available to the student group's executive board and arrive on time for meetings.

Coaching

Advisers who are good coaches help groups become more effective. For instance, they can play devil's advocates by encouraging students to look at the bigger picture and see hidden issues. Student leaders are easily excited (positively and negatively) about various plans and goals. Although this excitement allows them to motivate the group, it also can get in the way of decision-making. To promote independence and self-sufficiency, it is important for student leaders and the organization to take ownership of decisions, but advisers can coach them through reflective questioning and "what if" scenarios. This coaching style helps students to reach better decisions independently for their constituents without blatant direction from advisers.

Motivating and Recognizing Student Leaders

Student leaders volunteer their time and service to organizations to build résumés or to fufill personal passions. Identifying specifically what motivates student volunteers reveals ways to keep students involved and motivated and suggests the best ways to recognize efforts. Recognizing efforts and showing appreciation can range from simply appearing at events to developing student leadership awards programs. Books and online resources exist for advisers to learn how to appreciate and recognize student leaders appropriately. *The 99 Ways to Recognize a Person,* a document published by The National Residence

Hall Honorary, is a good resource found at www.nrrh.org.

Researching and Assessing

Advisers who have good research and assessment skills can convey these skills to student leaders to help direct decision-making. Understanding how research benefits goal setting, program planning, and proposal creation and knowing the appropriate methodology (i.e., surveys, journaling, focus groups) to gather the needed information are useful leadership tools. Promoting assessment and research deters student leaders from making decisions unilaterally for groups and teaches them how to become effective change agents for their organizations. In doing so, they leave their mark on the organization, a lasting legacy.

Roles In Advising

Advising roles vary based on the nature of the residence hall student groups and the way a specific campus structures student government or residence hall organizations. The following descriptions represent various roles first-time advisers might assume.

Educator/Trainer/Visionary

Student leaders often have predetermined ideas of their roles in organizations. It is important for advisers to provide strong leadership education for student leaders. Building strong foundations prepares groups for development and team building, and establishes realistic expectations and a healthy level of trust along the way. Assessment and research skills, details about the administrative and clerical duties student leaders will undertake, and information gleaned from what strengths and areas for growth students historically exhibit are examples of topic areas covered by advisers during training. The sooner groups know purchasing procedures and guidelines, avenues of reporting, job responsibilities, departmental expectations of the adviser's role, and how organizations fit within departments, the sooner groups can start to develop goal and mission statements and begin planning. Training helps student leadership groups buy into collaborative visions and understand boundaries. Training also allows groups to set individual and group decision-making boundaries. Successful advisers reinforce the results of their initial training through ongoing training, evaluation, and recognition throughout the academic year.

Information Resource

Successful first-time advisers have information on hand to help student leaders reach goals, and they familiarize themselves with departmental procedures and campus resources. This calls for advisers to be more visible to campus constituents. Successful new advisers introduce themselves to other student organization advisers and department heads of campus services with which the student group will interact. These organizations include but are not limited to: campus printing, dining services, student unions, service learning organizations, career services, counseling and mental health centers, the dean of students office, campus government, multicultural affairs, and athletics. A college or university also has relationships with the surrounding community in which it resides, and successful advisers familiarize themselves with community resources that might benefit student leadership. The more relationships an advisers build, the more they will be able to support student leadership endeavors.

Successful residence hall government advisers are conversant with procedures and current events of the National Association of College and University Residence Halls (NACURH). NACURH has numerous resources available to national and international residence-hall governments. NACURH offers documents on leadership advising through the National Information Center (NIC), National Residence Hall Honorary (NRHH), and various regional and national leadership conferences throughout the year. These resources will assist advisers and residence hall leaders with developing strong programming initiatives, organizational structures and procedures, and ways of recognizing outstanding student contributions.

Financial Consultant

In any situation where money is involved, successful advisers understand their role in accounting for funds. Although students assume primary responsibility for planning and budgeting, advisers ultimately are responsible for the ethical and legal use of funds. Successful advisers convene regular meetings with organization treasurers or business managers and expect sophisticated levels of budgeting and accountability from student leaders. To help them achieve this level, advisers train leaders in the proper way to develop budgets before the budgets go to the general memberships for approval. Assisting students in mature and ethical management of funds while allowing them to create systems of financial record keeping and reporting helps develop leadership skills.

Some of the most sensitive financial planning issues involve securing funds to pay for group travel to conferences and workshops. Advisers provide support by letting student leaders know what timelines, policies and financial approval procedures are necessary for travel or event planning.

Counselor and Student Development Practitioner

Advisers go on developmental journeys with student residence hall leaders. In the course of these journeys, advisers become trusted professionals to whom students turn for more than just organizational advice. Once advisers establish relationships with student leaders, the students may ask for academic or personal advice, requests that are appropriate and important. Knowing student cognitive and social development theories is crucial. Understanding what students go through at different junctures in their college years makes it possible for advisers to support student leaders in more effective ways.

In *Mentor: Guiding the Journey of Adult Learners* (1999), author Laurent Daloz discusses various aspects of healthy and effective adviser/student relationships and the guiding principles needed when working closely with students. The primary task, Daloz says, is to engender trust. This requires, among other things, having strong listening skills and taking time out from other work responsibilities to enter the students' world.

Successful advisers allow students to understand and voice their views. By not offering quick solutions, advisers help student leaders handle the various levels of conflict stemming from their organizational decisions and other key life experiences. Coaching students in decision-making allows them to face conflict and grow from it. When student leaders face conflict and experience growth, advisers can identify positive moments, restate them, and praise student leaders for their efforts (Daloz, 1999).

Group Facilitator and Conflict Manager

Effective one-on-one interactions with student leaders require great skill, but different skills are needed to keep groups working well together. Successful advisers begin relationships by getting on agendas to offer leadership development activities during meetings throughout the year or by regularly acknowledging groups for ongoing accomplishments. Team development activities start with low-risk exercises like name games then progress to higher levels of team trust-building like values clarifications and individual peer recognition activities.

Members of a group will not always agree with the direction of the organization or with the opinions of individual leaders. According to Dunkel and Schuh (1998), Bruce Tuckman's Group Development model recognizes that conflict in a group is normal. Without it, a group cannot truly meet its full potential and function as a performing team. It is through what Tuckman calls "storming," or conflict, that a group learns to process disagreements and conflict to come together to make decisions that make everyone feel part of the group (Dunkel & Schuh, 1998).

Successful advisers allow groups to work through conflicts, but recognize that when conflicts become dysfunctional, they need to intervene. It might be appropriate, for instance, for advisers to remind student leaders of the expectations, mission, and goals they established in the beginning of the year, pointing out how the current situation keeps them from meeting their full potential. Advisers also could facilitate discussions and have groups establish boundaries and guidelines, especially if conflicts have become heated. By mediating, advisers provide students with frameworks and models for discussing conflicts. Students independently must find solutions, however. If advisers immediately step in and fix situations, groups will never learn how to move through adversity. If advisers assess that conflicts lie between individuals, but affect others in the group, they can suggest private caucuses between those in conflict. Knowing when to speak up and suggest avenues to reach goals makes effective conflict managers.

Departmental Liaison

From a university and departmental viewpoint, the most important role of an adviser is to be the link between the student leaders and the department. Advisers help ensure that student leaders have structure and make informed organizational decisions, but also that they are conduits for communication flow back to departments. Keeping communication going both ways generates more support from departmental constituents and gives students feedback about decisions or projects so they can reassess and develop better final products.

The main role of first-year advisers is to build relationships between the organizational leaders and departments, not to serve as professional informants. As liaisons, advisers may invite the appropriate student leaders to schedule regular meetings with department directors or appropriate professional leadership. Effective student leaders attend various professional staff meetings to give updates and organizational reports. If all requests from the organization to the supporting department are filtered through advisers, the students and the groups do not develop.

Issues Facing First-Time Advisers

First-time advisers make mistakes. Many supervisors of new advisers have limited experience with advising. First-time advisers often find themselves alone attempting to identify roadblocks that lie ahead. They may freshly remember what it was like to be a student leader, but are not yet clear about what advisers do. First-time advisers must pay attention to professional and personal issues that can arise.

Creating Balance

For first-time advisers, creating a personal and professional balance is difficult. Watching students interact is a valuable experience. However, most organizational planning and activities occur during evening and late hours. If advisers are expected to be in the office during the day to complete other departmental responsibilities and also be available to students at night for planning meetings and events, there is no time left for personal lives. If advisers live in student housing, it can be even more difficult. Advisers must establish the appropriate balance between job responsibilities and wellness opportunities. Being overly visible not only keeps advisers from needed down time but also hinders the development of organizations and leaders. Students worry that they cannot make plans or decisions without advisers present and may seek constant approval.

Many advisers offer personal contact numbers in cases of emergencies. That is appropriate, but it is important for both advisers and students to respect boundaries by defining clearly what constitutes an emergency. Successful advisers are visible and available when promised, and they offer appropriate support and encouragement. Students return the respect by using good judgment during time spent with advisers. These actions help student groups become self-directed, taking risks without constant approval. Taking these actions help advisers develop appropriate relationships with students.

Professional Student Advocacy

A common trap for many first-time advisers is not being good student advocates. Strong student advocates support both the department and the student organization without compromising either group. Before jumping into discussions with department heads or supervisors, successful advisers research departmental precedents related to particular requests, then provide student leaders with information so they can formulate appropriate proposals that include full information. Advisers help students create fair and realistic requests and proof proposals before submitting them to departments for support. Departments will be more likely to recognize the students' efforts and students will properly prepare advisers to explain to upper-level administrators the rationale behind their requests. Advisers teach student leaders how to choose requests and "battles" wisely. If they do not, the department loses confidence in the student leaders or advisers, or both.

Adviser Versus Friend

When student leaders and advisers build relationships, there is a fine line between good professional support relationships and friendship. Friendship in an advisory relationship can make it difficult for advisers to disagree with students or withhold support for inappropriate initiatives that students want. Sometimes students do not understand that advisers can be trusted persons without being friends. And advisers can sometimes be flattered by the desire of some students to become close. Above all, successful advisers must make sure they are not placed in unethical situations. Successful advisers educate and inform students about appropriate boundaries surrounding the relationship. Once students understand the difference between adviser and friend, advisers will less likely encounter these difficult situations.

Advising Versus Participating

Many first-year advisers base advising styles on personal student leadership experiences when they were the ones doing the work. They become too hands-on with their approach, taking learning experiences away from student leaders. Successful advisers understand that they do not control all situations or decisions that effect organizations. Coming to this understanding is a struggle for advisers who like to get things done efficiently and perfectly. Advisers must fight urges to complete organizational tasks which are the responsibilities of student leaders, instead they should step back and encourage students to make their own decisions on their own time.

When students are struggling, student leaders may seek the personal opinions of advisers. Advisers need to beware of this the tendency to voice personal opinions, which could affect the group's decisions. Instead, advisers need to use these opportunities to state the facts and ask appropriate questions, thus relegating the actual decisions to the group.

It is okay for students to fail. Students learn from less-than-successful outcomes. Advisers who tend to jump in and make sure events do not fail aren't doing students any favors. Instead, successful advisers let students evaluate processes to identify key areas where performance could be improved and encourage students to integrate those performance objectives into the group's next experience.

Conclusion

Advising is an intricate process for which housing and residence life personnel rarely are well-trained. Knowing the various skills and roles will help first-year advisers focus on productive interactions with student leaders.

TIPS FOR SUCCESSFUL ADVISERS

- Suggest and provide education on topics but do not make decisions for the organization.
- Establish strong rapport with and offer genuine care to the group while remaining professional student advocates.
- Be visible and available to students when promised and establish a healthy balance between personal wellness and student development.
- Give "advice," not "do."
- Use appropriate levels of challenge and reflective questioning to help leaders make the best decisions for the organization.
- Provide key information on campus, community, regional, and national resources available to the organization.
- Research appropriate methods of motivating and recognizing the student leadership to instill and develop team spirit and personal success.
- See student failures as learning opportunities.
- Offer appropriate services to the organization's financial officer to ensure that funds are spent wisely.
- Set realistic expectations with the group to make sure everyone is aware of boundaries and needs.
- Ask groups to establish missions, goals, and objectives and help set boundaries and focus for the year.
- Take time to know active members and be visible at organizational meetings and activities.
- Offer performance feedback during individual advising meetings to assist in leadership development.
- Share in the group's successes and failures but avoid being in the spotlight.
- Research historical performances by past leaders of the organization, including advising styles.
- Understand university and departmental expectations of the adviser's role and the philosophies governing those expectations.
- Know group and student development theories and methods so they can better understand and plan for growth of the organization and its individual members.

Advising can be one of the most rewarding professional experiences. By being involved, advisers see all aspects of student development and leadership initiatives. By finding the right balance, these relationships can become avenues for lifelong mentoring and learning. Professionals should never pass on an opportunity to become an adviser, a journey of rewards and learning.

References

Costello, R. B. (Ed.). (2000). *The American Heritage® Dictionary of the English language (4th ed.). Boston: Houghton Mifflin.*

Daloz, L. A. (1999). *Mentor: Guiding the journey of adult learners.* San Francisco: Jossey-Bass.

Dunkel, N. W., & Schuh, J. H. (1998). *Advising student groups and organizations.* San Francisco: Jossey-Bass.

Evans, N., Forney, D., & Guido-DiBrito, F. (1998). *Student development in college: Theory, research, and practice.* San Francisco: Jossey-Bass.

Schuh, J. (Ed.). (1984). *A handbook for student group advisors.* Publication number 37. Alexandria, VA: American College Personnel Association.

2

The Responsibilities of Advising

Allan Blattner & Casey Tullos

According to the studies of Astin (1977, 1985), Boyer (1987), Kuh and Schuh (1991), and Pascarella and Terenzini (1981), student success and satisfaction in college are directly related to student involvement in extracurricular activities. They also contend that students get involved in organizations and take on leadership roles for a variety of reasons. These include to satisfy a sense of belonging, purpose, or accomplishment; to make a difference; to develop transferable career skills; and to achieve personal growth in leadership abilities. Given that these outcomes are of vital importance to the collegiate experience, colleges and universities routinely assign advisers to clubs and organizations.

Advising residence hall associations (RHAs) is an extremely rewarding experience filled with exciting professional opportunities. At the same time, the experience also can be exhausting and frustrating. This chapter identifies key responsibilities of successful advising and discusses issues within these responsibilities.

Identification of Roles

In 1988, Kenneth Stoner, former adviser to the National Association of College and University Residence Halls (NACURH) identified 11 responsibilities of RHA advisers. In 1996, Norbert Dunkel and Diane Porter expanded Stoner's list to 30 potential responsibilities of RHA advisers. Dunkel and Porter surveyed RHA advisers and presidents from 350 NACURH-affiliated institutions who rated the importance of these adviser responsibilities. Based on the results, the following were identified as the 10 most important adviser responsibilities:

Advisers' Responses

1. Meet with RHA executive board
2. Serve as an information resource
3. Interpret university policies
4. Attend meetings and activities
5. Motivate and encourage members
6. Understand student/group theories and models
7. Know the steps to develop a program
8. Provide continuity for the organization
9. Orient new officers to their roles and responsibilities
10. (tie) Reward and recognize others
    (tie) Understand how diversity affects the RHA

RHA Presidents' Responses

1. Meet with the RHA executive board
2. Attend meetings and activities
3. Serve as an information resource
4. Interpret university policies
5. Motivate and encourage members
6. Understand how diversity affects the RHA
7. Know the steps to develop a program
8. Attend regional and national conferences
9. Understand student/group development
10. Possess knowledge of NACURH and its services

Activity One at the end of the chapter is a useful tool that advisers and students can use as a conversation starter to help identify and clarify the roles of the adviser. This activity can assist in establishing expectations early in the year or in identifying and addressing problem areas later in the year.

Roles Within Context

After a 20-year study of group development, Tuckman and Jensen (1977) concluded that as groups grow and develop, they go through certain identifiable and predictable stages. These growth stages relate to the groups' purposes and interpersonal relationships that develop between group members. The stages are Orientation (Forming), Dissatisfaction (Storming), Resolution (Norming), Production (Performing), and Termination (Adjourning).

When student membership turns over, new members repeat Tuckman's stages and create life cycles. Members exhibit varying levels of skill and energy at different stages. Successful advisers are attentive to the life cycles of the groups they advise and to the members' levels of skill and energy in order to adapt roles to meet the current needs of organizations. For example, an RHA with low-energy membership that lacks experience or leadership skills may have very different needs from an RHA that has a highly enthusiastic membership and a knowledgeable, committed executive board. Recognizing the need to focus the enthusiasm of newly elected executive groups, advisers may spend considerable time meeting with individual students to build relationships and explain university policies. On the other hand, advisers with well-established student leaders engage primarily in listening to students' ideas and encouraging them to take action.

Activity Two at the end of the chapter is a series of four scenarios designed to serve as structured reflections for examining shifting roles of advisers at various group stages.

Using the previous information as a foundation, the following is a detailed look at six key adviser roles using organizational life cycles as rubrics to understand roles better.

Executive Board Guide

Advisers work with executive boards in a variety of ways: building teams; setting expectations and goals; communicating regularly and effectively; recognizing strengths and weaknesses; reflecting on organizational, academic, and personal issues; and evaluating programs and processes. The extent to which each of these areas can be explored depends on executive board members' skills and experiences.

Meeting regularly is important to advisers and executive board members. Meetings can be with the entire executive board, individual board members, or both. Ideally, advisers and executive board members meet together prior to general meetings to review agenda items, to seek input, and to address any questions or issues in preparation for general meetings. This is the time for advisers to ask the difficult questions regarding anything controversial that might arise in meetings. With highly skilled executive boards, advisers feel comfortable with the boards' ability to facilitate general meetings after pre-meetings adjourn. When executive boards are less experienced, it is important that boards have enough information to run general meetings with a clear understanding that they can rely on advisers for backup.

Successful advisers schedule individual weekly meetings with presidents to set goals and expectations, evaluate the progress of the executive board and the RHA membership, discuss solutions to potential problems, and plan for upcoming programs and events. These individual meetings give presidents opportunities to discuss new ideas with advisers, clarify information before sharing with executive boards, and discuss personal, academic, RHA, or executive board concerns. Through regularly scheduled individual meetings, advisers and presidents continue to establish and develop relationships. Depending on the skill levels of individual executive board members, similar meetings between advisers and other executive board members such as treasurers, programmers or national committee coordinators may be helpful.

Meetings and Activities Supporter

RHA presidents ranked attending meetings and activities second. The high ranking of this adviser responsibility indicates that it is very important to students that advisers be visible and show support for events and programs. As such, it is optimal to schedule meetings during times when both advisers and the executive board members can attend. When advisers cannot attend every meeting, executive board members need to be empowered and trusted to proceed in the absence of advisers.

Participation in programs and activities provides advisers with opportunities to visit with RHA members and other students in informal settings, thus helping students establish positive relationships with housing administrators. It is also important that advisers attend programs and activities to be of assistance if problems arise with such things as contracts, facilities, performers, and police. As institutional representatives, advisers ensure the health and well-being of students who attend programs or activities. Because many meetings and activities occur after work hours, this role can become taxing on advisers. Therefore, advisers and executive board members must set clear priorities and expectations about which programs advisers need to attend.

Information Resources Provider

Advisers are information resources providers on diverse topics including group conflict, organizational history, leadership skills training, and campus policies. Additionally, advisers inform student organizations about upcoming campus events, projects, or decisions that may influence students in the residence halls.

Time and energy spent executing various roles directly correlate to each organization's place in its life cycle. Successful advisers recognize student leaders' skill levels when deciding how and when to get involved. Experienced student leaders often know when they need additional information or clarification and will ask advisers for assistance. However, some experienced leaders can become overconfident or will not seek advice for fear it shows weakness. Leaders with less experience may need advisers to offer assistance more readily to save them from always needing to ask. When providing information, advisers offer just enough information to answer questions or address issues and are careful not to take control from the students.

University Policy Interpreter

As interpreters of college or university policy, advisers assist student organizations with understanding boundaries and developing plans to negotiate obstacles. Imagine the disappointment of RHA members when much anticipated late-night parties are cancelled because they did not get approval to have amplified sound after quiet hours have begun. Similar situations frequently occur when student organizations are full of energy and ideas but have not planned programs within campus policies or procedures. Successful advisers consult with campus authorities such as the director of housing or dean of students to provide RHAs with accurate information.

Another important aspect of policy interpretation is helping students make sense of the rules that govern RHAs. By highlighting the benefits of particular policies or explaining why certain procedures are in place, advisers demonstrate that most rules are actually effective rather than arbitrary or unfair. If RHA members understand that quiet hour policies exist to protect the primary rights of students to sleep and study without interference, they will understand why they must have approval to host late-night events that could potentially impact those primary rights. With increased awareness of university policies and deeper understanding of the reasons for particular rules and procedures, RHA members expand their ability to effectively plan events, relying less on advisers and more on their own troubleshooting skills.

Motivator and Encourager of Members

When surveyed by Dunkel and Porter, RHA presidents and advisers agreed that motivating and encouraging RHA members are two of the most important responsibilities for advisers. As motivators and encouragers, advisers lead by example. By fostering organizational environments that encourage the contributions of individual members, advisers teach RHA executive board members to value the participation and involvement of the general membership. Advisers encourage RHA executive board members by praising efforts and by challenging and providing support when they fail to reach their goals. Continuous encouragement from advisers helps executive board members face the highs and lows of leading student organizations.

To motivate student leaders effectively, advisers actively develop relationships with individual students. Each student is the best source about what he or she needs to stay enthusiastic about and committed to an organization. To tap into this valuable information, advisers structure opportunities through individual meetings and group outings in which students can reveal more of who they are and what they want to achieve. Ultimately, attention paid to individual students by advisers contributes to feelings of belonging and is essential for retaining and energizing RHA executive board members.

Keeper of Organization History

Another adviser responsibility is unofficial historian. Technically, student members of organizations fill the role of historian. Throughout each academic year, student historians play vital roles in documenting organizations' successes through pictures, newsletters, and information posted on web sites. However, from academic year to academic year, advisers provide organizations with continuity.

As keepers of the histories of organizations, advisers are responsible for ensuring that members know when and how organizations were formed. When organizations struggle to maintain consistent leadership, advisers communicate important information about operating procedures and programming traditions that might otherwise be lost or forgotten. Students have short-term views of organizations. Knowing an organization's history and accomplishments instills members with a sense of pride and energizes them to maintain the organization's momentum.

Actions to Avoid

While the focus of this chapter has been on six adviser responsibilities as identified by advisers and RHA presidents, it is equally important to describe two actions that inhibit successful advising.

Advisers do not run student organizations. Organizations are mechanisms students use to voice concerns, make policy suggestions and changes, and provide services and programs for fellow residents. Advisers have different forums to voice personal concerns about university policies, programs, and services on a more professional level. It is not appropriate for advisers to use student organizations for personal gain.

Advisers do not make decisions. Students have the rights and the capability to make decisions. Successful advisers seldom reverse student decisions. If student decisions violate university policies or break laws, advisers help students make alternate decisions. If decisions have serious financial ramifications, advisers help students think through their decisions. Advisers may ask challenging questions to encourage students to think about the implications of decisions. This can be done without making decisions for students. Most of the time, students will make the right decisions if advisers guide them through the process, empower them to make decisions, and trust them.

Conclusion

Each advising experience is unique and requires individualized application of the roles identified in this chapter. By understanding the roles and how they apply in each phase of the organizational life cycle, advisers will be prepared to help student organizations succeed. More importantly, advisers will be positioned to help students achieve personal goals and realize lifelong benefits of campus involvement.

References

Astin, A. (1977). *Four critical years*. San Francisco: Jossey-Bass.

Astin, A. (1985). *Achieving academic excellence*. San Francisco: Jossey-Bass

Boyer, E.L. (1987). *College: The undergraduate experience in America*. New York: Harper & Row.

Dunkel, N. W., & Porter, J. D. (1998). Residence hall association adviser responsibilities. *Journal of College and University Student Housing, 27*(2), 15–19.

Dunkel. N. W., & Schuh, J. H. (1998). *Advising student groups and organizations*. San Francisco: Jossey-Bass.

Kuh, G. D., & Schuh, J. H. (1991). *The role and contribution of student affairs in involving colleges*. Washington, DC: National Association of Student Personnel Administrators.

Pascarella, E. T., & Terenzini, P. T. (1991). *How college affects students*. San Francisco: Jossey-Bass.

Stone, K. (1988). *Residence hall advisor outline*. Unpublished manuscript.

Tuckman, B.W. & Jensen, M.A.C. (1977) Stages of small group development revisited. *Group and organizational studies, 2*, 419–427.

Activity One

PART ONE: Adviser Self-Reflection

For each item listed below, rate its importance as a responsibility of an RHA adviser on a scale of 1 (low) to 5 (high).

It is the adviser's responsibility to:	IMPORTANCE				
	Low				High
1. Serve as an information resource	1	2	3	4	5
2. Motivate and encourage members	1	2	3	4	5
3. Be a problem-solving agent	1	2	3	4	5
4. Maintain organizational records	1	2	3	4	5
5. Set goals	1	2	3	4	5
6. Provide vision	1	2	3	4	5
7. Attend meetings and activities	1	2	3	4	5
8. Run an RHA meeting	1	2	3	4	5
9. Reward and recognize others	1	2	3	4	5
10. Evaluate student volunteers	1	2	3	4	5
11. Orient new officers to their roles and responsibilities	1	2	3	4	5
12. Provide continuity for the organization	1	2	3	4	5
13. Recruit and retain members	1	2	3	4	5
14. Guarantee success of programs and activities	1	2	3	4	5
15. Be responsible for officer elections	1	2	3	4	5
16. Be an interpreter of university policies	1	2	3	4	5
17. Confront negative behavior	1	2	3	4	5
18. Know how to host a conference	1	2	3	4	5
19. Be a financial manager	1	2	3	4	5
20. Understand student/group development theories/models	1	2	3	4	5
21. Possess knowledge of legal issues	1	2	3	4	5
22. Know *Robert's Rules of Order*	1	2	3	4	5
23. Understand how diversity affects the RHA	1	2	3	4	5

It is the adviser's responsibility to:	IMPORTANCE				
	Low				High
24. Understand fundraising	1	2	3	4	5
25. Know the national and regional bid and award processes	1	2	3	4	5
26. Possess knowledge of NACURH and its services	1	2	3	4	5
27. Attend regional and national conferences	1	2	3	4	5
28. Meet with RHA executive board	1	2	3	4	5
29. Know how to conduct a programming needs assessment	1	2	3	4	5
30. Know the steps to develop a program	1	2	3	4	5

Based on your answers, select the five most important responsibilities of an RHA adviser. List them below in order of importance:

1.

2.

3.

4.

5.

PART TWO: Clarification with Group Members

Have members of the RHA complete the same survey and then compare the rankings. Based on all the responses, answer the following questions:

1. What do members perceive to be the most important adviser responsibilities?

2. Which responsibilities did you agree upon? Disagree?

3. How did the adviser's top five responsibilities compare? Top 10?

4. What issues need to be clarified and/or addressed given this information?

Activity Two

The following four scenarios describe an RHA at various points during its life cycle. In each scenario, try to identify the skill level (high or low) and the energy level (high or low) presented by the student members. Once participants have identified where the organization is in its life cycle, they need to consider how time spent in the various advising roles could be balanced in order to assist the group.

Scenario 1

RHA is a popular organization on campus. The current president has been an active member of the organization for two years. With some help from her adviser, she planned an executive board retreat where she and other board members set goals and planned events for the year. The general membership of the organization is excited about the organization because they see their ideas implemented into programs for their residence halls. Attendance at meetings is consistent and students are often overheard commenting on how productive and helpful the meetings are. The adviser is pleased because general students seem to be engaged and executive members understand their individual roles in the organization.

Scenario 2

RHA is a well-respected organization on campus. In previous years, the organization developed a reputation for always offering new and creative programs to a wide variety of students. However, the current executive board seems satisfied with continuing past programs rather than creating anything new. Most of the executive members are in their second or third year of service to the organization. General meetings are well-organized and attended by a core group of students. The organization does not seem to be attracting new members. The adviser is concerned that he is spending much of his time encouraging executive members to involve RHA representatives and hall council officers in generating ideas and planning programs.

Scenario 3

RHA is one of the oldest organizations on campus. Despite the organization's longevity, the organization is seeing its active membership decline. During spring elections, all of the candidates for executive positions ran unopposed.

Foregoing their usual planning retreat, the executive members have been using their weekly meetings to brainstorm program ideas leaving little time to conduct other business. General meetings average six or seven representatives rather than the 20 or 30 representatives who regularly attended in previous years. The adviser has noticed that executive members seem to communicate with each other only at the weekly meetings. He frequently finds himself following up on details so that RHA programs do not fail.

Scenario 4

RHA is increasing its presence on campus. The current executive board's goal is to ensure that every residential student knows he or she is a member of the organization. During their planning retreat, executive members pledged to actively involve each residential student in at least one RHA program during the year. Attendance at general meetings is up from previous years with 40 residents attending last week's meeting. Residents have been encouraged to share suggestions for programs whenever they see an executive board member. One month into the semester, RHA has yet to finalize a calendar of events. The adviser is concerned that the executive board is more excited about generating ideas than they are about actually planning and implementing specific projects.

3

Training Advisers

Julie McMahon & Sean J. Pierce

Providing training for advisers of residence hall governments is often an afterthought to schedules that focus on opening buildings for students' arrival. However, initial fall training and ongoing training is necessary to ensure the success of advisers and the groups they advise.

Before training schedules for advisers can be established, departmental adviser expectations need to be clearly identified. Adviser expectations are rarely established at the discretion of individuals, but rather collective decisions of professional staff within housing departments. Setting departmental adviser expectations impacts not only how adviser training is approached, but how extensive the training is. Typically, if staff members have advising listed as primary responsibilities on job descriptions, training focuses on all aspects of group dynamics and developmental theory; however, if advising is not a primary responsibility, adviser training is often a lower priority and not considered as crucial as conflict mediation and judicial training.

Advising student organizations is a task often delegated to entry-level professionals. Entry-level professionals have little to no advising experience but may have experiences as student leaders. A lack of advising experience places a burden upon the coordination of adviser training because there is often a lack of experienced advisers to lead training efforts. This situation can create an atmosphere of uncertainty, as new advisers may not understand adviser roles and may not know available resources. Other challenges related to delegating or assigning adviser duties include perceptions of lower or higher status advising duties related to the groups advised and equitably distributing workloads to co-advisers.

Adviser training needs to be incorporated into the overall staff training agenda to foster understanding as well as support from colleagues not advising student organizations. At various times, advising demands become overwhelming. The sense of being overwhelmed can be alleviated by creating supportive environments in which advisers can look to colleagues for assistance. Advising needs to be taken seriously, as the interaction with student organizations often affects not only departmental assessment, but overall staff recruitment as well. Future student staff members in housing and students affairs are often recruited from student organizations advised by the staff. It is imperative that advisers receive training, as they are often the first point of contact for the department.

This chapter discusses planning, scheduling, and facilitating initial and ongoing adviser training.

Identifying and Targeting Audiences

Identifying audiences is critical in all training, and adviser training is no different. Entry-level advising staff requires more comprehensive training than mid-level or veteran staff. Prior advising experience also dictates the depth of training. It is challenging to involve and engage entire groups at various stages of advising experience and ability. Training sessions and the organization of the training schedule varies greatly depending on the number of advisers, the staff level of advisers, and the advising experiences of advisers. Assessment of adviser skills may include informal personal conversations with advisers and supervisors to determine advising experiences and training expectations; roundtable discussions with veteran RHA advisers and hall or area level government advisers; and discussions with senior-level administrators.

All staff that advise student organizations or supervise others who advise student organizations should be included in adviser training. Inviting higher-level administrators or veteran advisers to attend adviser training offers them the opportunity to share experiences and visibly show support and commitment to developing student leaders. Inviting peer colleagues of advisers offers them the opportunity to support co-workers, while experiencing professional development.

Coordinators of adviser training need to address differences between supervising and advising. Often, new advisers juggle the demands of supervising student staff with the demands of advising student organizations. The responsibilities and approaches between supervising and advising differ in many ways. The most obvious difference is that student staff positions typically are compensated positions whereas student leader positions are volunteer positions.

Staff who volunteer or who are tapped to advise often have wide varieties of career and advising experiences. Coordinators of adviser training should not assume that advisers know everything or know nothing. A better approach is to set purposes or goals of training and address the knowledge and experience differences of advisers within the scope of training.

Most adviser training lends itself to lumping all levels and experiences of advisers together when information is relayed. However, key differences between groups must be addressed by facilitators. Professional staff adviser training may include greater emphasis on theories, philosophies, and core beliefs of the residential life programs. Graduate and undergraduate adviser training typically focuses on the "nuts and bolts," such as constitution writing, budget development and expenditures, and running meetings. As hall government student leader training typically occurs immediately after the opening of halls for the academic year, all training must include basic advising skills, overviews of universities and housing departments, the histories of student organizations, and the basic premise of "letting students take control."

Many professional staff members have previous adviser experience as graduate students. When training professional staff, coordinators of training may approach topics from the standpoint of the adult learning perspective and pitch from the middle. This allows facilitators to place value on the experiences of veteran staff and advisers while presenting knowledge to the middle ground. This approach tends to avoid boring those with lots of advising experience, while important information is relayed to all. Professional staff training can be roundtable format. Training coordinators need to identify what professional staff advisers need to know and create presentations to meet those needs. Often, professional staff is the most challenging group to train, as experience levels vary from no advising experience to many varied advising experiences at multiple universities.

Graduate advisers are open to more theoretical conversations during training. They often are learning about developmental theory and experiential growth in class. Prior experience is often limited, so facilitators need to be wary of assumed knowledge and address topics like conflict mediation with organization members, defining boundaries with students, and modeling appropriate behaviors.

Undergraduate student adviser training typically is more intensive. Undergraduate advisers have little knowledge or experience. Facilitators must explore every aspect of the topics and clearly define them. Often undergraduate advisers base advising style on previous personal experiences. What they define as "good" and "bad" advising may need to be addressed related to departmental adviser expectations. They may focus on a poor adviser experience they faced as a student leader. They may present with "all knowing wisdom" attitudes. A proven training approach is for facilitators to present best practices related to advising in an educational manner.

Adviser Training Calendar

Initial adviser training tends to occur in late summer prior to fall openings for full-time professional or graduate assistant staff. Adviser training builds upon a training framework that easily can be transferred to advising experience. Addressing topics such as ice breakers and team builders followed by studying the organizational structure of groups and ending with a review of group dynamics and developmental theory allows advisers to ease into the topic of advising without feeling overwhelmed. Dedicated time each month for training on advising issues provides an excellent venue for ongoing training. See Figures 1 and 2.

A topic for training may also include the "cycles" for the year. Many organizations begin in excitement or honeymoon phases, and advisers share that energy. As the year continues, the energy of some groups begins to wane and students stop attending meetings and events. It is important to address this phenomena and share ways to keep advisers motivated, which will subsequently help keep student organizations motivated. When groups lose motivation, advisers help with the energy rather than educate.

Adviser Training Topics

Utilizing the sample agenda in Figure 1, a curriculum might include approximately six hours of initial adviser training over sessions held in July and August. Successful initial adviser training schedules include introductions to organizational structure and incorporate RHA executive board members into training where they meet advisers and lead some presentations.

Staff members with Adviser Training and Recognition (ART) certification can be tapped to offer the ART sessions to staff when attendance at conferences where ART is traditionally presented is not feasible. Figure 2: Sample Monthly Training Schedule for Hall/Area Government Advisers includes the ART core curriculum and three electives which provides Novice Certification for advisers who complete the course work and experiential requirements. ART sessions provide real case studies, as well as address group development

and diversity. ART curriculum can assist coordinators of adviser training in setting expectations and goals. ART courses also aid in designing and implementing
teambuilding for student organizations.

Incorporating one-day, on-campus leadership retreats in September for
advisers is helpful. September retreats can focus on adviser training after halls
have opened when advisers can focus on discussions without being distracted
by opening preparation chaos.

Further clarification of key topics follows.

Communication

Successful adviser training includes strategies and techniques to build and
support communication between housing and student organizations. Student
organization updates should occur during departmental staff meetings, and
departmental updates should occur during student organization meetings. Student leaders may discuss upcoming events and organization progress. During
student organization executive board and general assembly meetings, advisers
may discuss upcoming department and university-wide projects and events to
keep students informed. Formally and intentionally supporting this communication exemplifies the importance of student organizations and advising to
students and staff, and promotes the reciprocal flow of information.

Philosophy, History, and Purpose

Adviser training also includes departmental philosophy and organizational
philosophy, history and purpose. Facilitators of these topics can include traditions and programmatic successes on campus. The National Residence Hall
Honorary is an organization that vastly differs from campus to campus. For
this reason, NRHH role and scope on specific campuses should be included
in adviser training. Facilitators need to be prepared to address advising vs.
co-advising, conference advising, and attendance expectations as well as committee involvement. Numerous student development theories focus on group
development and are addressed in higher education and student personnel curricula, but not all advisers now working in housing and residence life majored
in these academic disciplines.

Ethics and Conflict

Sessions on ethics and other teachable moments will bring the human element
to training programs. These sessions can be addressed in ongoing training
beyond initial summer training. While these topics are often addressed during
supervision training, they are not often addressed as issues for advising student
organizations.

Advisers may be "drama club" advisers, as well as RHA advisers. Differing student groups experience conflict as they typically are comprised of students from varying levels of psychosocial development. Advisers need to understand that conflicts between groups will arise and are healthy within reason. Providing case studies during adviser training allows advisers to identify and discuss ways of handling various student group conflict in an experiential format.

Training Topic Placement

After staff identify and communicate departmental advising expectations, those coordinating adviser training can determine training agendas. Strategic topic placement on agendas is important. Topics placed at the end of the day are perceived as less important as those that lead off the day. Topics placed early on agendas can be forgotten by the time information is needed. Placing topics late in training may not allow for preparations needed prior to opening and the beginning of the academic year.

Other Training Opportunities

Various resources are available to assist advisers with professional development beyond home campuses.

Ongoing professional development for advisers is available at a variety of conferences. Both student conferences and professional conferences offer program tracks aimed at assisting advisers with honing skills and sharing experiences. Conferences allow advisers to meet and network as well as to learn different approaches to developing advising style.

Also, the Adviser Recognition and Training Institute (ART) provides advisers opportunities to develop advising skills and to share expertise with new advisers. ART sessions are available at state, regional, and national student conferences coordinated through the National Association of College and University Residence Halls (NACURH). ART basic curriculum consists of the completion of five core components, the completion of three of seven electives, and three experiential requirements. See Figure 3 for descriptions of sessions and requirements for certification as an ARTist. The Master ARTist curriculum, developed in 2003, allows veteran advisers opportunities to continue advising professional development. Master ART curriculum consists of the completion of five additional master core components, additional advising experience, presentation of two ART programs, and publication of an adviser-related article in a regional or national publication. See Figure 4 for descriptions of master sessions and the requirements for certification as a master ARTist.

Resources for Advisers

Books and the Internet are excellent resources for advisers. Successful professionals build personal libraries of personal and professional development resources. Many personal libraries include books from undergraduate and graduate classes kept for future reference. Books like *Advice for Advisers* exist to provide advisers of all levels of experience with opportunities to continue self-directed professional development. Advisers can read this book from cover-to-cover, by chapters of interest, or as a reference when specific needs arise. Some chapters are written specifically for student organization advising, while others are written from the broader approach of human development and group interaction.

Several websites exist related to housing staff professional development and student leader development. Among them are the sites for the Association of College and University Housing Officers – International (*www.acuho-i.org*), Resident Assistant.com (*www.residentassistant.com*), ResLife.net (*www.reslife. net*), and Student Affairs.com (*www.studentaffairs.com*).

These websites offer ideas and suggestions for group development and programming, host information regarding conferences, and provide resource information to build professional libraries.

Other Adviser Training Considerations

When advisers have varied experiences, some will have the attitude that they are being re-trained. Coordinators of adviser training must develop training targeted to the individual. They need to emphasize to advisers that the overall goal of adviser training is to provide support for student groups. Often the first role of advisers is to get groups started by organizing hall level elections at the beginning of the academic year. Adviser roles may evolve and be re-defined in regards to interactions with the group. Advisers need to self-identify as hands-on or hands-off then be able to identify the pros and cons of each advising style.

Each institution varies in the composition of student groups and organizations. While most campuses share the traditional model of an RHA and individual hall or area governments, some institutions have other models. Coordinators of adviser training should keep in mind that most advisers are familiar with traditional models. If a program varies from traditional models, they need to share the history and rationale for decisions leading to less traditional models so that advisers can understand and support the concepts.

Hall council advisers should meet with RHA advisers monthly. All advisers need to be reminded to guide, not control, student groups. New professionals and graduate students may struggle with embracing their new roles as advisers while letting go of past roles as student leaders. Knowing when to step back and when to jump in and offer personal experiences for "teachable moments" is challenging to new professionals and graduate students. Keeping simplified approaches to adviser training with graduate staff or undergraduate staff recognizes that not all staff plans to pursue housing or student affairs as careers. For many larger institutions, systems may be so complex that graduate staff may understand their roles as advisers just before they graduate, and there is little continuity of advisers from year to year.

Successful advisers recognize and account for personal values that may differ from group values and group values that may differ from departmental values. All advisers need to be taught acceptable language for inclusive programming. Students will not always understand why programs such as "White Trash BBQs," "Redneck Olympics," or "Date Auctions" are not appropriate program promotions or how these programs are offensive to others.

Group Development Training

The adviser role in group development training is paramount. Advisers need to familiarize themselves with institution policies and procedures. These policies and procedures range from topics as basic as programming requirements and space reservations to those as challenging as legal issues and contracts. Often, advisers assume complete responsibility for the student organizations they advise. This responsibility is great and needs to be regarded as such.

Advisers should initiate the idea of training retreats with executive boards to promote planning for the upcoming year, as well as team building and unification. Assisting groups with planning of retreats involves more than selecting dates and locations. Generating of agendas, group needs assessments, and determining roles and responsibilities during retreats are just as important.

Ice breakers and team builders have large impacts on group development because they aid students in building trust and identifying strengths. Successful advisers constantly expand their group activity repertoires so as not to fall into the pattern of repeating the same activities. Working with executive boards to identify needs may seem simple, yet it is often overlooked. Once group strengths and areas of improvement are assessed, advisers can create training plans that continually build upon one another. At the completion of retreats, it is important for advisers to work with executive boards to determine future needs of groups based upon the outcomes of retreats.

The role of students in the training process should not be overlooked. They need to work with advisers to continually assess the needs of organizations.

This is a difficult task for students as they are not always prepared to be critical of themselves or their peers. Advisers can assist in this process by having students evaluate their familiarity with various members and the overall cohesiveness of the group. Once assessments have been accomplished, advisers can assist students with plans to incorporate ongoing group development throughout the academic year.

At the beginning of the year, either during retreats or within the first few weeks of school, students need to set goals for the coming year. Advisers need to assist them in brainstorming goals and creating action plans. One strategy is to have students list goals and identify the steps necessary in order to achieve the goals. Reviewing goals on a regular basis allows students to identify progress and adjust as necessary.

Another assessment option is to have student leaders solicit feedback from members related to overall group successes and failures. This can be done on a regular basis at general meetings or by surveying the group at given intervals. Student-leaders compile feedback and share with advisers feelings and general consensus. Student leaders can then work with advisers to strengthen, build, and maintain their organizations.

Diversity training is challenging with student groups. Increasing numbers of students are coming to campuses from varying cultures with different ideals and belief systems. Adviser and student leader training needs to include diversity training. Diversity training addresses issues such as inclusive programming, heterosexist programming, and traditions. Many new advisers struggle with the language needed to effectively express the importance of diversity to organizations, departments, and institutions.

It's important to recognize the hard work of student leaders. Student organizations are made up of officers who, depending on specific organizational structure, may be volunteers or may be compensated. Accountability of student-leaders may be viewed differently depending upon compensation issues and needs to be understood and addressed. Regardless, recognition is crucial to promoting the morale of students and retaining them in future positions.

Student session topics for group development are often similar to adviser training topics though the depth and scope of the topics differs. In fact, advisers can modify their adviser training materials or use the materials as a framework to effectively educate student leaders. Advisers need to address these topics with student leaders throughout the academic year:

- Programming (planning, implementing, and evaluating)
- Department philosophy

- Recognition (NRHH and OTMs)
- Community development – roles of Hall Council vs. Area Government vs. the RHA
- Student empowerment
- Leadership models
- Group Development
- Parliamentary procedure and running efficient meetings
- Money management

Housing Department Role

Because of the diversity of campus and housing department structures, it is difficult to generalize about the housing department's role within student organizations. Some housing departments fully fund student organizations, while others do not provide any financial assistance at all – and all points between. Student organizations may rely solely on fundraising efforts or support from other organizations on campus, such as campus-wide student governments. All housing organization roles and relationships have rewards and challenges.

Organizations that are fully funded by housing departments face many challenges. If housing departments solely provide financial support, student program efforts may require higher-level approval when funding is requested. Additionally, student organizations might be required to adhere to more stringent policies and procedures than other student organizations because of the level of housing organization involvement.

Advising RHAs may be part of job descriptions and considered to be very important to housing departments; however, housing departments may not provide any financial assistance to student organizations. Many reasons could explain the discrepancy. Institutions may have specific regulations guiding how monies can be distributed and spent, and supporting student organizations could be in violation of those policies. Conversely, housing departments philosophically may believe that student organizations are more frugal and appreciate earned money more so than money received as guaranteed handouts. If students rely on support from other student organizations, advisers need to fully understand how to secure funds for the next year, typically through a budget request process, and be able to effectively share information with groups they advise at the right time.

Advisers are challenged to explain housing department role and support differences when students attend state, regional, and national conferences and compare their situations with student groups from other institutions. These comparisons can result in frustration for those student organizations who receive little or no support from housing departments. Students rarely understand that each campus is unique and has positive attributes, as well as negative ones. Advisers need training on how to handle these situations.

Understanding the housing department's role is critical when designing an adviser training program. This topic needs to be covered appropriately, so all advisers are able to effectively communicate a department's stance on support and sponsorship as well as help the students to work within the established framework. This is an ongoing topic that needs to be addressed throughout the year.

Conclusion

Advisers touch the lives of many students. Adviser training is not inherent in housing programs and must be nurtured. Advising skills training could easily fill full training schedules. Though this is not practical, opportunities exist for those coordinating training to include advising skills training sessions in the fall and ongoing professional development opportunities. Successful adviser training programs require time commitment, departmental support, and collegial networking.

Advisers require continual support. Most coordinators of adviser training advocate "open door" policies as part of ongoing training and support for advisers. Consulting with coordinators of adviser training does not substitute for one-on-one meetings with supervisors, but rather provides forums for ongoing challenge and support.

TIPS FOR NEW ADVISERS OF STRONG ORGANIZATIONS

- Network as much as possible on-campus and off-campus.
- Think outside the box.
- Be willing to receive some training from the student organization.
- Ask lots of question. It's okay if students know more than you at the beginning. Even veteran advisers can gain knowledge from strong student organizations. Students respect advisers who credit the organizations' history.
- Develop close relationships with students. Just because you inherit a strong organization, doesn't mean they will still be strong in six months. Be mindful of what has made the organization strong. Do they have a long-standing tradition of strength? Are they coming off a period of hosting a conference where campus focus was on the organization?

- Learn about the organization, read everything you can regarding the organization and its history, and talk with students, colleagues, and administrators regarding their impressions of the group.
- Attend sessions for adviser development at conferences (ART and otherwise).
- Explore new possibilities and learn the ropes from students.
- Fill your bag of tricks.
- Sit back and observe.
- Read the Constitution and other official documents such as organization policy book, finance manual, position manuals, by-laws, state documents (i.e., Constitution and/or Policy Book), regional documents (i.e., ACURH Constitution, Policy Book, and Advisers Manual) and the National Articles of Incorporation (NACURH Constitution) and NACURH Policy Book. Advisers should be familiar with these documents.
- Don't try to change the world; see where you can help.
- Don't take students for granted if they say they don't need your assistance. Be involved and supportive. Thank them for their work.

TIPS FOR NEW ADVISERS OF ORGANIZATIONS IN TRANSITION

- Network on campus. Seek perceptions about the organization from others. How powerful is the organization? Are there political implications for the organization? Is the organization known for educational programming, socials-only, or a combination of both?
- Realize your role may be to keep the organization alive. Expect to spend significant energy on an organization in transition. Decide how much time you are willing to give; much will be after hours. Find balance with your personal life. Stay active; realize the line between being involved and being active. Negotiate with your department about time out of the office for executive board meetings. You will provide strength for a group in transition by organizing retreats and having one-on-one meetings with each officer. Trust your students to govern themselves.
- Be ready for change and think outside the box. Is the group ready for change if they are in transition? Are they meeting the needs of the members? Allow yourself to support, encourage, and empower student leaders. Explore what they could be, rather than what they are expected to be. Present options and vision for what they could be.
- You will not be hands-off with a group in transition; you will be engaged as a coach.

References

Day, D.V., Zaccaro, S. J., & Haplin, S. M. (Eds.). (2004). *Leader development for transforming organizations: Growing leaders for tomorrow.* Mahwah, New Jersey: Lawrence Erlbaum Associates Publishers.

McGill, I. & Brockbank, A. (2004). *The action learning handbook: Powerful techniques for education, professional development and training.* London: Routledge.

Storey, J. (Ed.). (2004). *Leadership in organizations: Current issues and key trends.* London: Routledge.

Figure 1.   Topics for Initial Hall/Area Government Adviser Training — July/August

- *Introductions/Share Advising Experiences/Distribute Manuals*
  - ➤ Words of Wisdom from Returning Advisers
  - ➤ Advising vs. Supervising
  - ➤ Expectations of Executive Board
  - ➤ Fall Leadership Training for Student Leaders and Members

- *Adviser Role/Expectations*
  - ➤ One-on-One Weekly Meetings with Hall/Area Government President
  - ➤ One-on-One Monthly Meetings with Hall/Area Government Treasurer
  - ➤ Attend two RHA meetings each semester
  - ➤ Attend Weekly Hall/Area Government Meetings
  - ➤ Attend Hall/Area Government Executive Board Meetings
  - ➤ Attend Hall/Area Government Programs
  - ➤ 4 hours per week of time
  - ➤ Audits and Equipment Checks

- *Hall/Area Government Relationships with RHA and Housing Department*
  - ➤ Hall/Area Government Status: Sponsored Organizations within Housing vs. Registered University Student Organization
  - ➤ Requirements of Student Members/Leaders
  - ➤ Full Time Students
  - ➤ Minimum 2.0 Cumulative and Last Semester GPAs
    - ✧ Not on Disciplinary Conduct Probation
    - ✧ Volunteers – But Accountable to Housing Department
    - ✧ Training

- *How RHA Executive Positions Interact with Advisers and the Groups They Advise*
  - ➤ NCC
  - ➤ Secretary
  - ➤ Business Manager (equipment checks)
  - ➤ Auditor (checkbook & audits)
  - ➤ Vice President
  - ➤ President
  - ➤ RHA Adviser (RHA attendance/RHA assignments)

- **_RHA President Shares Information with Advisers_**
  - ➢ Selling Activity Cards
  - ➢ Welcome Week Program Schedules/Budget
  - ➢ Hall/Area Government Liaisons to RHA
  - ➢ Selecting Hall/Area Government Officers
  - ➢ Constitutions

- **_General Information Sharing_**
  - ➢ Welcome Week
  - ➢ NRHH
  - ➢ NIC Office
  - ➢ ART Training
  - ➢ Conference Opportunities for Hall/Area Government Members and Advisers
  - ➢ Advising RHA Events and Committees
  - ➢ Hall/Area Government Programming and Events: Releases, Permits, Contracts
  - ➢ Hall/Area Government Offices and Equipment

- **_Case Study Training_**

- **_Suggested initial ART sessions: Working with Executive Boards and Motivation_**

Figure 2. Sample Monthly Training Schedule for Hall/Area Government Advisers

September	Benefits of Advising Discussion	ART — Motivation Elective
October	ART — CORE IV	Working with Executive Boards
November	ART — CORE III	Recruitment and Retention
December	ART —	Legal Issues Elective w/Case Studies
January	ART — CORE II Student/Group	Development Theories and Models
		Theories and Group Dynamics
February	ART — CORE I	Advisers as Information Resources
March	ART — CORE V	Meetings and Activities
April	ART — Conferencing Elective	

Figure 3: ART Basic Curriculum

When advisers complete the ART Basic Curriculum, they become *ARTists*. Certificates and pins are presented to qualified *ARTists,* and letters are sent to respective Chief Housing Officers or supervisors concerning the nature of the course and the accomplishment of the specific participant.

CORE I
Advisers as Information Resources
At this session, participants discuss information needed to assist students. Types of information discussed include campus information; departmental issues; state/regional/national RHA organizations information, ART history and organization; and general information such as travel requirements and financial structures. This session also addresses how to present and explain the structure/organization of student organizations to others at departments/institutions.

CORE II
Student/Group Development Theories and Models
During this session, participants discuss current student development and group development theories and models. The facilitator places special attention on the role of advisers in the development and planned growth of organizations. Multiple perspectives are presented from a variety of theorists.

CORE III
Recruitment and Retention
This session shares methods, strategies, and techniques advisers use to gain and keep members. Research data on involvement reflects the nature of students as well as what advisers do to take advantage of information to benefit the organization. Participants deal with daily, monthly, and yearly recruitment; retention efforts and the probability of success for each. Participants share successes and address campus-specific concerns as well as national trends. Special attention is paid to the retention of NRHH members, as members of this organization comprise the most active student leaders. Recognitions, rewards, and remuneration are addressed briefly.

CORE IV
Working with Executive Boards
Participants discuss how advisers work with student leaders in organizations. They discuss the purpose and goals of facilitating retreats; providing ongoing officer training; maintaining job descriptions; using group organization theories

and models; and providing ongoing developmental activities. Transition of officers, dealing with internal conflicts, and the adviser's role in these events is addressed also.

CORE V
Meetings and Activities

Participants discuss the responsibilities and duties of advisers during organizational meetings and events including seating, speaking rights, body language, and actions during events. They also address the changing role of advisers as groups mature and develop.

ELECTIVES

In addition to the five Core courses, participants must complete three electives. Core and elective courses support research data but also reflect regional concerns and other factors specific to a group. Additional electives may develop from research or follow-up efforts.

- Legal Issues

  Participants are introduced to legal terminology, sources of law, and issues that affect advisers of student organizations. This course does not give legal advice but rather creates an awareness of legal concerns and advises participants how to prepare for possible legal challenges.

- How Diversity Affects RHAs

  This elective is an interactive session that allows participants to explore how diversity both aids and hinders student organizations. Activities are designed to give participants opportunities to discuss specific diversity issues and to gather support and information from other advisers.

- Conferencing

  Participants discuss the nature of student leadership conferences and the adviser role during conferences. Issues focus on conference preparation, travel concerns, and conference activities. Participants also briefly discuss the role of advisers in hosting conferences.

- Motivation

  Participants discuss how advisers initially motivate students. Participants discuss strategies, techniques, and opportunities, and they share successful motivation efforts. Participants also discuss ways to transfer the responsibility for motivation to members so they become self-motivated.

- Working with the NCC

  To ensure that advisers understand the many facets of the NCC role, attention is paid to the NACURH regional business meeting format (regional conferences and No FRILLS) and related timelines. The program combines information from CORE I and IV as it pertains to working with an executive board member and understanding NACURH.

- **Advising NRHH Chapters**
  Within this session participants will be able to learn about the National Residence Hall Honorary organization. Conversations will allow advisers toexpolore challneges in working with students involved with your NRHH local chapter (whether active or honorary), and how this organziaiton can assist in motivating leaders on your campus. Resources will be provided in starting a lcation NRHH chapter, the Of The Month program, the affiliation process and working with the regional board.

- **Bids, Bid Writing, and Presenting**
  Course content includees information about bids in general, the bid process, writing and presenting. The bid process can be a daunting task for our student leaders, whether for

  ➢ regional/national awards (including SALT, POY, and others)

  ➢ a working knowledge of state/sub-regional awards

  ➢ bidding for conferences (regional, national, NO Frills, etc.)

  ➢ or running/bidding for office for SBD/RBD?NBD & NIC/NRHH.

Where does the adviser fit into this process? Sure, the expectation is that you are knowledgable of the policies and processes (Core I), but how much experience do you have to assist your students with the process from ideation and theme, to meeting the requirements of the bid, and developing a presentation (if one is called for)? Join us in this new elective (NA '06) as you gain pivotal knowledge in all things: BIDS.

EXPERIENTIAL REQUIREMENTS

In addition to course requirements, advisers must complete three experience-based requirements before qualification. These requirements can be completed at any time before, during, or after beginning the ART program.

1) Advise a residential student organization for two years. (Note: This advising experience must occur as a full time professional. Graduate advising experience counts ½ credit per year.)

2) Attend a NACURH-affiliated conference (not state conference).

3) Attend a NACURH business meeting (regional or national level).

Figure 4. ART Master Curriculum

MASTER CORE 1
Long-Distance Advising — State, Regional, National Boards

Advising state, regional, or national student organizations offers numerous new challenges. Many advisers feel these challenges and responsibilities are too great. In reality, these challenges can lead to meaningful professional experiences when the right tools and resources are provided. This session discusses the challenges and provides the tools and resources for advisers to accept the challenge of long-distance advising of state, regional, and national boards.

MASTER CORE 2
Conference Advising - From Bid Team to Completion

This session provides practical, business, and legal information to support advisers and student groups hosting conferences.

MASTER CORE 3
Teaching ART Concepts in Staff Training

ART Institute curriculum can be used in different contexts to support departmental staff training. This session creatively uses ART resources to address various aspects of undergraduate, graduate, and new professional staff training from judicial to programming.

MASTER CORE 4
Establishing Supportive Departmental Relationships for RHAs

Successful RHAs and student members need support from the top down. This session introduces ways to establish stronger relationships between student leaders and housing professional staff. Participants explore possible outcomes from student/professional relationships and partnerships.

MASTER CORE 5
Incorporating ART Fundamentals into other Advising Opportunities

This session assists advisers in transferring fundamental ART curriculum and concepts to advising groups or offering services to groups other than those associated with housing and residence life.

Experiential Requirements

In addition to the course requirements, advisers must complete three experience-based requirements before qualification as Master ARTists.

1) Complete three years post ART certification advising experience.
2) Publish an article for a regional/national publication on an aspect of advising student organizations.
3) Present at least two ART programs at professional or student housing/ residential life conferences.

4

Selecting a Style of Advising

Mathew R. Chetnik & Kathleen M. Neville

"Can you describe your advising style?" This is a typical interview question for individuals applying for jobs within student affairs. Simple and straightforward at initial glance, the request to describe advising style actually involves much more than a one-to three-minute response. Advising style is not consistent but rather a mixture of techniques, motivations, and methods. Choosing an advising style is like deciding what to wear in the morning. Without knowing the weather outside, the plans for the day, or even what is clean, individuals are not able to effectively select the clothes that will be most appropriate. Similarly, choosing an advising style requires professionals to have knowledge of a wide range of potential issues surrounding each situation. Thus, one's advising style is situational. Each individual student leader, each individual group, each individual task will require advisers to adapt style, focus on different aspects, and examine situations from different perspectives. In this sense, advisers need to be prepared to change and adapt their advising style to each unique situation based on an understanding of group dynamics and the individual needs of leaders. Advisers whose responses and actions remain consistently the same no matter the circumstances will not be as effective as advisers who are able to assess, monitor, and adjust.

There are few available resources that define advising styles. Supervision meetings, roundtable discussions, and generalized training sessions tend to concentrate more on the roles and requirements for advisers or on the organizational structure of groups rather than the development of a personal advising style. To gain a better understanding of advising styles, this chapter explores leadership theory focusing on styles of leadership.

Situational Leadership – Hersey and Blanchard

In the late 1960s, Paul Hersey and Kenneth H. Blanchard developed the Situational Leadership Model, which illustrates the interdependence between leaders and followers within group settings. The model stresses that the role leaders should play in order to be most effective depends on the amount of direction leaders deliver, the amount of socio-emotional support they give to followers, and the maturity or readiness of followers to complete specific tasks (Hersey, Blanchard & Johnson, 1996).

Followers are critical to the effectiveness of leaders because ultimately followers determine what power leaders may have. Leaders who can best adapt their style to each specific situation will better be able to influence members of the group. Therefore, leaders must appropriately assess the readiness, maturity, and willingness of followers before determining how best to lead.

Hersey and Blanchard's model illustrates that a leader's style should be determined by the maturity of followers in relation to performing given tasks, overall willingness and confidence. The authors define four leadership styles: Telling, Selling, Participating, and Delegating. Each style places a different emphasis on the leader's relationship with the group and the group's ability to perform the given task.

As the group develops skills and is able to perform tasks, the style of the leader also changes. This model is illustrated as four phases through which a leader moves as the group's readiness and ability changes. The "telling" style is most effective when the group is low in ability, low in willingness and needs direction. Other words for this style include guiding, directing, and structuring. The "selling" style is most effective when the group ability is low, but it's willing and trying. Other words for this style include persuading, explaining, and clarifying. The "participating" style is most effective when a group has just developed the ability to perform the task; however, they have not yet had the opportunity to develop confidence by performing the task alone. Other words for this style include collaborating, facilitating, and committing. The "delegating" style is most effective when the group has developed the ability to perform the task, and they have necessary confidence, willingness, and readiness. Other words for this style include observing and monitoring (Hersey et al., 1996).

Situational Advising Model

Utilizing the foundations presented in the Situational Leadership Model,

Kathleen E. Allen (1983) illustrates the methods in which college activities advisers can be most effective when working with groups and clubs in designing and implementing programs. Allen suggests that advisers' effectiveness and influence will shift as their styles react to environmental factors on campus. Allen also suggests that three factors can affect styles of advisers: universities' expectations of advisers; student groups' expectations of advisers; and the level of the students' development.

Universities' expectations are a continuum from administrations expecting that programs will be successful and that advisers will ensure the success by direct involvement to administrations that believe advisers merely serve as resources to groups.

Students' expectations of advisers may contradict the expectations of administrators. Students may expect advisers to plan all events or run all last minute errands for groups. If universities and students expect different things from advisers, it is difficult to establish appropriate adviser roles.

The level of the students' development measured by their ability, commitment, willingness to accept responsibility, and interpersonal skills affects advisers' styles. Not to be confused with chronological age but utilized for conceptualizing each stage of development, Allen defines the four stages of development as infancy, adolescence, young adulthood, and maturity through a quadrant model similar to Hersey and Blanchard's. Allen's definitions for each quadrant are:

Infancy: Students demonstrate low ability for programming, responsibility, and commitment to the organization. Advisers serve as program directors with a high focus on the product (task) and a low focus on the process (relationship with the group).

Adolescence: Students demonstrate increasing ability, skills, responsibility, and commitment. Advisers serve as a program teacher/ directors and have high focus for the product (task) and a high focus on the process (relationship with the group).

Young Adulthood: Students demonstrate competency in programming skills, increased willingness to take responsibility for actions, and overall commitment to organizations. Advisers serve as program advisers/teachers with low focus for the product (task) and high focus on the process.

Maturity: Students demonstrate high degrees of skills related to programming and group development, strong commitment to groups, and willingness to take responsibility for personal actions and actions of groups. Advisers serve as program consultants with low focus for product (task) and low focus on process (Allen, 1983).

A More Comprehensive View

Utilizing the foundation of Hersey and Blanchard's Situational Leadership Model developed in 1969 (Hersey & Blanchard, 1996), in addition to Allen's adaptation of the model (Allen, 1983), a comprehensive and practical model for advising style emerges. This generalized situational advising model, based on four quadrants can be applied to most organizations and expands to include working with students at all levels of involvement and development.

The Quadrants in Detail

Quadrant 1

Adviser Style: Telling
Adviser Role: Director/Initiator
Student Maturity: Infancy

In Quadrant 1, advisers provide high levels of guidance and lesser amounts of supporting behaviors. Advisers direct groups as to what, when and how to accomplish tasks. In this style, advisers have high focus on tasks and low focus on relationships with groups. In the event of crises, advisers utilize this style to manage situations effectively. Students within this quadrant exhibit low levels of skills for the specific tasks. They are not able or willing to do what it takes due to lack of knowledge or experience, fear of tasks because of the size or topic, or lack of self-confidence. They have little understanding of organizational history or the way things have been done to rely on. In this quadrant, advisers have high interest in ensuring that tasks are accomplished, which gives groups a sense of confidence and prevents them from falling into disarray. Advisers spend less time focusing on the developmental aspects of the process in order to ensure that groups achieve success. Advisers are visionaries who teach groups through role modeling skills needed to develop in order to be successful.

Quadrant 2

Adviser Style: Selling
Adviser Role: Teacher/Director
Student Maturity: Adolescence

In Quadrant 2, advisers provide significant amounts of direction due to students' overall lack of ability; however, groups need feedback and support to remain motivated and interested. Advisers help groups understand processes and answer questions which allow groups to become more invested and accept advisers' ideas while developing higher levels of knowledge and experience. In this style, advisers provide high focus on tasks as well as high focus on relationships with groups. Students increase skills and commitment because they have achieved success in one or both of the areas and are ready to independently move ahead with little handholding and direction from advisers.

Quadrant 3

Adviser Style: Participating
Adviser Role: Adviser/Teacher
Student Maturity: Young Adulthood

When groups have ability but begin to lose willingness due to motivation, Quadrant 3 style can be extremely effective. Advisers do not provide much direction at this point; however, advisers remain supportive and provide environments that encourage group communications toward problem-solving. In this style, advisers provide low focus on tasks and high focus on relationships and development of groups. Students demonstrate competency in tackling tasks and are willing to take responsibility for follow-through and hold groups accountable.

Quadrant 4

Adviser Style: Delegating
Adviser Role: Consultant
Student Maturity: Maturity

In Quadrant 4, groups have experience and feel ready to perform tasks without direction from advisers. Groups are ready to take control of tasks because they have confidence in their abilities. They no longer require the same level of adviser support as before. They have the confidence to ensure that groups are maintained. In this style, advisers provide low focus on tasks and low focus on relationships and development of groups. Students have achieved high degrees of competency and mastery over both tasks and the processes. Groups reaching this level of functioning are an adviser's dream. Groups quickly and efficiently identify how to handle tasks. They are willing to hold each other accountable and to identify issues on their own. They have become visionaries and work towards group success and growth beyond their elected terms of office. At this point, advisers are sounding boards and the advising role is minimal. This quadrant is the hardest to achieve, and may never occur. Certain individuals within student groups may reach this quadrant, but the entire group may not.

One of the most important aspects of this model is that it is fluid. Advisers (or groups for that matter) do not necessarily begin in Quadrant 1 and end in Quadrant 4. Instead, advisers adjust their style to meet the developmental needs and challenges of groups for each task. Although groups may be well formed with extensive leadership abilities (Quadrant 3 or 4), challenges may arise in which groups are unprepared (Quadrant 1.) Advisers need to adjust styles to assist groups working through challenges or accomplishing tasks. Successful advisers understand and are able to assess group dynamics and individual levels of development in order to be most effective.

Challenges in Selecting an Effective Style

Because the situational advising model is fluid, groups can exist in more than one quadrant at the same time. This requires that advising style change depending on individual needs or group tasks. For example, a group coordinating the fourth movie night of the year has group members who are experienced with the task, know what needs to happen, and have the skills to accomplish the task. The advising style may be Quadrant 4. Unfortunately, a serious conflict arises between two group members. This conflict has an adverse effect on the group functioning. Because members are not skilled in resolving personal conflicts, they need the adviser to operate from a Quadrant 1 or 2 perspective in order to resolve the conflict. Understanding the fine line between the two tasks is critical in helping the group succeed. The advising style must allow student leaders to plan the event independently but offer support in resolution of the conflict.

Another challenge in selecting the advising style is conflicting interests of institutions or departments with the needs of groups. For example, certain aspects of advising responsibilities may prevent providing the levels of attention that groups need. Groups operating in Quadrant 1 or 2 may need advisers present at events from a confidence-building perspective, but other job demands may necessitate advisers' absences from functions. Conversely, groups in Quadrant 4, who are coordinating events independently, may experience advisers moving into Quadrant 1 ("telling" mode) because of the nature of events and interests of institutions. Often, these perceived advising intrusions come from liability or fiscal responsibility mandates. Groups may be experienced and skilled in planning large events; however, because of liability issues, advisers may need to say "no." These are times when tensions between advisers and group members may arise. Often advisers are not given choices or freedom to determine how best to work with groups based on institutional expectations. Successful advisers clearly communicate institutional expectations and realities to groups.

Factors Influencing the Selection of Advising Style

Selecting an advising style requires that advisers examine internal and external factors. Advisers need to review the following internal factors within their control prior to interacting with students:

- **Have positive intentions and outlooks regarding advising.** Successful advisers recognize that advising student groups is not an opportunity to relive the "glory days" of their student leadership experiences. They put aside egos and do what is best for students. Advisers opting for low involvement with projects do so because the group has the skills, knowledge, and motivation to proceed independently, not because they are too busy with other projects or because it is not their responsibility to do student group work.

- **Utilize developmental theories in selecting advising style.** Understanding the needs of individuals and groups at various stages of development is key to determining how to most effectively advise. Many first-year students struggle with gaining confidence and competence. Effective advisers of first-year student groups take active, participatory roles within groups in order to ensure the success of events. Groups who have experienced leaders will function independently with little intervention of advisers.

- **Understand when to change advising style.** A key factor in successful advising is the ability to change advising style when individuals or groups need something different, require new challenges, or could benefit from different perspectives. An advising style described as "sitting back and letting groups work through issues and do their own thing because this is their time" does not recognize the fact that there are times when advisers need to step forward and become more involved in order to move leaders to the next level or to ensure successful events when successes are tied directly to the lives or reputations of organizations.

• **Provide strong rationale for choosing an advising style.** Advising requires thought, strategic planning, and foresight to intentionally work with leaders and groups to achieve high levels of success. If an adviser cannot justify high involvement with tasks, the selection of advising style may not be well suited for that group. However, if an adviser can justify high involvement with tasks because the group is comprised of primarily new leaders with minimal understanding of campus policies and procedures, the advising style is appropriate. The adviser understands that if the group does not experience a successful first event, they may struggle with feeling confident which could greatly impact the organizations' presence on campus or the success of future events.

Advising style also is determined by external factors outside the control of advisers. Advisers need to review and understand the following external factors that affect campuses or groups before determining advising style. The National Association of College and University Residence Halls (NACURH) White Paper (Dunkel & Spencer, ed., 1998) presents five elements that are critical to the development or improvement of a residence hall association. These elements, as well as the following external factors, are potential challenges for advisers:

• **Departmental support of advisers.** Support comes in various forms including the recognition of advising time by balancing workloads; training and development opportunities for advisers; and supervision of advisers that involves discussions and challenges in advising.

• **Campus political culture.** If campus culture dictates that advisers should make requests to upper-level administrators on behalf of students, then advisers need to take more active roles in groups instead of encouraging leaders to set up meetings with administrators to express concerns. Political culture also dictates consequences for organizations whose events are not successful or whose leaders make poor decisions. During the first stages of a group's formation, it is critical not to create conflicts with other groups or leaders on campus.

- **Student culture**. Taking a more active advising role in order to help groups achieve success may backfire, depending on student culture. If student leaders on campus do not have strong, collaborative relationships with administrators, they may view advisers as usurping their authority, if advisers choose more involved, direct styles of advising.

- **Organizational structure**. On some campuses, advisers are expected to take active roles within student groups. On other campuses, advisers are expected to be in the background and not participate. These examples represent two extremes. Successful advisers understand organizational structure and expectations on their campuses and operate within those limits.

- **Legal, liability, and risk management issues.** In an increasingly litigious society, successful advisers understand the importance of their roles in working with student groups. Those advising experienced, developed, highly involved groups of leaders may need to select advising styles that are more involved. Though less involved advising styles seem appropriate, the nature of particular tasks may require different approaches. For example, a group that wants to plan a skydiving trip may not understand the legal and liability issues surrounding such an event. Advisers need to be comfortable taking charge and saying "no" for the safety and well being of groups.

- **Finances and budget.** Finances and budget can be the driving forces in determining advising style. Initially, advisers may feel comfortable sitting back and allowing groups to take ownership of large programs. However, if program planning starts to deteriorate and a student group is at risk of losing large sums of money, the adviser needs to intervene. Risking or losing large sums of money is not an example when "failing as a learning opportunity" is going to be effective or beneficial. When the bottom line is budget, advisers must take more active roles, regardless of their preferred or natural advising styles.

- **Individual personalities within groups.** As advising styles change, so do student leaders' styles. Effective advising styles will often be determined by the personalities and needs of individual student leaders. Advisers may need to be less involved with experienced student leaders but take more active roles with less experienced student leaders no matter what their office levels. For example, an adviser needs to provide more support and attention to a president who is new to the leadership position than to an experienced vice-president who can easily perform the responsibilities of the position without adviser assistance. Successful advisers provide appropriate levels of involvement with students and communicate the rationale for the differing levels of involvement. Advisers may experience student leaders who resist adviser involvement no matter what the need. Successful advisers assess the potential benefits and consequences of "forcing" particular advising styles on leaders.

Practical Techniques for Working with Students

Advising student leaders requires advisers to focus on organizations or groups as a whole, particular tasks, and individual leaders as persons. The following are practical techniques that advisers can utilize when operating within each quadrant.

Quadrant 1

Suggestions for working with individual students or groups with regards to the organization:

- Discuss and review organizational history and files. Review with students historical files/memos/binders and teach the importance of keeping records.
- Coordinate and facilitate leadership training for groups. Coordinate, implement, and facilitate training, if necessary. Take the initiative to plan an afternoon/weekend workshop for teaching basic skills.
- Plan group cohesiveness activities. Coordinate activities that open discussions about setting goals and objectives, learning job descriptions and responsibilities, teaching processes including how to program, addressing and resolving conflicts, conducting strategic planning, etc. Be the facilitator for these discussions.
- Coordinate individual times with group members to determine thoughts and issues. If there are conflicts, work with individuals first to help them gain more confidence and skills to participate actively in resolving conflicts. If students do not understand their jobs or roles within groups, help them define their jobs or roles.
- Set clear expectations. Explore what it means to be student leaders.
- Visit students in their offices to show interest. Call during office hours to see how things are going.

Suggestions for working with individual students or groups with regards to tasks:

- Work with students step-by-step to plan events or tasks. Develop "to do" lists which include elements to implement the tasks.
- Walk with students to key campus offices and introduce them to staff so that hurdles of not knowing where to go or who to talk to are overcome. Sit with students at computers as they make advertisements.
- Attend committee meetings and planning meetings to monitor progress or lack of progress.
- Follow-up frequently to see if students need assistance.
- Provide high levels of recognition so students' confidence levels increase.
- Call to resolve problems on behalf of students. Bailing students out at this point allows for better conversations, which is more important than allowing students to fail.

Suggestions for working with individual students or groups with regards to academics/life outside groups:

- Be aware of what constitutions say about academics. Check grades at the start of the year, at midterms and at finals. Be firm about academic expectations and hold students accountable in some manner. If necessary place students on "warning" or ask them to step down from their positions. Relay that being student role models includes being academic role models and having a solid foundation in the classroom. Ensure that ongoing conversations include questions on academics. If there are no academic policies in place, encourage groups to develop policies in consultation with administrators.
- Review the "Student Learning Imperative" (American College Personnel Association, 1994) and incorporate it into advising style.
- Spend time getting to know each student. Develop trusting and mentoring relationships with students in advising relationships.
- Be consistent.

Quadrant 2

Suggestions for working with individual students or groups with regards to the organization:

- Solicit group members' feedback regarding processes and group dynamics. Fine-tune processes and develop better group dynamics.

- Ask individuals to take leadership roles for certain aspects of conversations or meetings. Teach students to do their own team building activities and facilitate discussions about topics.
- Continue to be firm and clear. Understand that negative student reactions can signify resistance to recognizing certain truths regarding individual performance or other aspects of group functioning. Communicate that organizations are students' organizations. Recognize the fine line between pushing students to recognize truths and allowing them to fail.
- Call "Family Meetings," but allow groups to work through issues. Put issues on the table, but allow group members to talk through issues themselves. Begin as an active participant then move into the role of observer to allow for student-leaders to develop within groups.

Suggestions for working with individual students or groups with regards to tasks:

- Ask students if they need help.
- Have contingency plans available to assist students who fail to carry through on particular tasks or responsibilities. Know how problems can be resolved in order to guide students through options when deadlines are missed. Provide reassurance, tempered with the reality, that failure to follow-through can jeopardize events, tasks, or groups.
- Provide both positive and constructive feedback in clear terms after events have occurred. Students/groups have enough confidence and self-assurance to be able to constructively hear ideas for improvements to systems and processes.

Suggestions for working with individual students or groups with regards to academics/life outside groups:

- Talk about priorities and goals.
- Challenge students on how academic performance potentially inhibits a group's development and success. Connect the two concepts.
- Have groups discuss grades and expected role modeling behaviors. Encourage groups to explore what academics mean to individuals and how different academic programs affect grades and requirements. Groups should be aware of academic commitments so that they can support individuals to ensure that tasks are being completed on time.
- Encourage groups to discuss grades, as well as upcoming academic commitments, during both executive board meetings and event planning meetings to properly structure workloads.
- Discuss issues surrounding going home for breaks, school and life stress, peer pressure, and financial stress. Engage in conversations about intense college experiences, like alcohol and drug use, which allow students to

begin connecting issues and developing positive habits. Discuss role modeling behaviors related to university policies.

Quadrant 3

Suggestions for working with individual students or groups with regards to the organization:

- Ensure that group and planning processes occur. Meet with executive board members to discuss and plan how those conversations will occur. Encourage planning sessions with presidents on communication skills, group processes, conflict resolution, feedback, avoiding cliques, and addressing rumors and other destructive complaining or communications.
- Ensure that expectations are reviewed. Encourage group members to hold each other to higher levels of accountability and resolve issues together in appropriate ways rather than complaining about each other. Remind groups that it is crucial to review how they are going to hold each other accountable before conflicts or issues occur.
- Challenge groups more forcefully and hold groups more accountable. If groups have not yet developed a high skills base, allow them to fail in order to learn and move to a higher stage of maturity.
- Share more. Groups need to hear honest, constructive feedback and views from advisers in order to grow and move to the next level.

Suggestions for working with individual students or groups with regards to tasks:

- Provide more critical feedback to group members. Students need to hear honestly how their performances and communication styles are impacting groups, how they are being perceived, and what their "reputations" are within groups.
- Discuss leadership qualities that students are learning, and point out what skills they have achieved, in addition to what skills they still need to develop. Relate these achievements to future life skills. Statements like, "I see you doing this within the group. How does this behavior affect you in your personal life?" assist leaders to become more reflective and aware of themselves.
- Allow programs to fail by not fixing problems. Teach students that emergencies because of poor planning or follow–through do not make emergencies for advisers. Allowing students to fail is discussed in previous quadrants, but this is the quadrant for action in this area.

Suggestions for working with individual students or groups with regards to academics/life outside groups:

- Give students more trust and responsibility to work though issues. Ask to be informed and updated about plans and progress, but allow students opportunities to "try again." Continue to check grades, but give students more autonomy and accountability in deciding what they can and cannot handle rather than forcing issues.
- Encourage "tough conversations" within groups with regards to account-ability. Groups need to have more conversations about how individual actions or inactions affect groups. Team is important, but so is individual responsibility.
- Be aware that the advising role as "mentor" is significant. Be aware how important support and guidance is to individuals in their pursuit of every-thing. Be aware that advising time commitments may decrease in this stage with regards to tasks, but increase with regards to personal issues. Individual meetings tend to focus more on relationships, career goals, and emotional crises.

Quadrant 4

Suggestions for working with individual students or groups with regards to the organization:

- Remind students that they need to keep advisers informed of activities. In Quadrant 4, groups tend to act independently.
- Ensure that group leaders mentor others to take their places. Students at this stage tend to forget they might not be around the following year.
- Help the group leaders understand that while they may not feel they need to be recognized for their individual efforts, they need to recognize the suc-cesses, achievements, and growth of the group membership.

Suggestions for working with individual students or groups with regards to tasks:

- Ensure that evaluation processes throughout the year, occur at the end of the year, and are well documented for future boards. Utilize outgoing executive boards to formulate outlines for incoming executive board sum-mer retreats.
- Encourage members as they are completing tasks to document the plan-ning involved. Encourage them to create "To Do" lists and timelines to pass on to future groups for the continued development and success of the organizations.

- Challenge students to think outside the box. Students easily fall into the trap of "This works, so let's do it over and over again the same way." Help them see the benefits of critically evaluating programs and processes to enable group members to develop into well-skilled, proactive, innovative leaders.

Suggestions for working with individual students or groups with regards to academics/life outside groups:

- Help executive board members define their positions for resume purposes. Assist them in understanding the magnitude of what they have achieved and how their achievements transfer to the work world.
- Provide guidance on how to achieve successful closure and how to move on. This is necessary for the health and success of individual student leaders and organizations.

Conclusion

"Can you describe your advising style?" A typical interview question that is not simple to answer. No one style of advising is effective in all situations. Effective advising style requires professionals to assess the maturity of individuals or groups; the external and internal factors influencing tasks; and the levels of challenge that groups need. Successful advisers continuously ensure that personal actions and commitments are for the benefit of groups and students. Without knowing the variables involved, advisers cannot determine advising styles that will assist groups effectively in accomplishing tasks. Therefore, advising style is situational. It depends. Often the most effective advising style is to sit back and allow groups to succeed or fail on their own. Other times, the most effective advising style is to participate with groups and take an active role because failure is not an option. Successful advisers act intentionally to assist individuals and groups grow and develop. Intentional action means being willing to adjust advising style in order to benefit groups while meeting the expectations of institutions.

References

Allen, K.E. (May 1983). Choosing the effective advising style. *Student Activities Programming*, 34–37.

Dunkel, N., & Spencer, C. L. (Eds.). (1998). *Advice for advisers*. Columbus, OH: ACUHO-I.

Hersey, P., Blanchard, K., & Johnson, D.E. (1996). *Management of organizational behavior: Utilizing human resources* (7th ed.). Englewood Cliffs, NJ: Prentice-Hall, Inc.

Pascarella, E., & Terenzini, P. (1991). *How college affects students.* San Francisco: Jossey-Bass.

Case Studies

The following case studies explore differing styles that can be utilized to effectively advise student groups. Consider these questions as case studies are discussed:

- Who calls the adviser if the group fails?
- Can the group handle the pressure or added workload at this point in time?
- What are the consequences of the group's decisions?
- What are the group's abilities?
- What is the group struggling with interpersonally? What are the individuals struggling with?
- What are the benefits and consequences of choosing a style?
- What time of year is it? What else is going on? How are group members performing academically? How does this impact the adviser's style?
- When is it most appropriate to challenge?

❖ Case Study 1

The National Communication Coordinator (NCC), a student leader within the Residence Hall Association (RHA), is in the process of conducting delegation selection and making travel arrangements for the national NACURH conference. The RHA budget will fund the air travel and conference registration for three individuals. The NCC is determined to take 15 students and is insisting upon driving to the conference in order to avoid air travel costs. The national conference site is approximately 15 hours driving time from your campus. The NCC also indicated that each delegate will fund raise $100 to cover some of the overall costs, including delegation t-shirts and give a ways.

- What are the college's expectations regarding student and staff travel?

- What are the college's expectations regarding fundraising?
- What are the staffing requirements depending upon the mode of travel?
- What are the potential consequences of either travel method?
- How should the adviser work with the NCC in Quadrant 1 vs. Quadrant 3 or 4?

✤ Case Study 2

The Residence Hall Association Executive Board is sponsoring the annual Spring Fling, a dinner/dance party, at an area hotel. In past years, both fundraising revenue and attendance at the event have decreased forcing RHA to seek last minute financial support in the amount of $1,000 to $2,500 from the Student Government Association in order to remain financially solvent. Additionally, ticket prices have increased from $15 per person to $30 per person due to increased food, transportation, and security costs. During the summer retreat, the Executive Board discussed the Spring Fling. They would like to hold the event this year at a more expensive venue, possibly a dinner cruise. This event is a favorite of the administration. In previous years when the group has considered canceling the event due to low initial ticket sales, the institution has directed the adviser to "make it happen."

- If the leadership in the group is in a particular quadrant, how does the advising style change?
- What are the bigger institutional issues surrounding holding or canceling the event?
- How much autonomy should the adviser give the leaders? What are the non-negotiable issues and decisions?

✤ Case Study 3

The group you advise decided to dissolve their constitution and operate in a more "free-flowing" manner. They have had several discussions focusing on developing an "authority-free" organization that is not hierarchical, one that allows the group to easily make decisions without red tape. In general, the group is rebelling against traditional organizational models and wants to operate more from a "committee" standpoint without students serving in designated leadership roles.

- What are the impacts for the group in relation to the rest of the institution?

- How will group decisions affect the role and style of the adviser?
- What advising style works best with this group of students? What are the expectations from the administration?

✤ Case Study 4

During the first week of classes, the group you advise is hosting a "Best-of -Town Pizza" event later this evening. The individuals coordinating the event have not kept the rest of the group informed about event details, have struggled with advertising and planning the event, and have requested assistance from the rest of the group at the last minute to pick up pizza from different locations around town. To further complicate matters, they have forgotten to purchase plates or napkins and have left to pick up pizza from one of the vendors. You are in the office with no other students around when you realize they do not have these items.

- On the surface, what quadrant do these leaders appear to be in?
- Do you head to the store to purchase plates and napkins? What are the consequences if you don't? What are the consequences if you do?
- How will you process this situation and help the group set expectations after the event?
- Under the same circumstances, would your advising style change if this event was held in March?

✤ Case Study 5

Two members of the group you advise are involved in a personal conflict, which has begun to impact the dynamics of the organization. You observed their interactions at meetings and events and have witnessed snide comments, unwillingness to help each other with tasks/projects, blocking of ideas and suggestions, etc. During your last individual meeting with the president, you expressed your concern about the situation; however, the president doesn't think it is that big of a deal.

- What approach do you take to the situation? When do you decide to step in, if at all?
- What are the potential consequences for the group? For the individual members?
- What would a conversation with the group members involve?

5

Residence Government Effectiveness

Gardiner Tucker

Student organizations on college campuses in the United States have existed since the 1800s and continue to play major roles in the lives of students. Student affairs practitioners engage student government organizations on a regular basis to cover a wide range of campus issues. These organizations are training grounds for student leaders and provide venues for practicing leadership, developing communication skills, developing decision-making skills, and advocating and representing students. The success of residence hall governments is pivotal to the student experience on campus.

This chapter links residence hall government and organizational effectiveness. How can advisers better understand effectiveness? What makes successful residence hall governments? Residence hall governments support complex sets of relationships. No single answer to improve effectiveness exists. Dimensions of effectiveness vary from year-to-year due to significant turnover of students and staff. What may be effective on one campus may be ineffective at another. Effectiveness is not a single idea, but rather a multi-dimensional construct. Advisers can improve effectiveness through awareness and application of organizational effectiveness principles. This chapter discusses residence hall government organizations and the elements of effectiveness that influence performance.

Residence Hall Government Organizations

Residence hall governments are defined as residence hall students organized into units titled Residence Hall Associations (RHAs). RHAs are defined by Stoner and Wyatt (1993) as "a leadership organization that [is] representative of the various halls on each campus." For the purposes of this chapter, RHAs are defined as the housing student governing body that operates within on-campus housing at a university or college. The structure of most RHAs includes a central governing body of students that represents the total residential student population on campus. Additionally, many campuses have hall or area student governments that operate within each hall on campus and floor (or "house") councils that report to hall governments.

Student leaders living in campus residence halls established RHA prototypes prior to 1954. Today, the National Association of College and University Residence Halls (NACURH), represents more than 450 RHA organizations (Dunkel & Schuh, 1998). RHAs serve these primary purposes: to advance the educational goals of students housed on campus (Stoner, Spain, Rasche, & Horton, 1993); to provide involvement opportunities (Komives & Tucker, 1993, 1998); to develop leadership skills; and to encourage a student voice in housing decision-making (Werring, 1984).

RHA advisers, often directors or assistant directors, serve as liaisons to RHAs. Successful advisers hold positions in housing departments that allow them to support decisions made by RHAs and to represent departments in most decisions (Komives & Tucker, 1993, 1998). Advisers provide important two-way communication between students and staff.

Clearly, RHAs are valuable educational commodities, benefiting both students and administrators. Current academic material on RHAs is primarily theoretical or conceptual focusing on theory to practice or on how to run RHAs effectively. Limited empirical research on RHAs exists; however, a qualitative study on RHA effectiveness (Komives & Tucker, 1993, 1998) and a quantitative study on dimensions of RHA effectiveness (Tucker, 2001) provide some insight. Limited published literature or research exists about area, hall, or floor councils. These organizations are often the initial leadership training ground for resident students and provide the preparation for entry into RHA positions.

RHAs include elements of non-profit organizations, volunteer organizations, government organizations, student organizations, and student government organizations. To more fully understand them, a general knowledge of organizations is worth examining.

Understanding Organizations

Societies created organizations throughout history to "pursue goals and objectives that can be more efficiently and effectively achieved by the concerted action of individuals" (Gibson, Ivancevich, & Donnelly, 1982, p. 3). Three elements are part of every organization: "behavior, structure, [and] processes" (p. v). When examined, these elements provide insights on how organizations are designed operate. Behavior includes the human dimension of activity in organizations, such as how members are affected by organizations and how to shape organizations. Structure is the way organizations are designed to meet purposes. Organizational designs or structure varies according to goals. Processes are the methods organizations use to accomplish goals. Processes include communication; decision-making; technological processes; and input, internal and output processes. Input processes are those that enter the organizational boundary, such as funding and supplies. Internal processes are those organizations use to accomplish work. Output processes produce products or services for customers (Gibson et al., 1998).

Organizational Theories and Application

To comprehend organizational effectiveness, an understanding of organizational theory must be developed (Goodman & Pennings, 1980). Because RHAs are organizations, to accurately assess effectiveness within institutional context, they must be understood from a theoretical framework of organizations.

Four Organizational Theories and Models

Organizations are viewed in multiple ways. No single theory completely explains the phenomenon of organizations (Cameron & Whetten, 1983; Dipboye, Smith, & Howell, 1994). The first theoretical organizational model is the closed system model, which assumes the preeminence of internal forces in organizational operation. The first widely used theory of this type espoused by Frederick Taylor was popular in the early 20th century and was known as scientific management or the "mechanistic" view of organizations (Morgan, 1986). This model stresses efficiency and control through bureaucracy. Jobs are narrowly defined and structure is emphasized.

A second theory describes organizations as "political arenas." This model, prevalent in the 1980s, focuses on power and negotiation with members having vested interests in certain decisions over others (Harrison, 1994; Morgan, 1986; Scott, 1981).

"Learning organizations," a third theory popular from the 1980s to today, views organizations as learning environments where self-reflection and change are readily accepted and human potential is realized (Morgan, 1986; Senge, 1990).

The fourth theory views organizations as "open systems" or as organic (Harrison, 1994; Morgan, 1986). This view emerged in the 1960s and emphasizes the interplay of the internal and external environments with continuous feedback from environments. In order to survive, structures must fit with environments. These models provide information that can be translated into criteria of effectiveness.

Application of Organizational Theories and Models

- **Mechanistic organizations.** The concept of mechanistic organizations sprang from the scientific management theory of Frederick Taylor (Morgan, 1986). Morgan (1986) describes mechanistic organizations as emphasizing power and control, putting efficiency and uniform productivity above all other concerns: "the mechanistic approach to organization tends to limit rather than mobilize the development of human capacities, molding human beings to fit the requirements of a mechanical organization rather than building the organization around their strengths and potentials" (p. 38). This reflects a view of organizations as linear in nature with members viewed as cogs in a wheel. For example, RHAs with meetings that are short and focused on business only are viewed as effective. This is efficient, but members miss opportunities to develop relationships. Effectiveness is equated with efficiency.

- **Political organizations.** The initial reaction to the term "political" may be negative, yet Bolman and Deal (2003) state, "Viewed from the political frame, politics is simply the realistic process of making decisions and allocating resources in a context of scarcity and divergent interests (p. 181)," which shows the essential role of politics in organizational decision-making. The political model defined by Harrison (1994) views members within organizations as forming special interest groups based on functions or responsibilities. Special interest groups have investments in decision-making processes though each group may have different interpretations of success and effectiveness. Members of special interest groups are constituents or stakeholders in the political view.

  Bolman and Deal (2003) elaborate further on the political perspective by offering five proposals. Political organizations: (1) consist of political groups and individuals who support specific initiatives such as recycling and vote as coalitions; (2) have ongoing differences between other groups and individuals indicating differences in values and beliefs; (3) distribute limited resources and may be required to make major decisions endorsing one cause over another; (4) view power as a major resource and conflict as an important process; and (5) negotiate between coalitions to achieve direction. Each proposal identifies different phenomenon that may be observed within organizations and explains the dynamics between members of organizations.

Morgan (1986) emphasizes that the political model helps to discredit the view that organizations are rational. He believes organizations have interests or investments in organizational operations: "The idea of rationality seems to be invoked as a myth to overcome the contradictions inherent in the fact that an organization is simultaneously a system of competition and a system of cooperation" (p. 195). The political perspective also challenges the view of organizations as harmonic unified systems that strive to cooperate internally and face the world to survive. Morgan cautioned, however, that politics can lead to greater mistrust and suspicion within organizations, causing internal strife.

- **Learning organizations**. Senge (1990) defines learning organizations as those "where people continually expand their capacity to create the results they truly desire, where new and expansive patterns of thinking are nurtured, where collective aspiration is set free, and where people are continually learning how to learn together" (p. 3). He emphasizes that in traditional organizations, problems develop from fragmented views of organizational parts derived from tendencies to view problems and processes as isolated from one another. To correct this, he emphasizes the need to see each part as a piece of the whole, connected.

  Learning organizations must question and self-criticize without undue censorship. Self-organization, innovation, and the ability to adapt quickly to changes in the environment are central concepts of learning organizations. Learning organizations have several central principles including challenging the organization's practices even when they are long standing; expanding the organization's capacity to work more effectively together; sharing knowledge with members; and making learning relate to the primary purpose of the organization (Senge, Kleiner, Roberts, Ross, & Smith, 1994). An example of challenging an organization's practices is questioning the continued use of Robert's Rules of Order to govern meetings. An example of expanding the capacity to work more effectively together is intentionally reviewing programs to improve them. An example of sharing knowledge is a member describing learned conflict management techniques with the group. Examples of making learning relate to the primary purpose of the group include planning structured retreats and training opportunities. Learning organizations are challenged when members take direction from "above" rather than self-organize and learn together.

- **Open system organizations.** Open system organizations are influenced by external forces and the impact of the environment on organizations (Morgan, 1986; Scott, 1998). External conditions impact internal functions. For example, university restrictions may affect RHA operations. Products or services provided are utilized to promote organization sustenance. For example, a communication skills program sponsored by a hall council may also benefit hall council members. Influence can come internally from members, in addition to from top down and from external forces. For example, new policies from the housing office may influence a floor council's activities. System elements affect one another instead of being isolated within the organization. For example, a floor president implements a program and informs the resident assistant in advance knowing the RA will be impacted. Constant change pervades open organizations. Success is related directly to adaptability to both external and internal change. Each area of the organization can be seen as a subsystem (Harrison, 1994).

  Open systems organizations are influenced by internal and external forces. Open systems organizations consist of interrelated components that operate together to receive input, process input, create output, receive evaluation of the output or services, and again receive input (Banner & Gagne, 1995; Gibson et al., 1982). Healthy open system organizations assume high degrees of harmony, which discount managed conflict as a possible benefit (Morgan, 1986). This assumption can lead to the suppression of different forms of thinking and decision-making.

These selected organizational theories and models describe organizations from various points of view and are a subset of the many organizational theories and models in the literature. Reviewing organizational theories and models helps advisers understand RHAs within a broader perspective. A broader perspective helps student leaders and advisers think beyond the RHA, allowing greater innovation and problem-solving. Each level of RHA can use organizational theories and models to gain insight into functioning and performance, critical elements to improving organizational effectiveness.

Organizational Effectiveness

Organizational effectiveness is a subset of general organizational theory. Effectiveness implies evaluation and "that some coherent set of interests and preferences is brought to bear" (Seashore, 1983). Miller (1991) defines effectiveness as "the degree to which a social system achieves its goals" (p. 103). This is differentiated from efficiency, which he defines as "cost relative to output" (Miller, 1991; Goodman & Pennings, 1980). Effectiveness is a central issue in organizational life, according to Whetten and Cameron (1994) because many decisions are made on the basis of perceptions of how well organizations meet goals. They make a unique link from traditional organizational effectiveness to more recent emergent concepts such as "excellence, quality, continuous improvement, transformation, revitalization, and so on" (p. 136). The effectiveness of organizations is a central concept in the literature on organizational research and can be traced to modern concepts of excellence theory in the operation of organizations today.

Gibson et al. (1982) lists three levels at which effectiveness can be defined: individual, group, and organizational levels. Cameron and Whetten (1983) concur on these three levels and add effectiveness on the "supersystem" level (Cameron, 1978). The supersystem level includes both the industry level of which the organization is a part and the broader level of society. Individual level of effectiveness is concerned with the performance of single members of the organization. Focus is on how well a member does a job. For example, how well does the National Residence Hall Honorary liaison perform in the RHA? The second level of group effectiveness concerns how well work groups perform on group tasks and projects. For example, how well does the area council programming committee perform? The third level is the organizational level of effectiveness. This level concerns the performance of the entire organization on dimensions such as market share, productivity, and profits to stockholders. The supersystem level of industry compares other organizations of similar type and concerns to an organization. For example, how does the amount of available resources one hall council controls compare to another in relation to performance? The supersystem societal level examines the impacts of organizations on society. For example, how does membership in NACURH impact or improve individual RHAs? Clearly, each level affects others, but effectiveness on one level does not necessarily cause effectiveness on other levels. Criteria of effectiveness operate on the individual, group, organizational, industrial, and societal levels of organizations.

Past Models and Theories of Organizational Effectiveness

Whetten and Cameron (1994) present an overview of past models and theories of organizational effectiveness. They caution that models and theories are competing and that no single one dominates. They trace various approaches to organizational effectiveness including ideal types, which examine unique sets of attributes; contingency theory; and multiple constituent theory.

Larger models and theories encompass goal attainment; the system resource model (Cameron, 1980; Scott, 1981; Yuchtman & Seashore, 1967); internal processes or organizational health; and participant satisfaction (Banner & Gagne, 1995; Cameron, 1980). Theories are examined below with examples of application to RHAs.

Ideal Types

Whetten and Cameron (1994) summarize the concept of ideal types as fixed types of organizational design that are consistent across organizations. One organizational type fits all, instead of varying approaches depending on members and environments of operations. Ideal types include the "rational-legal" form of bureaucracy, related to the mechanistic theory of organization, which has standard criteria, such as fixed hierarchy (Jacques, 1976); formalization of rules and processes; work specialization; and centralization of authority or decision-making (Hall, 1963; Price, 1968). The assumption of the ideal type is that organization leaders design organizations after prototypes or structures created by experts outside the organization. For bureaucratic organizations, ideal types of organizations are efficient (Banner & Gagne, 1995; Whetten & Cameron, 1994), which is the single most important decisive criterion of effectiveness for organizations based on Taylor's (Morgan, 1986) scientific management principles.

A divergent ideal type focuses on the concept of member contribution as opposed to bureaucracy. This means that organizations needed to optimally meet the needs of members in order to maintain the efforts of members toward organizational goals (Whetten & Cameron, 1994). For example, a hall council is considered effective if all members felt high satisfaction with their experience, even if they did no programming for the hall. This is the participant satisfaction approach (Hall, 1999). This model provides a challenge to the ideal type of a rational bureaucracy because it focuses on members and their wants and needs as the most important part of the organization instead of rules and efficiency.

Eventually, more ideal types emerge including the decision-making and the human relations types (Perrow, 1972). Each of these is formulated as an ideal type, often with conflicting criteria of effectiveness specific to the respective school of thought. The problem is choosing the ideal type to support because no consensus exists to place one above the others. Other conceptualizations of ideal types were goal-based models and models that emphasize internal processes (Scott, 1998; Whetten & Cameron, 1994).

The goal-based model, also called goal attainment, is the most popular form of ideal type (Banner & Gagne, 1995; Cameron, 1980). The name refers to the degree to which organizations reach stated goals (Harrison & Shirom, 1999; Seashore, 1983). The assumption underlying the goal-based model in general is that goals impact behavior (Locke & Latham, 1990). Goals are defined as "conceptions of desired ends--conditions that participants attempt to effect through the performance of task activities" (Scott, 1981, p. 16). In this view, organizations are mechanisms to reach objectives, and organizational objectives are established to influence organizational behavior or actions in specified directions. Organizations are considered effective as outputs and activities draw closer to goals. For example, if an area council reached all goals, it would be considered effective even if members overspent the budget or offered programs that were perceived as discriminatory.

The benefits of the goal-based model include ease of use; a focus on organizational purpose; the connection of values to goals; and the perception of "causal relationships" between conditions and goals (Seashore, 1983). Scott (1981) notes that organizational analysts are divided in how they view benefits of the goal model. Some think goals create emotional attachments that increase motivation; others believe goals supply cognitive direction and parameters to improve decision-making and outputs. Goals also allow group behavior to be evaluated in comparison to stated organizational goals (Scott, 1977).

There are several problems with the goal-based model approach, however. Goals are difficult to measure when products or services are not concrete. Multiple goals may mean that one goal is met through the sacrifice of another goal (Gibson et al., 1982; Yuchtman & Seashore, 1967). Organizations may not have widespread support for all of stated goals (Gibson et al., 1982), and goals are often set after behavior takes place (Scott, 1981). In spite of these limitations, setting goals is still considered an important feature of organizational effectiveness. For an in-depth discussion of goal models, see Banner & Gagne (1995) or Seashore (1982).

The internal processes ideal type, also labeled organizational health, refers to the presence of positive forces within organizations. These positive forces are low stress (Cameron, 1980) and good communication throughout the organization (Wheatley, 1992). Members support participative management, group decision-making, and management support of members (Likert, 1967). In this view, as the number of characteristics indicative of organizational health increase, the effectiveness of the organization also increases (Cameron, 1980). For example, if members of the RHA are participating fully, support one another, and have fun, effectiveness is enhanced even if the organization did nothing to improve residence hall living.

Benefits of this approach are illustrated in a management system labeled "System 4" (Likert, 1967), that includes internal processes. Examples of outcomes from healthy internal processes are increased loyalty and performance standards, improved cooperation, and higher productivity (Likert, 1967). A meta-analysis performed on the management literature by the Gallup organization (Buckingham & Coffman, 1999) supports several of these findings, including the belief that positive relationships between managers and employees result in higher employee productivity.

Shortcomings of internal processes are that many organizations continue to be successful, even when "healthy" processes are not in place (Cameron, 1980). The political model of organizations encourages internal conflicts as healthy processes (Bolman & Deal, 2003; Harrison, 1994).

Contingency Theory

The contingency theory emphasizes the fit between organizational "profile" and environments of operation; it arose from the competition between supporters of different schools of ideal types and situational leadership (Hall, 1999; Harrison & Shirom, 1999; Whetten & Cameron, 1994). Out of a focus on fit came ideas of system models such as the system resource model, organic or open systems, and mechanistic organizations that operate effectively in different environments (Whetten & Cameron, 1994). Contingency theory focuses on determining effectiveness criteria that relate specifically to environments of operation. Ideal types consist of standard criteria applied to all settings. Contingency theory implies that organizations have distinct effectiveness criteria that are best derived from examining organizations and environments. For example, RHAs vary depending on the university environments in which they operate, which makes each one unique yet effective.

System resource models are defined to the extent to which organizations acquire resources needed to operate (Cameron, 1980; Yuchtman & Seashore, 1967). Resources can be in the form of "materials, energy, information, and personnel" (Scott, 1981, p. 156), as well as financial resources. For example, an RHA with talented members and enough money to put on programs and services is considered effective. This approach isolates the input side of the organization, or the interface from the external environment, which is the source of the resources.

There are benefits to this view of effectiveness. Because all organizations must compete for limited resources (Hall, 1999; Scott, 1981), system resource models define effectiveness as the degree to which organizations gather resources to survive. This conceptualization helps focus the energies of organizations towards resource acquisition. Members emphasize enlarging resources and helping organizations compare themselves to similar organizations (Yuchtman & Seashore, 1967). Effectiveness is an organization's "ability to exploit its environments in the acquisition of scarce and valued resources to sustain its functioning" (Yuchtman & Seashore, 1967, p. 393).

Limitations to system resource organizations fall into several categories. Cameron (1980) illustrates that the model does not apply to all organizations because some organizations are effective even when they do not acquire preferred resources. An example is a floor council that is not able to acquire enough money to put on programs, but initiates creative options that include travel to free events.

Multiple Constituent Theory

Constituencies are groups of members who are dependent on or invested in organizations, Effectiveness from this perspective is defined as reaching goals set by the multiple constituencies of an organization (Cameron, 1980; Cameron & Whetten, 1983; Connolly, Conlon, & Deutsch, 1980; Whetten & Cameron, 1994; Zammuto, 1982). Responsiveness to constituents is another effectiveness factor, with the degree of satisfaction of the multiple constituents being the basis of determining effectiveness of an organization. For example, an RHA is viewed as effective when it receives high marks from the department of housing, area councils, hall councils, and residents, although a widespread consensus such as this is rare.

This approach to understanding effectiveness allows observers to be aware of the many perspectives that come to bear in determining what is important in organizations (Connolly et al., 1980). The approach highlights the need to identify values and to determine which constituents' values determine the criteria for effectiveness -- residents, department of housing administrators, RHA officers, etc. The multiple constituency approach moves away from the perspective that organizations are value free (Connolly et al., 1980) and focuses on making values visible in decision-making.

Weaknesses to the multiple constituency model of effectiveness include the pressure to balance the values of different groups of constituents and the reality that some organizations are considered successful even when they do not serve major constituents (Cameron, 1980). This model is also criticized for avoiding the issue of whose values should dominate (Keeley, 1984).

Multiple constituency theory highlights the role of coalitions or groupings of types of constituents. The dominant coalition is the group that has the most power and discretion to influence the organization (Thompson, 1967). Cameron (1978) emphasizes the importance of including dominant coalition members in the determination of organizational effectiveness because criteria of effectiveness are inherently value-laden and are always determined by the dominant or most powerful group. In addition, the dominant coalition consists of those who influence organizational policy and goals (Pennings & Goodman, 1977). These members are more likely to use information on organizational effectiveness (Campbell, 1977). Therefore, the consensus of dominant coalition members should be included in the generation of effectiveness criteria (Pennings & Goodman, 1977).

Summary of Past Models and Theories of Organizational Effectiveness.

Ideal types, contingency theory, and multiple constituency theory all illustrate organizational effectiveness in different ways. Each is applicable to RHAs, shedding light on the many ways advisers and students evaluate hall governments. Advisers and RHA members operate consciously and/or unconsciously using theories or models to evaluate performance. By intentionally considering various models and theories, advisers and RHA members can explore the appropriateness of adopting models and theories to particular student organizations and fine tune them to fit individual campuses. No single model or theory contains all the measures of effectiveness.

Student Organizations

A general and historic perspective of student organizations serves to illustrate the discussion of the effectiveness of RHAs. The first student organizations, literary societies and debate clubs, were established in the United States during the eighteenth century (Rudolph, as cited in Marine, 1984). Subsequently, class organizations, sports teams, and then college student councils developed. Student governments with greater political agendas proliferated in the early twentieth century (Marine, 1984). Over time, student activities became a prominent feature on modern college campuses.

Frederick (1959) identifies four periods of student activities in America: suppression, toleration, capitalization, and exploitation. The suppression period occurred during colonial times when survival was of utmost importance and leisure activities were minimal or nonexistent. The toleration period occurred in the 1800s when the country became more stabilized and refers to the tolerance that administrators and faculty began to show towards student-initiated ideas for self-organized associations and activities. During the capitalization period in the mid-20th century, student activities and organizations were supported actively by all the multiple publics invested in education because of the clear benefits derived by students. The exploitation period began in the 1950s and refers to the shift in priority from activities and associations to support students to the "main motivating force [becoming] rather some benefit to the institution, the teacher, the coach, or the administrator in the sponsoring role" (Frederick, 1959, p.29).

These four periods identify the evolving role of student activities and organizations throughout the history of the United States. Several key factors emerge from these periods. Student organizations were initiated by students. Student organizations are integral to the educational experience. Students benefit from involvement in student organizations. The major benefactors of student organizations and activities should be students, though this is not always the case. Thus, student organizations have been and are a central part of campus life, contributing to the growth and development of individual students (Astin, 1993; Dunkel & Schuh, 1998). Effectiveness as organizations is an important factor.

In general, involvement in student activities produces positive learning outcomes for students (Kuh & Lund, 1994). Astin (1993) found that election to an office was associated positively with a career as a lawyer, with undergraduate grade point average, with satisfaction regarding student life, and with self-perceived leadership development. The term "office" includes student government offices.

The positive benefits of student involvement in student organizations and the central role these organizations play in higher education point to the importance of determining what makes organizations work well. The assumption is that as organizations work more effectively, positive outcomes for students increase. Understanding organizational effectiveness is central to maximizing student benefits from participation in student organizations in general, and student government and RHAs in particular.

Student Organizations and Effectiveness

Bledsoe (1994) provides criteria for strong and weak student organizations. Strong organizations have relatively large, consistent memberships; are able to bring in new members; have high attendance at meetings; have minimal internal conflict; have signs of good leadership; reach goals set by the organization; have members who want to stay part of the organization; meet responsibilities to the institution; follow policies and procedures; and have positive impacts on student life. By contrast, weak organizations have inconsistent membership levels or very low numbers; have poor meeting response; have extensive personal conflict; have signs of poor leadership; are challenged to bring in new members; have little or no positive impact on student life; have signs of disorganization within the internal system; and have poor internal organizational communication.

Dunkel and Schuh (1998) provide multiple criteria for the effective operation of student organizations. They challenge universities and colleges to provide legal and contractual support; materials and supplies; office and meeting space; and academic encouragement to facilitate the success of student organizations on campus. They challenge student organizations to develop quality memberships; find funding also to operate; track budgets; effectively incorporate advisers; follow institutional norms for operation; examine legal implications of activities; and keep organized. They encourage student organizations to focus on communication (internally and externally) to address both academic and co-curricular activities, and to understand institutional decision-making. These challenges to institutions and student organizations illustrate the need for effective relationships between involved groups.

These criteria and challenges are valid for all student government organizations, including RHAs. RHAs are specific types of student organization and have distinct roles on campuses. To better understand the parallel functions and purposes of RHAs, a general review of student government organizations is required.

Student Government Organizations

Student government organizations are unique types of organizations though the criteria provided by Bledsoe (1994) and Dunkel and Schuh (1998) are relevant to effectiveness. Student governments typically represent student bodies on campuses to administrations with members selected by election (Cuyjet, 1994). Student governments also provide services that range from financial resource distribution to sanctioning other student organizations to providing free legal advice to lobbying for the sale of books at affordable prices (Cuyjet, 1994). From an educational standpoint, student governments provide extensive involvement activities for students, building leadership skills in a variety of areas.

In 1994, Cuyjet examined the effectiveness of a student government in one domain, service provision to students. He developed an instrument to determine both what services were being provided by the organization and what level of effectiveness was judged to be present for those services being offered. The sample consisted of members ($\underline{n}$ = 215) and non-members ($\underline{n}$ = 171) of the student government organization. Fifty-one services were included. Comparisons were made between members and non-members regarding the effectiveness of services provided. Cuyjet found significant differences on 21 services ($\underline{p}$ < .05), with non-member constituents appearing less aware of services than members. He also found significant differences between members and non-members in the perceptions of effectiveness on 11 services. His interpretation of these differences notes that constituents are often less informed than elected officers and members who have greater familiarity with the scope of activities. Cuyjet also notes that if gaps between members and non-members occur on a campus, the overall effectiveness of that student government is compromised. Based on these findings, he promotes the need for regular organizational assessments by campuses of student governments—including RHAs —to ensure constituents are informed of services.

This study also notes differences in rankings of importance of services provided. No services were ranked the same between members and non-members. Three were one rank apart. The top priority for non-members, addressing the issue of rising tuition, was eighth on the members' list. Cuyjet did not tie findings to organizational effectiveness research. However, a multiple constituency model predicts these findings because the findings show value differences between group constituencies. The disturbing theme in this study is that this student government, whose mission is to serve student constituents, may be addressing issues that are separate from the actual needs or priorities of students. This may be explained in part to conflicting goals between service to campus administration and services to students. This final aspect of the study indicates that student governments in general may need to consult constituents more actively to determine the outcomes most helpful to them.

Outcomes that students gain through participation in student government benefit both students and institutional communities (Kuh & Lund, 1994). The student government experience helps students apply and develop skills that enhance senses of self-competence and efficacy, especially through the process of working with diverse people. Additionally, academic knowledge is often applied and integrated through participation. Kuh and Lund (1994) call for increased student participation in campus government and for a focus on developing a sense of citizenship in students.

Student government organizations offer students unique experiences that build skills in multiple areas while contributing to universities. In parallel fashion, RHAs offer resident students unique opportunities to grow and learn while living on campus in addition to contributing to the effectiveness of housing departments as well as universities.

RHA Effectiveness

RHAs are complex organizations that contain multiple levels, serve multiple constituents, and have multiple goals. They are unique because part of their purpose is the education and development of their members. This purpose differs from the purposes of many student organizations, private sector companies, and non-profit. This uniqueness is indicative of the environments in which RHAs operate, institutions of higher education, which are complex and focus on the education of students. What makes RHAs work well? This varies depending on campus environments, but some guidelines exist. Each level of residence hall government—RHAs, area councils, hall councils, and floor councils—has unique features and common aspects that relate to effectiveness.

Residence Hall Associations

RHAs are typically the highest level of residence hall government. RHAs combine elements of various models and theories of organizations. RHAs are weakly linked to the mechanistic model of organizations. Although efficiency and organization are central RHA concepts and many have clear hierarchical designs, most are focused on the involvement and education of students which is counter to the "cog in a wheel" approach. One author (Komives, 1994) calls for more flexible, decentralized and empowering approaches to RHAs to allow for greater student learning and involvement, which is a compelling argument against over-relying on mechanistic practices.

The political model, considered an aspect of the internal system of organizations, has more parallels to RHAs. RHA members frequently are elected, which implies competition, yet they must also cooperate once elected. In addition, power is important and is defined positionally in the organization. Resources are acquired and distributed as integral processes of transacting business. Conflict is routine especially in advocacy roles between students and administration and in the distribution of limited resources.

RHAs as learning organizations are newer concepts. Few RHAs have flattened hierarchies to embrace decentralized, wide-ranging decision-making power. However, learning within organizations exists, with staff often acting as facilitators of student learning. Open systems theory fits with the environment in which RHAs operate. RHAs are nested within larger systems, including housing departments and universities. RHAs depend on and react to external environments including university administrations, residents, and hall/area councils. RHAs also parallel open systems models. They have inputs—students, budgets, supplies—from environments; have internal processes used to complete tasks; and produce outputs to environments such as programs and advice on policies and procedures.

RHAs have components of the political model, of learning organizations, and of the open systems model with some mechanistic concepts. Each of these perspectives brings different sets of variables to consider in determining what makes RHAs effective. Examining the nature of RHAs through organizational theory, models and types sets the stage for deeper understanding. RHAs have central purposes, associated educational philosophies, particular structures, internal systems, sets of activities they produce, relationships to other organizations, and are nested within larger organizations known as departments of residence life or housing.

Purpose of RHAs

Deciding purpose is a crucial step in the formation or success of RHAs (Stoner & Wyatt, 1993) and must be understood clearly at all levels (Komives & Tucker, 1993, 1998). The primary purpose of RHAs is to be multifaceted, including to develop "learning communities for students" (Dunkel & Spencer, 1998, p. iv) and to provide involvement opportunities for students on campus (Papish & Wall, 1998). RHAs are designed to develop leadership skills; encourage student voices in housing decision-making (Papish & Wall, 1981; Werring, 1984); make hall environments better; and engage residents in activities (Komives & Tucker, 1993, 1998).

Educational Philosophy of RHAs

RHAs are essential aspects of student learning outside the classroom. They can be part of an intentional educational design in residence halls. Levine (1994) endorses intentional education and identifies four areas to increase intentional education: out-of-class learning, which may be the most powerful; student-to-student interaction because students often have the greatest impact on one another; student culture because students themselves define culture or practices and transfer these lessons to other students; and student activities because activities that receive the most attention are created by other students. RHAs address Levine's four areas by providing forums for peer education; by developing academic skills; by transmitting peer culture; and by providing activities that meet student needs and desires.

RHA Structure

The structure of RHAs typically takes three forms: centralized RHAs that work with area and hall student governments; centralized RHAs comprised of voting members or representatives from each residential unit on campus with no separate area or hall student governments; and decentralized RHAs with governance solely in the form of area and/or building level student governments (Verry, 1993). RHAs do not include floor or unit levels of representation, hall levels of representation, or area-wide representation though these levels of governance may also be present within housing programs. Structures vary according to degree of formalization and centralization with highly formalized RHAs more rule-oriented than less formalized RHAs. Highly centralized RHAs may exist as single, all-campus units with no hall/area councils, and decentralized RHAs may exist with only area or hall functions and no central association (Cawthon & Underwood, 1998). For a more in-depth discussion of hall governance structures, see Chapter 6.

Other structural variables recommended for effective operations include designs that increase member participation and have levels similar to the housing structure yet allow for flexible responses to particular events and needs (Stoner & Wyatt, 1993). RHAs have elections; position descriptions for student leaders (Schaefer, 2000); constitutions and bylaws; executive boards or councils; and often belong to regional or national associations (Cawthon & Underwood, 1998). RHAs may have senates, which include members in positions other than executive board, or may have general assemblies that consist of students who attend meetings (Schaefer, 2000).

Resources needed for RHAs to function include funding (Grandpre & Kimble, 1998; Hudson & Tattershall, 1998; Komives & Tucker, 1993, 1998); rooms for meetings and offices (Miller & Blattner, 1998; Stoner & Wyatt, 1993); equipment and supplies (Miller & Blattner); and diverse members (Komives & Tucker, 1993, 1998). These resources allow RHAs to conduct work effectively.

Internal processes for RHAs include member leadership development; assessment of student needs; training in ethics, decision-making (Schaefer, 2000), group dynamics, and team development; meeting management motivation; general interpersonal skills (Stoner & Wyatt, 1993); evaluation of group performance (Sampson, 1998); conflict management (Boersig & Wallington, 1998); and recognition and reward systems (Komives & Tucker, 1993, 1998). Members should be involved in various aspects of RHA operations including voting on budget issues (Boersig & Wallington, 1998) and committing to enhance diversity within the organization and on campus through programming (Papish & Wall, 1998).

RHAs are expected to provide many activities and outcomes, including social activities (Dunkel, 1998) and outcomes related to the institution, such as examining university procedures that affect residents (Stoner & Wyatt, 1993) or fund-raising activities that provide services to residents, such as kits for exams or opening week. Other activities may include programs on academic success, fire safety, leadership, and social issues. Some activities happen off campus, such as community service activities, helping community organizations, or supporting national legislation (Miller & Blattner, 1998).

Other campus organizations in formal relationships with RHAs include housing departments, food services, campus student governments, and student press/media. Hall or area student governments are especially important as sources of support for RHAs (Stoner & Wyatt, 1993). To be effective, these relationships need to be characterized by mutual support (Miller & Blattner, 1998; Stoner & Wyatt, 1993) and by mutual communication (Komives & Tucker, 1993, 1998; Miller & Blattner, 1998; Stoner & Wyatt, 1993).

RHAs have staff advisers from housing administrations (Dunkel & Schuh, 1998) who support RHAs. Advisers educate members about organizations and institutions; train members in a variety of areas (Boersig & Wallington, 1998); act as role models; provide appropriate expectations (Mitchell & Munro-Krusz, 1998); provide oversight for budgets; inform groups about rewards at regional and national levels; meet regularly with executives; help groups understand university policies; support members' problem-solving and decision-making; and motivate members when necessary (Porter, 1998).

RHAs are frequently members of other larger organizations devoted to RHAs, such as NACURH at the national level and state and regional organizations (Schaefer, 2000; Stoner, Berry, Boever, & Tattershall, 1998). RHA members frequently attend conferences coordinated by these organizations (Spencer, 1998).

Housing Departments as Contexts and Environments

In the open system model, external environments play crucial roles in defining what makes organizations effective. External environments of RHAs include housing departments that administer facilities, programs, and staffing. Housing departments form part of the external environments influencing the organization of RHAs. Relationships between RHAs and housing departments must be included in RHA measures of effectiveness. Housing departments frequently have student development goals that include student involvement, leadership development, support of the academic mission, and educational activities. The most visible venues for these goals are RHAs, whose mission and goals should be consistent with the departmental missions (P. Mielke, personal communication, March 13, 1997). Mielke states that it is the collective responsibility of housing departments to take leadership in the development of RHAs as viable organizations. If there are strong relationships between housing departments and RHAs, the theory or model of organization operating in one most likely influences the other. Therefore, it is important to understand organizational theories that may influence RHAs.

Research on RHAs

A few empirical studies of RHAs have been conducted in the last 10 years. Empirical studies provide data that supports or challenges ideas of what makes RHAs work well. Three studies are summarized below: Komives and Tucker (1993, 1998) and Tucker (2001).

Komives and Tucker (1993, 1998)

Komives and Tucker conducted a national qualitative study on RHAs in 1993. The purpose of the study was to identify themes from select effective RHAs. These themes were identified as contributing factors to the success of organizations.

Ten university housing experts nominated RHAs that they believed maintained excellence over time. A snowball sampling procedure was used that confirmed the selected institutions. This process resulted in a final group of 13 select RHA programs. One or more housing professionals on each campus was interviewed, member checks were conducted by sending transcripts of interviews to interviewees for accuracy review, transcripts were reviewed for themes, and a document analysis of residence hall government materials was conducted. From the resulting data, Komives and Tucker identified five major themes with sub-themes that indicate RHA success.

The first theme is "staff values and beliefs regarding students" and includes these sub-themes: students matter and are highly valued; students are unique; student involvement is a commitment; strong RHAs are essential for residence life program success; staff commitment is endorsed in resource allocation; multi-directional communication is expected; and student input is sought and predetermined. These sub-themes indicate that staff beliefs and values support actions.

The second theme is "the role of the adviser" and includes these sub-themes: the role, placement, and commitment of advisers are central to the success of RHAs; advisers are professional educators; advisers understand how to work with volunteers; advisers are flexible and have high tolerance for ambiguity; advisers are highly engaged; advisers develop talent; and advisers possess multiple skills, beliefs, and values. Obviously, advisers play central roles in RHA effectiveness in these successful programs.

The third theme is "the purpose of the RHA" and includes these sub-themes: RHAs improve residence hall environments; RHAs provide activities for resident students; and RHAs are leadership training grounds for other campus organizations. Responses illustrate the importance of being aware of the purposes of RHAs.

The fourth theme is "organizational structure" and includes these sub-themes: structural designs vary; each campus has system-wide governance units; each system is perceived as coherently organized; each level of government has a central focus of activities; a trend exists to shift emphasis toward decentralization; successful governments provide continuity of officers; recognition and rewards are central to RHA success; successful RHAs have clear systems for communication to all levels of governance units and to residents; and clear sources of adequate funding and budget authority exist. Successful RHAs view structure as important.

The fifth theme is "leadership development" and includes these sub-themes: multiple levels of formal leadership training exist; strong commitments to develop leadership in underrepresented groups exist; officers benefit from experiences from other campuses; and residence life promotes leadership education. Intentional leadership development is associated with strong RHAs.

Five components of effective RHAs emerge from the studies: staff views students as mature, responsible, capable adults; advisers develop "mattering" relationships with student leaders; at all levels, the purpose of RHAs is clearly understood and supported by members and housing departments; organizational structures are designed to provide continuity, involvement, recognition and rewards, formal communications, and income streams; and ongoing leadership development takes place to identify emergent leaders and to ensure positional competence, student growth, and effective organizational maintenance. In general, these five components serve as guidelines or goals for RHAs.

Komives and Tucker caution that results of qualitative research are descriptive, not generalizable. Advisers must decide if findings are relevant to their institutions. The findings reveal less tangible issues such as staff values, mattering perspectives, and roles of advisers in relation to RHA effectiveness at participant institutions.

Tucker 2001

Tucker conducted an empirical, quantitative study in 2001 that examined the effectiveness of RHAs. This study included the development of a model of effectiveness and criteria for measurement derived from the literature and from constituents of RHAs. The study resulted in the design and validation of an instrument to measure RHA effectiveness based on criteria.

To build the model, conceptual elements were defined. Tucker developed a model for RHAs based on an extensive literature review of organizations and RHAs. The model had five constructs: resource acquisition/inputs; structure; internal system; productivity/outputs; and external environment. Each construct in the model was based on a multitude of models from the literature that highlighted dimensions of organizational effectiveness. All are applicable to the model development of effective RHAs because they provide concepts that apply to effective organizational functioning.

- **Model definition: Resource acquisition/inputs.** Resource acquisitions/inputs are materials, supplies, personnel, and space that come to RHAs and include processes used to acquire resources. Elements are funding; technology; office space; materials and supplies; talented members and numbers of members; and information and support from constituents and stakeholders, such as members, residence hall students, housing staff, and faculty-in-residence.

- **Model definition: Structure.** Structure refers to the internal structures of RHAs, including personnel reporting lines, procedures, and written documents. Elements are organizational design related to purpose such as number of officer positions; procedures for electing or appointing officers; meeting management; budgeting processes; written documentation of processes and practices such as constitutions; levels of clarity regarding roles and responsibilities; levels of formalization of rules, processes and procedures; voting procedures; levels of centralization; levels of decentralization; and degrees of organizational flexibility, such as the ability to change procedures when necessary.

- **Model definition: Internal systems.** Internal systems are processes used as RHAs accomplish work. Internal systems include the way members interact with one another and the use of political processes to influence organizations and to interpret organizational events. Elements are leadership, organizational vision, mission, member inspiration, communications, efficiency, group morale, group decision-making, allocating resources appropriately, reward systems, technological uses, member skills development, level of commitment, and creativity. Additional elements include the extent RHAs learn from experiences; the amount of constant change present within RHAs; the level of adaptability to changing internal conditions; the ability to clarify goals; the ability to plan activities; the ability to see RHAs as whole organizations; awareness and clarity of purpose; the satisfaction of primary members; the ability of RHAs to meet the needs of members; the extent to which values are the basis for actions; the amount of stress present among members; officer support of other members; levels of cooperation; training preparedness; meeting attendance; and evaluation and assessment activities.

Political processes are part of internal systems and include members advocating issues to affect decision-making; using negotiation as a frequent process to resolve differences, decide issues, or set direction; acting on personal interests; perceiving lasting differences between groups within the organization; emphasizing the importance of the distribution of limited resources; viewing power as important; and regarding conflict as necessary and important. Political elements are often overlooked in RHA effectiveness, yet they play key roles in how members interact. Political processes are important to how RHAs view and conduct work.

- **Model definition: Productivity/outputs.** Productivity/outputs are what RHAs do to fulfill missions and purposes. This construct includes secondary impacts to productivity such as resident satisfaction. Elements include responsiveness to the needs or wants of resident students; goal attainment; program delivery to residents; fundraisers that provide services to resident students; advice on policies and procedures to housing departments; performance in regional and national conferences; and advocacy regarding resident issues and concerns.

- **Model definition: External environment.** External relationships are relationships RHAs have with the external world and the external forces that influence RHAs, including universities and housing departments. Elements included adapting to changing external forces, such as new university or housing policies; seeking feedback from external constituents for self-improvement; building and maintaining relationships and reputations with other organizations; responding to and satisfying external stakeholders such as administrators, the campus student government, and national organizations; and building relationships with advisers.

Method of Study

The study was divided into two parts: defining the constructs that make up organizational effectiveness for RHAs (see above) and designing a valid and reliable instrument to measure those constructs. Tucker developed an item pool through a review of literature and by seeking input from a focus group of 73 respondents from three universities. The item pool was reviewed by a panel of experts, including 10 students who held RHA or NACURH officer positions and 10 professionals with extensive RHA experience. A pilot study was conducted, which included 275 respondents from nine institutions. A field test of the instrument included 2,042 respondents from 73 institutions.

Results

The study proves that RHA effectiveness can be defined and measured. A 94-item survey measures the effectiveness of Residence Hall Associations. The factor analysis merged the original five constructs of the model into three constructs renamed RHA Effects, Housing Relationship, and Formal Processes. RHA Effects combines the original constructs of internal systems and productivity/outputs. Housing Relationship construct is primarily the original external environment construct and shows the importance of the relationships between RHAs and housing departments. Formal Processes encompasses the formalized processes of RHAs that were present in all five previous constructs. The new constructs are represented in the final survey, which shows strong validity and reliability. This research defines organizational effectiveness as it specifically relates to RHAs instead of using generic models of effectiveness adapted from business to fit RHAs.

Summary of RHAs

RHAs are important student organizations within housing departments and involve multiple dimensions of effectiveness in function. They are unique organizations that combine elements of general organizations, non-profits organizations, government organizations, student organizations, and student government organizations. The research on RHAs is expanding and provides ways to measure and improve effectiveness, adding value to the experiences of thousands of students. Measuring effectiveness helps RHA members and advisers set goals and recognize ways to lead organizations to higher levels of performance, including member education and constituent satisfaction. The following case studies (Komives & Tucker, 1998, pp. 47–49) assist in the application of effectiveness presented in this chapter.

RHA Case Study One

Over the years, RHA advising has been shifted to one of the most recently hired hall directors. While it used to be in the job description of the associate director, other pressing demands, like facilities renewals, outsourcing food service, and a fire in a major residence hall meant that the associate director has to readjust duties, and RHA advising was shifted to hall director staff. The responsibility has remained there ever since. The RHA has become activist in recent years. Members are showing signs of wanting to protest rising food plan fees, and they are very dissatisfied with the limited serving hours during final exams. In addition, the RHA is considering recommending a major policy change regarding pets in the residence halls and are using the fact that hall directors are allowed this privilege as one of their arguments. The hall director adviser to the RHA is very nervous. She knows that central administration does not like addressing these issues, and she will be put in a tough spot being expected to defuse the agenda, yet believing the students have a right to be heard. How should she approach this dilemma with her supervisors and with the students? What communication systems might be helpful if she remains as the adviser?

RHA Case Study Two

You are the new director of residence life at Seesaw University (SU), which has 3,000 students housed on campus. The total student body is 10,000. The nine residential buildings on campus are divided into three distinct geographic areas. Each building has a full-time resident director (RD) and a part-time assistant hall director (AHD), and each geographic area has an area director (AD).

For resident student governance, each hall has a hall council advised by the AHD. The hall councils have two representatives who attend RHA meetings, but have no voting power. Hall council officers are elected once a year in the fall; RHA officers are elected in the fall. The RHA maintains budgetary control and entertains budget requests from the hall councils.

Parule Foster is the adviser to this RHA. She is a graduate assistant, working on her master's degree in college student personnel administration. She works on her assistantship responsibilities 20 hours per week, and also has responsibilities in the central office working with room assignments. She feels overworked and wants the students in the RHA to take leadership and run the organization themselves, consulting her only in emergencies. She meets with them when she has time.

When you arrive, you discover several concerns brought forth by various students and staff. You find from the campus student governance association that the RHA is seen as a group that implements programs similar to the resident assistants on campus, only on a larger scale, and even then their first program of the year does not take place until Halloween. Several of the AHDs tell you that the hall councils have little respect for the RHA. The RHA president comes to you individually, saying she feels her officers do not take her seriously. During this same meeting you ask her if she has sought ideas from NACURH, and she responds with, "What's that?"

After gathering these opinions, you examine the past annual reports for the department and uncover a gradual reduction in funding for the RHA from resident student fees, and an increasing emphasis on the RHA raising their own money through fundraising activities on campus. You also see that the Department of Resident Life sponsors an annual recognition ceremony for RAs, and that RHA officers are invited to attend, but do not partake in the actual ceremony.

To address these concerns you draw together your professional staff, including ADs and RDs, and the RHA president. Together you must (a) determine which aspects of the . . . [factors of effectiveness] involved in RHA success from this chapter are present, (b) figure out which aspects of the factors that are absent need to be in place to promote success for the RHA at SU, and (c) derive specific strategies to put needed aspects in place. Your group may create any information that is not presented in the case description. Choose someone in the group to act as the director—this person facilitates the discussion. Choose someone to act as RHA president—this person reports the findings and strategies of the group. After each group has reported, have a general discussion on how this case applies to actual participant cases.

Area Councils

Area councils are not as prevalent as RHAs and hall/floor councils. Area councils are unique and differ from RHAs in that they must cooperate with other area councils and represent multiple halls. When present in RHA systems, area councils often act as intermediaries between RHAs and hall councils because they work more closely with hall councils. The political model explains the level of effectiveness of area councils in building coalitions with other area councils and in negotiating for resources or discussing issues with RHAs and hall councils in their areas. Area councils collect opinions and perspectives of resident students through hall councils and represent them to or brief the RHAs on them.

Learning theory applies to area councils as one of the purposes of area councils is to educate members. Many programs have educational focuses. Open systems theory is more narrowly defined in area councils than in RHAs because the typical external organization that works with area councils are more limited, although input from students, resources, budget, supplies are still required. The outputs of area councils are focused on the halls under their purview, such as supporting hall leadership to put on programs, helping with problem-solving, and providing extra budget for hall capital improvements.

Purpose of Area Councils

Area councils are often created to parallel housing staffing structures that include area coordinators because this allows for effective communication and support between students and staff. Parallel structures are recommended by Stoner & Wyatt (1993), supported by a model by Osteen & Tucker (1997), and add layers of leadership development for residence hall students who can move from hall leadership to area council leadership positions. In addition, area councils help plan activities and coordinate needs between multiple halls.

Educational Philosophy of Area Councils

Area councils have similar educational purposes to RHAs. They create opportunities for peer-to-peer learning; academic skills development such as report writing, decision-making skills, and group projects; student cultural understanding; and activities that meet student needs and interests. They provide practice arenas for leadership and communication skills, which fit housing department goals.

Area Council Structure

Area councils are designed in a variety of ways. (see Chapter 6). Similar to leadership levels of RHAs, a chair or president, voting members, and representatives from each hall within the respective geographical living units comprise an area council. The level of centralization and formalization varies depending on campus environments and the educational philosophy of housing departments. The more decisions approved by area councils, the higher the level of centralization of authority. If area councils decentralize, they distribute greater degrees of decision-making to the hall level. Centralized organizational functions result in more efficient decision-making and allocation of resources. Decentralized organizational functions result in higher ownership in decision-making by hall councils.

Area coordinators or other staff members who oversee more than one hall typically advise area councils. Area councils usually direct two or more hall councils and representatives from hall councils attend area council meetings. Activities of area councils include providing programs to their respective halls; supporting individual hall programs; providing advice for hall leadership; advocating for issues facing halls; supplying resources for services desired by halls such as cable or laundry service; and providing information and opinions to RHAs

Area Council Research

No published empirical research specifically on area councils was found. Unpublished research data may exist on individual campuses. The themes found in the Komives and Tucker (1993, 1998) studies are transferable to area councils. Students mattering; students viewed as unique; commitments to student involvement; beliefs in strong government systems; resources allocated to student governments; extensive multiple direction communications; and clear methods of gaining student input are as relevant to area councils as to RHAs. The constructs found in the Tucker (2001) research are also relevant. Relationships with housing departments, strong internal mechanisms, and formal processes are crucial to the effectiveness of area councils. Although the RHA effectiveness surveys target specific organizations, area councils can use the results to measure effectiveness.

Summary of Area Councils

Area councils, though established less frequently, add to overall RHA effectiveness, especially at institutions that have area coordinators. They add extra layers of leadership development to systems, coordinate activities between halls, and provide closer support than RHAs alone.

Area Council Case Study

The housing department added area coordinator positions to the staffing model this year in conjunction with area councils. The RHA is concerned that it will lose power and influence with the housing department and, as a result, is running its operations as it had before this year and is avoiding providing any funding support to the councils for larger scale programming. Using organizational theory and organizational effectiveness models (such as the political model and multiple constituency theory), frame the problems presented and create a strategy to improve the effectiveness of communication between the RHA and area councils, and between housing and the residence hall government.

Hall Councils

Hall councils are student organizations in specific buildings within housing systems and are as prevalent as RHAs on campuses. The hall/floor councils are immersed in living environments of halls, which challenge these organizations because of the blurred boundaries between living together and acting together as distinct organizations.

Purpose of Hall Councils

Hall councils provide leadership opportunities for residents in the hall; produce programs and services for residents; create a sense of community in halls; and support goals of housing staff members who live and work in close proximity. Hall councils represent residents to area councils or RHAs, as well as to housing staff; solicit resources for activities in the halls; and communicate campus issues to residents. Hall councils impact student life by enriching the co-curricular experience.

Educational Philosophy of Hall Councils

Hall councils exist in accordance with the philosophy that human involvement is beneficial for individuals and communities. Hall councils allow for residents' voices in hall, area, and campus activities, which enhance involvement and set the stage for residents to contribute to the communities in which they live.

Hall council structure

Hall councils are designed with central governing groups that are elected or appointed, usually either in fall or spring terms. They often have representatives from each floor, sometimes called "floor presidents." Hall councils are usually advised by hall directors and focus activities on the hall, while working closely with housing staff. Many have budgets that consist of a portion of student fees collected from residents. The procedures and internal processes are often more informal than those associated with area councils or RHAs.

Hall Council Research

No published empirical research specifically on hall councils was found. Unpublished research data may exist on individual campuses. The concepts of RHA effectiveness are transferable to hall councils. The same staff beliefs and values that matter with RHA effectiveness apply to hall council effectiveness. Concepts of organizational effectiveness that work for RHAs also work for hall councils, but priorities may be different. For example, formal processes may be lower priority for hall councils, but relationships with housing staff may be higher priority because hall council leaders typically are first-year students, while RHA leaders are experienced leaders. Advisers also can apply group development and effectiveness, other areas of research and conceptualization, to hall councils, (see Chapter 11 on group development concepts).

Summary of Hall Councils

Hall councils are often the first student organizations experienced by residents at institutions. They are pivotal in creating hall communities that are healthy and involving, and they provide levels of engagement important to student satisfaction. Although no published research about hall councils exists, many housing staff has extensive experience advising them. Using RHA effectiveness concepts will assist advisers in making hall councils successful and memorable.

Hall Council Case Study

You are a hall director hired mid-year. You eagerly await your first hall council meeting so you can hear about the successful activities that have happened first semester and about the plans for second semester. Instead of positive stories, you find that the hall council had very low numbers, had few people showing up to meetings, had extensive personal conflict, had signs of poor leadership, were challenged to bring in new members, had little or no positive impact on student life in the hall, were disorganized, and had poor internal communication. Using the concepts presented in this chapter, lay out a strategy to improve hall council functioning through the end of the academic year.

Floor Councils

Formal floor councils are in place at some institutions while other campuses allow RAs to develop community on floors without formal structures. Organizational theory and group development concepts are applicable to floor councils, although much of the observable behavior on floors falls within the personal, not floor council responsibility such as roommate conflicts. Learning organization theory fits floor activities as floor members learn from experience and apply classroom learning to floor interactions. Open systems theory is applicable too, as hall events and dynamics affect floor functioning, although floors can be quite isolated from the rest of the hall.

Purpose of Floor Councils

Formal floor councils set basic levels of community-building. The added structures of floor councils focus resident attention on positive rather than destructive involvement. Floor councils are typically advised by resident assistants (RAs). Floor councils provide information, student help, and opinions to hall councils. They also communicate hall level issues to floor residents, organize floor activities, develop residents' skills, and work closely with RAs. They provide initial training for leadership and hall/campus citizenship.

Educational Philosophy of Floor Councils

Involvement is essential to student development (Winston & Anchors, 1993). Floor councils can be the first organization in which students become involved. The impact of involvement can be seen immediately on floors. Many residents learn through interaction, so floor councils provide arenas for interaction and learning in halls.

Floor Council Structure

Floor councils can be informal small groups with leaders or more formal structures. Formal structures might include electing floor presidents, providing floor president manuals, providing formal training, having other elected positions, and scheduling regular floor community meetings. Floor president may represent floor issues and opinions in a formal way to hall councils and may have budgets to manage (see Chapter 6 for further discussion).

Floor Council Research

No published research on floor councils was found. The RHA effectiveness related to group development and research are relevant to the dynamics that take place in floor communities, especially if informal floor council structures exist.

Summary of Floor Councils

Floor councils are the smallest governance unit in residence hall systems. They operate at the local floor level and may have the greatest impact on floor residents. Floor councils provide ways for residents to have their opinions heard; help residents practice interpersonal skills; and accelerate resident involvement in university activities and communities. Floor council effectiveness is key to housing goals, and concepts from this chapter can help staff better address challenges facing floor councils.

Floor Council Case Study

Your RA comes to you as the hall director with the issue that vandalism is increasing on the floor. In anger at the perpetrators, the floor put up signs stating that those who caused the damage will be found and arrested and that they will be kicked off the floor. Using the concepts presented in this chapter, analyze what may have led to the vandalism and diagnose how to help the RA and floor president intervene at this time.

Conclusion

Clearly, RHAs are central and important aspects of housing organizations. They provide opportunities for residents to develop and become engaged and involved in educational communities within residence halls. The effectiveness of all levels of governance in the halls can be determined by examining select-ed organizational and effectiveness theories and research targeting residence hall government. Each level of residence hall government is unique yet has parallels with the others. Effectiveness can be assessed by taking these steps:

- Decide on the purpose of assessment. Is the assessment about resource allocation, for goal setting, to compete against other organizations, etc.
- Choose an assessment technique, such as survey or focus group approach.
- Collect data on current performance.
- Inform members and other constituents about assessment results.
- Compare results to current goals and desired results.
- Set goals to close gaps and enhance strong areas.
- Re-assess to determine performance improvement.
- Celebrate or recognize progress. Keep in mind that "students matter and are highly valued" is a primary belief and balance the pursuit of effectiveness in that light (see Chapter 19 for an in-depth discussion of assessment).

References

Astin, A. W. (1993). *What matters in college? Four critical years revisited.* San Francisco: Jossey-Bass.

Banner, D. K., & Gagne, T. E. (1995). *Designing effective organizations: Traditional and transformational views.* Thousand Oaks, CA: Sage.

Bledsoe, T. (1994). *Use of organization development interventions to enhance perceived effectiveness of student organizations.* Unpublished doctoral dissertation, University of Georgia, Athens.

Boersig, P., & Wallington, E. (1998). The first advising position. In N. W. Dunkel & C. L. Spencer (Eds.), *Advice for advisers: The development of a residence hall association* (2nd ed., pp. 9–23). Columbus, OH: Association of College and University Housing Officers - International.

Bolman, L. G., & Deal, T. E. (2003). *Reframing organizations: Artistry, choice, and leadership*. San Francisco: Jossey-Bass.

Buckingham, M., & Coffman, C. (1999). *First, break all the rules: What the world's greatest managers do differently*. New York: Simon & Schuster.

Cameron, K. S. (1978). Organizational effectiveness: Its measurement and prediction in higher education (Doctoral dissertation, Yale University, 1978). *Dissertation Abstracts International, 40,* 341A–342A.

Cameron, K. (1980, Autumn). Critical questions in assessing organizational effectiveness. *Organizational Dynamics,* 66–80.

Cameron, K. S., & Whetten, D. A. (1983). *Organizational effectiveness: A comparison of multiple models*. New York: Academic Press.

Campbell, J. (1977). On the nature of organizational effectiveness. In P. S. Goodman, J. M. Pennings, & Associates (Eds.), *New perspectives on organizational effectiveness* (pp. 13–55). San Francisco: Jossey-Bass.

Cawthon, T. W., & Underwood, S. J. (1998). The organizational structures of RHAs. In N. W. Dunkel & C. L. Spencer (Eds.), *Advice for advisers: The development of a residence hall association* (2nd ed., pp. 51–63). Columbus, OH: Association of College and University Housing Officers - International.

Connolly, T., Conlon, E. J., & Deutsch, S. J. (1980). Organizational effectiveness: A multiple-constituency approach. *Academy of Management Review, 5,* 211–217.

Cuyjet, M. J. (1994). Student government as a provider of student services. In M. C. Terrell & M. J. Cuyjet (Eds.), *Developing student government leadership* (New Directions for Student Services, 66, pp. 19–30). San Francisco: Jossey-Bass.

Dipboye, R. L., Smith, C. S., & Howell, W. C. (1994). *Understanding industrial and organizational psychology: An integrated approach*. New York: Harcourt Brace.

Dunkel, N. W. (1998). The future of advising. In N. W. Dunkel & C. L. Spencer (Eds.), *Advice for advisers: The development of a residence hall association* (2nd ed., pp. 227–235). Columbus, OH: Association of College and University Housing Officers - International.

Dunkel, N. W., & Schuh, J. H. (Eds·). (1998). *Advising student groups and organizations*. San Francisco: Jossey-Bass.

Dunkel, N. W., & Spencer, C. L. (Eds.). (1998). *Advice for advisers: The development of a residence hall association* (2nd ed.). Columbus, OH: The Association of College and University Housing Officers – International.

Frederick, R. W. (1959). *The third curriculum: Student activities in American education*. New York: Appleton-Century-Crofts.

Gibson, J. L., Ivancevich, J. M., & Donnelly, J. H. (1982). *Organizations.* Plano, TX: Business Publications.

Goodman, P. S., & Pennings, J. M. (1980). Critical issues in assessing organizational effectiveness. In E. E. Lawler, D. A. Nadler, & C. Cammann (Eds.), *Organizational assessment: Perspectives on the measurement of organizational behavior and the quality of work life* (pp. 185–215). New York: John Wiley & Sons.

Grandpre, E., & Kimble, G. (1998). An introduction to raising money. In N. W. Dunkel & C. L. Spencer (Eds.), *Advice for advisers: The development of a residence hall association* (2nd ed., pp. 145–160). Columbus, OH: Association of College and University Housing Officers - International.

Hall, R. H. (1963). The concept of bureaucracy: An empirical assessment. *American Journal of Sociology, 69,* 32–40.

Hall, R. H. (1999). *Organizations: Structures, processes, and outcomes.* Upper Saddle River, NJ: Prentice Hall.

Harrison, M. I. (1994). *Diagnosing organizations: Methods, models, and processes* (2nd ed.). Thousand Oaks, CA: Sage.

Harrison, M. I., & Shirom, A. (1999). *Organizational diagnosis and assessment: Bridging theory and practice.* Thousand Oaks, CA: Sage.

Hudson, M., & Tattershall, B. (1998). The money management of RHAs. In N. W. Dunkel, & C. L. Spencer (Eds.), *Advice for advisers: The development of a residence hall association* (2nd ed., pp. 133–144). Columbus, OH: Association of College and University Housing Officers - International.

Jaques, E. (1976). *A general theory of bureaucracy.* Hampshire, England: Gregg Revivals.

Keeley, M. (1984). Impartiality and participant-interest theories of organizational effectiveness. *Administrative Science Quarterly, 29,* 1–25.

Komives, S. R. (1994). Increasing student involvement through civic leadership education. In C. C. Schroeder, & P. Mable (Eds.), *Realizing the educational potential of residence halls* (pp. 218–240). San Francisco: Jossey-Bass.

Komives, S., & Tucker, G. (1993, 1998). Successful residence hall government: Themes from a national study of select residence hall government structures. In N. W. Dunkel, & C. L. Spencer (Eds.), *Advice for advisers: The development of an effective residence hall association* (pp. 27–43). Columbus, OH: Association of College and University Housing Officers - International.

Kuh, G. D., & Lund, J. P. (1994). What students gain from participating in student government. In M. C. Terrell & M. J. Cuyjet (Eds.), *Developing student government leadership* (New Directions for Student Services, 66, pp. 19–30). San Francisco: Jossey-Bass.

Levine, A. (1994). Guerrilla education in residential life. In C. C. Schroeder & P. Mable (Eds.), *Realizing the educational potential of residence halls* (pp. 93–105). San Francisco: Jossey-Bass.

Likert, R. (1967). *The human organization.* New York: McGraw-Hill.

Locke, E. A., & Latham, G. P. (1990). *A theory of goal setting and task performance.* Englewood Cliffs, NJ: Prentice Hall.

Marine, J. (1984). Student groups and advisers: Historical perspective. In J. H. Schuh (Ed.), *A handbook for student group advisers* (pp. 9–22). Carbondale, IL: American College Personnel Association.

Miller, C., & Blattner, A. (1998). Relationships residence hall associations have with their institutions. In N. W. Dunkel & C. L. Spencer (Eds.), *Advice for advisers: The development of a residence hall association* (2nd ed., pp. 109–117). Columbus, OH: Association of College and University Housing Officers - International.

Miller, D. C. (1991). *Handbook of research design and social measurement* (5th ed.). Newbury Park, CA: Sage.

Mitchell, S., & Munro-Krusz, K. (1998). The motivation of students: From theory to practical application. In N. W. Dunkel, & C. L. Spencer (Eds.), *Advice for advisers: The development of a residence hall association* (2nd ed., pp. 65–79). Columbus, OH: Association of College and University Housing Officers - International.

Morgan, G. (1986). *Images of organization.* Newbury Park, CA: Sage.

Osteen, J., & Tucker, G. L., Jr. (1997). Advice, authority, and accountability: Understanding the unique roles of residence life staff and hall government leaders. *Journal of College and University Student Housing, 27* (1), 34–40.

Papish, R., & Wall, V. (1998). The role of the RHA in developing inclusive communities. In N. W. Dunkel & C. L. Spencer (Eds.), *Advice for advisers: The development of a residence hall association* (2nd ed., pp. 101–108). Columbus, OH: Association of College and University Housing Officers - International.

Pennings, J. M., & Goodman, P. S. (1977). Toward a workable framework. In P. S. Goodman, J. M. Pennings, & Associates (Eds.), *New perspectives on organizational effectiveness* (pp. 146–184). San Francisco: Jossey-Bass.

Perrow, C. (1972). *Complex organizations: A critical essay.* Glenview, IL: Scott, Foresman and Co.

Porter, D. (1998). Responsibilities of a residence hall association adviser. In N. W. Dunkel & C. L. Spencer (Eds.), *Advice for advisers: The development of a residence hall association* (2nd ed., pp. 25–33). Columbus, OH: Association of College and University Housing Officers - International.

Price, J. L. (1968). *Organizational effectiveness: An inventory of propositions.* Homewood, IL: Irwin.

Sampson, K. (1998). Group development concepts. In N. W. Dunkel & C. L. Spencer (Eds.), *Advice for advisers: The development of a residence hall association* (2nd ed., pp. 81–100). Columbus, OH: Association of College and University Housing Officers - International.

Schaefer, K. (2000). *Working with residence hall associations.* (PaperClip Communications Residence Life Management Manual). Garfield, NJ: PaperClip Communications.

Scott, W. R. (1977). Effectiveness of organizational effectiveness studies. In P. S. Goodman & J. M. Pennings (Eds.), *New perspectives on organizational effectiveness* (pp. 63–95). San Francisco: Jossey-Bass.

Scott, W. R. (1981). *Organizations: Rational, natural, and open systems.* Englewood Cliffs, NJ: Prentice-Hall.

Scott, W. R. (1998). *Organizations: Rational, natural, and open systems* (4th ed.). Upper Saddle River, NJ: Prentice Hall.

Seashore, S. E. (1983). A framework for an integrated model of organizational effectiveness. In K. S. Cameron & D. A. Whetten (Eds.), *Organization effectiveness: A comparison of multiple models* (pp. 55–70). New York: Academic Press.

Senge, P. M. (1990). *The fifth discipline: The art & practice of the learning organization.* New York: Doubleday.

Senge, P. M., Kleiner, A., Roberts, C., Ross, R. B., & Smith, B. J. (1994). *The fifth discipline field book: Strategies and tools for building a learning organization.* New York: Doubleday.

Spencer, C. L. (1998). State, subregional, regional, and national conferences. In N. W. Dunkel & C. L. Spencer (Eds.), *Advice for advisers: The development of a residence hall association* (2nd ed., pp. 207–214). Columbus, OH: Association of College and University Housing Officers - International.

Stoner, K, Berry, K., Boever, C. L., & Tattershall, B. (1998). History and services of the national association of college and university residence halls, inc. (NACURH). In N. W. Dunkel, & C. L. Spencer (Eds.), *Advice for advisers: The development of a residence hall association (*2nd ed., pp. 181–205). Columbus, OH: Association of College and University Housing Officers - International.

Stoner, K, Spain, J., Rasche, C., & Horton, R. (1993). History and services of NACURH. In N. W. Dunkel, & C. L. Spencer (Eds.), *Advice for advisers: The development of an effective residence hall association* (pp. 163–185). Columbus, OH: Association of College and University Housing Officers - International.

Stoner, K., & Wyatt, K. (1993). A NACURH "White Paper" on residence hall government. In N. W. Dunkel & C. L. Spencer (Eds). *Advice for advises: The development of an effective residence hall association* (pp. 1–7). Columbus, OH: Association of College and University Housing Officers - International. (Reprinted from *Journal for College and University Student Housing,* 14(1), 3–6, 1984).

Thompson, J. (1967). *Organizations in action.* New York: McGraw-Hill.

Tucker, G. L. (2001). *The development of an instrument to measure the effectiveness of residence hall associations.* Unpublished doctoral dissertation, University of Maryland.

Verry, B. (1993). The organizational structures of RHAs. In N. W. Dunkel & C. L. Spencer (Eds.), *Advice for advisers: The development of an effective residence hall association* (pp. 45–53). Columbus, OH: Association of College and University Housing Officers - International.

Werring, C. J. (1984). The purpose of residence hall student government: One conceptual model. The *Journal of College and University Student Housing,* 14 (1), 40–43.

Wheatley, M. J. (1992). *Leadership and the new science: Learning about organization from an orderly universe.* San Francisco: Berrett-Koehler.

Whetten, D. A., & Cameron, K. S. (1994). Organizational effectiveness: Old models and new constructs. In J. Greenberg (Ed.), *Organizational behavior: The state of the science* (pp. 135–153). Hillsdale, NJ: Lawrence Erlbaum Associates.

Winston, R. B., Jr., & Anchors, S. (1993). Student development in the residential environment. In R. B. Winston & S. Anchors (Eds.), *Student housing and residential life* (pp. 25–64). San Francisco: Jossey-Bass.

Yuchtman, E., & Seashore, S. E. (1967). A system resource approach to organizational effectiveness. *American Sociological Review,* 32, 891–903.

Zammuto, R. F. (1982). *Assessing organizational effectiveness: Systems change, adaptation, and strategy.* Albany: State University of New York Press.

Traditional and Alternative Organizational Models for RHAs

Phyllis McCluskey-Titus & Janet W. Paterson

University housing departments have attempted to foster stability and predictability by providing for well established structures within their organizations to include residence hall associations (RHAs). RHAs have been established across the United States in virtually all colleges and universities that have mature residential life programs. The specific purpose of these associations varies by institution, but, in general, they formalize the involvement of residents in hall governance, and they open communication channels between residents and their institutional leaders.

This chapter briefly overviews three major organizational typologies and how RHAs operate within each framework. In addition, the chapter presents findings on the dominant RHA organizational structure in use today, discusses hypotheses of why this model remains dominant, and illustrates alternative models for RHA organization exemplified through three case studies. Finally, the authors provide a framework for establishing and maintaining model RHA programs as well as discuss the implications for allowing the bureaucratic model to continue to be used without an exploration of whether it provides the best possible co-curricular learning opportunities for students.

Note: Sections in italics are taken directly from Cawthon, T.W. & Underwood, S.J. (1998). The organizational structures of RHAs. (in Advice for Advisers, 2nd ed. Dunkel, N.W. & Spencer, C.L. eds.). Columbus OH: Association of College and University Housing Officers—International, and are used with the permission of the authors.

Brief Overview of Organizational Theory

To appreciate how and why RHAs have been structured, a basic understanding of organizational theory is needed. Beginning with the turn of the [20th] century and well into the middle of the century, theorists viewed organizational behavior as operating within closed systems. From this perspective, now known as the conventional view, institutions, such as colleges and universities operated with little concern or influence from outside forces. The conventional view was predicated on the desire of organizations to maintain stability and predictability at all costs, creating structures which were highly hierarchical, rigid, formal, and controlling (Kuh, 1996).

Two examples of conventional organizational structure are the bureaucratic and the rational model.

Bureaucratic Model

Developed by Max Weber (1946), the bureaucratic model is characterized by specialization and competence; consistent procedures and policies; and high levels of structure. In RHA organizations, the bureaucratic model manifests itself as campus governing organizations with representatives and officers from across the institution. Senior-level housing staff members serve as advisers and/or provide significant direction to groups. Decision-making is limited to executive council officers with strong adviser input. Other aspects of a bureaucratically organized RHA include formal charters for existence, formal channels of communication, and formal policies and rules. This is a highly controlled and ordered way in which to operate and is a very common model in higher education organizations, particularly in residence hall associations.

An example of how an RHA operating within this model would address a modification to the organizational structure was described by Ellen Herion, vice president of the Association of Residence Halls (ARH) at Illinois State University (personal communication, December 8, 2004).

Early in the school year, Merion and the president planned several new programs and initiatives, which would require additional students being appointed to chair planning teams/committees. Following the prescribed procedures of the organization, the idea for the program first had to be submitted as an agenda item for a meeting of the assembly. (In some situations the item might require submission at one meeting to be placed on the agenda for the next meeting.) At the assembly meeting, the program idea was presented and discussed. Area representatives then were expected to take it back to their area government meetings for further discussion and a recommendation of how their representative should vote. At the next assembly meeting following the area government meetings, a motion was made to adopt the idea for the new program and also the need for a new chairperson and a vote was taken. When the motion passed without major modifications (which would require it being sent back out to the area governments) then a change to their by-laws or constitution was enacted and submitted to the Student Life Office as an updated constitution/bylaw. The organization then began the process of marketing the leadership position and accepting applications from potential chair candidates. By the time a person was appointed to the position, several months had passed, and the need for the intended program was potentially moot.

Rational Model

The rational model works best when everyone associated with the organization is familiar with and supportive of the organization's purpose and mission and when the environment is predictable and stable. An organization that operates under the rational model is characterized by logic, order, direction, and predictable behavior, but tends not to be highly structured (Barr, 2000). Typically, RHAs operating using this model have sets of officers with designated leaders or chairpersons and advisers, who can be either highly involved with new groups or more laissez-faire with experienced organizations. Decisions are made by executive councils that have sought input from constituents affected by the decisions. This model works best for campus governance groups with responsibility for one residence hall or a smaller residential area than with the traditional campus-wide RHA.

The Postconventional View

Since the 1960s, the postconventional view of organizations has come into vogue. In this view, organizations such as colleges and universities are considered to be complex open systems shaped by external influences and pressure. According to this theory, today's institutions of higher education not only are, but must be, ever changing as they adapt to fluid environments. Roles, predictability, and stability are no longer paramount. Instead, open communication and responsive structures are valued (Kuh, 1996).

One example of the postconventional view is the collegial model of organization.

Collegial Model

The collegial organizational model, put into practice within RHA, consists of work accomplished by using a committee structure rather than the traditional officer structure. When using this model, decision-making takes place by coming to a consensus of the group in a meeting or other formal setting. Using this model assumes that all participants have a valid and mostly equal voice in determining programs and polices. In this model, the adviser can be either an active part of the group or a consultant. Although the collegial model is preferred in theory, it is a very time-consuming and inefficient method to operate, particularly in the political world of higher education.

Although admittedly oversimplified, the primary difference in these organizational views [and associated models] might be summed up with two words: static vs. dynamic. Conventional organizations have structures which preserve the status quo, whereas postconventional organizations encourage input and hold structure as a secondary goal. For RHAs to work most effectively, the group must understand the context in which it operates. The mission, structure, and expectations of the college or university, the housing department, and perhaps student government or other related organizations all dictate the level of freedom or control each RHA organization has to organize according to a specific model. The following section will provide an overview of RHA organizational structures that are currently in use.

A Review of Current Organizational Structures

In summer 2004, the authors examined 45 RHA constitutions and websites that represented various campus types, including large and small; public and private; urban and rural; and religious and secular (Appendix A). This study reveals that organizational structures consistently reflect a traditional bureaucratic organizational model. Most RHAs examined utilize executive boards of officers, representation from the different living units, and advisement from staff in the housing department.

Residence hall associations, like many student organizations at colleges and universities, suffer from the limited ability to enact significant change because of the fluidity in membership, the limited amount of time any particular administration is in office, the high turnover in student leadership, the natural tendency to retain the status quo, and because enacting change takes time and is difficult. This is confirmed by Schein (1992):

One of the major dilemmas that leaders encounter when they attempt to change the way organizations function is how to get something going that is basically countercultural, that does not fit the paradigm. The use of quality circles, self-managed teams, autonomous work groups or other kinds of organizational devices that rely heavily on commitment to groups may be so counter cultural in the typical U.S. individualistic competitive organization as to be virtually impossible to make work. (p. 140)

Students who rise through the ranks of leadership in residence hall associations have been successful in the current bureaucratic and rational structures and therefore are unlikely to focus on the limitations inherent in those models. Students who are frustrated with the status quo are more likely to seek leadership opportunities in other settings rather than remain within the organization long enough to achieve a position of influence or authority to make changes. Students with rebellious tendencies are not always encouraged by housing staff, who often exert significant influence over student-leaders by providing access to and growth opportunities for those more in sync with the administration and advisers' viewpoints.

How often do students campaigning for RHA leadership positions base their platform on restructuring or remodeling the organization? The concept of organizational remodeling likely is construed to be a dull, routine initiative or overwhelmingly difficult. Generally, the platform issues put forth by these candidates are more tangible and related to addressing students' wants and needs, like room and board costs, programming desired by the students, wireless Internet access in rooms, and refurbishing lounges or study areas. Whether due to a lack of interest or a limitation of ability or imagination, organizational or structural changes are not commonly pursued by RHAs.

Organizational Variations within Hierarchical RHAs

Within existing hierarchical RHAs, three representative variations were identified: centralized, decentralized, and blended.

Centralized RHAs with Building or Area Representation

RHAs with a highly centralized structure have a strong central association and no individual building or area governments. Representatives from individual residence halls or areas are elected or appointed, as delineated in the constitution, to serve on a central RHA. This central or oversight RHA establishes policies and procedures to govern the overall residence life program for all residence halls or areas. The RHA has a constitution and bylaws detailing the structure of the executive council, membership, offices, responsibilities, and committee, as appropriate. Building-level quality of life issues are handled through existing residence life staff or informal governing procedures or bodies.

Although less common than a blended structure for RHAs, the centralized structure might be suitable for a campus with a small residential program or one where the administration desires to maintain tight control over residence life issues or greatly values consistency. The absence of building or area governments would limit the number of residents involved in residential governance. Additionally, the centralized structure is less appropriate for a campus that highly values diversity and flexibility in their residence life program. Individual areas or buildings might have a more difficult time expressing their individuality in the structure.

Figure 1 represents one example of how a centralized RHA would be structured and would function.

Decentralized Structure: Buildings or Area Governments with No Central RHAs

In the decentralized structure, individual buildings or areas have their own organizations with no central or oversight RHA. Each residence hall or area government operates independently of the others on campus. Each organization establishes its own governing documents, policies, and procedures. This structure affords no formal means of coordination between buildings or areas. Theoretically, distinctly varied residential life programs could be generated in this structure. Regardless of the distinctiveness of each organization within the decentralized structure, invariably some buildings or area government will be stronger than others, producing potential difficulties for residence life administrators.

Figure 1. Centralized RHA Structure

The decentralized structure might be appropriate for a campus with a relatively small number of individual residence halls or defined areas, or where diversity is the overriding value in the residence life program. For example, a campus with a number of theme halls or halls with distinct interests might benefit from a decentralized approach to residence life governance. One drawback of this structure is the lack of formal avenues for dialogue among the building or area organizations. Little or no communication among them could create an environment of competition and unnecessary duplication of effort.

Figure 2 shows an example of a system with a decentralized RHA.

Blended: Buildings or Area Governments with Central RHAs

The blended structure is by far the most common on today's campuses. Blended RHAs have individual building or area governments and a central RHA providing oversight and/or coordination among the individual organizations. Building or area level governments are made up of voting and nonvoting members. The majority of members have voting privileges and are elected to serve as representatives in the individual building or area governments. Nonvoting members, on the other hand, may include alumni members or advisers. The ability of each building or area organization to operate independently is detailed in the governing documents; however, a fairly significant level of independence is typical of a blended system. Furthermore, the individual organizations will elect officers who make up the governing body for the RHA.

The oversight or central RHA is made up of elected or appointed members form the individual governments. An executive council comprised of elected officers from the body of representatives and oversees the operation of the central RHA. Through its members and executive council, the central RHA

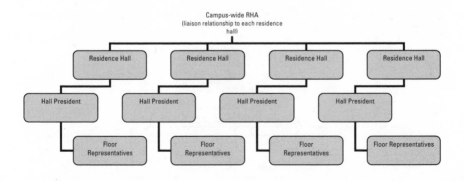

Figure 2. Decentralized RHA Structure

provides coordination, guidance, and direction for the building or area govern-ments. This structure attempts to maximize the potential gain to be realized from building or area level organizations, while minimizing the shortcomings inherent in the decentralized structure with its lack of coordination.

The organizational structure of a blended RHA system is depicted in Figure 3.

These three approaches, though varying in scope and representation, all adhere to a traditional hierarchical and conventional model form of governance and do not utilize alternative organizational structures and systems. While the bureau-cratic model can be highly effective and efficient for student organizations, the role of RHA advisers is to provide developmental out-of-class learning experiences for students involved in the organization. The Student Learning Imperative (ACPA, 1994) cites that "optimal benefits are more likely to be realized under certain conditions, such as active engagement and collaboration with others on learning tasks" (p. 2). A collegial organizational model, which is networked or more collaborative, provides more opportunities for students to be meaningfully involved in the organization and to build collaborative rela-tionships outside of the hierarchy.

Underlying Causes for the Predominance of Bureaucratic/Structural RHAs

With few and limited modifications evident, the use of the bureaucratic model as a single approach apparently results from one of three choices: first, students may be unaware of alternative structures or models for RHAs or are unable to access information about alternative organizational models; second, students

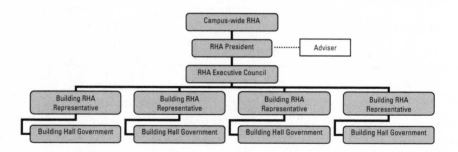

Figure 3. Blended RHA Structure

may not have been challenged by advisers to consider alternative models for organization; and third, students may be convinced that current organizational structures best meet the needs of students and the purpose of campus RHAs.

Unaware of Alternative Structures

For many RHA leaders, the National Association of College and University Residence Halls (NACURH) is an organization that provides information through a national office and website; education through training workshops and programs; annual regional and national conferences; and ongoing support to campus-based residence hall leadership. The *Resource File Index* on the NACURH website (www.nacurh.org/rfi/), while very comprehensive, does not list any topics pertaining to organizational structure or alternative models of organizational structure for RHAs. This suggests that alternative residence hall association organizational models, if they exist, are not a common topic of discussion for student leaders within NACURH or for campus RHAs. Additionally, a review of programs presented at recent regional meetings of NACURH, available on the various regional websites (www.nacurh.org/JACURH/, www.web.umr.edu/~macurh/, and www.nacurh.org/SAACURH/), shows a great variety of informative programs about leadership, ethics, membership, diversity, innovative programming, running meetings, and personal/career development, but no sessions about organizational models or what to consider when making a change in structure.

Not Challenged by Advisers

For a number of housing professionals who advise RHA organizations, the RHA advising responsibility is one of many work-related duties that compete for time. A related article (McCluskey-Titus, 2004) reveals that advising student organizations is not an area where housing professionals invest the same time or effort that they might invest in supervising staff, even though both groups have similar needs. The work and research associated with proposing organizational change then following through with that change may not be feasible for overworked professionals or for inexperienced student leaders who often are in charge of RHA groups. Perhaps advisers could benefit by educating themselves about varying organizational models or bringing the topic up for discussion with RHA officer groups. Taking the initiative to present programs on this topic at state, regional, or national conferences is a service to other campuses that are unaware of options, that seem to struggle organizationally, or that would benefit from "organizational analysis." Advisers have the ability to serve as educators for student groups and within that role can present other alternative structures or ask hard questions about organizational effectiveness that might make major contributions to organizations.

Current Structure Best Meets Needs

A final possible reason for not changing from a conventional model of organization for RHAs is that the traditional model has historically been effective and efficient. American students have been raised in a country of hierarchical organizations. Although Kuh (1996) suggests that postconventional models of organizations are emerging, most churches, governmental entities, schools, and civic organizations are organized predominantly in a bureaucratic or rational organizational structure. This finding is supported by Love and Estanek (2004), who remind student affairs professionals that "most of the research and writing in student affairs that addresses leadership focuses on organizationally designated leaders. This emphasis on hierarchical structure has inhibited the development of alternative versions and visions of leadership" (p. 40). As a result, it is difficult for students to create or envision organizations using purely collegial or networked models for RHAs without concrete examples to emulate. Students are content to maintain a traditional hierarchical representative model because it is known and understood, which makes for efficient transition between student leadership each year. It is still an organizational model which is used so regularly and successfully by so many campus and community organizations that it is accepted as functional.

Given what is known about membership, leadership, activities, and purposes of these RHA organizations, the current lack of variety in the organizational models employed by RHAs is probably a combination of the reasons mentioned above. The following section provides some alternative models for rethinking RHA organizations. As educators, advisers can provide the stimulus for organizations to examine and consider how RHAs might better serve the needs of students to practice and hone leadership skills. If students are not challenged to reconsider the organizational structures of RHAs by advisers, then advisers have missed opportunities to use the RHA experience as applied learning labs.

Alternative Approaches

Zand (1974), Love and Estanek (2004), and Allen and Cherry (2000) have suggested three different collegial organizational models: collateral organizations, the pervasive leadership model, and the systemic leadership model.

Collateral Organizations

Contrary to what is on paper, many times organizations designed with a traditional hierarchical structure, including hierarchical leadership and representatives, actually operate outside that structure through informal means. Labeled "collateral organizations," Zand (1974) describes a supplemental informal organization that actually co-exists within the usual formal one. Zand (1974) further asserts that traditional organizational models were designed to best address well-defined repetitive problems, perhaps not the standard function of all RHAs because RHAs tend to face a combination of anticipated and unanticipated concerns. A collateral organization emerges when ill-defined and unforeseen problems and opportunities arise. In the RHA, a problem might arise if there is a need for funds for an upcoming program, but the RHA has already met and did not act on the request for funding. Perhaps the adviser, president, and treasurer might meet with the program chair to find a way to resolve the problem without having to reconvene the entire RHA. As in this example, hierarchical organizations often handle the business and non-business activities of an organization in informal ways by capitalizing on personal relationships and informal networks and ignoring the prescribed way of doing things in order to be more efficient and effective. As a new organizational model, perhaps there would be a way to designate or recognize these informal networks through a task team system rather than a structured hierarchy. The organizational model (Figure 4) shows how an organization using the collateral structure might operate in practice.

Pervasive Leadership Model

In a second alternative model, Love and Estanek (2004) propose a pervasive

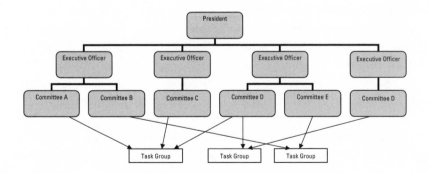

Figure 4. Collateral Organization with Acknowledged Informal Networks

leadership model where "organizational members are connected...through a system of relationships, and that the organization is connected to other organizations and systems through relationships as well (p. 45) ... Pervasive leadership does not imply that there is no internal structure or no hierarchy to the organization or that there should not be. In fact, there are both formal and informal structures in the organization" (p.42). This model is similar to Zand's (1974) but also recognizes the impact of alliances and resources *outside* the organizational structure. In RHAs, this might include other student-run organizations on campus, companies within communities with whom RHAs do business, organizational alumni, or the NACURH organization. Again, developing models that incorporate feedback from interested others (such as advisory boards) or more formally recognizing the influence of these interested others by re-working relationships with them is up to individual organizations.

One way to envision the Pervasive Leadership Model of an organization would be as a solar system (Figure 5). At the center, like the sun, is a centralized leadership team providing vision and resources to various organizational entities. Circling this center orb are the functional units represented in the diagram as planets. Although each of these units has a relationship to the central leadership, they also have relationships among and between each of the other units. At different times in the life of the organization, function units are highly aligned and interdependent with each other. There is a continuous ebb and flow of which units are in close alignment and which are farther away and more independent, but at all times every unit within the system impacts the other units, even if they currently are not working closely together on an initiative. The stars shown in the diagram represent the outside alliances and resources, which although they are not a formal part of the organization, still have an impact on its functioning.

Systemic Leadership Model

In light of many new changes to how people communicate and work together, Allen and Cherry (2000) developed the Systemic Leadership Model to better explain and apply networking concepts within organizational structures. They challenge the old paradigm of one- and two-way communication and encourage organizations where information is sent and received through many unrelated sources. Proponents of systemic leadership encourage ignoring formal communication and reporting structures because "restricting information also restricts the organization's ability to renew itself. The traditional paradigm of management believes that it is important to control the amount, timing and direction of information...Our continued attempts to control information may

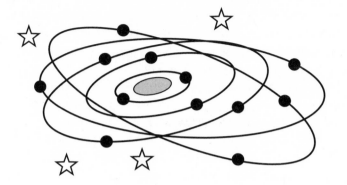

Figure 5. Pervasive Leadership Model

not only be damaging our organization's ability to learn, but may be impossible to maintain" (Allen & Cherry, 2000, p. 32).

This model emphasizes an organization with overlapping and interdependent responsibilities and strong relationships with other campus groups. If an RHA is sensitive to this type of communication model, then decisions would be made in collaboration with many others who have information or who might be affected by the decision. The role of advisers is to help make useful connections between offices, individuals, or organizations that might have information helpful to groups and to serve as additional information sources in decision-making. When following this model, the need for traditional meetings is not necessary, as work can be done among individuals through ongoing communication using technology, telecommunications, and written documents, as well as face-to-face interactions. Differences between a networked model and the more traditional models discussed earlier are that information-gathering processes are very complex in the networked organization, and it is impossible to know every bit of information before taking action or making decisions. Another difference is that the organization is never static; it is constantly in flux, and the group recognizes and embraces changing opportunities. Lastly, the whole system must be examined rather than individual aspects of it. It is a model that values process rather than a concrete product.

Throughout this chapter both traditional organizational models as well as potentially more effective newer models, have been introduced. These alternative models are more fluid and help students take proactive approaches to self-governance or problem-solving. Many bureaucratic organizations wait for issues to be brought forward, while these alternative models tend to promote action before it is necessary. Students may become more engaged in the processes associated with RHAs (program development, problem-solving, student advocacy) rather than be mired in a hierarchically organized process to get things accomplished. Students might focus on learning how to "do" rather than navigating or circumventing the structures. This chapter continues with two case examples showing alternative RHA structures and how each structure works on the different representative campuses. Following those cases is an example of a national model RHA, which has operated successfully using a more structured bureaucratic model.

An RHA Structured by Committee

Adviser Michelle Massey, University of Louisville, shared her perspective on the RSA (Resident Student Association) committee structure (personal communication, October 4, 2004). On the University of Louisville campus, the director of housing and residence life is extremely interested in meaningfully involving students in the organization in order to receive feedback. As a result, the traditionally organized RSA, comprised of four representatives from each residence hall (president, vice-president, public relations officer, and treasurer), plus a group of traditional officers that included a president, vice-president, secretary, treasurer, public relations officer, National Communications Coordinator (position associated with NACURH), and an NCC in training, became involved as members of four specific housing-related committees.

The Food Advisory Board is comprised of RSA presidents and meets each month over lunch with Chartwells and university administrators from contract administration who oversee the dining contract. The main purpose is to provide significant feedback on the dining program and serve as liaisons between campus food service and residents of their individual halls. They also have significant responsibilities, as in the recent changes and redesign of restaurants on campus.

The Resident Advisory Council meets monthly with the housing and residence life director and is made up of the RSA vice-presidents. The purpose of this committee is to provide specific input about what is happening in the residence halls from the student perspective, as well as provide input on the housing department annual budget and expenditures. In addition, the director meets monthly with RAs to confirm what is happening in the halls and share feedback from the Resident Advisory Council.

Resident student association treasurers are participants in the Facilities

Advisory Committee. Chaired by the associate director of facilities, this group is responsible for prioritizing all facility replacement and repair decisions and facility-related expenditures.

The Public Relations Committee is comprised of the public relations officers from each hall and serves as a special events planning and organizing group. They select the theme, plan the annual awards banquet, and coordinate fund-raising and community service for the RSA. They also work cooperatively with the National Residence Hall Honorary (NRHH) to plan the awards banquet.

The general body of the RSA (about 35 people) meets weekly, but much of the meeting is set aside for committee reports. The overall mission of the RSA organization is for student advocacy and programming, both of which take place through the various committees. Massey provided several examples of how committees are able to resolve student concerns, e.g. what action to take when someone receives a call from a fraudulent credit card company or when students express dissatisfaction with the temperature of the facilities. The RSA committee members work directly with the appropriate central office level housing staff to resolve issues rather than having to work through several layers of staff before issues are resolved.

This is not to imply that entry-level or graduate housing staff is not involved with resident students in the resolution of problems or with hall governance. At the University of Louisville, graduate hall directors advise hall councils and receive extensive training provided by Massey and RSA members. In addition, the hall council and RAs work collaboratively under the direction of the hall director to provide joint programming for residents. This model provides a sense of unity for the campus.

But what happens when RHA organizational structure is directly opposed to the campus philosophy? The second case study provides an interesting example of a drastic campus measure used to remedy this situation.

Disbanding a Traditional Campus RHA and Creating Something New

The University of Illinois at Urbana-Champaign is a large housing system with 8,800 on campus residents, 80% of whom are first-year students. Prior to fall 2003, University of Illinois sponsored a traditional, structured, hierarchical RHA organization for residence hall students, including programming, governance, and funding board components. The members of the former RHA were involved nationally, regionally, and statewide. In fact, University of Illinois hosted the Illinois Residence Hall Association conference as recently as spring 2003. It was that experience, as well as the adoption of a new campus philosophical direction, that led to the dissolution of RHA on campus (Jodie Leasure, personal communication, September 16, 2004).

The Illinois Leadership Philosophy was adopted by the U of I campus May 1999 and focuses on the idea of leadership to serve the common good. It is by nature non-positional and non-hierarchical (see www.illinoisleadership .uiuc.edu for more information). This philosophy stood in direct opposition to the RHA organization that had been in existence at the University of Illinois for many years. In addition, there were several other concerns expressed about the RHA, including the basic level of leadership skills training provided when some students needed more advanced skills development and the unwilling-ness of students to run for RHA officer positions. When the university hired a new RHA adviser, that person organized a retreat in the summer to regroup and plan for the year. Fully five months later, the organization was floundering, and people raised the question of whether RHA needed to exist. The answer to this question was, "No."

So what replaces the functions typically performed by the RHA at the University of Illinois? Who plans programs? Who allocates funding? Who pro-vides feedback to central housing staff? The University of Illinois has a num-ber of highly effective leadership teams that carry out the functions that many campuses associate with RHAs. For instance, a Student Involvement Team, comprised of the assistant director for student involvement and two full-time program coordinators for leadership and multicultural programs, plans and executes leadership activities and multicultural programming. This Involve-ment Team and several students attended a national leadership conference sponsored by PaperClip Communications and returned to campus with ideas and models for activities and programs that would bring people together. The Student Involvement Team also works with a departmental Student Involve-ment Committee to develop the direction to be taken and programs to be implemented within the department. This committee is made up of the assistant director, area coordinator(s), residence directors, program coordinators and learning community staff.

The Residence Life Leadership Coalition is a group of 10 to 40 stu-dents and staff who represent various residence hall constituent organizations, including area councils, Black student organizations, the Latino organization, and the National Residence Hall Honorary. This coalition is not organized hierarchically and has no formal leadership group. Two central housing staff members conduct the meetings, but do not dictate the direction of the group.

The purpose of the coalition is to gather together students involved in leadership in the halls and share information, provide feedback about housing issues, make decisions as appropriate, and participate in more advanced leadership training. The director of housing and other housing staff use the group to seek feedback about specific issues, such as room and board rates, building new halls, fees, and staffing.

The former RHA received income through an activity fee. These funds are now allocated by a Central Residential Funding Board. Comprised of volunteers, this organization makes decisions about the $30,000 to $60,000 available for organizations to program each year. This organization is advised by the assistant director for student involvement who convenes the group, provides training, and supports bi-weekly meetings as needed. The adviser has no vote and has a limited voice in the discussions and decisions.

The Residential Fundraising Council coordinates the major fundraising initiatives for student organizations, such as carpet and linen sales and the Microfridge rental program. This group is run like a business, and involved students get hands-on business experience as they manage multiple sales and rental programs, maintain an inventory of fridges, and manage a budget of approximately $60,000 a year. The Residential Fundraising Council gives most of this amount to the funding board for allocations. All other funds are used for expenses of the group and programs. One of the program coordinators for Leadership and Multicultural Programs advises this group, which falls under the supervision of the assistant director.

Two additional working groups that operate at the University of Illinois include the Marketing Feedback Group and the Director of Housing Feedback Group. Both of these groups function as non-structured associations with no parliamentary procedures employed and no allocated funding or operating budget. The purpose of these groups is to provide direct student input to marketing and survey items, as well as general housing issues. These two groups are often made up of first-year students, most of whom are not particularly involved in housing organizations. The groups meet several times per semester to provide opinions to the staff who are seeking feedback.

Overall, these "central housing organizations" are operating well. The university has found that the limited structure imposed on these student-run groups promotes problem-solving and discussion about common issues. There is no competition or campus activism expected of these groups, so they encourage honest sharing between students and staff. Most groups are "governed" with the student empowerment philosophy in mind. Students are fully responsible for the organization and the coordination of what happens in the groups.

One drawback that has been observed with this process is that if students are not taught to effectively organize, groups become adviser-run organizations. A number of the groups started off slowly because leadership training was not geared to assist students with the types of responsibilities faced with loosely structured systems. Staff developed a new organizational development curriculum this year in an attempt to respond to the lack of training and provide residents the skills needed to operate successfully under the campus leadership philosophy. The University of Illinois campus has made a minimum two-year commitment to this process and will formally and regularly evaluate effectiveness. While the future of a traditional RHA is uncertain on this campus, students have made no indication of a need for its return. The administration is determined to support student decision-making about this issue, whatever they should decide to do in the coming years.

The Bureaucratic RHA Operating Successfully

One campus that has a highly structured RHA system that is also very effective as a learning laboratory for students is the Inter-Residence Hall Association (IRHA) at the University of Florida. A discussion with their adviser, Julie McMahon (personal communication, September 13, 2004), reveals how the IRHA organization functions. As a large organization, there are six main officers including a president, vice president responsible for Residence Hall Week, an auditor, business manager, secretary, and a National Communications Coordinator (NCC). Several of these positions report directly to a central housing staff person or to the University's Student Government Association. In addition, each of these officer chairs is a member of a significant housing committee (e.g. dining services, Of the Months, finance, and judiciary), as well as a major campus program. An IRHA representative is also an active member of every housing committee, including search committees, and a member attends the housing professional staff meeting each week to provide significant input.

As campus leaders, much is expected of IRHA officers and representatives, so the organization serves as a learning laboratory for campus leaders and potential future staff members. This is done through the emphasis on giving students real tasks and duties and educating them as to the responsibilities associated with their roles. All IRHA officers and members are proficient in Robert's Rules of Order, which is practiced at IRHA meetings, and they have been used as consultants and trainers for other campuses. Students with meaningful campus roles are trained and educated about the politics of their positions, as well as the specific skills necessary to be successful. Students also assume full responsibility for large-scale campus programs, including six concerts per year, the Weeks of Welcome held in the fall, Gator Nights Friday programming, and a Winter Ball, which benefits a charity. In addition, the expectation exists that a new initiative will be developed each year. As a recent new program initiative, the IRHA planned a Gator Rock Café promoting voter registration.

In spite of being highly structured, the responsibilities and learning experiences provided to officers and members help foster strong leaders who know how to work within a bureaucracy and understand the value of building strong relationships. These types of educational experiences are consistent with the *Learning Reconsidered* philosophy statement (2004) that emphasizes knowledge acquisition and application (p. 18), as well as civic engagement, and inter/intrapersonal competence as major student outcomes (p. 19) acquired through student involvement with campus organizations, such as IRHA.

A National Model for RHA Excellence

What makes for a nationally recognized model RHA? We were able to develop a rubric for establishing and maintaining a model RHA program based on conversations with a number of recognized RHA advisers, as well as a review of the websites from most schools recognized with national awards by NACURH.

Involvement in the National Association of College and University Residence Halls (NACURH) Organization

Whether state, regional, or national leadership and participation, advisers cite the ability for students to network with other leaders at conferences and to hold leadership positions within these organizations as reasons RHAs are effective and strong. Campuses with strong RHA organizations usually report active NRHH (National Residence Hall Honorary) chapters on campus as well. Involvement in NACURH also provides both advisers and students opportunities to discuss organizational structure and how alternative models might be applied in practice.

Relationship with Housing Offices

Strong RHA organizations have active working relationships with housing/residence life offices. RHA members are often asked to serve on important housing selection and procedure committees; are given early notification of rent increases or policy changes and asked for reactions; or regularly attend professional staff meetings. In addition, student members of RHA work cooperatively with professional staff in finance, food service, assignments, and facilities on related RHA projects, such as cable TV programming, wireless computer access, monitoring expenditures for the organization, dining hall assessment processes, and facility renovation and rehabilitation. Even highly bureaucratic RHA organizations practice some of the "systemic leadership" skills through informal networks developed between student-leaders and housing staff. Perhaps RHA officers or members can develop informal relationships with housing directors through contact at meetings or task forces where both are present. This informal networking provides occasions for discussion about campus-wide problems or concerns that students may have outside of the established chain of command.

Developed Traditions Through Large-scale Programs

RHAs that are most effective offer residence hall students programs each year that are anticipated and celebrated by returning students, and the excitement is passed along by staff and upperclass students to first-year students. These events are meaningful opportunities for students to meet others, contribute to local or national charities, celebrate living in campus housing, hear music, or participate in community service activities. An opportunity to plan and implement programs is another way that RHA members can practice leadership skills outside formally organized and run meetings.

Understand and appreciate the History of Organizations

When current students involved in an RHA (as leaders or as members) know and know about former student-leaders and the importance of the traditions and values of the organization, it tends to be a stronger organization. There is a sense of history and being a part of something that is bigger than current individual officers that supports involvement and allows for stronger commitment to organizations. Past leaders come back as speakers for events or banquets and keep in touch with organizations through e-mail, letters, and in some cases financial donations. There are awards named in honor of past leadership. These awards are presented by the persons for whom they are named, or presenters share stories about those persons at the award ceremonies. Written, video, and pictorial scrapbooks, along with oral traditions, allow for a culture of appreciation and understanding to be built among organization members. Oral histories are strong cultural elements and allow for understanding and appreciation of the important role that RHAs play in the education and development of civic and community leaders well beyond the college experience.

Support from Residence Hall Staff

When student, graduate, and professional staff in housing support organizations, RHAs tend to be stronger. In some cases, residence hall student staff were members or co-advisers of RHAs. In other cases, RHAs allow for unique leadership opportunities for students not employed through housing offices. Those RHA organizations where members and residence hall staff participate in joint programming efforts and work more closely on policy and procedure implementation tend to be more successful. RHA leaders are often encouraged to apply and are selected for resident assistant (RA) positions the next year, thus assuring a supportive base for RHA organizations campuswide. Choosing RAs who have exposure to alternative organizational structures through previous RHA experiences contribute to RA staffs that work more collaboratively and understand the value of developing relationships across a broad spectrum of offices and organizations.

Support from Housing Offices

In addition to involvement, housing offices that show financial support to RHAs tend to have more involved and active organizations. Some housing offices support RHA leadership with small stipends or by allowing leaders a choice of residence hall rooms either at reduced fees or as benefits for service. Others pay for transportation and registration to national or regional conferences for officers or selected members. Other housing offices support RHAs through meal stipends, parking, advanced course registration, or book allowances. Support also is demonstrated through assignment of RHA advisers who are truly committed to RHA organizations and to student growth and education.

Committed Advisers

Finally, few RHAs are successful without advisers who are interested in student leadership development and committed to the mission and purpose of RHA organizations. These advisers tend to give students responsibility for projects and programs and give them support to complete the tasks on their own. They invest time and energy in the organizations and enjoy working with student leaders rather than seeing the advising duties as chores or something else that needs to be done in a day. Many current advisers mention that they had been involved as residence hall leaders and had advisers who served as mentors to them. Others mention having "a passion" for advising and seeking housing positions that allow them to follow that passion. Advising is as important as staff supervision, but not all professionals take the opportunity to work in the same way with RHA student-leaders.

Conclusion

Paul Bloland (1967) in his monograph on student group advising encourages student affairs professionals to think of student organizations as co-curricular classrooms and advisers as teachers. As with any class that offers a lab section to practice the concepts learned, a residence hall association should provide student participants the opportunity to learn about leadership and organizational functioning and management — all skills which are transferable to post-college life. Learning labs are places for students to experiment with new ways of doing things yet provide somewhat controlled environments which act as safety nets for failing with limited negative consequences.

The bureaucratic or rational models employed by many RHA organizations may be effective when campus environments and missions of organizations support and value the hierarchical structure and decision-making procedures employed. Since there are newer, alternative models available and emerging, this provides advisers who are interested in student growth the opportunity to present these newer models to student organizations and allow students the chance to explore and struggle with new concepts. Astute advisers do not allow organizations to accept the bureaucratic model because it is familiar or easy to work within; instead, astute advisers advocate testing whether rational concepts are applicable to RHAs and how RHAs really operate in practice.

"Prior to Burns's work on transformational theory in the late 1970s, all leadership theories had in common a focus on hierarchy, authority, control, competition, separation of the leader from the led, organizations as closed systems, and a focus on change as incremental" (Love & Estanek, 2004). The predominant existing model for residence hall organizations appears to be reflective of this genre. As the evolution in organizational models de-emphasizes hierarchical structure and emphasizes networking and collaborative relationships among and between organizational members, it is recommended that residence hall associations provide students with the opportunity to experiment with alternative models of organizational structures.

The educational value of exposure to alternative models to the students involved in RHA includes: 1) allowing students to work in a collaborative organization and to develop the skills necessary to be successful in them in future work or organizational settings (knowledge acquisition); 2) bringing knowledge of how that approach works within a bureaucratic setting with them into organizations they join in the future and possibly improve them (knowledge application); and 3) practicing skills requiring cognitive complexity which results in outcomes of improved critical thinking, reflective thinking, intellectual flexibility, and identity/cognition integration (*Learning Reconsidered*, p. 18.).

One role as adviser/teacher is to provide "structured experiences which contribute to their [the students'] intellectual or personal growth" through "educationally desirable" organizational activities (Bloland, 1967, p. 6, 8). Challenging students to evaluate the effectiveness of current organizational structures and explore alternative organizational models is one way to accomplish this responsibility.

References

American College Personnel Association. (1994). *Student learning imperative*. Washington, D.C.: Author.

American College Personnel Association & National Association of Student Personnel Administrators (2004). *Learning reconsidered*. Washington, D.C.: Authors.

Allen, K. & Cherry, C. (2000). *Systemic leadership: Enriching the meaning of our work*. Lanham, (MD): University Press.

Barr, M.J., Desler, M.K., & Associates. (2000). *The handbook for student affairs administration*, (2nd edition). San Francisco: Jossey Bass.

Bloland, P.A. (1967). *Student group advising in higher education*. Alexandria,VA: American College Personnel Association.

Cawthon, T.W. & Underwood, S.J. (1998). The organizational structures of RHAs. In N. W. Dunkel and C. L. Spencer (eds.), A*dvice for Advosers: The development of a residence hall association* (2nd ed.). Columbus OH: Association of College and University Housing Officers-International.

Kuh, G.D. (1996). Guiding principles for creating seamless learning environments for undergraduates. *Journal of College Student Development, 37* (2), 135–48.

Love, P. & Estanek, S. (2004). *Rethinking student affairs practice*. San Francisco: Jossey-Bass.

McCluskey-Titus, P. (January 20, 2004). Student organization adviser as mentor: A different paradigm? *NASPA Net-Results*. Available on-line: http://www.naspa.org/membership/mem/nr/article.cfm?id=1312

National Association of College and University Residence Halls (NACURH) website. Available on line: http://www.nacurh.org/

Schein, E. H. (1992) *Organizational culture and leadership* (2nd ed.). San Francisco: Jossey-Bass.

Weber, M. (1946). *Essays in sociology*. New York: Oxford University Press.

Zand, D. (1974). Collateral organizations: A new change strategy. *The Journal of Applied Behavioral Science, 10* (1), 63–89.

Appendix A

Residence Hall Association Websites Reviewed

1. Arizona State University Residence Hall Association
2. Bucknell University Residence Hall Association
3. Butler University Residence Hall Association
4. California State University - Chico Residence Hall Association
5. California State University - Northridge Residence Hall Association
6. Carnegie Mellon University Student Dormitory Council
7. Clemson University Residence Hall Association
8. College of New Jersey Residence Hall Association
9. Eastern Illinois University Residence Hall Association
10. George Washington University Residence Hall Association
11. Georgia College & State University Residence Hall Association
12. Gonzaga University Residence Hall Association
13. Indiana University of Pennsylvania Residence Hall Association
14. Juniata College Residential Hall Association
15. Kansas State University Association of Residence Halls
16. LaSalle University Resident Student Association
17. Lehigh University Residence Hall Association
18. North Carolina State University Inter-Residence Council
19. Northern Illinois University Residence Hall Association
20. Radford University Residence Hall Association
21. Saint Louis University Residence Hall Association
22. San Francisco State University Residence Hall Association
23. Santa Clara University Residence Hall Association
24. Southern Methodist University Residence Hall Association
25. Stephen F. Austin State University Residence Hall Association
26. Syracuse University Residence Hall Association
27. Texas Tech University Residence Hall Association
28. University of Alabama Residence Hall Association
29. University of Arizona Residence Hall Association
30. University of Florida Inter-Residence Hall Association
31. University of Houston Residence Hall Association
32. University of Idaho Residence Hall Association
33. University of Iowa Associated Residence Halls
34. University of Maryland-College Park Residence Halls Association
35. University of Michigan Residence Halls Association

36. University of Minnesota Residence Hall Association
37. University of Missouri-Rolla Residence Hall Association
38. University of Southern Mississippi Residence Hall Association
39. University of Utah Residence Hall Association
40. University of Wisconsin-Oshkosh United Students in Residence Halls
41. University of Wisconsin-Platteville Residence Hall Council
42. Wake Forest University Resident Student Association
43. Western Michigan University Residence Hall Association
44. Western Washington University Residence Hall Association
45. Winthrop University Resident Students' Association

7

Advising Student Organizations in Residential Learning Communities

Diane Porter

This chapter provides an overview of considerations for advisers working with residence hall associations housed in residential learning communities that are affiliated with academic programs or other campus administrative offices or organizations. There is some truth that "an adviser is an adviser is an adviser" no matter the circumstances, and there are some basic skills that all advisers ideally should possess. However, there are also situations that advisers of student organizations in residential learning communities should be aware of that may cause changes in advising paradigms. The chapter provides four residence hall governance vignettes from institutions with residential learning communities at different stages of development using different approaches.

What Are Residential Learning Communities?

Residential learning communities have existed in higher education for decades. These communities are structured using a variety of approaches that are all intended to complement students' college experiences beyond the classroom by providing supportive learning environments, community development programs, educational programs, and opportunities for stronger relationships with faculty and staff. Within these communities, students live and learn in seamless environments surrounding specific themes, topics, or academic disciplines. Students in residential learning communities typically are assigned to the same residence halls, floors, or areas; mentored by upperclass peers who also reside in the same location; and are immersed in programs, activities, and sometimes university courses taught on-site related to the theme of the community. For the purpose of this chapter, "residential learning communities" is used as the all-inclusive term for any living-learning programs located in residence halls, from theme floors to residential colleges and anything in between.

Vignette #1: Starting from Scratch

In the summer of 2000, the department of housing and the honors program at a large public research institution in the Southeast began collaborating on a new Honors Residential College. This college was to be the first of its kind in the United States built from the ground up. The facility and program was to represent a shared vision of all involved persons – honors students, honors program staff, the university provost, housing administrators, architects, engineers, and the construction crew. Housing staff initiated and coordinated extensive planning for the physical structure, as well as for the program, which needed to be in place for residents in two years.

The program planning initially involved four faculty members from the university honors program, three housing professionals, and four students. Two more students joined the group. Students represented the existing student honors organization, the hall government from the hall that formerly housed honors students, and the campus-wide residence hall association. This large planning group met monthly at first, then bi-weekly, and then weekly for two years, until the residential college opened. Initially, meeting agendas addressed topics like programming space, programming themes, educational components, policies, faculty involvement in the hall, and utilization of the faculty-in-residence. Then the time came to tackle student governance and representation.

This campus has a long, rich history of successful and nationally-recognized residence hall governance. The student honors organization enjoys the same long, rich history. Via the student members on the planning committee, committee chairs invited each of the three represented student organizations— the student honors organization, the hall government from the hall that formerly housed honors students, and the campus-wide residence hall association—to submit and present proposals to the entire committee on the desired organizational structure of the new organization. Each proposal included a rationale, an organizational structure with officer selection procedures, and a sample constitution. The proposals were well written and professionally presented, but there was a problem. All the proposals looked exactly like the organizational structures of the three existing organizations with few ideas on how to incor-

porate "the others" into one new organization. The committee chairs congratu-
lated the students on their hard work and then challenged them to combine the
three proposals into one organization to represent their interests, as well as the
interests of future residents of the Honors Residential College. It took a year's
worth of lively meetings to get student representatives to the point where they
could agree on a functional area government organizational structure.

What took so long? What were the issues involved? If individually these
student organizations had successfully represented honors students, planned
and implemented social and educational programs, and served as "governing
bodies" for the hall or this specialized group of students, why was merging
into one representative organization such a long and tedious process? Among
the ideas considered:

Organizational Structure

- Which parts of each proposal should be utilized?
- What structure would this new organization take?
- What is the mission of the new organization?
- What is the name of this new organization?

Executive Board

- Which positions would best meet the needs of the proposed structure?
- What are the requirements or duties of each position?
- Are officers elected, selected, or appointed?
- Is there an application process? Interview? General election?

Funding

- Which funding source best serves the needs and interests of
  the organization?
- Are there limitations or parameters in terms of utilizing funds from
  various sources?
- What is the process to access the funds?

Registered or Recognized

- Is this new organization a registered student organization with the
  institution?
- Is this new organization a recognized student organization within a
  specific academic or administrative department?
- Is it possible to be both?
- How is this defined by the institution and/or student government?

Constitution

- Are there institutional guidelines for student organization constitutions?
- Will the group utilize specific parts of an existing constitution, or will a new constitution be written to address the needs of all parties involved?
- What is the process for amending the new constitution?
- What is the timeline for submitting the new constitution to the appropriate offices at the institution for funding, recognition, etc.?

Meetings

- If this new organization falls under an umbrella organization, which officers or members will be required to attend which meetings?

Membership

- Since the Student Honors Organization serves all honors students, both on and off campus, how will the new organization located in a residence hall meet the needs of Honors students who do not live in the residential college?

Adviser

- Will this new organization be advised by a housing professional? A housing graduate student? A staff member from the Honors Program? All of the above? None of the above? A combination of all of the above?

These issues were addressed by student members of the planning committee both in formal committee meetings with faculty and staff present and among themselves outside of formal planning committee meetings. It was not unusual for the student committee members to meet late into the night to work through issues, argue with one another, and formulate alternatives to bring to the larger committee for input and help in decision-making and problem-solving.

A newly proposed organization was in place when the residential college opened. However, it was not a finished product. Faculty and staff were comfortable with the product, but student members of the planning committee had a difficult time starting the year with unresolved issues. The students eventually agreed to having an unfinished basic structure in place and then addressing issues as they arose throughout the year. The planning committee of faculty and staff continued to meet with students to work through issues together after the facility opened. After a successful inaugural year, the new Student Honors

Organization was named runner-up for the Office of Student Activities Student Organization of the Year, a campus-wide award, based on flexibility in creating an organization to meet the needs of constituents and by thinking outside of the box.

Vignette #2 – It Happened By Chance

Fall 2001, the housing staff of a mid-sized, private university in the Northeast assembled a group of students from residential learning communities to gather feedback about experiences in the communities. After a successful session, staff inquired about the possibility of meeting with the students again a few more times throughout the year to further assess how things were going. The students wanted to continue to meet, but asked to meet on a weekly basis instead of occasionally throughout the year.

As the students continued to meet and discuss issues related to learning communities, they also began to plan programs and activities for learning community students and to network with each other. Eventually, they decided to create a constitution and become a recognized student organization through the Office of Residence Life. The new organization became the Learning Community Advisory Board (LCAB). This organization is not to be confused with the campus-wide residence hall association or the individual hall community councils also in existence on this campus. LCAB is a separate organization serving only students living in learning communities and runs a somewhat parallel organization to the RHA and community councils. Recently, LCAB decided they wanted a more formal relationship with the RHA, due to similar missions and student representation, so the LCAB/RHA liaison position was created on both the RHA board and the LCAB board to maintain relations between the two groups, as well as other groups represented through the RHA.

The creation of LCAB has not altered the structure of the established RHA on this campus except for the addition of the LCAB representative to the RHA. A positive outcome is that the RHA is more aware of and focuses more on academic-related issues than they have in the past. The only real challenge that has arisen is that learning community floors have both a floor president, who reports to the community council and/or the RHA, and an LCAB representative. The creation of LCAB also serves as a recruiting tool for learning communities. Prospective students were reluctant to sign up to live in learning communities because they were afraid they would not meet students outside their specific learning community. With LCAB in place, programs and activities are planned for all learning community students, and there are ample opportunities for residents to mingle across learning communities. LCAB programs are either self-supporting or funded through the Office of Residence Life. LCAB also has the option of applying for funds through other campus organizations. Figure 1 is an example of the LCAB Constitution.

Vignette #3 – Co-Existing Organizations with RA Advisers

Three types of learning communities exist at a large, public research institution in the Midwest: thematic communities, freshman interest groups (FIGs), and academic communities. Residents in these learning communities share governance and decision making for the group and plan academic and social programs and activities tailored to the specific majors or interests in each community. The formal group that guides the governance and programming processes is the Leadership Council. Depending on the size of the learning community, the respective Leadership Council could be made up of residents from one floor or from several floors all from the same learning community. Therefore, there are as many Leadership Councils on the campus as there are learning communities. Resident assistants on learning community floors serve as advisers to Leadership Councils. If a learning community, is larger than just one floor, the graduate supervisor serves as the overall adviser to the Leadership Council for that community while working closely with the resident assistants in that learning community.

Since many residence halls also have regular communities (not designated learning communities) in the same building or area, separate governance and programming groups exist. These groups are called Board of Governors and are comprised of representatives from the regular communities and sometimes representatives from learning communities in the hall or area, depending on the constitution for a particular hall or area Board of Governors. The role of the Board of Governors is to provide a student voice for all residents in a particular hall or area and to provide representation to the campus-wide Residence Hall Association. The Leadership Councils are responsible for learning community students only. A hall or area Board of Governors is aware of the learning communities in their respective hall or area. While there is not typically much crossover between groups in terms of leadership, the groups do collaborate on occasion.

Most learning communities on this campus require students to pay either a $50 or $100 per semester activity fee, which provides the funding for learning community programs and activities. This larger pool of programming money allows students in learning communities the unique opportunity to plan how funds will be used and to be creative in the wide variety of activities offered to

FIGURE 1. LEARNING COMMUNITY ADVISORY BOARD CONSTITUTION

established Fall 2001

◆ **ARTICLE I: Name**

Our organizational name shall be: Learning Community Advisory Board, here-after to be referred to as LCAB.

◆ **ARTICLE II: Mission Statement and Goals**

The mission of the Learning Community Advisory Board (LCAB) is to provide recognition for learning community (LC) students, faculty, and staff; create opportunities for idea-sharing across learning communities; provide a voice for LC students in the development and implementation of learning communities; and to develop leadership skills in its members. LCAB strives to enhance the lives of LC students by planning events and programs designed to demonstrate the core values of the University and to round out the learning community experience.

Goals

A. To work as a student advisory committee to University learning community students, faculty, and staff.
B. To fund and plan a variety of activities and materials which improve the learning community experience.
C. To provide a voice for LC students.
D. To assist in recruitment of future LC students.
E. To create a forum for University students, faculty, and staff to learn about the different learning communities.
F. To provide a worthwhile leadership experience for members, including team building and opportunities for growth and development.
G. To establish and maintain relationships between LCAB and University offices, University organizations, and the University community.
H. To work with RHA and NRHH to provide students with a quality living experience.

◆ **ARTICLE III: Membership**

A. *The membership of LCAB should consist of representatives from each of the following learning communities:*

1. Arts Adventure LC 1 and 2

Figure 1. Learning Community Advisory Board Constitution *(continued next page)*

2. Citizenship Education LC
3. Education Living-LC
4. The Creativity, Innovation, and Entrepreneurship LC
5. International Relations LC
6. School of Management LC
7. The Wellness LC
8. The Service LC
9. Women in Science and Engineering LC
10. Interfaith LC

B. *In addition to those members, students who are learning community alumni/ alumnae may participate as well.*

ARTICLE IV: Executive Board

A. *Co-Chief Executive Officers (CCEOs)*

1. Call and run all meetings of LCAB and set the agenda.
2. Work as a liaison between LCAB and LC faculty and staff.
3. Meet with the LCAB advisers weekly to coordinate the administration of LCAB.
4. Serve as the representative and spokesperson of LCAB or appoint as need arises, a person to the position.
5. Create and appoint positions within the organization, which may not serve on the Executive Board, as s/he sees fit.
6. Hold a term of office for one calendar year, from April to April.
7. In the event that the Chairperson is unable to complete his/her term, s/he must give two meetings notice before resigning.

B. *Chief Programming Officer (CPO)*

1. Attend all LCAB meetings.
2. Serve as the liaison to the student activities program adviser.
3. Oversee the planning of programs, as well as delegate responsibilities.
4. Hold a term of office for one calendar year, from April to April.
5. In the event that the CCEOs are unable to complete his/her term, the CPO will assume the position of the interim chairperson, until a new CEO can be elected.

C. *Chief Financial Officer (CFO)*
1. Attend all LCAB and Executive Board meetings.
2. Keep current records of all LCAB finances.
3. Prepare all requisition and purchasing forms for LCAB.
4. Meet regularly with treasury adviser appointed by the LCAB adviser.

Figure 1 (cont'd). Learning Community Advisory Board Constitution

5. Report weekly all LCAB expenditures and the current balance.
6. Hold a term of office for one calendar year, from April to April.

D. *Chief Internal Communications Officer (CICO)*

1. Attend all LCAB and Executive Board meetings.
2. Hold a term of office for one calendar year, from April to April.
3. Take minutes at every meeting to be distributed to all members.
4. Maintain a directory of all current LCAB members.
5. Maintain LCAB's listserv and email account.
6. Oversee the LCAB webpage.
7. Take pictures at LCAB events and keep a photo library (digital and paper photos).

E. *Chief External Communications Officer (CECO)*

1. Attend all LCAB and Executive Board meetings.
2. Hold a term of office for one calendar year, from April to April.
3. Develop an overall external communications plan for LCAB (i.e., press releases for campus and local newspapers, etc.)
4. Coordinate LCAB representation at Spring Receptions.
5. Oversee LCAB representation at various campus events and functions.
6. Write articles for the Learning Community Newsletter (or delegate this to appropriate people).
7. Work with programming committees to develop and implement advertising and marketing.

F. *Residence Hall Association Liaison Officer (RHALO)*

1. Attend all LCAB meetings.
2. Serve as LCAB liaison to the Residence Hall Association.
3. Attend RHA meetings.
4. Hold a term of office for one calendar year, from April to April.

ARTICLE V: Selection of Officers

A. *Qualifications*

1. Officer candidates must be current or former participants in a learning community.
2. Elections will be held every April.
3. All current LCAB participants may vote.
4. Officers will be determined by a majority of votes.

Figure 1 (cont'd). Learning Community Advisory Board Constitution

B. Resigning Office

1. If an officer should leave office for any reason during his/her term, s/he shall submit a letter of resignation two weeks in advance.
2. If an officer should leave office for any reason during his/her term, a general election will be held.

ARTICLE VI: LCAB Representatives

A. LCAB Representatives

Each Learning Community can have an unlimited number of attendees at LCAB meetings.

B. Representative Responsibilities

1. Participate in LCAB meetings.
2. Participate in the planning and implementation of LCAB programs and activities.
3. Assist with the recruitment of future LC students.
4. Attend LCAB events.
5. Keep in general communication with LCAB concerning the business of their LCs.

ARTICLE VII: Voting

A. Each LC representative will receive one vote. Members of the Executive Board are inclusive of those votes. Total votes for each LC can total no more than three. The votes will be yes, no, or abstain.
B. Abstentions will be subtracted from the total number of votes. If more than 1/3 of members who are present abstain, a re-vote will be conducted.
C. A vote will be passed if there is majority agreement of the vote.

ARTICLE VIII: Advisers

A. Will be the Director of Learning Communities for Student Affairs and the Graduate Assistant for Learning Communities in the Office of Learning Communities.
B. Attend all LCAB meetings.
C. Meet with the LCAB CCEOs on a weekly basis.
D. Give a report during each meeting.
E. Work with LCAB CCEOs to:
   1. Establish group goals.
   2. Design retreats.
   3. Develop group cohesiveness.
F. Advise and provide leadership for the organization.

Figure 1 (cont'd). Learning Community Advisory Board Constitution *(continued)*

G. Serve as a liaison between the Learning Community Program and LCAB.

H. Keep LCAB up-to-date on policies affecting them.

I. Has the option to appoint and substitute additional organization and committee advisers as necessary.

ARTICLE IX: Funding of Activities

A. All events and activities funded through LCAB must meet University expenditure guidelines.

B. Programs may be funded which serve to improve the learning community experience for the learning community population.

C. Rationale:

1. Funding proposals shall come through LCAB representatives and LC members.

2. Co-sponsorship must be consistent with available funds within the group requesting or providing assistance.

3. Funds accrued through any revenue producing event will be redistributed to all co-sponsoring agents proportional to their original investment.

4. All proposals will be submitted to the CFO at least two meetings prior to the event.

5. LCs that submit funding proposals must have current LCAB representation to be considered.

ARTICLE X: Amendments

A. The Constitution will be reviewed and amended by the membership of LCAB at any time during the semester, at the discretion of the Executive Board, with regards to time constraints for the agenda.

B. Suggested amendments to the Constitution will be submitted, discussed, and decided upon by the voting procedures discussed in Article VI.

Figure 1 (cont'd). Learning Community Advisory Board Constitution

learning community residents. It is not unusual for this money to be spent on large-scale trips or tickets to cultural events that support and enhance the learning community theme. The Office of Student Organization Accounts (SOA) is responsible for providing fiscal oversight, banking, and bookkeeping services, as well as training and budgeting guides for the Leadership Council, since the group is recognized by the Student Activities Office.

While this system has been in place for many years and works quite well on this campus, it is not without challenges. Due to the large amount of funding available to the Leadership Councils, they are sometimes perceived as being the "haves," while the Board of Governors and the RHA may be perceived as the "have nots." It is not unusual for Leadership Councils to be approached by other groups for programming or activity funds. This is usually remedied through some co-programming. The other challenge also deals with money. It is difficult to teach resident assistants how to advise students to spend the large amount of money they have access to. As a result, money tends to go unused and rolls over to the next year for another group of students. On the positive side, this split system serves this campus well, and all students take ownership in their respective communities and residence areas.

The Leadership Councils, Boards of Governors, and the Residence Hall Association all go through training together at the beginning of fall semester and engage in teambuilding and intentional conversations about how the groups interact with one another. Figures 2 and 3 are sample exercises from those training sessions. Figures 4 and 5 are training materials for RA advisers of Leadership Councils.

Vignette #4 – The Well-Oiled Machine

This mid-sized land grant research institution has a rich history of successful learning communities in residence halls and residence hall governance. Each residence hall floor or learning community has its own floor government. Representatives from floor governments make up the individual residence hall or area governments. Representatives from the residence halls or area governments make up the campus-wide residence hall association at one representative per 250 residents per hall/area. Since approximately 64% of bed spaces are located in sponsored learning communities, learning communities are just as much a part of the norm of campus housing as traditional halls. Staff members at this institution report no differentiation in residence hall governance between learning community governments and traditional floor governments.

LEADERSHIP COUNCIL EXPECTATIONS EXERCISE

It is important to establish a set of expectations for each other. What does the adviser expect of the group, the group of the adviser, and the group of each other? First, reflect on the questions below individually and write down your responses. Then, spend time discussing these topics and develop a set of expectations you all can agree on. Keep in mind why you joined the community, what you hope to gain from your experience, and the relationships you wish to have. Have someone keep notes to type up and distribute to all after the retreat. Ask additional questions to the ones below if needed.

1. *What is your understanding of your responsibilities and of others' responsibilities?*

2. *What do you expect of your fellow officers?*

3. *What do you expect of your adviser (RA)?*

4. *What can others expect of you?*

5. *When community meetings are called, who is expected to attend?*

6. *How often should community meetings occur?*

7. *Are Leadership Council members and RA(s) expected to attend all community programs?*

8. *How will I communicate with my floor (include how and when)?*

9. *How will information be shared?*

10. *How will communication regarding meetings occur (e-mail, phone, etc.) and in what time frame?*

11. *How will meetings be run (i.e., agenda, free flowing, reports, parliamentary procedures, etc.)?*

12. *Should the RA meet with the chairperson before meetings to establish the agenda, determine who needs to make a report, etc.?*

13. *If someone is upset with something or someone, how should it be handled?*

14. *What role shall the RA (adviser) take in meetings? (Have time for their individual report; remain quiet, except to explain University or residence hall policies; be a regular member of the group with voting rights; serve as a tie breaker; recommend or plan programs themselves for the community; make sure additional training is available to members; mediate conflicts among the group; keep the council on track with budget and goals; etc.)*

Figure 2. Leadership Council Expectations Exercise

LEADERSHIP COUNCIL GOAL-SETTING-EXERCISE

Spend some time brainstorming what the Leadership Council would like to accomplish for the year. Use the following questions to guide this session. Have someone record what the group identifies as possible goals. After coming up with a list, look at the items realistically. Can they be accomplished during the year? Will there be enough money to accomplish them all? What steps will be needed to accomplish the goals? Keep notes and create a document that can be shared with the entire community at a later time.

1. *What does the community hope to accomplish this year?*
2. *What traditions would we like to establish or maintain?*
3. *What type and how many programs should we do?*
4. *How do we want to work together with the Board of Governors?*
5. *What needs to be done to successfully meet our goals?*
6. *How will we know we have been successful?*
7. *What deadlines or time schedules do we need in order to be successful?*
8. *Discuss anything additional that would be important to include.*

Figure 3. Leadership Council Goal-Setting Exercise

In terms of academics, the residence life program on this campus actively supports academic programming for each community including traditional floors and floors that are sponsored learning communities. The Residential Life Department designates a specific dollar figure per resident that each community can access for educational programming purposes like study bucks, dining with a faculty member, field trips, etc.. Program plans and budgets are submitted to the Office of Residential Academic Programs where programs are approved and funds are allocated. These funds are in addition to the traditional funds collected via the social fee and distributed to the residence hall association, hall/area governments, and community governments.

During the spring semester, the residents in each community are responsible for planning "Fall Welcome" for new residents who will be joining the community the following fall. Current staff and residents are asked to reflect on their first semester experiences and then plan programs accordingly to meet the needs of incoming students. On floors that are sponsored learning communities, this process is guided by each community stakeholder group comprised of faculty or staff from the academic program or college affiliated with the learning community as well as the hall coordinator, student staff, student leaders, and floor government representatives from the community. Fall welcome plans

ADVISING THE LEADERSHIP COUNCIL:
A GUIDE FOR RAS

An ideal student group has established leaders with previous experience in that group. They know the traditions, goals, opportunities, and potential of the group for which they work. They know how to plan programs, run meetings, motivate the members of the community, and how to lead responsibly and ethically. However, the vast majority of Thematic Communities do not fit this ideal, as their membership is comprised almost entirely of freshmen, except for the resident assistant. The RA is an established student-leader who needs to step to the front with confidence and provide the leadership that is in many ways absent from a community of freshmen. RAs will be the central players in defining and maintaining the traditions, goals, opportunities, and potential of the community. They will mentor and advise new leaders of the community to plan programs, run meetings, motivate residents, and act responsibly as leaders.

If RAs do the job well, the RA job will change as the year progresses. Early on, RAs will effectively hold the hands of Leadership Council members. Eventually, they will encourage and empower Leadership Council members to strike out on their own and develop skills independent of RA direct involvement. RA influence will be explicit and direct in August and September and should be implicit and indirect by April and May.

The following outlines effective advising practices that typically provide positive results. Many are intuitive and common sense. They are included because they are simple and remarkably effective.

Provide the Foundation

1. Set a positive atmosphere immediately. Strive to make time together fun and productive.

2. Involve everyone in attendance and ensure that opinions, perspectives, and personalities are respected and valued.

3. Make sure the group understands its history as a community. Share with them the community's traditions and goals, and help them understand their role in maintaining and creating new traditions and goals.

Help Them Get to Work

1. Make sure Leadership Council members know their roles and how to work together. Discuss how they want to conduct meetings, how they will deal with conflict and disagreement, and what kind of expectations they have of one another and of the whole council.

Figure 4 (cont'd). Advising the Leadership Council: A Guide for RAs

2. Spend time discussing goals. Help the group understand which goals are realistic and achievable. Remind the group of goals they should have that cannot be neglected.

3. Help the chair develop an agenda for each meeting and have enough copies for all participants, plus one for official records. Provide suggestions and other feedback as needed. Always be sure to allot time to provide feedback on the agenda.

General Advising Advice

1. An adviser's ultimate role and purpose is to serve as an educator to those he or she advises. Start in a very active role, and encourage others to assume responsibilities as the year progresses. The membership learns how to lead, how to run a meeting, how to plan an event, etc., especially as you provide support and guidance through that experience.

2. Know how to listen, observe, and understand the ever-developing dynamics of the group. Take notes at meetings; connect with those who are distracted or who are distracting the rest of the group. Support those who want but cannot find a voice in the group.

3. Be aware of body language. Find out why members look distracted, annoyed, or bored and help them seek ways to remedy the dynamic. The reasons could be as divergent as wanting to be more involved or no longer wanting to be involved at all.

4. Understand that each member will have different experiences, interests, and areas of expertise. While it is natural to be drawn to individuals whose styles compliment your own, an adviser's role should encourage and support all members of the group and seek to provide each of them opportunities for growth and development.

5. Do not pretend to know everything, and do not be afraid to make mistakes. Be prepared to admit you may not know the answer, and if you have made a mistake, admit it and move on.

6. What is your own behavior? Are you alert? Do you pay attention? The members of the group will take their cues from your behavior.

7. If there is an obvious problem in the group, address it appropriately and immediately. Problems that linger quickly grow larger. Share your concerns with the chair and work with her or him on a remedy.

Encouraging Group Productivity

Two things common to any group are that they usually have something to do – a task – and a specific means by which they seek to accomplish that task – the process. These are referred to as task functions and process functions.

Figure 4 (cont'd). Advising the Leadership Council: A Guide for RAs

Task functions include planning a program, developing a budget, or running a meeting. Is everything organized? Does the needed task get accomplished? Is everything planned for and taken care of? Problems in the task functions area are usually connected to lack of organization, planning, or vision. Slip into educator role and ask the kinds of questions that help members develop a better structure to their endeavors.

Process functions are how tasks get accomplished. Is everyone involved?

Do they respect each other and pay attention to each other? How do they work as a group when they are trying to accomplish a task? Problems in this area are usually going to be social – members not doing what they agreed to or members not getting along. Problems resemble roommate conflicts, except with more direct connection to the rest of the community. The mediation techniques you were trained with are transferable and should empower you to help the individuals involved come to an understanding of how to proceed.

Though task and process functions are different, they are interrelated. Problems in one easily can lead to problems in the other. It is important to be a good observer so you may more easily identify the root of a problem.

Figure 4 (cont'd). Advising the Leadership Council: A Guide for RAs

THEMATIC COMMUNITY LEADERSHIP COUNCIL JOB DESCRIPTIONS

In developing the Leadership Council for your Thematic Community, you will want to recruit and elect the positions listed below. There are some optional positions for you and the council to consider. Feel free to develop positions to fit your community's needs or add to the responsibilities listed below. In Thematic Communities with more than one floor, you will only need to elect one group of officers for the entire community. You may still elect a floor/house governor, vice governor, or any other officer or position required by your center student government or needed on your floor/house.

Chair: This person leads/directs the council. The chair sets meeting times and agendas and serves as a liaison to the RA and other student leaders. In conjunction with the council and the RA, the chair helps establish the purpose, goals, budget and programs for the community. There could be co-chairs to share responsibilities.

Vice-Chair: The vice-chair serves as community leader in the absence of the chair. If the chair is unable to convene a meeting or set an agenda, the vice-chair fulfills those responsibilities. The vice-chair would be in direct contact with the RA and other student leaders and would assist in the development of the purpose, goals, budget, and programs for the community. A specific role could be designed for the vice-chair as defined by the council.

Treasurer: The treasurer assists in developing and managing the budget for the community's funds, oversees the allocation of funds, and maintains the SOA account. The Treasurer approves expenditures based on the budget and writes check requests to the SOA Office for reimbursements. The treasurer serves as co-signatory on the community's SOA account with the graduate supervisor. The treasurer works directly with the RA and the Center's VP of Finance. The treasurer also assists in the development of the purpose, goals, budget, and programs for the community.

Secretary: The secretary takes minutes at all council meetings, posts the minutes for the community to read, and keeps community records as well. The secretary works directly with the RA and the chair. The secretary also could serve as the floor/house historian. The secretary assists in the development of the purpose, goals, budget, and programs for the community.

Historian: (Optional) The historian serves to create and maintain floor/house records of the community's events during the academic year. This may mean

Figure 5 (cont'd). Thematic Community Leadership Council Job Descriptions

taking photographs, developing a scrapbook, or other creative ways to develop and preserve the traditions of the community, like creating a slide show for the year.

Special Projects Chair: (Optional) The special projects chair works on special projects that the community wants to develop. An example is organizing a volunteer service activity such as working on a Habitat for Humanity project. Another example is coordinating a special program related to the theme that the community requests or the Leadership Council develops. The special projects chair develops a committee of community members to work together and communicate via email and meetings the kinds of activities requested. The special projects chair also could develop projects as a committee.

Librarian: (Optional) If the community wants to establish a resource area of written materials related to the theme, the librarian coordinates, purchases, and organizes the resources. In some cases, special rooms or space could be designated to house the resource materials for the community. Lounge space could be considered for such a purpose. The librarian works with the RA to facilitate the space needed and could develop a committee of residents to help in selecting materials.

Residential Fellow (RF) Liaison: (Optional) Each Thematic Community has a faculty member, staff member or other related professional working with the community as a volunteer. The role of the residential fellow is negotiated with the community's members but typically includes friend, resource person, and program planner. In the case of a residential fellow for a Thematic Community, the RF should have some expertise in the thematic area and should be able to share that expertise with the community. The RF liaison is the contact person for the RF for invitations to events and activities and assists in getting community members involved with the RF. The RF also could serve on the Leadership Council or programming committee themselves.

Intramural Coordinator: (Optional) In some centers this position might already exist as a floor officer position. If not, then having a community member or group of members to coordinator floor/house intramurals is beneficial to the development of community. The intramural coordinator is the liaison to the Recreational Sports Office and the center's intramural director to sign up community teams for the various sports offered. This person organizes informal competitions within the community or organizes other sports-related activities for the community.

Member(s)-At-Large: (Optional) Members-at-large of the council attend meetings, represent the interests of other community members, work on pro-

Figure 5 (cont'd). Thematic Community Leadership Council Job Descriptions

grams and projects, and communicate the activities of the council to the community (formally or informally). The member(s) roles could be discussed and clarified by the council early in fall semester.

Programming Committee Chair: (Optional) The programming committee chair is directly responsible for coordinating a committee of floor/house members to plan and implement programs based on the community's goals, needs and interests. The chairperson assists with the development of the purpose, goals, budget, and programs for the community with the rest of the council. The programming committee chair could also be the vice governor and attend the Board of Vice Governors' meetings.

Governor: It is recommended that in Thematic Communities, the chair serves to lead the Leadership Council, while the governor serves as a member of the council. The governor represents the community at the center Board of Governor meetings. The governor voices his or her opinion, and those of the community, on how center student government activity fee funds should be spent, on what programs should be sponsored in the center, and on what policies and procedures should be implemented in the center. The Board of Governors is a decision-making body for the entire center, and the governor serves as liaison to the community and the board. The governor also assists in the development of the community's purpose, goals, budget, and programs as a member of the council.

Vice Governor: It is recommended that there be both a vice Chair of the Leadership Council and a vice governor for the community. The vice governor is a member of the council and represents the community at the Board of Vice Governors' meetings. The Board of Vice Governors might also be called the Board of Educational Programmers. It is the primary responsibility of the vice governor to represent the opinions and ideas of the community on the board. The Board of Vice Governors generally serves as the center programming body to plan and implement center-wide programs and activities. The vice governor could also serve as the community's programming committee chair. The vice governor would assist in the development of the community's purpose, goals, budget, and programs.

Figure 5 (cont'd). Thematic Community Leadership Council Job Descriptions

and budgets are submitted to the Office of Residential Academic Programs for feedback and approval.

What is the advising role for a residence hall organization that is a well-oiled machine? Throughout this vignette, a scenario is described where lines between learning communities, floor governments, hall governments, and the residence hall association are blurred. Seemingly, all of the groups work together as one entity to represent and support residence hall students. Advisers may be involved on many levels—on the floor, within the hall or area, and on the campus-wide level. It is important that advisers understand the history, the big picture, and the expectations of various housing and other institutional entities—the stakeholders. It is important for advisers to understand the organizational structure of the offices, programs, or communities involved; the funding intricacies; and the ultimate purpose of the Residence Hall Association.

This scenario is unique in that it represents a well-oiled machine, and all parties work well together—and separately—to accomplish shared goals. Of particular importance is the intentional focus on educational programming and welcome activities planned by residents, for residents.

Conclusion

The purpose of this chapter was to provide an overview of considerations for advisers of Residence Hall Associations housed in residential learning communities affiliated with an academic program or other campus administrative office or organization. The four institutions represented here all have strong learning communities, rich histories of student governance in the residence halls, and different approaches when it comes to combining the two. While there is no one right answer, there is also no need to reinvent the wheel when implementing new learning communities in residence halls and designing student governance in support of these communities. The following are tips for advisers in residential learning communities:

- Get students involved in the process, whether starting from scratch or changing an organization to meet the needs of the learning community. Student input in planning will lead to commitment to the organization.
- Help students define the organization's mission. Typical Residence Hall Association advisers know that the purpose of the RHA is community development, programming, serving as a voice for residence hall students, and representing student concerns to the appropriate authorities. While this also may be in the mission of the RHA in a residential learning community, it is probable that this

mission will be more focused on the goals of the academic community it represents. Mission statements will affect key topics like the constitution and by-laws of the organization, leadership and committee structure, needs assessment and programming efforts, constituents, policy development, and funding.

- If the community is linked to an academic department, involve faculty members in the organization beyond a typical faculty adviser role. Faculty members are able to offer insights and perspectives from their areas of expertise and experience that can enhance the organization's ability to plan, implement programs, assess and meet student needs, and access resources.

- Be willing to spend time with faculty members explaining such topics as housing/residence life philosophy, mission, history, lingo, procedures, rules, regulations, staffing patterns, and facilities. Spend time providing the historical perspective about the learning community and student governance in the residence halls. Ask faculty members to explain the academic side of the institution and learning community to housing staff who will be working with the student organization. Have a clear idea of what faculty members' goals are for students and how they conceptualize/define student learning and success. Ideally, all faculty and staff at the institution are working for student success, so it is helpful to find out what "student success" means to everyone involved.

- Be open to new ideas. Think outside the box. Be willing to change the traditional advising paradigm.

- Be flexible. It is acceptable (and probably preferable) not to have everything in writing when initiating a new student organization in a learning community. Be willing to learn from experience.

- Be patient.

- Listen to students.

- Get resident assistants involved.

- Understand the make-up of the constituency. Explore any political issues that may be involved.

- Compromise – with students, with faculty, with administrators.

- Become knowledgeable about sources of funding, stipulations on use of funds, etc.

- Have an understanding of basic student development and group development theory. This knowledge will provide comfort during frustrating times.

There are differences between advising typical residence hall associations and those in learning communities affiliated with academic programs or other campus administrative offices or organizations. Identifying and addressing these differences will result in less frustrating advising experiences. Advisers are encouraged to enter into the venture with a sense of wonder and open minds and to listen to students and faculty before uttering, "That's not the way it's done around here." Advisers should heed the guidance of the *Student Learning Imperative* (1996):

> Both students and institutional environments contribute to what students gain from college. Thus, the key to enhancing learning and personal development is not simply for faculty to teach more and better, but also to create conditions that motivate and inspire students to devote time and energy to educationally-purpose-ful activities, both in and outside the classroom....Student affairs professionals attempt to make "seamless" what are often perceived by students to be disjoint-ed, unconnected experiences by bridging organization boundaries and forging collaborative partnerships with faculty and others to enhance student *learning*.

Together, residence hall associations in residential learning communities enhance students' college experiences beyond the classroom by providing supportive learning environments, community development programs, edu-cational programs, leadership opportunities, and stronger relationships with faculty and staff. Within these communities, students can live and learn in seamless environments.

Reference

American College Personnel Association (1996). *The student learning imper-ative: Implications for student affairs*. Washington, DC: Author.

8

Motivating and Recognizing Student Leaders and Student Organizations

Jacque Bollinger

"You get the best effort from others not by lighting a fire beneath them, but by building a fire within them" (Nelson & Spitzer, 2002).

No truer words have been poken, particularly when it comes to advising. This statement is the essence of what effective advisers do. They discover the fire within each student and determine how best to feed that fire. It is a priority for advisers to determine what motivates students to seek leadership roles and what keeps them happy and productive in those roles as well as allows them to grow and develop further as leaders.

Residence hall association (RHA) and hall government advisers need to understand the importance and value of motivation and recognition to student organizations. The responsibility often falls to advisers to discover what inspires and motivates students. This responsibility is challenging as there is no magic formula to motivating students. Each student is diverse and unique. Each comes from varying life experiences and rarely is inspired by the same things. One standard formula for motivating students does not exist; motivation is individual and unique to each student.

Challenges to Advising Student-leaders

Advisers of student organizations and student-leaders are fortunate. Most students who get involved in student organizations choose to do so. They made the decision to be involved. It is rare that students feel forced to be part of RHAs or other student organizations. Typically, students are attracted to organizations for particular reasons and find something within a student organization that is of interest to them. They feel they can contribute and feel some type of affinity for the work. While it may often feel like student-leaders are not motivated, it is important to remember that they started from a place of motivation.

What are the challenges in advising student organizations, particularly RHAs or hall governments? What makes the motivation of these students and student organizations unique? The following provides some insight.

Transitory Nature of College Students

Students are in college for a short time and may live in the residence halls for even shorter periods. Often, when advisers think they have organizations figured out, the year is over, and it is time to elect yet another executive board.

Limited Adviser Contact with Students

RHA or hall government adviser contacts with students can often be limited. Advisers may see students they advise at weekly individual and/or executive board meetings, unlike staff who they may see on a daily basis. It is difficult to get to know student-leaders well enough to determine skill levels and what motivates them to succeed.

Advising Not Supervising

Students who choose to get involved with RHA or hall governments are volunteers. They choose to be involved. For the most part, advisers have little leverage with student-leaders in terms of power. In most cases, advisers cannot fire student-leaders, deduct wages, or put them on probation. Advisers must find what intrinsically motivates student volunteers.

A New Group of Students Each Year

Advisers may find it monotonous to start over again every year. The degree to which they feel this is often dependent upon the return rate of the organizations they advise and the skill levels of those returning to positions. Often in this case, it is not a question of motivating students, but motivating advisers.

Student Organizations Resist Change

While students like to believe advisers are resistant to change and new ideas, it is often the students who are resistant. Student organizations often perpetuate unhealthy organization procedures and culture as student-leaders cannot see beyond their time within organizations. Residence hall student-leaders make decisions for students who come after them, rather than the students who are presently living in the residence halls. Many of the student-leaders that advisers work with today will not be around tomorrow to see the results of their work. On many campuses, change occurs slowly. Organizations may take beginning steps to initiate new policies or programs, but the final results may take years for fruition. The challenge becomes motivating existing students to do work now, although they may not see the benefits.

Academic Demands

Students' top priority is education. The academic demands of classes, mid-terms, finals, group projects, and major papers often cause stressful emotional highs and lows. Depending upon academic demands, the commitment of student-leaders to student organizations may be inconsistent with spurts of activity and times of non-production.

Advantages to Advising Student-leaders

Despite the challenges to motivating student-leaders outlined above, there are advantages to advising student-leaders who reside in residence halls.

Transitory Nature of College Students

The transitory nature of college students is a challenge and an advantage or blessing. Director of Residence Life and Dean of Students at the University of Wisconsin Oshkosh, Jim Chitwood, is fond of saying, "Time and graduation heals all things." This quote can be particularly true in advising scenarios. If advisers find themselves unable to resolve situations with leaders who are less than competent or if they are advising dysfunctional student organizations, eventually the dynamic will change due to graduation or the urge of students to move off-campus.

Each Year Begins Anew

In the world of higher education, there is a beginning and an end to each school year. New beginnings are quite motivating as there is always hope for what is possible.

Student-leaders Live in Residence Halls

Students are busy. The fact that residence hall student-leaders live in residence halls increases the ability of RHA or hall government advisers to communicate with them. This is not true for advisers of other student organizations.

Resources for Advisers in Residence Halls

RHAs and hall governments tend to enjoy consistent sources of funding and also tend to receive more funding than other student organizations. In addition to financial support, RHAs and hall governments also may receive other perquisites from housing or residence life offices, such as office space, telephone access, printer and copier access, computer support, transportation/vehicle availability, and additional advisers. This is not true for other student organizations.

Residence Hall Leaders Are the Cream of the Crop

While it is often easy to become frustrated, advisers need to remember that students who are attracted to residence hall leadership positions tend to be high achievers. Most come to positions self-motivated with some skills. This is not necessarily true of the general student population or students who tend not to get involved.

Common Terminology

Before proceeding, terminology related to motivation and recognition must be clarified. Nelson and Spitzer (2002) use the following definitions which support the purposes of this chapter:

- **Motivation:** The internal human energy available to inspire a person to act.
- **Motivator:** Anything that increases motivational energy.
- **Demotivator:** Anything that reduces motivational energy and/or triggers negative behavior.
- **Recognition:** A positive consequence provided to a person for behavior or result. Recognition can take the form of acknowledgement, approval, or the expression of gratitude. Recognition means appreciating someone for something he or she has done for you, your group, or your organization. Recognition can be given while an employee is striving to achieve a certain goal or behavior, or once he has completed it.
- **Reward:** An item or experience with monetary value (but not necessarily money) that is provided for desired behavior or performance, often with accompanying recognition. Harvard Business School professor and management consultant Rosabeth Moss Kanter defines a reward as "something special—a special gain for special achievements, a treat for doing something above and beyond."

- **Incentive:** Recognition or reward that is promised in advance for an anticipated achievement based on meeting certain criteria. Incentives create anticipation and excitement and thus can result in stronger, clearer motivation. (Nelson & Spitzer, 2002, p. xxv)

According to Nelson and Spitzer's (2002) definition of motivation, the energy to act is internal and therefore individual. Not all individuals are motivated similarly; however, Nelson and Spitzer do find common themes and motivators among employees in work environments:

- **Action:** Being actively engaged in productive work.
- **Fun:** A work environment that includes enjoyable activities—not just drudgery.
- **Variety:** Opportunities to perform new and different tasks.
- **Input:** Feeling that one's opinion matters.
- **Stake-sharing:** Being empowered to make discretionary decisions.
- **Responsibility:** A role in decision-making, such as being responsible for a whole task, rather than just doing piecework.
- **Leadership opportunities:** A chance to manage a team, meeting, or event.
- **Social interactions:** The freedom to communicate with other employees at work without being reprimanded for loitering.
- **Teamwork:** Being a member of a productive team.
- **Using strengths:** Being encouraged to do the things one does well.
- **Learning:** Enhancing one's capabilities.
- **Error tolerance:** Being allowed to fail, without punishment, and being helped to learn from the experience.
- **Measurement:** Being encouraged to keep one's own score, rather than being micromanaged by a supervisor.
- **Goals:** Being encouraged to set one's own goals, rather than having them imposed by others.
- **Improvement:** Being in an environment that enables individuals to become a little better every day.
- **Challenge:** Being given appropriately difficult tasks that cause one to stretch, without feeling anxious.
- **Encouragement:** Being in an environment in which others believe in individuals.
- **Appreciation:** Receiving acknowledgement of contributions.
- **Significance:** Feeling part of a "mission that matters" (Nelson & Spitzer, 2002, p. 51).

Though Nelson and Spitzer's research was done within work environments and not volunteer student organizations, themes and motivators are similar. The terminology may differ, but student-leaders need the presence of these same elements to feel valued and inspired. Student-leaders are looking and seeking out these same organizational traits. It is the responsibility of advisers to assure that these exist within organizations. The degree to which individual members of student organizations need these themes and motivators will vary from student leader to student leader.

In addition to determining what motivates individuals, Nelson and Spitzer's (2002) research determines what demotivates individuals. Again, this research was conducted in work environments; however, the findings are relevant to student organizations as well. Common demotivators are: organization politics, unclear expectations, unnecessary rules, poorly designed work, unproductive meetings, lack of follow-up, contact change, internal competition, dishonesty, hypocrisy, withholding information, unfairness, discouraging responses, criticism, capability underutilization, tolerating poor performance, being taken for granted, management invisibility, over control, take-aways, and being forced to do poor quality work.

Students may use different terminology, but similar themes represent the frustrations or disappointments student-leaders have when working within student organizations. Astute advisers work with organizations to assess if demotivators exist within their organizations and to what degree, and then they develop strategies for eliminating or turning demotivators into motivators.

Nelson and Spitzer's (2002) research also assesses why individuals stay within organizations. What exists within organizations that motivates individuals to stay and to continue to do quality work? The top 10 reasons individuals stay in organizations are:

1. Career growth, learning, and development.
2. Exciting work and challenge.
3. Meaningful work, making a difference and a contribution.
4. Great people.
5. Being part of a team.
6. Good boss / good adviser.
7. Recognition for work well done.
8. Autonomy, a sense of control over one's work.
9. Flexible work hours and dress code.
10. Fair pay and benefits (Nelson & Spitzer, 2002, p.7).

If given the opportunity to create a list of Top Ten Reasons Student-leaders Stay in Student Organizations, student-leaders would answer similarly. In place of "flexible work hours and dress code" might be "flexible schedule to accommodate academics." In place of "fair pay and benefits" might be "fair work distribution." Otherwise, the list is the same. Student-leaders get involved in student organizations to meet others, to gain skills for careers, to make a difference, to be part of something bigger, to be recognized for jobs well done, to have control over what they do, and to work with good advisers.

Motivating Students

"Believe in 'em, hold 'em accountable, and give 'em supportive feedback," (Connellan, 2003, p. 37) offers this quote to explain how to bring out the best in others. He believes three factors must be present when working to develop and motivate others to achieve and succeed: expectations, responsibility, and feedback. Whether a supervisor, adviser, coach, or parent, these three factors are crucial in developing the potential of others.

Expectations

Student organization advisers enjoy unique roles. They suggest and provide input, but do not necessarily possess decision-making authority. Though not voting members of organizations they advise, advisers are responsible for assisting organizations to become productive and purposeful. Although not supervisors, it is reasonable for advisers to have expectations of organizations they advise. Student-leaders often fail because they do not know what is expected from them (Connellan, 2003).

Successful advisers set high expectations for themselves and for those they advise. These expectations are powerful because they can set the tone for student organizations. Research on the phenomenon of self-fulfilling prophecies provides ample evidence that people act in ways that are consistent with others' expectations of them. If advisers expect students to fail, they probably will. If advisers expect them to succeed, they probably will.

The strongest and most powerful influences in times of uncertainty and turbulence are advisers' expectations. When accepted ways of doing things are not working, then advisers' strong expectations about the direction of organizations and manner in which they operate will allow organizations to continue. High expectations make positive impacts on the perceptions and feelings that members of organizations have about themselves and increase self-confidence (Kouzes & Posner, 2003).

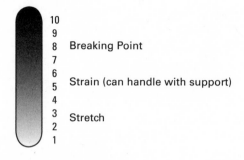

Figure 1. Gradient Stress Scale

Successful advisers link high expectations to what's important to the success of student organizations they advise. They make sure that expectations are consistent with the goals and values of group members. Expectations must be realistic and associated with the current status and situation of advised organizations.

Accountability

Part of the role of advisers is to assure that group members hold each other accountable and follow through on missions and commitments. Lack of accountability is an indicator of problems within student organizations and leads to mediocre results.

Connellan (2003) outlines four steps to successful accountability: establish accountability, set goals, develop action plans, and engage. Successful advisers acknowledge the link between goal setting, action planning and student motivation. These processes allow advisers to hold student organizations accountable which in turn allow them to evaluate progress. The task of advisers is to help student organizations reach mutual goals, NOT adviser goals, and reach the goals with a sense of togetherness (Kouzes & Posner, 2003). Advisers are part of larger missions, and their language needs to reflect the sense of "we," the sense of being a part of a team. Progress toward goals allows for growth and development which is a main reason listed for staying with organizations. Goals are what organizations expect to see accomplished by carrying out action plans. Successful advisers hold organizations accountable for reaching goals.

Connellan (2003) discusses a concept called "gradient stress," which offers a strategy to assist advisers in supporting the goals of student organizations while challenging and motivating them to reach higher on future goals. In the following scale (Figure 1), 1 represents little stress and, 8 to 10 represents the breaking point. If students are at stress level 1 and advisers take them to stress levels 2, 3 and 4, the students are stretched. At stress levels 5, 6, and 7, the students may be strained, but if advisers give students the support they need to make the adjustment, students can handle it.

If advisers go straight from level 1 to level 8, 9 or 10, students will be at a breaking point. No matter how much support advisers give, students won't be able to handle the stress. Too many advisers and leaders try to accomplish goals without advisers giving even modest amounts of support, and then they wonder why organizations don't perform.

The key to using gradient stress is to tailor the strategy to each individual. Advisers can challenge student-leaders to grow by "adjusting" for stress comfort. For example, a student leader who is comfortable at stress level 5 can be challenged to make that level a new level 1. Now the point that was stress level 9 or 10 becomes stress level 5, which the person can handle with support from an adviser or other students. So levels of performance that seemed out of reach a few months before become doable, as long as advisers or organizations provide the necessary support. The means to making this strategy work is providing support. "The more support you put into the system, the faster you can grow people" (Connellan, 2003, pp.63-65).

Connellan (2003) offers other strategies for advisers working with student organizations to set and achieve high goals. He outlines two theories of goal setting: setting high goals will motivate individuals to do what is necessary to achieve them, and setting low goals will allow individuals to reach them, therefore, inspiring them to reach higher goals in the future. Neither strategy is necessarily correct.

If there is a 100 percent probability of success, little motivation exists. If there is no probability of success, little motivation exists. Maximum motivation exists when there is high probability of success, but some risk and challenge (Connellan, 2003).

Feedback

Effective advisers understand the importance of giving feedback to students. It is a common misconception that advisers shouldn't give feedback, as they are not supervisors of student organizations. However, if advisers do not provide feedback, who will? How do student-leaders or organizations know how they are doing if others do not hold up mirrors and allow them to see themselves as they are? "The reason someone isn't doing his best is rarely willful negligence —it's usually simple misunderstanding" (Connellan, 2003, p. 71). This statement is true of most student organizations. Student organizations do not want to fail. They want to be successful. When they are not successful, it is often because they are unaware of what they are doing wrong.

Connellan (2003) discusses three types of feedback: motivational feedback, informational feedback, and developmental feedback. All are important to student organizations and the students working within organizations.

Motivational feedback can come in three forms: positive feedback equals reinforcement, negative feedback equals punishment, and no feedback equals extinction.

Negative feedback is typically the feedback that comes to mind when "feedback" is mentioned. Most fear it and avoid it. Successful advisers rarely use negative feedback. Successful advisers view positive feedback as the most necessary type of feedback in advising situations. Positive feedback validates. It acknowledges work well done. It finds the positives in situations that are not necessarily positive.

Successful advisers know the difference between reinforcement and punishment (positive and negative feedback). Unfortunately, few advisers are aware of the effects of no feedback (extinction) and how devastating the effects can be to student organizations. Giving no feedback may seem harmless. However, poor performance that is not addressed is repeated or escalates; positive performance that is not acknowledged offers no motivation for improvement or further development. Failure to provide feedback can be devastating to individual students and organizations.

Positive reinforcement makes students want to keep doing what they're doing. If advisers want improvement, they need to reinforce improvement. Reinforcement should be immediate and specific and should be given for any improvement, not just excellence. Continuous reinforcement is best for developing new behaviors. Successful advisers use continuous positive reinforcement with newly-elected student-leaders and students who are improving skills. However, once individuals and organizations reach solid levels of performance, advisers should switch to intermittent reinforcement (Connellan, 2003).

In addition to motivational feedback, successful advisers use informational feedback. Informational feedback is more immediate and is used to track progress. Common ways to give informational feedback are to chart meeting attendance, tally program numbers, assess students served in the office, or acknowledge the effectiveness of marketing campaigns.

Developmental feedback is the most effective form of feedback for advising purposes. Developmental feedback allows advisers to individually meet with students to openly discuss issues or problems. Developmental feedback involves several steps. First, advisers define issues or problems. They let students know what the issues or problems are and how they became aware of them. Second, advisers ask students if they view issues or problems similarly.

If so, can students offer thoughts or solutions to the issues or problems? The third step involves working together to explore possible options for resolving the issues or problems. Advisers then acknowledge and reinforce any positive responses or strategies that students offer. Finally, advisers conclude the feedback session by reviewing what was discussed and summarize the strategies for improving issues or problems (Connellan, 2003).

By using expectations, accountability, and feedback, advisers establish solid foundations for organizations that motivate students and increase student organization productivity.

The Importance of Recognition

"People will forget what you said. People will forget what you did. But people will never forget how you made them feel" (Nelson & Spitzer, 2002, p. 15). A chapter on motivation is not complete without discussing recognition. Recognition and performance are closely linked. While recognition is not solely the responsibility of advisers, recognition typically is initiated at the adviser level. Someone within organizations needs to model recognition and assure that recognition becomes part of organization culture. That someone is usually advisers.

Researchers conducted many studies on the importance and outcomes of recognition. Nelson and Spitzer's (2002) research on the benefits of recognition has been adapted to include language for student organizations.

Benefits of Recognition

• **Improved morale.** One of the more immediate effects of increased recognition is improved morale. When students are recognized for doing good work, they feel special and consequently happier and more satisfied in leadership roles.

• **Enhanced productivity.** Students who feel good about leadership roles tend to perform at higher levels; performances become further motivation for wanting to continue to perform at higher levels.

• **Increased competitiveness.** When student organizations recognize and reward performance that is aligned with the key objectives of organizations, organizations become more successful, competitive, and efficient in reaching goals.

• **Decreased stress.** A fine line exists between stress and excitement. Recognition makes work fun and exciting, which increases the likelihood that student-leaders will rise to challenges when needed, rather than feel overwhelmed in their positions.

• **Decreased absenteeism.** When students are thanked and valued for the work they do, they begin to look forward to the time they spend within organizations. Meeting and office hour absenteeism declines. Involvement in activities increases.

• **Decreased turnover.** More recognition equals better relationships, decreased turnover, and increased length of involvement in the organization.

Improving Adviser Recognition Skills

After reviewing the benefits of recognition, it is difficult to understand why organizations or advisers do not adapt ongoing policies of recognition. The following are tips for improving adviser recognition skills.

Common Excuses for not Recognizing

The following are common legitimate—and not so legitimate—excuses for not recognizing student-leaders and organizations:

- "I don't know how best to recognize my student-leaders."
- "I don't feel that providing recognition is an important part of my job."
- "I don't have time to recognize."
- "I'm afraid I might leave somebody out."
- "Students don't value the recognition I have given in the past."
- "Students begin to expect recognition for simply doing their job."
- "I don't have the resources to recognize effectively."

Effective Praise

Nelson and Spitzer (2002) offer guidelines for effective praise using the ASAP3 formula:

• **As soon.** Timing is critical. To be effective, a thank-you should come soon after the achievement or desired activity has occurred. If advisers wait too long, the gesture loses significance. Students assume that other things were more important to advisers than thanking them.

• **As sincerely.** If not sincere, words alone can seem hollow if not sincere. Adviser praise should be based on true appreciation of and excitement about successes. Otherwise the thanks may be viewed as manipulative or a strategy used only when advisers want students to take on additional tasks. As the saying goes, "People don't care how much you know, until they know how much you care."

• **As specifically.** Advisers should avoid generalities in favor of details of achievements. Compliments that are too broad tend to seem insincere. Specifics give credibility to praise. Recognition that states what students did and why efforts were of value are the most successful.

• **As personally.** The most effective forms of recognition are personal. Making recognition personal shows that recognition is important enough for advisers to put aside everything else to focus on individuals. Advisers have limited time. The things they do personally for students indicate the high value they place on students. Recognition by quick e-mails or voice mails is appreciated, but praise in person means much more when time allows.

• **As positively.** When advisers say to students, "You did a great job on this newsletter, but there were quite a few typos," the "but" erases all that came before. Successful advisers save constructive criticism for future similar projects and remove it from praise and recognition.

• **As proactively.** Successful advisers praise progress toward desired goals. They do not wait for perfect performance but rather praise improvements and behavior that are approximately right. This strategy yields end results faster (Nelson & Spitzer, 2002, p 78).

Essence of Recognition

The essence of good recognition communicates:

• "I saw what you did." (This makes sure others know what was seen.)
• "I appreciate it." (This places value on the behavior or achievement.)
• "Here's why it's important." (This provides a context.)
• "Here's how it makes me feel." (This gives recognition an emotional charge.)

Incorporating Recognition

In order for recognition to occur regularly, advisers must build time for recognition into their schedules by reserving specific time each day or each week to work on recognition activities. If recognition becomes part of daily or weekly "to do" lists, advisers are more likely to make recognition a priority. Recognition does not have to be cumbersome. It can be as simple as e-mails

FIGURE 1. Questions to Ask Yourself Before Recognizing

Individual Recognition	Team Recognition
• What do I want to recognize? The best recognition is contingent; that is, in response to a specific behavior or performance. • Who do I want to recognize? Identify the person or people most responsible for the desired behavior or performance. • When should the recognition be done? The best recognition takes place soon after the desired behavior or performance. • Where should the recognition be done? The best recognition is personal; that is, delivered directly to the individual being acknowledged – ideally, in person. • How should the recognition be done? The best recognition is done in a way that enhances its motivational value to the recipient. Who performs the recognition? Is it done in public or private?	• Who should be recognized? • What should be recognized? • Where should recognition be done? • When should recognition be done? • How should the recognition be done?

FIGURE 2. Recognition Mistakes

Individual	Team
• Missed recognition opportunities. • Recognition that's not timely. • Insincere or mechanical recognition. • Public recognition for private people. • Undercutting praise with criticism. • Giving recognition that is not rewarding.	• Treating everyone the same. • Leaving someone out. • Not letting the team determine rewards. • The rush to recognition. • Rewards that aren't rewarding. • One size does not fit all. • Loss of freshness or relevance. • Confusing priorities and alignment. • Subjective recognition. • Entitlement recognition. • Recognition take-aways. • Inappropriate recognition. • Zero-sum recognition. • Untimely recognition.

or phone calls. It can be public acknowledgement in meetings or individual acknowledgement in private meetings. Before recognizing someone, Nelson and Spitzer (2002) suggest advisers ask themselves the questions outlined in Figure 2. They also discuss common mistakes that are made when recognizing in Figure 3.

Recognition Considerations

Before advisers begin developing new recognition programs, they must assess existing recognition programs. It may not be necessary to develop new recognition programs if existing campus recognition programs are underutilized. Most universities support numerous programs for recognizing and rewarding work well done. Advisers are encouraged to explore some of the following recognition resources on their campuses:

- National Residence Hall Honorary (NRHH)
- Of-the-Month Program (often associated with NRHH)
- Academic Honoraries
- Campus Student Organization Awards (often associated with Campus Unions or Dean of Students Offices)
- University Scholarships (often coordinated by Financial Aid or Foundation Offices)
- Regional and National NACURH Awards
- State RHA Organizations (WURHA, MORHA, etc.)
- Departmental End-of-Year Awards
- Division of Student Affairs Recognition
- Departmental or Organizational Newsletters
- University Newspapers

Motivation and Recognition Tools for Advisers

Exercise 1. When holding student organizations accountable, Connellan (2003) suggests using After Action Reviews (AARs) following each activity or event. Think of the last activity that your student organization planned, and ask yourself the following questions below.

After Action Reviews – (AARs)

1. What was supposed to happen?
2. What actually happened?
3. What accounts for any difference?
4. What can be learned?

How could you adapt AARs for regular use within organizations you advise?

Exercise 2. On a single sheet of paper, write the answers to the following questions for the students you advise:

1. What are the key areas of responsibility or accountability for this individual?

2. In each of these key areas, what are the critical metrics or performance indicators that should be used to measure results?

3. For each indicator, specify the performance level you expect the person to achieve and the date by which you think it should be achieved?

Without revealing your responses, ask students you advise to answer the same three questions. Compare responses. If responses don't match, there are potential problems. It is unlikely that students can or will perform as you expect.

Advising Tool

Kouzes and Possner (2003) offer this model to bring structure to individual student advisement meetings:

1. Where are we going?
   - I'll tell you where I think we're going.
   - You tell me where you think we're going.
2. Where are you going?
   - I'll tell you where I see you and your group going.
   - You tell me where you see you and your group going.
3. What are you doing well?
   - I'll give you my sense of what you're doing well.
   - You give me your sense of what you're doing well.
4. What suggestions for improvement do you have for yourself?
   - I'll tell you the suggestions I have.
   - You tell me the suggestions you have.
5. How can I help you?
   - I'll add anything else I think I can do.
   - You tell me what I can do to help and support you.
6. What suggestions do you have for me?
   - I'll tell you what I think I need to do.
   - You tell me what you think I need to do.

Conclusion

Exemplary advisers make those they advise feel strong. They encourage them to take responsibility for successes of organizations by enhancing skills. They help build students' confidence levels of students by listening to ideas and allowing students to act. Good advisers empower those with whom they work and acknowledge good work by giving credit to students for contributions. By applying the concepts of motivation and recognition, advisers can foster student-leader competence and student organization success.

References

Connellan, T.K., (2003). *Bringing out the best in others*. Austin, TX: Bard Press.

Kouzes, J.M., & Posner, Z., (2003). *The leadership challenge*. San Francisco: Jossey-Bass.

Nelson, B., & Spitzer, D., (2002). *The 1001 rewards and recognition fieldbook*. New York: Workman Publishing Company.

9

Understanding Today's Students

Gary Kimble & Lakecia A. Johnson-Harris

Today's college students are tech-savvy, hardworking, and ready to achieve goals. They grew up using computers in school and at home. They had their parents' undivided attention and believed the sky was the limit. They've come to campus expecting the same kind of treatment. According to the National Association of College Admissions Counselors in the State of College Admissions Report (2004), the percentage of students completing high school and going on to college has increased steadily since 1976. Enrollment in postsecondary institutions is expected to increase well into the 21st century, and college enrollment is expected to grow by 10% over the next 10 years. This report also notes that African-Americans and Hispanics together constitute 31% of the American population. However, they represent only 17% of students enrolled at four-year colleges and universities. In addition, women have led admissions since 1970 rounding out at 8 million enrolled compared to 6 million enrolled men.

Selecting a college is a huge undertaking. Students pour over admissions material to narrow the search. During the application phase, they typically make several in-depth campus visits and schedule time to go back for a second visit before final decisions are made. They are meticulous in their planning efforts and set their minds on the perfect choices for them.

Whether a novice adviser or seasoned veteran, this is a remarkable time to be employed in higher education. There are unprecedented opportunities to work with and impact this unique group of college students unlike any previous generations. The optimism observed among today's students is not over-stated or inflated. In examining individual characteristics of members of the current generation, there is much evidence for this enthusiastic outlook. As a group, they have been tagged the Millennial Generation. The first members of the Millennial Generation were members of the high school graduation class of 2000. They arrived on campuses and set new tones and expectations. History might very well look back upon this period as higher education's Renaissance period for student affairs.

This new generation of students should cause higher education administrators and researchers to pay closer attention to historians Neil Howe and William Strauss, who wrote the books *Millennials Rising: The Next Generation (2000)* and *Millennials Go to College: Strategies For a New Generation On Campus (2003)*. This chapter provides a brief overview of the characteristics of the Millennial Generation based on these books, shares implications for advisers, and poses questions for deeper reflection.

The Millennial Generation

The first class of the Millennial Generation was born in 1982 and graduated college in 2004. Most contemporary American generations are defined in terms of birth date. A generation encompasses the period of time in which the group's members reach adulthood. Generally, adulthood is identified as between ages 18 and 21. Howe and Strauss (2000) note, "that of the past nine generations, the age of 'generational maturity' has been between the ages of 17 and 24" (p. 40). Using an accepted 20-year measure for the Millennial Generation, individuals born in 2002 will comprise the ending boundary for this generation.

Clearly the members of the Millennial Generation are a force to be reckoned with for higher education administrators. Members of this generation born in 2002 will be first-year college students in 2020. For most advisers, students of the Millennial Generation will encompass the majority of their higher education advising experiences and careers.

Howe and Strauss (2000) state that students in this group "are unlike any other youth generation in living memory" (p. 4). In addition, they note, "over the next decade, the Millennial Generation will entirely recast the image of youth from downbeat and alienated to upbeat and engaged—with potentially seismic consequences for America" (p. 4). Furthermore, Howe and Strauss (2000) state, "By the time the last Millennials come of age, they could become the best educated youths in American history, and the best behaved young adults in living memory" (p. 30). This statement is not meant to cast shadows on previous generations, for history has recorded the triumphs of GI Generation, as well as others. Like the Greatest Generation, something catastrophic happened to the members of the Millennial Generation, the events of September 11, 2001. They are technologically smarter, volunteer more, care about grades and education, are more involved in religion, and have better relationships with parents than most other generations. The evidence appears substantial that dramatic changes are being witnessed in the attitudes and behaviors of members of this generation.

While demographics are important, understanding today's students beyond demographics will enable advisers to be more effective. Effective advisers comprehend how students arrive at colleges, how they think and act, how they confront issues, how they interact with their peers, and how events and forces shape their attitudes. The intent of this chapter is to arm advisers with a clear understanding of this generation so that they will enthusiastically embrace opportunities to work with individuals of the Millennial Generation.

Understanding the Millennial Generation begins with sensing the power of this group. Demographers and historians alike agree that there are more members of the Millennial Generation than any previous generation. Millennials may be America's first 100 million-person generation. Comprising the eventual 100 million members will be future immigrants, along with the more than 80 million present members (The Echo Boomers, 2004). Of course, much of this population increase is due to the dramatic reversal in falling birth rates since the 1980s. This generation is expected to average 3.9 million native births per year, towering over every other earlier generation in America.

Beyond numbers, Howe and Strauss (2000) identify seven distinguishing traits and supporting rationale for understanding the Millennial Generation: "Special, Sheltered, Confident, Team-Oriented, Achieving, Conventional, and Pressured" (pp. 43–44).

Special

Millennials have a sense that "they are *special* to their parents' sense of purpose and vital to the nation" (Howe & Strauss, 2000, p. 43). Evidence of this stems in part from the extent to which children's issues moved to the center of the nation's political and social agenda during their lives. This is a generation of wanted individuals born to parents who planned for them. It has been said of the Millennial Generation, "They came along at a time we started re-valuing kids" (The Echo Boomers, 2004). Although busy, their parents show commitment to this generation. Cell phones allow parents and children to be in constant contact. This generation appears more affluent than previous generations. One possible factor contributing to this is the increase in two-income families. Another factor that may account for affluence may be the increase in parental education with "one of every four Millennials having at least one parent with a college degree" (Howe & Strauss, 2000, p. 81). Parents worked longer hours, and during the economic boom of the 1990s, families generally faired well economically.

Millennials are the most racially and ethnically diverse generation to date, which contributes to their sense of being special. Millennials are the least Caucasian generation in U.S. history. As of 2002, non-whites and Latinos accounted for 37 percent of the 20 and under population (Howe & Strauss, 2003; The Echo Boomers, 2004). The Millennial Generation college student represents more global diversity. One of five Millennials has at least one immigrant parent, and one in 10 has at least one non-citizen parent (Howe & Strauss, 2003, p. 38). Asian teens are a rapidly growing group, and Latino youths have surpassed African-Americans in number (Howe & Strauss, 2003, p. 39).

Sheltered

Millennials have been sheltered and have been the focus of the most sweeping youth safety movement in American history (Howe & Strauss, 2000, p. 43). Beginning with the "Baby on Board" signs in the early 1980s, Millennials have been buckled into car seats, fitted with bike helmets, carpooled to numerous after-school activities and generally hovered over, leading to the term "helicopter parents" (Howe & Strauss, 2003, p. 11, 19). Parents continue to shelter Millennials at college. Advisers should not expect to see changes in parent or student behavior in the area of sheltering for some time. Dr. Mel Levine, professor at the University of North Carolina believes, "Parents feel as if they're holding onto a piece of Baccarat crystal or something that could shatter at any point. Parents really have a sense their kids are fragile. Parents therefore are protecting them, inflating their egos, massaging them, and fighting their battles for them" (quoted in The Echo Boomers, 2004).

A number of other factors support the concept of Millennials being a sheltered generation. As a group, they are the offspring of older parents (Howe & Strauss, 2000, p. 80). Their mothers' average age is 27, up from a previous average of 24, and they are growing up in families with the smallest numbers to date (Howe & Strauss, 2000, p. 80). More of them are single children (Howe & Strauss, 2000, p. 81). Fifty percent of Millennials have no siblings, and roughly 40% of them are first-borns (Howe & Strauss, 2000, p. 81). During their lifetime so far, federal spending on children (as opposed to spending on adults and seniors) rose for the first time (Howe & Strauss, p. 111). In 1990, Congress expanded Medicaid to all poor children born after 1983. Other visible signs of sheltering this generation include the numerous cities, state, and federal laws passed to protect them. New laws curtail harm to children, including tougher punishments of child offenders. Work places and businesses have adopted more child-friendly policies (Howe & Strauss, 2000, p. 132). Curfews have been instituted in more than 300 American cities (Howe & Strauss, 2000, p. 114). There is now more rapid response to suspicion of child abuse; increased ratings on music and movies; stricter vaccination and child health protocols; school buses equipped with seat belts; school uniforms; and zero tolerance policies at schools; and more closed campuses. Taken in totality, these new regulations are clear indicators of the value parents have placed on the security and protection of today's generation. Parents expect similar protections from higher education administrators, as their children arrive on campuses.

Confidence

More support for the origin of the high sense of optimism toward today's generation stems from this group's exhibited level of confidence. Millennials, nicknamed the "Sunshine Generation," are optimistic, positive, happy, satisfied with their lives, and confident in their futures (Howe & Strauss, 2003, p. 54). Research supports these statements. In fact, 92% percent of today's students agree with the statement, "I am usually happy" (Howe & Strauss, 2003, p. 15). Suicide rates are declining. Millennials in general are upbeat, engaged, closer to their parents, and more comfortable with authority. Millennials appear to trust authority and organizations. They are used to structure and value close family ties. According to the Harris Poll of the class of 2001, 88% indicate that they have established goals for themselves for the next five years, and virtually all (98%) feel they will some day get to where they want to be in life. This is inspiring for advisers and student affairs professionals working with these students.

Team-Oriented

The development of strong team instincts and tighter peer bonds are worth noting about this generation (Howe & Strauss, 2000, p. 44). The concept of team extends well beyond conventional ideas of teams. To Millennials, the development of close personal friendships and staying close to high school and college friends is a priority. The use of the Internet and cell phones provide more options for staying in touch with an even larger number of friends in ways never before imagined. This is a trend no one expects to see diminish. In public schools today, teamwork is stressed in areas like team teaching, team grading, collaborative sports, community service, service learning, and student juries. Students in campus organizations have intense interests in helping others. Their commitment to service learning, is strong and is manifested through the huge number of hours they devote annually to community service projects. In no other area is the idea of team more pronounced than in the cooperative activities that exist on campus. Millennials appear destined to be involved in volunteer and community activities that focus on more than the individual. Howe and Strauss (2003) clearly believe student governments and student judiciaries will assume new importance, especially if college administrators expand their authority over student rules, discipline, campus activities, and community service (p. 100). A poll conducted in 2002 on behalf of the Council for Excellence in Government found that 40% of young adults aged 18 to 30 indicated a career in government was very or fairly appealing to them (Howe & Strauss, 2003, p. 103). Maybe due to the emphasis on team, Millennials appear to be very conventional, non-confrontational and identify with the mainstream. This generation is comprised of very respectful individuals who will arrive on campuses with high expectations.

Achieving and Team-Oriented

As a group, Millennials are achieving and team-oriented. With new accountability measures and higher school standards at the heart of America's political agenda for educational policies, Millennials are on track to becoming the best educated and best behaved young adults in history (Howe & Strauss, 2000, p. 44). After all, high expectations have defined their lives. Within the group, there is an increase of aptitude test scores for every racial and ethnic group, and SAT scores are at a 30-year high. Due to their sheer numbers, the effect they are having on society is evidenced by the increases in school construction and college enrollments. Howe and Strauss (2003) note that Millennials are probably the most all-around capable teenage generation this nation, and perhaps the world, has ever seen (p. 123). In addition to their achievements academically, Millennials out-of-classroom achievements are equally impressive. Advisers are inheriting a generation of young individuals who are highly interested in clubs, community service, and student government. Administrators will be well advised to enhance meeting rooms and student offices for this generation.

Traditions are very important to Millennials, and they will have great interest in developing school spirit activities or those things that will endure students to the university. It is widely believed that campuses will witness an intense return to activities such as pep rallies, awards and award ceremonies, school songs, and proms.

Conventional

As a rule, Millennials exhibit more positive social habits, behave more modestly, and exhibit better conduct. More often than not, they are in favor of tougher rules against misconduct, and they believe in the concepts of honesty and hard work. The group tends to identify with their parents' values. Within this generation, violent crime is down 60 to 70%, the use of tobacco and alcohol are at all-time lows, teen pregnancy is down, and nine out of 10 Millennials indicate they "trust" their parents (The Echo Boomers, 2004).

Pressured

Millennials are a pressured generation. This trait explains the challenges advisers face with these students. Some may be concerned about the extent to which Millennials have been sheltered with parents hovering near; other may feel a sense of satisfaction with the support students are receiving from families. The "all work and no play" mentality Millennials have experienced may be more detrimental to this group than any other factor. As a group, Millennials experienced a decline in free play time and outdoor activity; a significant increase in the amount of time spent in school; more time doing household work; and considerably more time studying throughout their lives. Millennials have been discouraged, as a group, from taking risks. It is imperative for advisers to establish trust among students to create or enhance their sense of security to take necessary risks (Howe & Strauss, 2003, p. 44).

Collectively, Millennials have been pressured to succeed academically. At the same time, institutions are being more selective and scaling back or eliminating remedial classes. There is increased competition with the group, and the development of campus polices regarding honor codes, cheating, and behavioral standards add even more pressure.

Another issue to address is the declining number of men attending college. At this point, the Millennial Generation is dominated by women (Howe & Strauss, 2003, p. 4). Statistics indicate fewer men are applying for college, and even fewer are being accepted. In addition, the dropout rate for men is higher the first two years of college (Howe & Strauss, p. 95). Campuses must focus on creating or expanding locations where men experience greater comfort and where they can apply their masculinity in socially constructive ways (Howe & Strauss, p. 102). With the emphasis on teams generally displayed by Millennials, advisers and student affairs professionals need to be more aware of loners or students not making connections within groups, regardless of gender.

Advantages of Advising the Millennials

Although advisers experience challenges from this generation, the evidence seems to weigh heavily on the side of the advantages of advising this generation. Millennials are probably the most all-around capable teenage generation this nation, and perhaps the world, has ever seen (Howe & Strauss, 2000). Howe and Strauss (2000) also note, "Millennials are attending college for traditional reasons – to learn, to grow, to make new friends, to develop intellectually, to become fully functional adults" (p. 124). In comparison to the students of the previous generations, the Millennials' positive attitudes and sense of purpose present very hopeful signs. To be effective, advisers must be aware of their needs and be prepared to meet them.

There are a number of ways to help meet the needs of the Millennial Generation student. Advisers need to maintain positive, upbeat, and optimistic attitudes to match the attitudes and high expectations of today's students. Advisers who help build traditions or who focus on the institution traditions will be more successful. It will be important to showcase groups, team skills, and community service. Advisers should stress friendship and support the college experience as a bonding one. Advisers need to be prepared for obsessive parents and to assume that parents, the media, and the nation are paying close attention to the Millennials' safety and protection. Advisers should expect high standards of behavior and provide quality leadership opportunities. The events of September 11, 2001, might have had less of an emotional effect on Millennials as a group, since they experienced their own version in 1999 with the school shootings in Columbine, Colorado. In the book, *Millennials Go To College*, Howe & Strauss (2003) note that since the events of September 11, the positive traits exhibited by Millennials include an enhanced orientation to personal safety; more family closeness; greater community and political action; more long-term planning; enhanced patience; a "good for the group" mentality; an enhanced respect of norms and institutions; and a greater commitment to extracurricular activities (p. 32). College life in the Millennial Era will be dynamic, energizing, and inspiring. As advisers, it might be difficult to imagine a better atmosphere for working with students.

Today's Advisers

If today's generation of students is cast in a very positive light, the era in which the generation of today's advisers grew to adulthood could not have been more void of light. A large number of mid-level housing professionals, who have advising as primary job responsibilities, are members of Generation X. Reviewing the generational differences and the social, political, and cultural landscapes of the different generations help to better understand the development of its members. Just as it would be unwise to categorize individuals of the Millennial Generation as the same, it would equally unwise to do the same for members of the preceding generation.

Most historians identify members of Generation X as being born between 1960 and 1981. Growing up a member of Generation X was in stark contrast to growing up a member of the Millennial Generation. In the book, *Generations: The History of America's Future, 1584 to 2069* (Howe & Strauss, 1991), Economist Robert Kuttner describes the Generation X as "a generation of economic disease" and a "depression of the young" (p. 320). While Millennials are politically active, Generation X'ers have been described as apathetic and disengaged from the political process. It has been noted that Generation X'ers grew up as kids whose low test scores and high rates of crime, suicide, and substance abuse marked a postwar extreme for American youth (Howe & Strauss, 1991, p. 317).

As a generation, older Americans perceived Generation X'ers as a "lost generation, an army of Bart Simpsons, possibly armed and dangerous" (Howe & Strauss, 1991, p. 317). They have been portrayed as a wasted generation, and the 1983 book, *Nation at Risk*, despaired of a "rising tide of mediocrity" emerging from America's schools (Howe & Strauss, 1991, p. 320). Similarly, a blue ribbon Carnegie Foundation report labeled them "shallow" and criticized them for their "uncivil speaking" and "deteriorating campus culture" (Howe & Strauss, 1991, p. 320).

Unlike Millennials who are team focused, Generation X'ers were encouraged to be self-reliant, independent, and self-actualizing individuals (Howe & Strauss, 1991, p. 321). Whereas Millennials were provided nurturing, Generation X members were taught to grow up fast; theirs was a generation of "self immersed parents, disintegrating homes, schools with conflicting missions, confused leaders, and new public health dangers" (Howe & Strauss, 1991, p. 321). Unlike the protected Millennials, Generation X'ers basically were told that "whatever bad things strike people their age—from AIDS to drug addiction, from suicides to homicides—were mainly their own fault" (Howe & Strauss, 1991, p. 322). When asked about their generation, one student responded, "My generation was born on Friday the 13th" (Howe & Strauss, 1991, p. 324). It is somewhat interesting that many historians refer to this generation as the Thirteenth Generation.

Everywhere one looked, the news about this generation was less than positive. While Millennials are reporting an actual and first-time decline in suicide rates, suicide rose in 1976 above the previous record set in 1908 (Howe & Strauss, 1991, p. 326). Generation X'ers faced divorce rates higher than most other generations. Just as significant was the number of children with two once-married parents, the number of working mothers, latchkey children, and possibly the first generation to be less college educated than its previous generation (Howe & Strauss, 1991, p. 326). As a generation, this group had a much higher risk of dying from accidents, murder, and suicide, and nearly 8% of school-aged children reported they missed one day of school per month from fear of going (Howe & Strauss, 1991, p. 326). The portion of the population in jail rose by one-third, while the proportion of the population owning their own homes fell by an equal number. Lastly, in surveys conducted during this period, adults often ranked automobiles ahead of children as necessary for the "good life" (Howe & Strauss, 1991, p. 328). Indeed, this is a stark contrast from today's generation. Although Generation X has experienced overwhelming societal and family issues, those who have entered the housing profession have continued to advance professionally and build positive relationships with students. Advisers from this generation can look forward to working with students who are driven, organized, and have experienced personal successes. In establishing relationships with Millennials, the Generation X adviser can look forward to students who want to be the best and are truly concerned with making and reaching goals.

Implications for Advisers

Ethics and accountability are topics of concern for both advisers and Millennials. Due to the previously discussed character traits of Millennials, these issues could manifest themselves in opposing ways. With the pressure to succeed and the emphasis on being special, the Millennial Generation students could display "need to win at all costs" attitudes. Ethical decision-making and ethical behavior might prove challenging for Millennials, if these traits conflict with personal goals—or the opposite situation may occur. Millennials might be so focused on conventional values that they expect all decisions and behaviors by peers, advisers, and campus administrators to be above reproach and ethical. Millennials with high expectations regarding accountability and ethical behavior might become easily disillusioned, if they do not feel decisions are ethical. Effective advisers need to be keenly aware of the need to clarify and offer genuine and positive rationale should this arise. Today's students demand honesty and integrity. If advisers tell them something, they expect documentation and verifiable proof.

Advisers need to focus attention on educating students to effectively challenge authority. Members of this generation often hesitate to question those in authority. When accountability issues arise, students have the responsibility to question authority. Millennials may hesitate to do so. This generational trait failed to develop in the Millennials' formative years. Parents of today's students did not encourage these skills in their children, though the parents learned these lessons quite well. This situation presents advisers with a precarious and challenging duty.

Several other areas or issues warrant attention from advisers. Much has been noted regarding the technological capabilities of today's students. Most are fully skilled in all forms of communications technology, including cell phones and computers. Although technology presents great avenues for communicating, many Millennials appear less comfortable in face-to-face communications. It is not uncommon to see today's students walking and talking on the phone, listening to iPods or downloaded music, or chat rooms or instant messaging. Even with all of today's forms of communications available, Millennials need support in developing personal communication skills.

Widely popular technology advances have made it easier for students to stay in touch with each other. Advisers need to stay in the communication loop by learning how to use mediums, such as cell phones, instant messaging, and text messaging. Students will expect advisers to use these methods to stay in touch with them. One of the key skills of leadership is communication. The downside of using technology to communicate is that students may hide behind it when they are confronted with situations where they are avoiding face-to-face meetings. Although some personal communication experiences won't be personally pleasant, the information gained from taking the time to meet with other students or advisers is necessary. Advisers confidently can model interpersonal communication skills so students can see first-hand the benefits of cultivating meaningful relationships.

Advisers have many opportunities to positively impact today's students. None is more important than recognition. Members of the Millennial Generation have grown up being praised. Generally speaking, advisers are nurturing individuals, and offering recognition is not only natural, but also affords them opportunities to use their creative talents. The challenge will be to maintain high levels of creativity. The members of this generation respond well to praise and recognition, even more so than in previous generations. Many traditional, low-cost forms of recognition are effective. The National Association of College and University Residence Halls' (NACURH) lists of ways to recognize students are effective tools. Recognition does not need to be complex to be effective. Today's students respond positively to simple forms of recognition. Key elements to successful and effective recognition are that recognition should be genuine or sincere, timely, and address the recipients'individual personalities. Recognition can be offered publicly and privately. Effective recognition also can be offered in writing.

Millennials are returning to or more accepting of traditional campus activities. Much has been written about their support of traditions, such as award banquets, campus cheers, songs, and pep rallies. Today's students are receptive to the creation of new campus traditions or following long accepted ones. Today's advisers will find success in working with Millennials promoting and elevating events to new levels. To attract today's students, savvy advisers offer realistic, practical, and quality program ideas. Promotional materials that make use of bright colors, cool designs, graphics, strong images, and show concern for the environment gain points in the eyes of Millennials. Today's students are bright, technically astute, and sophisticated. They are participatory and experience oriented. They desire to be engaged and caught up in the experience. This is why reality television programs and extreme sports on television are enjoying levels of popularity.

Advisers must recognize the need to involve Millennials' parents. Parents today are more involved in the lives of their children and can be considered positive untapped resources. Beyond simply communicating with them, it will be more beneficial and feasible for advisers to collaborate with them. Parents today tend to be more educated and may have had campus living experiences. In fact, many may have shared campus leadership experiences with their children. This familiarity can lead to partnerships. Advisers today have opportunities to seek out parents who have resources to enhance student organizations. These resources extend well beyond financial support. Many parents are entrepreneurs, business owners, speakers, and technology savvy individuals. Today's advisers need to seek innovative ways to involve them. Many parents have a desire to be involved. There will less resistance from today's students to have parents involved. Parents enjoy being involved, not only because of their positive experiences, but because they believe in the benefits of student organizations. After all, many of them were involved in similar organizations. Like advisers, parents are aware of the value of campus organizations. Today, one can see parents who are architects offering design support; parents who are employed as chefs or bakers offering goods, as well as fund-raising ideas; and bankers offering training in money management and fiscal matters. Advisers must create innovative avenues for involvement and seek ways to enhance parents' knowledge of the needs of the organization. There may never be a better time for advisers to connect with parents and to make them campus partners.

Advisers need to take proactive steps to make sure that organizations are inclusive. This means actively seeking the names of diverse students from other students and administrators to invite to be part of the organizations. In seeking diversity in organizations, advisers need strongly to consider race, sexuality, religion, and socio-economic status. In most cases, campus populations are not as diverse as one would like in the higher education environment. Specifically, the numbers of African-American and Latino-American students are remaining about the same with little growth. Regionally and geographically, there are differences in race and customs that impact and affect diversity. It is not uncommon on some campuses for students to self-segregate, not only in social circles, but also within clubs and organizations. RHAs have strong histories of being diverse and representative of all students residing on campus. Advisers and housing professionals need to do more to ensure that RHAs and hall governments are diverse. Socio-economic factors also have to be taken into consideration to guarantee our organizations are inclusive along the lines of class as well.

International students residing on campuses also should be encouraged to get involved. In some cases, language barriers may deter them from seeking out involvement. Including students from other countries within RHA organizations helps to prepare American students for working in the global community. Students have opportunities to communicate with others who are different from them. In some cases, this contact may be their first experience, since many local schools, churches, social circles, and neighborhoods are segregated directly or indirectly along racial lines.

Advisers are the leaders and role models for students on diversity issues. They must have strong self-awareness of biases that may affect how they interact with students to ensure that they don't isolate or alienate students who bring diverse perspectives and different beliefs to organizations. Advisers should encourage student-leaders to examine projects and issues closely to make sure the minority voices are heard. Millennials pose different views on diversity and social justice issues. By the second decade of the Millennial Generation, campuses will be less race conscious and more female dominated than ever before in history. The Millennials will have less patience with the internal politics of universities and will rebel against any university policies viewed as separatist.

Summary Questions

The following offer readers questions to contemplate when working with today's Millennial Generation college students.

1. Have you considered ways to involve parents in student organizations?
2. Are efforts in place to enhance the understanding of multiculturalism and diversity among students in place?
3. Are handbooks available for students that define roles within organizations and that offer guidelines and procedures to follow?
4. Are recognition programs in place for members of organizations?
5. Are intentional efforts being made to ensure diversity within organizations?
6. Are avenues emphasizing teamwork available for today's students?
7. Do organizations reinforce healthy and safe behaviors among students?
8. Do officer and/or member training programs focus on decision-making skills and goal-setting for members?
9. Do programs exist to teach students to confront positively?
10. Is the development of effective communication skills a component of officer/member training?
11. Are students making positive connections/relationships with peers?
12. Are you aware of the potential need for additional support for male students?
13. Are students encouraged and supported to take risks?
14. Are you aware of the pressure on students today to succeed academically?
15. Are accountability measures in place to justify decisions for programs and expenditures?
16. To what extent is alcohol abuse an issue among students in organizations?
17. Are students provided office space to conduct organization business?
18. How will you relay the benefits of and encourage students to program with diversity and social justice issues in mind?
19. What are key issues on campus regarding how students relate to or fail to relate to one another?

20. Have you considered attending a technology conference, or have you maintained a high level of knowledge regarding rapidly advancing technology? Do you use this knowledge in presentations and demonstrations?

References

Harris Interactive Poll. (2001). *Millennium's first college grads are "connected, career minded and confident-way!"* Retrieved October 1, 2004, from http://www.harrisinteractive.ccom/news.index

Howe, N. & Strauss, W. (2000). *Millennials rising: The next great generation.* New York: Random House.

Howe, N. & Strauss, W. (2003). *Millennials go to college.* American Association of Collegiate Registrars and Admissions Officers and LifeCourse Associates.

Howe, N. & Strauss, W. (1991). *Generations: The history of America's future, 1584 to 2069.* New York: William Morrow.

National Association for College Admissions Counseling (2004). *High school graduation and college enrollment* (chap. 1). Retrieved November 5, 2004, from http://www.nacac.com/research_trends.html

The echo boomers. (October 3, 2004). Retrieved October 18, 2004, from CBSNews.com. Web site: http://www.cbsnews.com/stories/2004/10/01/60minutes/main646890.shtml

U.S. Department of Education. (1983). *A nation at risk: The imperative for educational reform.* National Commission on Excellence in Education.

10

Current Issues

Paula Bland

Residence hall associations (RHAs) have been at the forefront of current issues on college campuses for decades. Many residence hall associations trace their origins and histories to campus issues involving coed housing options, visitation policies, funding for programs, conduct and dress codes, room decoration, and other quality of life concerns in residential living. Though they may not seem so today, at one time these issues were very controversial. Administrators and trustees were reluctant to allow students more freedom and decision-making in campus living. Residents expressed their need for self-governance and self-determination in living environments and joined coalitions to bring issues to university administrations and boards of trustees. They learned campus politics in order to get changes they wanted for residence hall life. Residence hall students today continue to want and need a voice.

The successful actions of students to lobby for rights established the practice of allowing them the freedom of speech on campuses today. Before the student movement for free speech on college campuses in the 1960s, administrators limited student conduct and activities. Decisions regarding living situations were tightly controlled. Often, men and women were treated very differently, in regards to lifestyle or living options and conduct regulations. Women had curfews and were required to be in residence by midnight or earlier, while men typically had no curfews. *In loco parentis* was the standard operating procedure for university administrators. Today, it is common practice for college or university administrators to involve students in decision-making regarding issues concerning quality of life on campus. As a result, residence hall student-leaders have taken the lead on addressing these issues.

Residence hall associations or other campus living organizations can get involved in a variety of issues that impact student lives. The following list illustrates the types of issues that interest residence hall student-leaders:

- **Residence hall policies including:**
  - o Campus living requirements
  - o Room assignments and switching rooms
  - o Resolution policies for roommate conflicts
  - o Bathroom usage for same or different gendered students or transgendered students
  - o Pet policies
  - o Computer usage policies (i.e. Internet use, wireless use, website development, etc.)
  - o Codes of conduct and student conduct boards

- **Residence hall costs including:**
  - o Involvement in the housing department budget and planning
  - o Funding for student organizations and activities
  - o Allocations to outside departments

- **Residence hall services including:**
  - o Vending, laundry, and campus identification card services
  - o Telephone and computer connections
  - o Cable television and movie channels
  - o Recreational space, furniture, and equipment
  - o Convenience store and other vendors
  - o Room painting and decorations
  - o Housekeeping and custodial services
  - o Repair and maintenance practices

- **Meal plan, menu, and dining options**

- **Renovation and construction of housing facilities**

- **Environmental issues and the impact on residence hall life including:**
  - o Energy conservation
  - o Mass transportation
  - o Use of Styrofoam in packaging

- o Use of pesticides and chemicals
- o Recycling and reusables

- **Higher education funding including:**
  - o Tuition and fees
  - o Scholarships, grants, and loans
  - o Student fee referenda to finance capital construction and renovation

- **Recruitment and retention of underrepresented populations of students**

- **Free speech and academic freedom including:**
  - o Website information
  - o Protests and rallies
  - o Student resolutions on institutional or residence life issues

- **Academic calendar and scheduling issues**

- **Current political events including:**
  - o State and federal elections
  - o Federal foreign policies, including war and the draft
  - o Global economy
  - o Health issues, such as AIDS

- **Alcohol and drug abuse**

- **Sexual misconduct issues including:**
  - o Holding students responsible for sexual misconduct
  - o Informing the community members of incidents of sexual misconduct
  - o Housing rights for individuals accused of sexual misconduct or sex offenders

- **Safety and security on campus including:**
  - o Key policies and management
  - o Security cameras and monitoring systems

- **Leadership development including:**
  - o Identifying leaders and getting students involved

- ○ Establishment and organization of student groups
- ○ Organization constitutions and by-laws
- ○ Election policies and election violation issues
- ○ Recruitment and motivation of members
- ○ Funding and fee allocation control
- ○ Skill development workshops

Advising Students on Current Issues

Residence hall communities provide ideal opportunities for students to experiment with the practices of self-governance and self-responsibility. Students in living/learning communities can apply principles learned in classrooms to everyday life. Students who study social change models can use new knowledge to improve the quality of life in residence halls. These opportunities to experiment with self-governance and self-responsibility also can produce challenges. Some student-leaders are more concerned with personal or political agendas than protecting the rights, needs, and desires of residents who they were elected to represent. Some student-leaders embrace personal styles of leadership that appear to oppose every popular or generally accepted opinion, sometimes just for sake of opposition. These challenges to student-leadership development and group dynamic issues are not addressed or resolved easily. Advisers have opportunities to develop students in many different ways.

Residence hall associations generally limit themselves in scope and purpose or are limited by administrations. Clearly, residence hall students have the capacity to serve in positions that benefit whole student populations; however, these positions usually are incorporated into campus-wide governance or representative systems, such as SGAs. This hierarchy allows RHAs to tackle problems, issues, and programs that deal primarily with the unique needs of students living on campus.

Larger issues, such as higher education funding or recruiting and retaining students from underrepresented populations, impact residence hall communities. Residence hall student-leaders can support larger campus-wide issues by relaying information to constituents and encouraging resident involvement. However, residence hall associations that focus only on larger campus-wide issues often lose sight of their primary mission, to improve the quality of life in residence halls. When residence hall student-leaders from the 1960s and 1970s lobbied for change in visitation hours and coed living, they also continued to make residence halls fun and exciting places to live. New options for programming occurred because of changes in financial resources and control of fees for residence hall associations. Conference attendance grew because of these resources, which helped residence hall student-leaders identify trends, issues, and strategies in residence hall communities.

Residence hall student-leaders must be challenged to determine the varying needs of residents. Every year brings new and different issues for discussion, as well as new and exciting opportunities for programs and activities. Some residents never care about environmental issues or participate in recycling programs, but they are concerned about how basketball tournaments are planned and whether enough teams will enter to host competitions. Conversely, other students actively focus solely on environmental issues. Neither basketball tournaments nor energy conservation programs alone make the residence hall experience. Successful advisers remind student-leaders with single focus issues that constituents have diverse interests and concerns.

Successful advisers are adept at developing and coaching groups on establishing roles, boundaries, expectations, and goals. Student-leaders who attempt to focus groups on single issues or narrow political agendas will not find support in high-functioning groups. Groups that commit to meeting the needs of residence hall populations will develop goals and objectives in a variety of areas. It is the responsibility of advisers to help residence hall student-leaders seek out the diverse interests and needs of all residents. Political-minded student-leaders can be coached to broaden their perspectives to share in these responsibilities or to channel their interests into other student groups or organizations on campus.

Student groups typically have at least one member who chooses to oppose every idea or thought that is put forward. This includes opposing ideas or issues brought forward by housing administrators. Student-leaders with this style of leadership pride themselves on working against administrations. Advisers are seen as administrators who cannot be trusted. The key to working with these leaders is to develop relationships where advisers communicate the value of the student voice and can advocate for student concerns. When students understand that advisers and other administrators are trying to accomplish the same goals and objectives, then negative styles of leadership are appeased. Experienced advisers communicate the desire for student leader success.

Professional staff and student-leaders may disagree about how to accomplish goals. All styles of leadership and ways of doing things should be valued. Discussion and dialogue result in developing the best or most effective way to accomplish goals. Advisers should challenge students to think differently. One-on-one discussions between student-leaders and advisers can build trust in relationships. Advisers can find ways to introduce contentious students to new information, which aids in understanding other points of view. Synergistic relationships and groups accomplish more than individuals.

Negative students, at time,s draw energy away from groups instead of helping groups succeed, but successful advisers use negative students' insights to help groups understand obstacles or barriers to face in accomplishing goals. Addressing negative issues can prepare groups for overcoming barriers. In this way, negative students actually help groups succeed, overall. Advisers are cautioned, however, to not allow the same students to play the negative role repeatedly. Students may feel it is the only way of fitting into a group. Relationships with other group members will deteriorate over time, if students do not find other ways to feel valued. Successful advisers look for opportunities to direct negative students to positive, effective communications and achievements.

Issues of Free Speech

The First Amendment to the United States Constitution limits the right of government to restrict individual citizen's beliefs and the expressions of those beliefs by providing freedom of speech. Groups and individual citizens cannot be penalized or punished for voicing opinions or beliefs or for reporting facts and truth. The First Amendment promotes the free expression of beliefs, ideas, and thoughts. A democracy thrives on the ability of citizens to speak the truth and debate issues. An informed, knowledgeable population is more prepared to participate in the ongoing process of democracy. Educated citizens demand accountability of elected representatives.

The university promotes free speech through co-curricular and extra-curricular opportunities, as well as in academic classrooms. The limitation of the right of government to restrict free speech has been applied broadly to include colleges and university situations, though public institutions tend to be less restrictive than private institutions. For public institutions, the meaning of "government" extends to university administrations because public universities are established and governed by state governments for public education purposes. For private institutions, which are established and governed by institutions other than governments, more limitations on student expressions may be made. For example, a private university established by a religious organization may limit the establishment of certain types of student groups that would oppose that religious organization's doctrines. Often in efforts to promote the free expression of truth and the academic debate of such truth, private institutions allow students many of the same rights of self-governance, free speech and self-determination in living situations that are offered to students in public universities.

Principles of Free Speech

There are several foundational principles that are incorporated in the right of free speech. These principles also are derived from the democratic philosophy that citizens must participate in free and open exchanges of beliefs and ideas to be prepared for self-governance.

Principles of the Right to Organize

Students have a right to organize and express their rights of free speech through organizations. Student or college unions (student governments) are generally regarded as campus-wide entities formed to represent student bodies of universities. Representation comes in many forms. Students organize to meet the needs of constituents for planned activities, programs, and events. Students use student unions as forums to voice opinions and needs to each other, as well as to administrations. Today, most student governance or representational bodies are not called "student or college unions," but instead are the buildings in which students gather to express views. Campus-wide student organizations also permit the formation of special interest or smaller, more uniquely purposed groups to be formed. Special interest groups focus on topics that have smaller, more clearly defined purposes, such as environmental issues, or activities, such as homecoming events.

RHAs are special interest groups. Residence hall student-leaders share the common interest of addressing the needs and activities of residents living on campus. RHAs represent residence hall student communities to administrations. They focus efforts primarily on serving the needs of residents. Addressing resident student needs may involve political agendas from time to time. However, successful RHAs are like their housing administrative counterparts; they are generalists. RHA leaders are knowledgeable in many different areas and extend themselves to address only the concerns of residents. Programming and events that enhance the living/learning experiences of residence hall students are also focus areas of RHAs. RHAs can partner with SGAs when issues arise that directly relate to the needs of residence hall students, if the influence and support of SGAs support the communication of those needs to administrations.

Principle of Non-Discrimination

Student organizations cannot discriminate in regards to free speech. All voices need to be heard within organizations. Any exclusion of opinions is against the basic principle that each person's voice is important and valued. Democratic organizations promote free and open debate so that citizens can weigh issues and make informed personal decisions. Citizens express opinions and beliefs to representatives through voting. In democracies, the majority ultimately decides organizational position. In residence hall associations, elected representatives debate residence hall policies, such as visitation rights. Representatives solicit opinions and feelings of hall constituents through discussions or conversations and represent those opinions and feelings to residence hall associations. RHAs develop resolutions stating majority opinions and have representatives vote to support positions. Resolutions are sent to administrations to express the collective voice of residents in efforts to influence the ultimate policy decisions. In some situations, residence hall associations are given decision-making authority on issues by administrations. In either case, every student's voice must be permitted in the debate. All opinions must be valued and included, or organizations will appear to discriminate against those voices and not have permitted the free speech of some individuals. Once the majority opinion is determined by vote, the majority view is acted upon. Advancing the majority opinion does not preclude sharing minority or dissenting opinions. All beliefs and opinions are welcome in debates.

Principles of Time, Place, and Manner

The courts have upheld that universities have the right to limit the rights of free speech based on time, place, and manner. Universities and entities such as departments of residence life, can make regulations and policies which determine the time, place, and manner for individuals or groups wishing to exercise free speech within the university setting. The mission of universities is the education of students, the advancement of research, and service, including the expansion of the general knowledge base of society. Universities are encouraged to balance group and individual rights of free speech with their missions of education, research, and service. For example, universities typically permit students to protest or rally on current political issues, but will avoid officially supporting or not supporting issues. In doing so, universities promote discussion and debate on issues, and thus promote the education and preparation of individuals in the community for decision-making in a democratic society. Universities, however, limit rallies and protests to designated times or locations that do not interfere with classes or the business operations of campuses.

Housing administrators establish rules or guidelines to restrict behaviors that are considered disruptive to residence hall environments. Quiet hours are established so students may study or sleep in their own rooms. The rights of individuals to play stereos loudly are subordinate to the rights of residents to study. Other regulations limiting certain kinds of behavior in residence hall environments support the challenges of group living. To avoid having unwanted solicitation and protect the educational environment in residence halls, RHAs or administrations impose rules to restrict commercial companies or vendors from presenting programs in residence facilities.

Restrictions of Free Speech

Principles of free speech cannot be used to justify violence, slander, libel, subversion, or obscenity. Nor can they be used to incite racial or ethnic violence. The courts clearly state that freedom of speech cannot be used to justify various types of harmful forms of expression. The courts do not protect speech that promotes violence or unlawful activity. For RHAs, this means that any activities that have the potential to incite riots on campus or promote violent or destructive behavior will not be permitted and should be avoided. Lawful, peaceable protests executed within guidelines and regulations can be advertised and promoted. However, nothing in promotional materials should encourage destructive or unlawful behavior or any behavior not permitted by university regulation. Universities have the right to restrict organizations and cancel protests if destructive or unlawful behaviors are imminent. For example, a student group receives permission to promote a silent protest in a classroom building while classes are in session. If students arrive and commence talking over bullhorns during the silent protest, the administration most likely would cancel the protest immediately if students using bullhorns refuse to immediately cease the activity. The administration would not be in violation of the free speech rights of the students at that point.

In another scenario, a housing administration may decide to install new low-flow showerheads in each shower in residence halls in an effort to conserve energy. To address the issues and concerns of residents regarding the ineffectiveness of the new shower heads, the RHA may engage in conversations with the administration about residents' concerns. RHA leaders may send out information regarding the issues over e-mail, website, and newsletters, as well as hold "town hall" meetings. However, the RHA leaders cannot promote the removal of or damage to showerheads by the residents in protest of the decision.

No student group or individual can slander or libel a faculty person, staff person, administrator, or another student for any reason. During campaigns and elections, students running for office do not have free speech protection to publicly make false or defaming statements or reports against other candidates. Such statements are slander and written forms of those statements are libel.

Students or organizations that accuse faculty persons of unfair treatment may not make slanderous statements to the press or file reports that include libelous information. The right of free speech only provides for accurate information and facts to be communicated.

Free Speech and RHAs

Written communications and websites. RHA student-leaders need to consider the principles of free speech when designing communications and building websites. RHAs address various issues and topics that relate to residence hall living. Written communications, like flyers and newsletters, as well as websites, efficiently communicate with the total residential population. RHAs disseminate information regarding policy change proposals or to advertise programs and speakers via written communications or over websites. RHAs can administer surveys over websites. RHA student-leaders should present facts truthfully in ways that members of organizations can make informed decisions. Program advertisements should not include obscene material or encourage illegal activities. Surveys should be designed to be without bias and seek constituent opinion neutrally. These principles apply to all written forms of communication including, brochures, fliers, posters and e-memos, and websites.

Advisers should monitor written forms of expression, including websites. Together, leaders and advisers should develop policies and procedures for advisers to review and approve written communications before they are copied or posted. This can be included in discussions of expectations between advisers and student-leaders. Successful advisers develop relationships with student-leaders so that the review and monitoring of information is not perceived as censorship, but rather a routine adviser duty in support of student-leaders' success.

Open meetings and records. Residence hall association meetings including hall council meetings, floor council meetings, and resident adviser council meetings, should be open to those recognized as constituents or stakeholders. Open meetings and records ensure that all constituents understand the reasoning and rationale of decisions. Successful advisers teach and encourage student-leaders and officers to prepare and distribute agendas so all interested individuals can participate. The rules of organizations may vary in allowing non-elected representatives or officers to speak, however. Organizational rules may dictate that only voting or ex-officio members may be recognized by chairs to speak. Members with speaking rights may be permitted to yield speaking rights to non-voting individuals to express opinions or share appropriate information.

Rules also may be formulated to permit others to speak, if time allows. In some situations, chairs may recognize voting members first, and if time allows, non-voting members may be recognized to speak. Allowing and encouraging participation from all constituents benefits everyone. Student-leaders receive larger quantities of varying input and information to review. Decisions and actions reflect the larger groups' needs rather than the needs of a select few. Student-leaders should keep and post records and minutes of all meetings, including keeping official records of decisions.

Interfering with the educational opportunities of other students. Residence hall association activities should not interfere with the educational mission of universities. Planning activities and programs that draw students away from academics or class should be avoided. Meetings should be scheduled at times when most students are not in class. On many campuses, residence hall meetings and programs are prohibited from occurring during finals week.

When residence hall leaders organize public protests, the protests should be organized to follow all the policies of the university concerning time, place, and manner. Organizers should not inhibit students from attending class or set up physical barriers to keep students from attending classes. Large public speakers should not be located outside classroom buildings or residence hall buildings during class time. Student-leaders soon discover that the method and manner of using their voices are often as important as what they say.

Agree to university policies regulating time, place, and manner. Savvy residence hall student-leaders realize that success lies in working with administrators rather than developing adversarial relationships. In the same manner, complying with the university regulations for time, place, and manner helps student organizations gain credibility with administrators. Student-leaders who are willing to hold each other accountable and accept responsibility for their actions, both individually and organizationally, tend to develop solid, trustworthy relationships with administrators. Those student-leaders will be entrusted with information or difficult situations to resolve. Their influence will increase, and they will better serve constituents in the process.

Promote no illegal activity. Residence hall associations should not plan illegal activities. Residence hall associations should not promote the use of illegal substances or encourage the violation of any laws. Advisers may need to remind student-leaders that certain actions of groups or individuals may be illegal, like the defamation of individuals or groups; involvement in sexual misconduct or harassment; use of discriminatory language; and use of inappropriate graphics or photos in advertising.

Successful advisers develop relationships of trust and communication with student-leaders in organizations. At the beginning of each year, student-leaders and advisers should discuss and establish expectations of each other. As part of expectations communications, advisers can clearly state that illegal activities cannot occur and, in fact, participating in illegal actions will not accomplish the goals or objectives of organizations. If student-leaders choose to proceed with illegal activities, it is the responsibility of advisers to intervene. For example, to protest university policies regarding alcohol use on campus, student-leaders may want to purchase alcohol and drink in public on campus. When informed of this plan, it is the adviser's responsibility to do whatever is necessary to keep students from proceeding. One option is that the adviser could call a meeting to address the illegal behavior, and inform students that if they chose to proceed, the students may be referred for judicial action and removed from the residence halls. The adviser may need others to support their efforts, including other administrators and the campus police, so that appropriate action can be taken. Student-leaders promoting illegal activities should be removed from office and/or no longer allowed to advocate for residence hall issues.

Speakers and addressing all points of view. When controversial speakers are invited to campuses, efforts should be made to offer alternative perspectives on controversial topics. For example, if a speaker is invited to speak on issues in the Middle East from the Palestinian perspective, efforts should be made to present other perspectives, perhaps the Israeli perspective, at the same time or another time. This ensures that a variety of information and opinions are presented for students to make informed choices. Panel discussions are another way to ensure the presentation of various points of view.

Speakers, as well as entertainers, who are invited by RHAs should be cautioned against using inflammatory or defaming language. The right of free speech does not protect speakers and entertainers if slander, libel, subversion, or obscenity is part of their program, or if they incite racial or ethnic violence. When considering speakers or entertainers for RHA-sponsored programs, advisers need to be informed of the content of presentations or the beliefs and values of speakers. If possible, advisers should review tapes of previous performances or speeches. If controversial speakers are invited to campus, RHAs and advisers should work with the university regulations and officials to ensure safe, and peaceful assemblies of community members.

The Role of Advisers

Advisers play key roles in working with students who embrace political or current issues. Most students have little knowledge of university bureaucracy. Advisers educate students in the regulations of the university. When addressing issues with political implications, the role of the adviser is to assist student-leaders in clarifying the relationship of issues to the lives of residence hall students. Student-leaders may determine that RHAs will not get involved with political issues that do not directly relate to the operation of or the quality of life in residence halls. They can refer residents and other students who wish to take on those topics or concerns to other organizations.

Conclusion

Addressing current issues presents real-life learning experiences for student-leaders and opportunities to learn skills in dealing with difficult issues. They learn communication skills to ensure that appropriate and helpful information is presented to constituents so better, more informed decisions can be made. Student-leaders learn critical thinking skills and are able to present various sides of issues to others. They better understand the merits and responsibilities of the First Amendment, including rights of free speech. These situations make the residence hall experience part of the overall education of students.

The following is a list of suggestions for advisers to consider when working with residence hall student groups on current issues.

- Set up relationships with students in such a way as to be consulted and included in plans.
- Plan time and sessions to help leaders understand the role of advisers.
- Help students establish clear missions and purposes for groups.
- Remind leaders of their purpose and help them develop and revisit goals.
- Discuss and identify clear boundaries and the authority of groups.
- Train leaders in setting expectations of each other and advisers.
- Help student-leaders learn how to hold each other accountable.
- Take students through processes to determine how decisions will be made in groups.
- Set standards for addressing appropriate ways to communicate with each other.
- Learn the art of asking appropriate and timely questions.

Case Studies

❖ Case Study 1

The Residence Hall Association (RHA) president contacts the RHA adviser to get advice concerning a resolution that will be presented to the RHA senate at the next meeting. This resolution is being presented by two RHA senators who are interested in keeping candidates for office from the Student Government Association (SGA) or any other student club or organization from entering residence halls and going door-to-door to solicit votes for elections. The resolution would prohibit any student from walking through residence halls and knocking on doors to discuss elections or campaign issues. The residence halls on campus are locked 24-hours per day, and residents must show IDs or swipe ID cards to gain entry into buildings. Residence hall policies already prohibit companies and outside agencies from entering the residence hall living areas with or without resident escort to solicit business. It has been the practice, however, for students who are running for SGA offices to find hall residents to escort them through the halls to talk with residents during elections. The SGA candidates usually live off-campus and see the residence hall population as easy, captive audiences for their campaigns. The candidates are reluctant to schedule campaign forums in hall lounges or common areas because of time limitations and the belief that residents would not attend. The candidates are usually respectful of residents and are not considered to be security risks.

The two RHA senators have concerns about this practice because of the potential for safety or security concerns and the general annoyance that candidates bring into hall communities. They feel that candidates knocking on doors interrupting study or sleeping time should not bother residents. The senators feel that the residence hall living areas should be free from "outsiders pushing agendas." The issue of being able adequately to inform residence hall students of issues and of candidate opinions on issues does not concern the senators. They feel this can and should be accomplished in a different manner. They don't feel that the RHA has any obligation to inform SGA of this potential change.

The RHA president will facilitate the resolution discussion in the senate meeting. He works closely with SGA officers on campus-wide issues and feels he needs to inform them of this resolution. He thinks this is an issue of free speech, and they should be permitted to voice their opinion and concern for the resolution, if they choose. The RHA president believes that this could be a one-sided discussion, if the SGA officers are not present to voice their perspective.

The SGA officers have not often attended RHA senate meetings. The RHA senate agenda is regularly posted on the RHA website.

Questions to consider:

- Should the RHA president personally inform the SGA officers of this resolution?
- How could the adviser help the RHA president make this decision?
- What interpersonal or political risk does the RHA president take if he chooses to inform or chooses not to inform SGA officers of this resolution?
- Is this a free speech issue?
- What things should the RHA senate consider in passing this resolution?
- Does the role of the SGA on campus factor into making a decision on the resolution? If so, how?
- What role does the RHA adviser play in the senate discussion?
- If the RHA Senate fails to consider all the aspects of this policy change, what should the adviser do?

❖ Case Study 2

The Student Government Association (SGA) of a public university has asked the campus Residence Hall Association (RHA) to join their efforts to lobby the state legislature for an increase in state appropriations for higher education. An increase in state appropriations for higher education would result in maintaining the same tuition and fee rates for in-state students as the past five years. The SGA has planned several campus rallies, as well as a trip to the state capital to lobby legislators directly. All appropriate university policies have been followed by the SGA to set up the rallies and organize the trip to the state capital. The SGA has asked the RHA members to attend the rallies and the capital trip, as well as to help fund the project. The funding would help cover expenses for the transportation to the state capitol and t-shirts for all students to wear. The SGA would also like to set up tables in each residence hall lobby to gather signatures from residence hall students for their petition to the state legislature.

The housing department allocates money from student room and board fees for the RHA budget. The Residence Hall Association and the housing department do not receive any state appropriated money for their budgets. Most of the RHA budget generally is allocated for various programs and activities, community service projects, conference attendance, organizational supplies, and officer compensation. The budget does, however, include a small amount of unallocated monies for unanticipated requests. The RHA senate is permitted to allocate money to any project or activity it deems appropriate, as long as the activity is conducted within the guidelines and policies of the university.

The RHA is involved in representing the residence hall student voice in many campus issues and concerns. The vice president of student affairs on general issues regarding students often consults the RHA president. RHA officers and representatives from the halls are asked to sit on many different campus committees to address campus concerns, such as alcohol abuse, safety, and security. They often are included in search committees for new staff or administrators. The RHA president is invited to speak to the board of trustees once a year to give a report on the state of the residence halls and to discuss any upcoming plans for changes in residence hall living.

The SGA proposal is scheduled for the next RHA senate meeting. The RHA president has allocated a significant amount of time to consider the SGA proposal. The RHA has not been involved in state political issues or questions of higher education funding in the past.

Questions to consider:

- What does it mean for the RHA senate to entertain this proposal?
- How should the RHA adviser prepare for the RHA meeting?
- What questions should be addressed to the SGA presenters?
- What issues may arise from the proposal?
- If these issues were not being considered in the discussion, what impact would it have on the decision of the RHA senate?
- Is this an appropriate use of residence hall student money?
- Should residence hall students be concerned and spend time in addressing higher education funding?
- Will a precedent be set in the senate's decision, either in a situation for the proposal or against the proposal?
- What impact, if any, will the decision of the senate have in the perception of other students, staff, faculty, or administrators of the university?
- What role does the adviser play in helping the RHA senate make a decision on this issue?

✤ Case Study 3

The writings of a popular university professor recently have been called into question by the university's administration for potentially libelous statements toward various state government officials. The targeted officials have made public statements demanding the professor's immediate release as a university employee. The university professor is tenured with over 20 years of service on the campus. The university president has set up a committee, in accordance with the established review procedures for tenured professors, to examine the writings in light of the allegations. The tenured professor teaches English and is extremely popular with students. His classes include controversial topics and writings and are considered by most students to be very engaging. In response to the allegations from the state officials and the resulting administrative review committee, the professor has issued statements to the press indicating that he believes he has the right of academic freedom to publish his opinion about the government officials.

The residence hall association president receives an email from a hall senator who indicates that she wants to introduce a resolution in the next RHA senate meeting. This resolution would support the right of the professor to publish his opinions regarding state officials, as a right of academic freedom. The senator submits a copy of the resolution to the RHA president in advance, in accordance with the senate's rules. In reviewing the resolution, the RHA president believes the language of the resolution is inflammatory and goes beyond the statement that the RHA supports academic freedom for this and all university professors. If passed by the senate, he believes the resolution indicates that the RHA also supports the stated opinions of the professor. The resolution also calls for the RHA senate to sit in protest of the review committee in the university president's office. The RHA president personally is against the idea that the RHA Senate should make a statement supporting this professor or his right of academic freedom. He also feels that the protest would damage the good reputation of the RHA organization with the housing and university administrations.

The RHA president brings the resolution to the RHA executive meeting for discussion. It has been the practice of this RHA president to develop each week's agenda with his executive board. This year the RHA senate has been very busy addressing residence hall issues concerning student alcohol abuse on campus, new policies for room re-applications and assignments and the need for increased security measures and equipment to monitor the outside doors to the residence halls. The RHA senate previously has not addressed issues that go beyond the quality of living in the residence halls. The RHA executives are divided on how this resolution should be handled. The rules of the RHA senate allow the president to ultimately determine when and/or if any resolution will be added to the agenda for senate consideration.

Questions to consider:

- Is this an appropriate issue for an RHA organization?
- How does the adviser help the RHA president make a decision on whether to add the resolution to the RHA senate's agenda?
- Does the issue involve the right of free speech for the residence hall students? For the professor?
- What options does the RHA president have?
- Should the president allow the resolution to be presented, but also communicate his feelings about the resolution to the senate?
- If the president does not allow the senator to present the resolution for consideration, what risk is he taking with that senator? With the executives? With other senators, leaders, or residence hall students? What risk would he take if he did permit the presentation of the resolution for consideration?
- What role should the adviser play in these issues?
- How should the adviser communicate with other administrators about what is being considered by the RHA?

11

Group Dynamics, Theory, and Evolution

Tony W. Cawthon & D'aun Green

Working with groups in an advisory capacity, whether volunteer or as part of job expectations, provides opportunities to observe, support, and assist in the development of groups and group members. Additionally, the experience offers growth and professional development experiences for advisers. Studying groups and group behavior is important because group formation is a naturally occurring process within the environment of human behavior. Johnson and Johnson (1987) state, "All day long we interact in one group and then in another" (p. 3). Extensive information exists that addresses concepts and theories regarding groups, group dynamics, and group leadership. This chapter addresses the foundational issues related to working with groups through theories, models, approaches, and practical applications that are easily understood and implemented. It is designed to help advisers process, understand, and implement strategies to aid in the analysis and development of groups and group behavior. Much of this chapter is dedicated to discussing foundational issues related to defining groups, group dynamics, and stages of group development. Furthermore, several prominent theories, models, and approaches concerning group roles, communication, conflict, and leadership are discussed. Theoretical foundation is provided so that advisers have a general understanding of the resources available for facilitating the practical application of advising skills and assessing various group interactions. The final portion of this chapter offers several different types of application exercises for practicing group concepts.

This chapter also offers information about the benefits and challenges of working with groups. Understanding benefits and challenges of working with groups can prepare advisers for the realities and the rewards of advising. No matter how small or large the group, group dynamics determine whether the group will attain its purpose. Komives, Lucas, & McMahon (1998) advocate that "being purposeful means having a commitment to a goal or activity" (p. 82). This chapter offers a foundation of context for advisers to gain insight into the formation, development, and analysis of groups. For, as Schein (1992) indicates, "Every group must learn how to become a group" (p. 92).

Benefits and Challenges

Working with groups is like playing a musical instrument. It takes a basic understanding of theory, practice, attention, and a willingness to try new things. Accepting the responsibility of being an adviser is a serious commitment. This commitment comes with benefits, as well as challenges. The balance between benefits and challenges is dependent upon the group and the leadership of that group.

Benefits

The benefits of working with well-functioning groups can be significant and far-reaching. Few things compare to the feeling of accomplishment when groups of individuals pull together to fulfill common purposes or activities. The opportunity to watch student development theory in action is a great benefit for advisers. Advisers observe the development of critical thinking skills, identity development and emotional control in students and student-leaders. Observing student-leaders struggle in accepting diversity and observing them educate fellow students about the inappropriateness of words when they use phrases such as, "Oh, that's so gay" is an invaluable experience. This maturation process allows students to move beyond simply understanding concepts to being able to skillfully manage group dynamics. They move from practicing to mastering various leadership skills.

Observing the development of purpose and identity are also benefits of working with groups. When groups and student-leaders begin to focus on their reason for existing, they have taken the first step towards group purpose. A good resource for understanding personal identity development is Chickering and Reisser's book, *Education and Identity* (1993), which refers extensively to personal identity development as part of Chickering's seven vectors. Many of the same concepts can be utilized to understand and work with group identity development. Once groups have identity and purpose, group members can begin to set goals. Every group, regardless of purposeful intent, establishes identity, purpose, and goals. An example is a group of students who follow set procedures to form a student rugby organization. Simply stated, their purpose and goals are to play rugby, but this implies much more. It implies that individuals have a common purpose and are looking for opportunities to gather together and share a passion and love for the game of rugby. The relationships that form as a result of the organization may continue for a lifetime. Thus, joining a group to play rugby may afford some members the added value of making lifelong friendships.

Advisers, as well as students and members of groups, benefit from the growth and development that occur from belonging to groups. Observing and assessing group roles, as well as observing human nature and behavior at work, allows advisers to add tremendous amounts of data to their understanding of how groups and individuals interact. These observations assist advisers become more aware of personal behaviors and the intent behind those behaviors that leads to being better listeners and problem-solvers.

Often advisers are supervisors as well. Advising is different than supervising. However, the basic skill set for both roles shares many common components. Both the supervisor and the adviser grow and develop through interactions with others. Advisers and supervisors learn through experience. Every role—directing, observing, coaching, mentoring, or advising—provides learning opportunities. Developing skills builds strong professional foundations.

Challenges

Unfortunately, not every experience working with groups is positive. Sometimes growth comes through adversity; however, addressing and resolving challenges can be extremely detrimental to groups and members and exceedingly time-consuming. One of the most common challenges is dysfunctional group behavior. Within this category, there can be a host of different issues: the need for power and influence; negative specific member behaviors; hidden agendas; communications; decision-making and follow through; and ethics.

The need for power and influence is a prevalent challenge of dysfunctional groups. Stewart, Manz, and Sims (1999) state, "inherent in the process of socialization is the notion that team members influence one another. Power is defined as the capacity to influence others" (p. 90). Power can corrupt even the most sensible persons. Hazing is an example of dysfunctional power in a group setting. Greek and non-Greek organizations are equally vulnerable. Waking new National Residence Halls Honorary initiates at 6 a.m. and taking them to the local pancake house for breakfast can be considered hazing.

Other dysfunctional group behaviors can manifest in specific member behaviors. Often members and leaders assume roles that negatively impact groups. An example is the SGA senator who blocks both the discussion and/or vote on a particular bill. This person is perceived as disagreeable and disrupts the group's ability to move forward. (Group roles will be discussed in-depth later in this chapter.)

Hidden agendas can be disruptive to group development if they are not properly confronted and defused. Hidden agendas come in many forms and functions. One effective way of confronting and defusing hidden agendas is for groups to work extensively on purpose and identity. It is much easier for group leaders to deal with dysfunctional behavior if there is an agreed upon road map and a clear set of expectations for group behavior.

Communication is a challenge for all groups because groups are made up of individuals who bring different strengths. An example of a communications challenge is demonstrated by playing the communications game. A circle is formed, and a phrase is whispered into the ear of one person. It is then whispered around the circle. When the phrase is whispered back to the originator, it is often vastly different the original phrase. Gender, stress, and fatigue significantly impact groups and group member communications pattern. Johnson and Johnson (1987) suggest:

> Groups that display a high cooperative orientation, groups whose members are good listeners, more accepting of the ideas of others, and less possessive of their own, generally demonstrate greater sending and receiving skills. … One sound means of improving the communication among group members is to increase their cooperativeness and decrease their competitiveness. (p. 194)

Another common challenge in working with groups is the decision-making process and subsequent follow-though. Johnson and Johnson (1987) report, "The purpose of group decision-making is to decide upon well-considered, well-understood, realistic action toward goals every member wishes to achieve" (p. 83). The dysfunctional side of the decision-making process occurs when members cannot civilly come to consensus about decisions. Compounding these situations, depending on the group's makeup, leaders of groups may exert positional power and make unilateral decisions that groups are neither part of nor supportive of. This concept is reflected by Komives, Lucas, and McMahon (1998) who state, "More and more participants in groups expect to be involved in decision-making, and indeed, involvement is essential to a relational, empowering approach" (p. 182). Table 1, which is a visual representation of Johnson

Methods of Decision-Making	Disadvantages	Advantages
1. Decision by authority without discussion	One person is not a good resource for every decision; advantages of group interaction are lost; no commitment to implementing the decision is developed among other group members; resentment and disagreement may result in sabotage and deterioration of group effectiveness; resources of other members are not used.	Applies more to administrative needs; useful for simple, routine decisions; should be used when very little time is available to make the decision, when group members expect the designated leader to make the decision, and when group members lack that skills and information to make the decision any other way.
2. Expert member	It is difficult to determine who the expert is; no commitment to implement the decision is built; advantages of group interaction are lost; resentment and disagreement may result in sabotage and deterioration of group effectiveness; resources of other members are not used.	Useful when the expertise of one person is so far superior to that of all other group members that little is to be gained by discussion; should be used when the need for membership action in implementing the decision is slight.
3. Average members' opinions	There is not enough interaction among group members for them to gain from each other's resources and from the benefits of group discussion; no commitment to implement the decision is built; unresolved conflict and controversy may damage group effectiveness in the future.	Useful when it is difficult to get group members together to talk when the decision is so urgent that there is no time for group discussion; when member commitment is not necessary for implementing the decision; and when group members lack the skills and information to make the decision any other way; applicable to simple, routine decisions.
4. Decision by authority after discussion	Does not develop commitment to implement the decision; does not resolve controversies and conflicts among group members; tends to create situations in which group members either compete to impress the designated leader or tell the leader what they think he or she wants to hear.	Uses the resources of the group members more than previous methods; gains some of the benefits of group discussion.
5. Majority control	Usually leaves an alienated minority, which damages future group effectiveness; relevant resources of many group members may be lost; full commitment to implement the decision is absent; full benefit of group interaction is not obtained.	Can be used when sufficient time is lacking for decision by consensus or when the decision is not so important that consensus needs to be used and when complete member commitment is not necessary for implementing the decision; closes discussion on issues that are not highly important for the group.

Source: From *Joining together: Group theory and group skills* (Fifth edition) (pp. 238-239), by D. W. Johnson and F. P. Johnson, 1994, Boston: Allyn and Bacon. Copyright 1994 by Allyn and Bacon. Reprinted/adapted with permission.

Table 1. Advantages and Disadvantages of Decision-Making Methods

and Johnson's work (1994 as cited in Komives, Lucas, & McMahon, 1998, pp. 183-185), presents an overview of the advantages and disadvantages of decision-making methods that can used for enhancing decision-making strategies.

The final and most difficult challenge to deal with that impacts group dynamics is ethics. Most previously presented challenges can be localized and contained. Today's students have trouble separating ethical from unethical behavior, in part because the media constantly bombards them with unethical behavior that is often rewarded. Examples of unethical behaviors are the misuse of official letterhead for unethical purposes or not telling the whole truth on reimbursement paperwork so that university officials do not question expenditures. For advisers and group leaders, "leading by example is a powerful way to influence the values and ethics of an organization. This means aligning your own values with the worthy values of the organization" (Komives, Lucas, & McMahon, 1998, p. 92). Successful advisers strive to be positive ethical role models for students and fellow professionals. Actions have the greatest impact on others.

Advising comes with benefits and challenges. Benefits allow advisers to see growth and development in group members and groups as a whole. Challenges create dissonance among group members, and this dissonance can either make groups stronger or destroy them as they work through conflicts. Advisers have critical impact on the resolution of conflicts by giving sound counsel and by role modeling appropriate behaviors. The balance between these two outcomes—stronger groups or destroyed groups—is a true test of group dynamics and of advising skills.

Group Dynamics: Stages of Group Development

In recent years, attention has been focused on establishing community on college and university campuses (McDonald, 2002; Boyer, 1990; Kuh, 1991; Miller, 1994). Typically, university housing and student activities are key components in community development programs. For university housing, residence hall governments are links for establishing, maintaining, and continuing community. If residence hall government systems and other campus student organizations are working effectively and productively, they are visible groups on campuses.

College students living in university housing participate in many campus organizations. They likely participate in residence hall governments, as well as in class groups, work groups, and other student organizations, both formal and informal. Prudent advisers are knowledgeable about group processes, development, and dynamics. This section addresses issues related to definition of groups; types of groups and group membership; and the evolution of groups, group performance, and productivity.

Definition of Groups

Numerous researchers have attempted to answer the question, "What is a group?" (Mills, 1984; Fiedler, 1967; Lewin, 1951; Sherif & Sherif, 1964; Cartwright & Zander, 1968; Stogdill, 1959; Cattell, 1951; Brown, 2000; Shaw, 1976; Bass, 1960; Homans, 1950; Johnson, 1995; Turner, 1985; Bales, 1950; McGrath, 1984). Each researcher defines the term slightly differently based on key criteria. These criteria include goals (Mills, 1984), mutual influence (Shaw, 1976), shared identity (Brown, 2000), interrelations (McGrath, 1984), motivation (Bass; 1960, Cattell, 1951), communication (Homans, 1950), structured relationships (Sherif & Sherif, 1964), interaction (Johnson, 1985), interdependence (Fiedler, 1967; Cartwright & Zander, 1968; Lewin, 1951), interpersonal interaction (Stogdill, 1959), psychological significance (Turner, 1985), and perceptions of membership (Bales, 1950). To date, no clear comprehensive definition is accepted.

In answering the question, "What is a group?," particular attention is paid to how the term *group* differs from similar terms, such as *gathering, aggregate, crowd, assembly, congregation,* and *meeting*. The American Heritage Dictionary of the English Language (1992) defines a group as "(a) a number of individuals or things considered together because of similarities, and (b) an assemblage of persons or objects gathered together or located together (p. 800);" a gathering "as bringing or coming together in a mass (p. 751);" and a crowd as "a large number of person gathered together (p. 447)." Glanz and Hayes (1967) identify three ways groups differ from other types of gatherings. The traits that characterize groups are that members have face-to-face contact, members are highly interactive, and are working toward common goals that have value for them.

Advisers working with individuals in student organizations are well aware that groups are more than simply an assortment of individuals coming together. They are individuals interacting to achieve common goals, individuals who are motivated to enhance the campus environment and are interdependent upon one another for success. After reviewing numerous definitions of groups, the authors believe the definition provide by Gladding (2002) most reflects student organizations. He defines groups as "a collection of two or more individuals, who meet in face-to-face interaction, interdependently, with the awareness that each belongs to the group and for the purpose of achieving mutually agreed on goals."

Types of Groups

In understanding and recognizing the numerous definitions of groups, one should also be familiar with the numerous types of groups. Kottler (2001) identifies seven types of groups: task groups, educational groups, process groups, experiential groups, self-help groups, counseling groups, and inpatient therapy groups. While extensive writing and research is available on counseling inpatient and self-help groups, these groups are beyond the scope of this text and typically do not employ strategies and techniques that would be used with residence hall governments. They are not discussed in this chapter; however, the hall government experience reflects characteristics of the first fours types of groups: task groups, educational groups, process groups, and experiential groups.

Kottler (2001) defines task groups as those groups working on specific tasks, purposes, and objectives. These groups focus less on member needs and group process and more on accomplishing their purposes. Conyne, Wilson, and Ward (1997) state that tasks being managed revolve around problem-solving and decision-making. Examples of task groups include task forces, committees, study circles, and neighbor associations. The weekly hall government meetings with set agendas or student organizations participating in campus homecoming activities reflect a task group orientation.

One type of task group is "teams" (Pfeiffer, 1994). Reilly and Jones (1974) indicate that teams different from other groups in that teams have shared group goals rather than individual goals; stress interdependency; dictate high member commitment; and are responsible to those higher than they in the organizational structure. To achieve effectiveness, Johnson and Johnson (1997) purport that teams must operate in structured environments and be supported. Katzenbach and Smith (1993) identify three guidelines when establishing teams. These guidelines are to keep teams small; to select members based on current or potential knowledge, skills, and expertise; and to provide teams with the necessary resources for success.

Educational groups differ from task groups in that educational groups tend to be concerned with both content and process. Like members of task groups, members of educational groups focus on meeting desired objectives, but also focus on assisting members in meeting personal needs as well. Educational groups employ techniques, such as role playing, active learning, and group presentations, to assist members in mastering both group content and process (Kottler, 2001). Students participating in campus and community organizations are afforded opportunities for learning self-confidence; public speaking; interpersonal and communication skills; and decision-making.

Effective advisers also incorporate characteristics from process and experiential groups in member interaction. Process groups place primary emphasize on learning and less emphasis on content (Kottler, 2001). Effective advisers utilize strategies and techniques in advising styles and relationships that enhance member learning. For example, advisers who work with students on planning end-of-the-year banquets would spend more time evaluating processes by focusing on what students learned, experienced, and felt about the events, rather than the actual details and specifics of the events themselves. Allowing students to make decisions and accept responsibility for consequences and engaging students in dialogue about these decisions and responsibilities focuses student learning more on process and less on content.

Experiential groups concentrate on feelings and interpersonal engagement (Kottler, 2001). These groups allow members to engage in direct experience to enhance learning. The basic concept is that by experimenting and observing, individuals gain insight into what they can and cannot achieve. Johnson and Johnson (2000) identify four factors that reflect experiential groups: participants learn by doing, not simply talking about subject; participants role play the acquisition of new talents; participants engage in structured practice, until the new talents are incorporated into their behavioral repertoire; and participants develop personal awareness through direct experience. By participating in student organizations, students are participating in experiential groups. They have numerous opportunities for examining others; practicing new skills in challenging and supportive environments; and integrating new behaviors. These opportunities are enhanced as they interact with other members and advisers. By providing positive and constructive feedback to members, advisers enhance members' confidence and self-concept.

Evolution of Groups, Group Performance, and Productivity

Student organizations like all groups evolve. The pace and type of change is impacted by numerous factors, such as group size, membership, experience of group leaders, and adviser style. Despite ongoing change, research supports the theory that groups progressively develop through predictable stages and patterns that have unique characteristics. Understanding where groups are in development allows advisers to assess what groups need to continue growth (Yalom, 1995). Numerous researchers have proposed group development models (Bennis & Shepard, 1956; Vander Kolk, 1990; Wheelan, 1994; Yalom, 1995; La Coursiere, 1980; Tuckman, 1965; Corey, 2004; Peck, 1987; Hare & Naveh, 1984; Kottler, 2001; Napier & Gershenfeld, 2004; Wheelan & Hockberger, 1996). Applicability and space does not permit a discussion of all models. Nine perspectives on group development applicable for assisting individuals working with student organizations follow.

Shambaugh (1978); Johnson and Johnson (2000); and Napier and Gershenfeld (2004) state that perspectives on group development typically reflect either sequential-stage perspective or recurring-phase perspective. Theories reflecting the sequential-stage perspective critically examine the order of stages using linear focus, whereas the recurring-phase perspective examines those reoccurring issues that may recycle throughout group evolution. Understating both approaches is important because with participation and turnover high for hall governments, advisers may perceive that groups are seemingly in constant states of evolvement and frequently address the same issues over and over.

Tuckman's Model of Forming, Storming, Norming, Performing, and Adjourning.

Tuckman and Jensen's (1977) model clearly reflects taking a sequential-stage approach. Building upon the earlier work of Tuckman (1965), these researchers evaluated literature from the past 20 years on group evolution. They studied varying types of groups and determined that task groups evolve through five basic stages of development. Tuckman (1965) originally proposed a four-stage model distinguished between stages of social domain (social or interpersonal activities) and task domain (group activities). He stated that it was important to view stages from both angles. In social domain, the four stages are testing dependence; tension; unity; and functional roles then adjournment. In the task domain, the stages are orientation and defining of the task, emotional reactions to the task, sharing of perspectives, and, finally, the emergence of solutions then adjournment. All groups struggle to balance tasks to be performed and interpersonal relationships within the group.

The five stages of group development later identified by Tuckman and Jensen (1977) are forming, storming, forming, performing, and adjourning. The forming stage is characterized by members' feelings of ambiguity and insecurity as they attempt to determine group membership, functions, roles, and procedures (Johnson & Johnson, 1997). Advisers easily can identify this stage during initial hall government meetings as participants address these issues. Critical skills for advisers when assisting groups in the forming stage are serving as experts by being knowledgeable and prepared, serving as facilitators, and helping members establish rules as they create group identities.

The storming phase is characterized by member reactions. In this stage, conflict emerges and members respond to conflicts and the demands associated with resolving group tasks. Groups typically exhibit resistance to group influence, challenge authority, and resist completing tasks (Napier & Gershenfeld, 2004). At this stage, effective advisers prepare to use their skills in managing group conflict, spend time with groups as a whole and members individually, and incorporate both work and fun activities into group activities.

Entering the norming phase allows members to establish new group rules and procedures regarding behavior. Clarifying these norms allows for group cohesion as members begin buying into groups and express commitment to achieving group tasks. Members understand their reliance and impact on one another in this stage. Advisers ensure that members have skills needed to succeed, and they encourage members.

Performing reflects actual work being accomplished. In this stage, group issues in previous stages have been resolved and members now work to solve tasks. Members are flexible in how they achieve tasks and recognize that numerous methods may be employed in successfully mastering tasks. In this stage, advisers maintain lesser roles, keep groups on target toward goals, and encourage groups to become more responsible.

The final state of adjourning occurs when groups achieve conclusion of tasks and anticipate that group relationships will be changing (Napier & Gershenfeld, 2004). At this stage, the advisers encourage and thank members individually and as groups, allow time for reflection on group experiences, and recognize group productivity. Effective advisers recognize in what stage groups are operating and what must be done to assist groups to reach the performing stage. They also comprehend that the stage a group is operating may change as circumstances change, such as when new members join the group or when conflict among members emerges.

Corey's Stages of Group Development

Corey (2004) is one of the most prolific authors on issues related to groups. While his theory appears to be more therapeutic, the stages of group development he proposes are applicable to the stages that student organizations evolve. Corey clearly states the stages should not be perceived as discrete stages. Like groups in real life, stages overlap, groups may reflect characteristics of multiple stages, and groups reach the stages at various times.

Corey identifies six stages of group development. Stage one is pregroup issues-formation of the group. Issues in this stage include selecting new members, determining size and meeting place, determining frequency and length of meetings, setting group goals, and exploring member and leader functions. Stage two is initial stage-orientation and exploration. In this stage, groups develop trust, members become acquainted, members share and clarify expectations, and members facilitate roles. Transition stage-dealing with resistance is Corey's third stage. High levels of anxiety, conflict and defensiveness distinguish stage three. Members struggle for control, learn how to handle and work through conflict, and remain concerned about being rejected. Stage four is the working stage-cohesion and productivity. This stage builds on work accomplished in the previous stages, and in this stage, individual members become part of a group. They are less dependent on leaders, focus on producing results, and feel included in the group. Members connect with established goals, listen to one another, and exhibit high levels of trust and cohesion. Groups in this stage welcome conflict and follow through on commitments. Corey's fifth stage, consolidation and termination, reflects members becoming concerned about groups coming to a close. Participants express emotions about being group members, withdraw from the group, and express the importance of the group in their lives. The final stage, post group issues-evaluation and follow-up becomes most pertinent for advisers. This stage involves assessing group experiences and establishing mechanisms for future improvements.

Peck's Stages of Development and Community

Peck (1987) explores the stages of development that groups experience when developing community. Peck identifies four stages of community develop: pseudocommunity, chaos, emptiness, and community. In psuedocommunity, participants interact on a surface level. They engage in friendly and neighborly exchanges so as not to address substantive issues that might raise conflict. As communities experience chaos, previously avoided conflicts emerge and dominate groups. Many ideas are presented and multiple perspectives offered. In the emptiness stage, participants realize that this excessive conflict, lack of communication, and nonacceptance of others' opinions stifle community development. Groups achieve the final stage, community, when participants are able to value and embrace diverse and multiple opinions.

Hare and Naveh's Stages of Development and Problem-Solving: The LAIG Model

Hare and Naveh (1984) examine the stages of group development in terms of problem-solving. They propose that as groups engage in problem-solving, they experience four predictable periods. Phase one is the latent (L) stage and reflects group orientation issues. In this period, participants focus efforts on establishing purpose, participant roles, and member expectations. Clarifying these issues assists problem-solving development. Adaptation (A) is phase two. In this stage, participants identify necessary information needed to address problems under consideration and determine member tasks. In integration (I), members explore and create solutions to problems by constantly assessing and reevaluating options. After exploring these options groups, the group reaches the final stage, goal attainment (G).

Bennis and Shepard's Theory of Group Development
Human Relations

Bennis and Shepard's (1956) group development model examines group development as evolving conflict between dependence and independence around issues of power, love, authority, and intimacy. Experiencing these issues assists the group mature. Group evolution includes two phases, each with three subphases. Phase one is dependence and is comprised of dependence/flight, counterdependence/flight, and resolution/catharsis. Phase two is interdependence and is comprised of enchantment/flight, disenchantment/flight, and consensual validation. The mature group is one that resolves internal conflict, maximizes resources, and engages in effective problem-solving.

Phase one is characterized by members searching for common goals; looking to the leader for direction; dealing with potential subgroups; and discussing group member roles and responsibilities. In phase two, members are comfortable and cohesive. Members engage in productive discussions and effective problem-solving. Bennis and Shepard (1956) also identify the following group personalities: dependent members who are most at ease with group structure; counter-dependent members who dislike authority; over-personal members who must become overly intimate before achieving a level of group comfort; counter-personal members who elude closeness; conflicted members who exhibit any compulsion in the adoption of previous types; and independent members without compulsion.

Schutz's Fundamental Interpersonal Relations Orientation (FRIO)

Schutz's (1958, 1982, 1992) FRIO model examines how groups develop related to interpersonal relations and individual emotional needs. He initially identifies three stages of group development and the basic needs that are satisfied by group participation. The stages and corresponding needs are: dependence (inclusion); independence (control); and interdependence (affection/openness). Schutz views group development as cyclical and states that as groups near the end of stages, groups actually recycle back. In a 1982 update to his theory, he describes five stages of group development: gaining inclusion, gaining control, gaining openness, giving up control, and giving up inclusion. Gaining inclusion deals with establishing initial group norms. Individuals decide whether to become group members or not and if a fit exists between them and the group. Gaining control is characterized by leadership struggles and conflict about everything related to the group. Movement to the next stage does not occur until members begin taking responsibilities. In gaining openness, members develop emotional intimacy and discover they like functioning as a group. By giving up control, members achieve this comfort level, and the group moves toward effectiveness and efficiency. In essence, they are now functioning as a collaborative group. The final stage, giving up inclusion, is about celebrating the conclusion of the group experience (Kormanski, 1999).

As advisers, understanding stages of group development allows for better advising. If group members are struggling with inclusion and approval, effective advisers might incorporate icebreakers and team-building activities at the beginning of all meetings. If groups are achieving interdependence, effective advisers design mechanisms for members to celebrate successes and growth.

Wheelan and Hochberger's Integrative Model of Group Development

Wheelan and Hochberger (1996) developed the Integrative Model of Group Development. Their perspective is that group development is more cyclical and less linear. They state that while groups develop in predictable order, groups also recycle through stages as membership changes, crises occur, or expectations change.

This model comprises five stages. Stage one is dependency and inclusion. Like other initial stages of other models, this stage is about fitting it. Leaders take active roles with groups, while members focus on getting along, being accepted, and satisfying leaders. Stage two is counterdependency and flight. In this stage, participants more freely express ideas and opinions, and they labor over roles to be played. This free expression of ideas and struggles with roles lead to conflict and the emergence of factions and subgroups. Trust and structure is stage three. Groups achieving this stage have utilized the conflict in stage two for growth. Struggling with conflict leads to trust and an understanding that groups can be productive by developing structured ground rules and practices toward goals. Members focus less on power struggles and more on productivity. Groups achieve stage four, work, when there is evidence that groups are exhibiting constructive communication, collaboration, and high productivity. To achieve this work, groups have resolved group orientation issues, such as structure, roles, and aspirations. Stage five is termination. This stage allows members to reflect, assess, and share experiences, as well as what they have learned.

Kottler and Parr's Stages of Group Development

Kottler and Parr (2001) present a four-stage group development process. In developing their model, they reviewed numerous models (Bennis & Shepard, 1956; Vander Kolk, 1990; Wheelan, 1994; Yalom, 1995; La Coursiere, 1980; Tuckman, 1965; Corey & Corey, 1997; Peck, 1987; Hare & Naveh, 1984;

and Napier & Gershenfeld, 2004) in an attempt to seek common elements and principles and to present a more simplified model. Their model identifies four stages: induction, experimental engagement, cohesive engagement, and disengagement.

The primary focus of the induction stage is learning what it means to be in a group. In this stage, participants rely on leaders for direction. They feel unsure about being in the group and being accepted. While groups often provide new members with some type of orientation, they have yet to learn the rules of what it means to be a good group member, and it becomes the role of advisers to teach them. Kottler and Parr (2001) state that if the rules of groups are personalized and followed, moderate trust is evident and effective communication processes are in place, groups will move to the next stage.

Stage two is experimental engagement. In this stage, participants become more active. Participation, including the amount of time committed and the expression of opinions, increases. At this stage, varying levels of member participation exist and conflict usually arises. Overall, there is minimal engagement. Effective advisers typically seek ways to enhance engagement in this stage.

Cohesive engagement, stage three, is the working stage. Members are close, trust one another, are productive, and view leaders as facilitators. Participants understand their roles in organizations and know what it means to be effective group members. Advisers in this stage fight the need to determine the direction of organizations and find ways to further constructively challenge groups.

The final stage is disengagement. Groups in this stage understand and begin to prepare for an ending to the process. Emotions are high as members prepare for the future and deal with changing relationships. Helping participants reflect, process experiences, and set future goals becomes the leaders' role. Effective advisers find ways to honor both the achievements and efforts of group members.

Bion's Group Development

Bion (1961) states that in every group two types of groups exist: the basic assumption group and the work group. The work group functions as a mature group with members being knowledgeable about task, purpose, and direction of the group. The assumption group represents those unconscious behaviors that exist causing groups to perform as if group members were holding certain assumptions. The three assumption groups are the dependent group, the fight-flight group, and the pairing group. Kormanski (1999) identifies the predominant behavior at each stage of the assumption groups. In the dependent group, the dominant behavior is the need for authority; in the fight-flight group, the dominant behavior is conflict; in the pairing group, the dominant behavior is extreme support; and in the working group, the dominant behavior is performance.

In the dependent group, the leader is supreme. Unsure of their roles, group members struggle with being group members. The dependent group is not sure of how to address group tasks, so no member takes any responsibility. In the fight-flight group, the group either attacks or shuns tasks. Conflict is central to this stage, and members remain unsure of how to work cohesively. In the pairing group, members participate more as the group seeks cohesiveness. As the group achieves the working stage, they are effective problem solvers who are task-oriented and learn from both leaders and peers (Kormanski, 1999).

Individual Development: Theories, Models, and Approaches

Often advisers think that to be effective, they must be experts on group dynamics and group development. The most effective advisers, however, are well-versed and knowledgeable about individual development. Since groups consist of individual members, possessing an understanding of individual development is necessary. This section examines three theories, models, or approaches to individual development.

Maslow's Hierarchy of Motivation

Maslow (1954) is probably the best-known *needs* theorist. He states that individuals are motivated by unmet needs, and lower level needs must be met before higher level needs. Maslow presents a positive theory in response to what he believes are the rather depressing theories of Sigmund Freud and B. F. Skinner. He believes people are fundamentally trustworthy and able to determine their own lives.

Maslow identifies seven needs: physiological, safety, love and belonging, esteem, self-actualization, desire to know and understand, and aesthetic. General needs must be satisfied for individuals to behave unselfishly. What motivates individuals is fulfilling needs. As long as individuals move toward satisfying needs, growth leading to self-actualization is possible. Clear patterns are identified and generally only one need is addressed at a time, but there can be some overlap of needs.

Physiological needs—the need for air, water, food, sleep, and sex—are basic human needs. It is not possible to move toward fulfillment of higher level needs if physiological needs are not satisfied. How well individuals satisfy basic needs impact behavior in groups. The degree to which individuals fulfill the needs of belonging, esteem, acceptance, and confidence impact how they contribute or detract from groups. Napier and Gershenfeld (2004) report that any working group contains members who are influenced by their own needs, and these needs often impact communication with others. Effective advisers identify needs students are experiencing and find ways to support the satisfaction of these needs.

Student Development Theories: Psychosocial, Cognitive, Environment, and Typology.

To effectively work with groups, advisers require a general understanding of student development theory. Numerous student development theories are useful in examining student behavior. Although most of these theories focus on individual development, advisers must be knowledgeable about how college students develop identity. Specifically, advisers should be knowledgeable about psychosocial theory (issues and tasks); cognitive theory (meaning making); environment theory (conceptualization of the environment); and typology theory (individual difference). An example of each theory follows.

- **Psychosocial Theory: Chickering.** Psychosocial theory explores individual personal and interpersonal experiences. Chickering (1969) expands on the concepts of Erik Erikson's (1968) work on identify development. Chickering states that identity development is the central issue for individuals between the ages of 18-25 as they explore life tasks typical for this age group. Successful mastery of these life tasks is not easy and occurs due to repeated exposure and practice.

  Chickering and Reisser (1993), in an updated version of the original theory, propose seven vectors of development that comprise individual identity development students experience at varying rates of development. These vectors include: developing competence, managing emotions, moving through autonomy toward interdependence, developing mature interpersonal relationships, establishing identity, developing purpose, and developing integrity. Also important in impacting students' psychosocial development are environmental conditions, such as institutional size and objectives; student affairs programs and services; curriculum and teaching practices; and faculty-student interaction. Progression of development through these vectors is not sequential but rather cyclical in that an individual's mastery of earlier vectors is necessary for success in developing identity and for integration of tasks related to each vector.

- **Cognitive Theory: Kohlberg and Gilligan.** Cognitive-structural theories investigate changes in how people create, think, and reason. These theories also purport that cognitive changes are due to assimilation and accommodation of information. Assimilation involves incorporating information into existing cognitive structures. Accommodation also involves revising current structures or creating new ones to incorporate information (Evans, Forney, & Guido-DiBrito, 1998). Effective advisers are knowledgeable of cognitive-structural theories, such as Kohlberg's Theory of Moral Development (1976) and Gilligan's Theory of Women's Moral Development (1982/1993) because understanding students' reasoning abilities provides insight into decisions students make that impact their lives and their interactions with peers (Evans, Forney, & Guido-DiBrito, 1998), and moral reasoning impacts decision-making, which is a primary task of most student organizations.

Kohlberg's Theory of Moral Development (1976) has three levels with two stages per level. At the core of the theory is the concept of justice. The levels and stages are: preconventional level with stage one—punishment and obedience orientation; stage two— instrumental-relativist orientation; conventional level with stage three—interpersonal concordance and stage four—law and order orientation; post conventional level with stage five—social contract and legalistic orientation; and stage six—universal-ethical principle orientation. At the preconventional level, individuals maintain perspectives that are self-centered. At the conventional level, individuals adopt societal perspectives. At the postconventional level, individuals make deliberate efforts to clarify moral rules and principles at this level, they also allow these self-determined expectations and principles guide their behaviors. Students at the preconventional level view participating in groups as an equal exchange of favors. They are motivated by reciprocity. For example, if they do something for the group, they expect something in return. At the conventional level, student participation is about being good group members by maintaining group structure.

Gilligan (1982, 1993) studied moral development in women and concludes that justice is not the only factor on which individuals make decisions. She states that care and responsibility are also factors influencing moral decision-making. Her model considers moral development as occurring in three levels and two transition periods, with each level representing a changing view on the relationship between self and others (Evans, Forney, & Guido-DiBrito, 1998). The first level is orientation to individual survival followed by the first transition from selfishness to responsibility. Level two is goodness as self-sacrifice followed by the second transition from goodness to truth. The final level is the morality of nonviolence. In the first level, decisions are made based on individual needs. In level two, individuals become concerned about being accepted by and taking care of others. In level three, individuals realize that taking care of themselves is as important as is taking care of others (Gilligan 1982, 1993).

Evans, Forney, and Guido-DiBrito (1998) identify several researchers who have shown the applicability of both Kohlberg and Gilligan perspectives to student affairs work. Examples of this applicability include Clark and Dobson (1980), who apply Kohlberg's theory in group counseling situations; Rodgers (1983), who advocates listening to both voices when handling roommate conflicts; Picard and Guido-DiBrito (1993), who state that student organizations' advisers must recognize how group members are impacted by both voices; and Komives (1994), and Fried (1994) who illustrate how understanding both voices allow student-leaders and practitioners increased insights into their positions (cited in Evans, Forney, and Guido-DiBrito, 1998). Additionally, Porterfield and Pressprich (1988) advocate that university housing staff should listen to both voices in developing staff training activities.

- **Environmental Theory.** Applying environmental theory allows advisers to explore the connections college students have with their environments. There are numerous environmental theories. Strange and Banning (2001) categorize them into four perspectives of campus environments: physical, organizational, human aggregate, and constructed. Each type offers insights into how the environment influences student behavior. Particularly useful to advisers is the constructed perspective that attempts to understand the environment by obtaining the perspectives of participants within the environment.

  Of the constructed theories, the social climate theory of Moos (1979) is applicable for group work. Moos studied the social climates existing in an environment. To understand social climates, Moos states it is necessary to recognize the physical settings, the human beings, and the organizational structures within the environment (Grandpre, 1995). Moos (1979) identifies three components of social climates. These components are relationship dimensions; personal growth dimensions; and system maintenance and change dimensions. Moos identifies the social climates of social or task group environments, work environments, residence hall environments, family environments, classroom environments, hospital settings, and military units (Strange & Banning, 2001).

- **Typology Theory: Jung and Myers-Briggs.** Typology theory examines how individuals develop preferences. These preferences are styles that remain stable over time and impact how individuals react to changing situations, changing environments, and comprising personality types. One preference is not perceived as better than another, but indicates only that an individual favors one type of behavior over another. Jung's (1921, 1960) theory of conscious personality type and Myers (1980) adaptation of this theory are useful in understanding individuals' personality types.

Jung proposes that human behavior is not random, but predictable and consistent. He distinguishes two dimensions of personality types: attitude-types and function-types (Mattoon, 1981). Attitude-types include extraverts and introverts. Functional-types include thinking, feeling, sensing, and intuition. Thus, eight possible types emerge. Jung believes attitude-types appear early in our lives, with function-types appearing later (Von Franz, 1971), and individuals possess all four functions to varying degrees (Hopcke, 1989). Adapting this theory, Myers (1980) adds another set of functions based on Jung's ideas about judging and perceiving. Both believed that an individual's personality is a preference on each of the four dichotomies: extraversion/introversion, thinking/feeling, intuition/sensation, judging/perceiving. These combinations result in sixteen personality types.

Space does not allow discussion of the Myers-Briggs 16 personality types, but it is useful to understand attitude-types and function-types. The extraversion and introversion type refers to how individuals deal with the world and how they relate to others. Extraverts are influenced by the external world with energy being focused on people and things. They tend to be action-oriented and impulsive. Introverts are influenced by the subjective world within themselves; their energy is focused on ideas and thoughts. They prefer reflection, thinking alone, and quiet time.

The thinking/feeling dichotomy examines how individuals evaluate and make decisions with information. Thinking types use logic and analyses to make objective decisions using facts and impersonal criteria. In contrast, the feeling types make decisions based on emotions and feelings. In making decisions, they rely on personal and subjective values and judgments, not facts. They are sociable and highly interested in others.

Intuition/sensation refers to how individuals learn about the world and their preferences for incorporating information. Sensing individuals take in data in a literal, concrete fashion. They understand facts and receive data based on their five senses. They rely on results, not theory, for learning. Intuitive individuals receive data from the unconscious and use insights to generate possibilities for all information. They look for symbolism, relationships and connections. Then they theorize based on such observations.

Individuals differ in how they bring order to their lives and worlds through judging or perceiving. Those who perceive prefer to live spontaneously and have lives of possibilities. They are flexible, open-ended, and prefer taking in new information as they explore new possibilities. Those who judge prefer organized, planned, and structured lifestyles. They are decisive and prefer following plans to keep life orderly and stable.

Understanding these types can assist advisers in multiple ways. Types can be used to match assignments and tasks for group members. Effective advisers assist students with discovering tasks they are most suited to perform in groups. Teaching members about types allows for better communication and understanding when conflicts arise. For example in meetings, thinking types enjoy debating issues, even if issues are not ones they believe in or feel strongly about. However, feeling types are uncomfortable with debate and perceive it as conflict with potential for someone to be hurt. Understanding and appreciating different types teach members how diversity of types can lead to increased and more diverse problem-solving. Type knowledge improves group relationships and communications.

Group Dynamics: Roles

Effective advisers are knowledgeable of the different theories relating to group roles. This information assists advisers by allowing them to identify the basic characteristics of these roles to either encourage or defuse them. Roles are about behaviors and how behaviors impact both individuals and groups. Stewart, Manz, and Sims (1999) define roles as "a set of behaviors that is characteristic of a person in a specific situation" (p. 38).

Much of the early research and theory development begun in the late 1940s was dedicated to dividing groups into specific role areas. The group areas were divided further to explain specific behaviors exhibited by group members. For example, the member or executive officer who mediates conflict and attempts to smooth over feelings and "keep the peace," according to Lifton (1967) is characterized as a *harmonizer*. Benne and Sheats (1948), Knowles and Knowles (1959), and Lifton (1967) conducted early studies about group roles. A compilation of the typology used by these authors and an excellent example of the common roles of groups can be found in the book *Exploring leadership: For college students who want to make a difference* by Susan Komives, Nance Lucas, and Timothy McMahon (1998). This information is in table form and is helpful becuase it lists task roles, role descriptionxs, and examples of the roles in use. The table offers a connection between the wrtitten example (theory) and an actual instance of observed behavior (practice).

Additionally, Lifton (1967) identifies three roles played by both group members and the group itself. These are group task roles (roles played in engaging in problem-solving and decision-making); group growing and vital-izing roles (roles that solidify group development and cooperation); and anti-group roles (roles that meet individual needs, not group needs). A complete listing of Lifton's (1967) typology follows:

Group Task Roles

- **Initiator/contributor.** Offers new ideas or changes ways of handling group problems or goals. Suggests solutions for handling group difficulties. Establishes new procedures and new organization for the group.

- **Information seeker.** Seeks clarification of suggestions in terms of factual adequacy and/or authoritative information and pertinent facts of factual accuracy; authoritative information; and pertinent facts.

- **Opinion seeker.** Seeks clarification of values pertinent to what the group is undertaking or of values involved in suggestions made to understand.

- **Information giver.** Offers facts or generalizations which are authoritative or relates own experience pertinent to group problem.

- **Opinion giver.** States belief or opinion pertinent to suggestions. Emphasis on proposal of what should become the group's views on pertinent values.

- **Elaborator.** Gives examples or develops meaning. Offers rationale for sug-gestions made before. Tries to deduce how ideas might work out.

- **Coordinator.** Clarifies relationships among ideas and suggestions, pulls ideas and suggestions together, or tries to coordinate activities of members of subgroups.

- **Orienter.** Defines position of group with respect to goals. Summarizes. Shows departures from agreed direction or goals. Questions direction of discussion.

- **Evaluator.** Subjects accomplishment of group to standards of group func-tioning. May evaluate or question practicality, logic, facts, or procedure of a suggestion or of some unit of group discussion.

- **Energizer.** Prods group to action or decision. Tries to stimulate group to greater or higher quality activity.

- **Procedural technician.** Performs routine tasks (distributes materials, etc.) or manipulates objects for group (rearranging chairs, etc.)

- **Recorder.** Writes down suggestions, group decisions, or products of decisions. Provides group memory. (Sampson as cited in Dunkel, Spencer & Associates, 1998, p. 90-92)

Group Growing and Vitalizing Roles

- **Encourager.** Praises, agrees with, and accepts others' ideas. Indicates warmth and solidarity in attitude toward members.

- **Harmonizer.** Mediates intergroup scraps. Relieves tensions.

- **Compromiser.** Operates from within a conflict in which personal idea and position is involved. May yield status, admit error, discipline him/herself, and "come halfway."

- **Gatekeeper and expediter.** Encourages and facilitates participation of others. "Let's hear." "Why not limit length of contributions so all can react to the problem?"

- **Standard setter or ego ideal.** Expresses standards for group to attempt to achieve in its function or applies standards in evaluating the quality of group processes.

- **Group observer and commentator.** Keeps records of groups processes and contributes these data with proposed interpretations into group's evaluation of procedures.

- **Follower.** Goes along somewhat passively. Is friendly audience. (Sampson as cited in Dunkel, Spencer, & Associates, 1998, p. 91)

Antigroup Roles

- **Aggressor.** Deflates statements of others. Expresses disapproval of values, acts, or feelings of others. Attacks group or problems. Jokes aggressively. Shows envy by trying to take credit for others' ideas.

- **Blocker.** Negativistic. Stubbornly and unreasoningly resistant. Tries to bring back issues group intentionally rejected or by-passed.

- **Recognition-seeker.** Tries to call attention to self. May boast, report on personal achievements, and in unusual ways, struggles to prevent being placed in "inferior" position.

- **Self-confessor.** Uses group to express persona, non-group oriented feeling, insight, ideology, etc.

- *Playboy.* Displays lack of involvement in group's work. Actions may take form of cynicism, nonchalance, horseplay, or other more-or-less studied, "out of field" behavior.

- **Dominator.** Tries to assert authority in manipulating group or some individuals in group. May use flattery, assert superior status, or right to attention, gives directions authoritatively, interrupts contributions of others, and so forth.

- **Help-seeker.** Tries to get sympathy response from others through expressions of insecurity, personal confusion, or self-deprecation beyond reason.

- **Special interest pleader.** Verbally for "small business owner," "grassroots community," "homemaker," "labor," and so forth. Actually cloaking personal prejudices or biases with stereotypes that best fit individual need. (Sampson as cited in Dunkel, Spencer, & Associates, 1998, p. 92)

The impact of these roles varies from group to group and person to person. This theoretical information is extremely useful for advisers when reviewing group and/or group member behaviors in efforts to validate positive behaviors or defuse negative behaviors.

Current scholars, such as Komives, Lucas, and McMahon (1998), focus on two group roles, group-building and task roles. They state:

Group-building roles are actions that focus on the group as people, including the relationships among members. These have also been called group maintenance roles. Task roles focus on accomplishing the purposes of the group, including giving information and opinions and moving the group along on tasks by summarizing and by using various decision-making strategies. Task roles focus on the content of the group discussion. (p. 173)

Komives, Lucas, and McMahon (1998) also write about dysfunctional roles. Behaviors such as the special interest pleaders, the blockers, and the clowns are examples of dysfunctional behaviors.

Stewart, Manz, and Sims (1999) approach group roles from a team perspective. They believe that team formation falls into two specific categories: functional perspectives and interpersonal perspectives. Within both perspectives are various explanations for why individuals form groups and for why they join groups. The functional perspective sees group membership and roles as necessary for survival. Individuals use groups as a way of survival. Stewart,

Manz, and Sims (1999) state when writing about functional membership that groups "help us to improve the quality of our lives" (p. 5). Improvement occurs because of the strengths that each member brings that permeate all members of the group. The interpersonal perspective suggests that individuals join groups because they need to be with others. This belonging is manifested in the need to affiliate and have power over others or to give and receive affection. Another perspective of interpersonal membership is that individuals need to share information and compare themselves to one another.

Scholars of group roles reinforce that groups are going to happen, and it benefits both the environment and groups to understand the particulars of why and what kinds of behaviors impact group dynamics. Chickering and Reisser (1993) state, "Once a student identifies with a particular group, it becomes both an anchor and a reference point." (p. 394.) This identity and grounding are the basis for student affairs professionals working to positively impact the growth and development of groups and group members. A solid foundation of understanding group roles and dynamics serves students both now and as they enter other phases of their lives.

Group Dynamics: Communication

Komives, Lucas, and McMahon (1998) state, "While communicating and working together make organizational (and common) sense, they do not always exist" (p. 291). Communication is a complicated aspect of group dynamics. The primary reason communication is difficult is because groups are made up of individuals. Each person brings different life experiences and lenses to the communication process. This diversity of insight contributes to the richness of human interactions, but also adds significant complexity to the process. Communication is a complex process of talking and listening. Komives, Lucas, and McMahon (1998) state, "In every communication, each person has a right to be heard and a responsibility to listen" (p. 157).

Hackman and Johnson (2000) believe, "Human communication is: (a) a process, (b) circular in nature, (c) complex, (d) irreversible, and (e) the characteristic that defines the total personality" (p. 27). The challenge for advisers, leaders, and members of groups is to keep communication lines open. Kouzes and Posner (1995) suggest that "Whatever the technique, the leader must keep communication pathways open and vital" (p. 47).

Communication takes many forms. It can be spoken, written, and nonverbal in nature. Although the focus of this section is on groups and communication patterns, it is important also to examine the role of the individual in communication. Communication patterns of individuals within groups, especially the communication of leaders, positively or negatively impacts how successful groups are in accomplishing goals. Sometimes negative behavior is an issue with group behavior and impacts communication patterns. Burgoon, Heston, and McCroskey (1974) provide the following advice regarding communication for advisers and groups who may wish to avoid defensive behavior:

1. It is important that individuals avoid criticizing other group members who express different views.
2. Communication that is perceived as an attempt to control others will probably result in negative reactions or behaviors.
3. People who bring "hidden agendas" into the group breed distrust.
4. If the group is to have a genuine relationship of trust, it must learn to cope with signs of defensive behaviors by providing a supportive climate.
5. The appearance of a lack of concern for the feelings of other members will likely produce defensiveness.
6. An attitude of superiority arouses defensive behavior.
7. The more close-minded people are in their beliefs about "truth," the more likely others are to react defensively. This situation is especially true for those who disagree." (Sampson as cited in Dunkel, Spencer, & Associates, 1998, p. 93)

By practicing these key concepts, groups and group leaders can avoid the pitfalls of defensive behavior.

Another aspect that impacts group communication pattern is size. Small groups have more intimate communication patterns than large groups simply by virtue of size and accessibility to individual dialogue. Burgoon, Heston, and McCroskey (1974) identify seven unique characteristics of small groups regarding how they communicate. Sampson (cited in Dunkel, Spencer, & Associates, 1998) states, "Small groups are more likely to have frequent interaction, develop a group personality, establish group norms, cope with behaviors, have defined roles, establish independent goals, and benefit from assembly effect bonus" (pp. 92–93). These characteristics suggest that by working as groups, they are able to accomplish more than if they were individuals working independently (Sampson as cited in Dunkel, Spencer, & Associates, 1998). Because of the challenges associated with trying to get large groups of people to accomplish tasks, large groups are commonly divided into smaller groups because this division enhances the likelihood of goal accomplishment. These smaller groups, such as committees or task forces, give members more fulfillment from group membership because they have greater opportunities to interact with others on a more personal basis.

The extensive nuances of communication and how communication impacts behavior makes it essential that group advisers and leaders are committed to continually learning about the art of communication. Hackman and Johnson (2000) report, "Leadership effectiveness depends on our willingness to communicate, as well as on developing effective communication skills" (p. 27). The more advisers and leaders study and practice communication and communication theory, the better communicators they become.

Group Dynamics: Conflict

Much of the information presented in this chapter targets resolving conflict in groups through understanding group development, roles, communication, leadership, and student development. Effective advisers also need basic knowledge of types of conflict that can occur within groups and teams. Stewart, Manz, and Sims (1999) identify specific types of conflict. "The most basic and useful distinction between conflict types seems to be between relationship-oriented conflict (sometimes referred to as affective conflict) and task-oriented conflict (sometimes labeled as cognitive conflict)" (p. 95). Conflict, just as group roles, centers on relationships and task roles. Relationship conflict can be damaging to groups because it is often personal in nature or geared toward individuals; however, task conflict can be beneficial to groups. The presentation of divergent thoughts and ideas often produces outstanding products.

Conflict is inevitable. However, with successful conflict resolution, groups can be positively impacted. Stewart, Manz, and Sims (1999) present four specific types of group reactions to conflict and resolution: avoidance, imposition, compromise, and integrative bargaining

Avoidance is not dealing or confronting the conflict. There are situations where avoidance is acceptable. Stewart, Manz, and Sims, Jr. (1999) state, "long term avoidance can allow conflict to build up to the point where team members become so angry with each other that they are unable to continue to working together" (p. 97). Advisers should encourage students to discuss problems. Another strategy to address avoidance is assisting students in role-playing conversations to reach conflict resolution. These role plays increase student confidence about the confrontation process.

Imposition occurs when group members are forced to do things that they do not agree with or see as beneficial. Many times, the members do not have the "power base" to influence others. This "forced participation" can lead to dissatisfaction. A suggestion for defusing imposition is being aware of project assignments and allowing for volunteer participation rather than mandatory participation.

Stewart, Manz, and Sims (1999) state, "Compromise requires that each side of a dispute make concessions. Relying too much on compromise may cause team members to get too comfortable with using it whenever conflict arises and thereby rob the team of the benefits of constructive disagreement and the potential to reach more optimal solutions" (p. 97). Maintaining balance is key as some compromise is effective, but too much enhances group problems.

Integrative bargaining is characterized as assertive problem-solving and win/win resolution. Stewart, Manz, and Sims (1999) report, "Team members engaged in integrative bargaining work cooperatively to determine the source of conflict, and then explore alternatives that eliminate the conflict without significantly damaging the interests of either person" (p. 97). Advisers facilitate integrative bargaining by bringing conflicting factions together to openly discuss and work toward finding win/win resolutions to issues.

Regarding how conflict is handled, most groups benefit from open communication and group standards. Open discussion about conflict is critical during the forming stage of development. Clear expectations set standards for group behavior. Open communication, problem identification, specific expectations, and willingness to compromise are all necessary components of successful conflict resolution.

Group Dynamics: Performance

Effective group performance includes how groups make decisions, how they engage in effective problem-solving, and how motivated members are. Factors, such as group composition and size, impact group performance. Smaller groups have increased member interaction and cohesion. The more similar the group members, the less conflict the group experiences (Forsyth, 1999). A number of theories address group performance, especially the functions of decision-making and effectiveness. Five of the more common ones are the theory of social facilitation; social impact theory; social combination theory, Hackman and Morris's process model of group performance; and Johnson and Johnson's elements of group productivity.

Social Facilitation

Social facilitation is based on the 1898 work of Triplett (Forsyth, 1999) and Zajonc (1965). Social facilitation examines how individual performance of tasks might be influenced by the presence of others. In essence, social facilitation examines how member performance is impacted if performing alone or with an audience (Johnson & Johnson, 2000). Zajonc explains that having an audience increases the likelihood that an individual will display dominant responses (those behaviors and responses that are easy to master) and decreases the likelihood that an individual will display nondominant responses (those behaviors and responses not mastered). Responses may be correct or incorrect. Zajonc believes that individuals do better if performing dominant tasks with an audience. If tasks are complex and call for nondominant responses, audiences obstruct performance (Forsyth, 1999).

Social Impact Theory

Social impact theory and the concept of social loafing also address group performance. Social loafing (Williams & Karau, 1991) suggests that groups often experience a lessening in individual effort when there are numerous individuals working on a task. In short, individuals often exert less effort than they would if performing the task alone. It could be argued that often group members often reap the benefits of the group's productivity, while maintaining anonymity and feeling no social pressure to perform. Napier and Gershenfeld (2004) report that social loafing is more common in groups with the following characteristics: large; unclear group member roles; little to no group cohesion; unbalanced division of labor; limited decision-makers; evasion of conflict; and member insecurity about levels of ability. Effective advisers employ numerous strategies to minimize social loafing. These strategies include rewarding group for good performance, holding members accountable for individual behavior, assisting members in internalizing group goals, increasing member motivation, increasing member personal involvement, dividing larger groups into smaller groups when possible, and increasing the value of the group goals for members (Forsyth, 1999).

Social Combination Theory

Steiner's (1976) social combination theory maintains that group performance and effectiveness depend on group composition and the types of tasks confronting the group. Of particular concern to Steiner was whether or not group members have sufficient skills and abilities to fulfill tasks. Steiner differentiates types of tasks using a three-prong approach: task components, task output, and task group member combinations. He argues that some tasks can be broken down into component parts (divisible tasks) and some cannot (unitary). He also argues that some tasks value quantity produced (maximizing) and some value quality of performance (optimizing). He identifies six types of tasks related to how groups combine members' contributions: additive, compensatory, disjunctive, conjunctive, and discretionary (Forsyth, 1999). In examining these tasks, Steiner (1976) believes groups perform best when the tasks being addressed are additive.

Hackman and Morris

Hackman and Morris (1975) developed the process model of group performance that focuses on member interaction. Hackman and Morris identify three factors that impact group performance: group members' skills and intelligence, amount of energy members invest, and strategies utilized for addressing group tasks. They propose that if members utilize necessary skills, increase effort, and have effective performance strategies, performance will be enhanced. They also identify three types of inputs that impact groups: individual-inputs, which are group member skills and attitudes; group-level inputs, which are group structure issues (such as size, composition, roles, and unity); and environmental-inputs, which are types and structure of group tasks. By manipulating these three factors, group performance is enhanced.

Johnson and Johnson Elements of Group Effectiveness

Johnson and Johnson (1997) offer a practical model for group productivity. Saying that truly effective and productive groups are uncommon, they believe that for groups to become fully functioning and to create conditions that enhance productivity, the following five elements must occur:

1. **Positive interdependence** is the concept that all participants must contribute for groups to reach maximum performance. Members must be connected and understand that no one can succeed without working to help one another.
2. **Individual accountability/personal responsibility** is the idea that everyone must pull his/her own weight when addressing tasks. Individuals must possess some personal sense of responsibility and must work hard to ensure group success. Members cannot engage in social loafing, and all must be actively engaged in solving tasks.
3. **Promotive (face-to-face) interaction** is members being willing to assist other group members by sharing resources, providing feedback, challenging and supporting others, and creating environments of trust.
4. **Social skills.** For members to succeed, they must possess social skills,

interpersonal and small group social skills. Lacking social skills dooms good performance.

5. **Group processing** allows participants time for reflection on the group experience. Taking time to evaluate group performance in specific and systematic ways enhances productivity.

Groups and Leadership

One of the primary reasons students join residence hall governments, fraternities, sororities, and student organizations is for involvement, meeting new people, leadership opportunities, and a sense of belonging. Alexander Astin's (1993) research on student involvement indicates that students who are engaged and involved in groups on campus are more likely to succeed and be retained to graduation. Hallenbeck, Dickman, and Fuqua (2004) state, "On most university campuses, the two primary organizational structures that provide the setting for a large percentage of students and identified student-leaders are residential life and Greek life" (p. 24).

One benefit to belonging to a group is the opportunity to become a part of that group's leadership. Often students begin leadership skill-building and practice in high school. They join groups or clubs and take on leadership positions within those organizations. College is a continuation of these activities. Hallenbeck, Dickman, and Fuqua (2004) believe, "Leadership experiences, while in college, can be powerful tools in the development of the individual" (p. 24). Understanding leadership theories provides advisers with the necessary tools to support personal development and the development of student-leaders. Being an adviser is a leadership position, as well as a role that fosters leadership in others.

Bensimon, Neumann, and Birnbaum (1989) outline six theories and models of leadership: trait theories; power and influence theories; behavioral theories; contingency theories; cultural and symbolic theories; and cognitive theories. They say, "The boundaries of these categories are fluid, and they are neither mutually exclusive nor consistent" (p. 7).

Trait Theories

Trait theories identify specific traits and characteristics that individuals possess or develop which support their ability to function successfully as leaders. In the early 1900s, the study of leadership traits was new and developing. Northhouse (2001) reports, "These theories that were developed were called *great man* theories because they focused on identifying the innate qualities and characteristics possessed by great social, political, and military leaders [e.g. Thomas

Jefferson, Abraham Lincoln, and Mohandas Gandhi]" (p. 15). Early scholars believe that leadership traits were part of the physical make-up of individuals and were not learned behaviors. Later findings support that a combination of personality traits and situational factors influence leadership characteristics.

Charismatic leadership is an example of trait theory. Johnson and Johnson (1987) state, "To be charismatic, a leader must have an extraordinary power or vision and be able to communicate that to others, or unusual powers of practical leadership that will enable her/him to achieve the goals that will alleviate followers' distress" (p. 44). Many prominent leaders in history are considered charismatic in their leadership. Examples of charismatic leaders are John F. Kennedy, Bill Clinton, Martin Luther King Jr., and Oprah Winfrey. Ethical leadership is one of the greatest challenges for charismatic leaders. Adolph Hitler and David Koresh are examples of leaders who used their charismatic strengths to the detriment of society. Peter Dricker (as cited in Hackman & Johnson, 2000) states, "Charisma becomes the undoing of leaders. It makes them inflexible, convinced of their own infallibility, unable to change" (p. 121).

Power and Influence Theories

Power and influence theories focus on the issues of power and influence, the source of these components, and how leaders utilize power. The source of and the manner in which leaders wield power and influence impact their ability to lead. There is some discrepancy about exactly which theory to categorize transactional and transformational leadership. Bensimon, Neumann, and Birnbaum (1989) categorize these leadership styles within power and influence theory. They believe these theories are further delineated into "social power theory (specific power bases listed below), social exchange/transactional theory, and transformation theory" (pp. 37–43). Recognizing bases of power assists advisers and leaders in developing positive power structures within groups. French and Raven (as referenced in Bensimon, Neumann, and Birnbaum, 1989) identify bases of social power:

- Leaders can influence others through their offices because of the legitimacy provided by our social and legal systems (legitimate power) and through the ability of leaders to provide rewards (reward power) and to threaten punishments (coercive power). Leaders can also influence others through their own personalities in two ways—their perceived expertise (expert power) and the extent to which other personally identify with and like them (referent power). (p. 9)
- **Social Exchange/Transactional Leadership Theory.** Transactional leadership can be compared to the phrase, "quid pro quo" or "this for that." In a group

setting, Bensimon, Neumann, and Birnbaum (1989) describe this theory as the relinquishment of self-governance. They report, "A group may relinquish the ability to govern themselves and follow a leader if they believe that the leader can reward them and is competent (p. 10). Northouse (2001) indicates, "Transactional leadership refers to the bulk of leadership models, which focus on exchanges that occur between leaders and their followers" (p. 132). These exchanges can be anything from political favor to monetary rewards. Bensimon, Neumann, and Birnbaum (1989) state that transactional leadership involves entering into a bargaining process, not relationship, with sustained purposes. Transactional leadership is considered the foundation of leadership, and transformational leadership is considered the process of taking leadership to the next level.

- **Transformational Leadership Theory.** A new approach to understanding leadership is transformational leadership. Northouse (2001) indicates, "This approach stresses that leaders need to understand and adapt to the needs and motives of followers" (p. 158). Furthermore, skilled leaders understand that participants often need a transactional approach to satisfy their needs for dynamic leadership and a transformational approach to satisfy their needs for substance, empowerment, and change. Ralph Nader (as cited in Hackman & Johnson, 2000) appropriately summarize both transactional and transformational leadership by stating, "The function of a leader is to produce more leaders, not more followers" (p. 90).

  Transformational leaders are often characterized as passionate, creative, and visionary. Contrasting transformation leadership to transactional leadership, Northouse (2001) suggests, "transformational leadership refers to the process where by an individual engages with others and creates a connection that raises the level of motivation and morality in both the leader and the follower" (p. 132). Bensimon, Neumann, and Birnbaum (1989) suggest that it may benefit leaders to approach transformational leadership in a transactional manner. A charismatic transactional leader may be more successful in bringing about successful organizational change because of the personable approach and the ability to reward those who can embrace change.

Behavioral Theories

Lewin, Lippitt, and White (1993) are recognized pioneers of behavior theory which purports that leadership styles have an impact on groups and how they function. Much work on behavioral theories was conducted in the 1950s and focused on the theme that "there is one best way to lead" (Komives, Lucas, McMahon, 1998, p. 36). A criticism of this theory is the lack of a match between leadership behaviors and specific situations. Researchers support the idea that there is an impact of leadership style on groups, but they do not pinpoint the exact correlation. As Bensimon, Neumann, and Birnbaum (1989) report, "It is relatively easy to call certain behaviors of leaders *effective* once the desired outcomes are observed, but much more difficult to stipulate in advance the behaviors of leaders that will have the desired outcomes" (p. 14).

McGregor's theory X and theory Y are behavioral theories and contextually referred to as a human resource frame. Bensimon, Neumann, and Birnbaum (1989) state, "Rather than emphasizing control and supervision, leaders who adopt the human resource frame give attention to removing organizational constraints on workers and to such self-enhancing processes as increased participation in decision-making and job enlargement" (p. 29). McGregor (1960) developed the theories of X and Y to support the human resource frame that organizations should serve people rather than people serving organizations. Theory X workers are characterized as not needing direct supervision and not being goal-oriented whereas, theory Y workers are characterized as goal-achieving and needing little additional motivation.

Contingency or Situational Theories.

Contingency or situational theories are based on the premise that "different situations require different patterns of traits and behaviors for a leader to be effective. Because effective behavior is contingent on the situation, they are collectively referred to as *contingency theories*" (Bensimon, Neumann, & Birnbaum, 1989, pp. 14–15).

- **Fiedler's Contingency Model.** Fiedler (1967) advocates that leader effectiveness is dependent on style and the favorableness of the situation. Leader style is either task or relationship focused. Fiedler's early work centers on assessing co-workers. He believes leadership styles are impacted greatly by the characteristics exhibited by those who others do not like to work with. Fiedler's work has been criticized extensively because of the assessment he used to collect data and the application of this theory. Fiedler and Garcia (as cited in Bensimon, Neumann, and Birnbaum, 1989) report, "More recently, Fiedler has further developed the contingency model by incorporating into it two factors that have largely been ignored or found to be related to a leader's performance—the leader's intelligence and the leader's competence and expertise" (p. 16).

- **Path Goal Theory.** Path goal theory is grounded in the belief that leadership is understanding what motivates participants or group members. Northouse

(2001) explains, "The stated goal of this theory is to enhance employee performance and employee satisfaction by focusing on employee motivation" (p. 89). Path goal theory is based on the theory of motivation, and it assumes that a worker's job satisfaction and effort are influenced by expectancy and variance. Northhouse (2001) identifies this theory as being one of the first to help leaders understand the impact of a chosen leadership style, a task, and an employee's ability to complete the task as its strength. A criticism of path goal theory is that it is complex and can be confusing.

- **Hersey and Blanchard's Situational Leadership Model.** Hersey and Blanchard's (1977) situational leadership model assumes that leaders are flexible in leadership styles. They propose it is possible for leaders to alter their behavior in response to varying circumstances and worker readiness. These scholars believe, "The appropriate degree of task and relationship behavior exhibited by a leader depends on the maturity level of the followers" (Hackman & Johnson, 2000, p. 73). The greater the necessary control exerted by the leader, the lower the maturity level of the follower and visa versa.

Cultural and Symbolic Theories

Cultural and symbolic theories approach leadership from a non-linear perspective. Bensimon, Neumann, and Birnbaum (1989) state, "These theories proposed that leadership functions within complex social systems whose participants attempt to find meaningful patterns in the behaviors of others so that they can develop common understandings about the nature of reality" (p. 21). As individuals in organizations work and grow together, specific cultures develop. Organizational culture presents through group norms, values, communications, artifacts, and celebrations. Bensimon, Neumann, and Birnbaum (1989) state that for leaders to be successful "a major factor in the success is the degree to which they are able to articulate and influence cultural norms and values" (p. 21). The symbolic aspect of these theories is manifested in the celebrations that exist within organizations. These theories "assumed that organizational structures and processes are invented, not discovered" (Bensimon, Neumann, & Birnbaum, 1989, pp. 20–21).

Cognitive Theories

Cognitive theories maintain that organizational members create leaders, and the expectations of participants in an organization or group setting dictate the success of the leader. This control of group members is illustrated by Bensimon, Neumann, and Birnbaum (1989) who state:

Leadership is associated with a set of myths reinforcing organizational constructions of meanings that helps participants to believe in the effectiveness of individual control. These myths influence the perceptions of leader, as well as to followers, so that leaders are likely to have exaggerated beliefs in their own efficacy" (p. 23).

This group of theories examines leadership as cause and effect. Leaders believe that they are the reason for the groups' success, and followers believe that also. Cognitive theories offer different perspectives on leadership development, but additional research is necessary to fully understand their impact (Bensimon, Neumann, & Birnbaum, 1989).

References

American Heritage Dictionary of the English Language (3rd ed.) (1992). Boston, MA: Houghton Mifflin Company.

Astin, A. (1993). *What matters in college? Four critical years.* San Francisco: Jossey-Bass.

Bales, R. (1950). *Interaction process analysis.* Reading, MA: Addison-Wesley.

Bass, B. (1960). *Leadership, psychology, and organizational behavior.* New York: Harper & Row.

Benne, K. D., & Sheats, P. (1948). Functional roles of group members. *Journal of Social Issues, 2,* 42–47.

Bennis, W. G., & Shepard, H. A. (1956). A theory of group development. *Human Relations, 9,* 415–437.

Bensimon, E. M., Neumann, A., & Birnbaum, R. (1989). *Making sense of administrative leadership: The 'L' word in higher education* (ASHE-ERIC Higher Education Report No. 1). Washington, DC: School of Education and Human Development, The George Washington University.

Bion, R. W. (1961). *Experiences in groups.* New York: Basic Books.

Boyer, E. (1990). *Campus life: In search of community.* San Francisco: The Carnegie Foundation for the Advancement of Teaching.

Brown, R. (2000). *Group processes: Dynamics within and between groups* (2nd ed.). New York: Blackwell.

Burgoon, M., Heston, J., & McCroskey, J. (1974). *Small group communications: A functional approach.* New York: Holt, Rinehart & Winston.

Cartwright, D., & Zander, A. (Eds.). (1968). *Group dynamics: Research and theory./* (3rd ed.). New York: Harper & Row.

Cattell, R. (1951). New concepts for measuring leadership in terms of group syntality. *Human Relations, 4,* 161–184.

Chickering, A. W. (1969). *Education and identity.* San Francisco: Jossey-Bass.

Chickering, A. W., & Reisser, L. (1993). *Education and identity* (2nd ed.). San Francisco: Jossey-Bass.

Conyne, R. K., Wilson, F. R., & Ward, D. E. (1997). *Comprehensive group work.* Alexandria, VA: American Counseling Association.

Corey, G. (2004). *Theory and practice of group counseling* (6th ed.). Belmont, CA: Brooks/Cole.

Corey, M. S., & Corey, G. (1997). *Groups: Process and practice* (5th ed.). Pacific Grove: CA.

Dunkel, N. W., Spencer, C. L., & Associates. (1998). *Advice for advisers: The development of a residence hall association.* Columbus, OH: The Association of College and University Housing Officers — International.

Erikson, E. E. (1968). *Identity: Youth and crises.* New York: Norton.

Evans, N. J., Forney, D. S., & Guido-DiBrito, F. (1998). *Student development in college.* San Francisco: Jossey-Bass.

Fiedler, F. E. (1967). *A theory of leadership effectiveness.* New York: McGraw-Hill.

Forsyth, D. R. (1999). *Group dynamics* (3rd ed.). Belmont, CA: Wadsworth Publishing.

Gilligan, C. (1982, 1993). *In a different voice: Psychological theory and women's development.* Cambridge, MA: Harvard University Press.

Gladding, S. (2002). *Group work: A counseling specialty (4th ed.).* Upper Saddle River, NJ: Prentice Hall.

Glanz, E. C., & Hayes, R. W. (1967). *Groups in guidance.* Boston, MA: Allyn & Bacon.

Grandpre, E. (1995). *Comparison of the real and the ideal perceptions of a student living environment by psychological type.* Unpublished dissertation. The Ohio State University.

Hackman, J., & Morris, C. (1975). Group task, group interaction process and group performance effectiveness: A review and proposed integration. In L. Berowitz (Ed.), *Advances in Experimental Social Psychology: Vol. 8* (pp. 47–99). New York: Academic Press.

Hackman, M. Z., & Johnson, C. E. (2000*). Leadership: A communication perspective* (3rd ed.). Prospect Heights, IL: Waveland Press.

Hallenbeck, D. A., Dickman, M. M., & Fugua, D. R. (2004). Dimensions of leadership and motivation in relation to residential setting. *Journal of College and University Student Housing, 33,* 23–31.

Hare, P., & Naveh, D. (1984). Group development at the Camp David Summit. *Small Group Behavior, 15* (3), 299–318.

Hersey, P., & Blanchard, K.H. (1977). *Management of organizational behav-*

ior (3rd ed.). Englewood Cliffs, N.J.: Prentice-Hall.

Homans, G. C. (1950). *The human group.* New York: Harcourt, Brace, & World.

Hopcke, R. H. (1989). *A guided tour of the collected works of C. G. Jung.* Boston, MA: Shambhala Publications, Inc.

Johnson, A. G. (1985). *The Blackwell dictionary of sociology: A user's guide to sociological language.* Cambridge, MA: Blackwell.

Johnson, D. W., & Johnson, F. P. (1987). *Joining together: Group theory and group skills* (3rd ed.). Englewood Cliffs, NJ: Prentice-Hall.

Johnson, D. W., & Johnson, F. P. (1997*). Joining together: Group theory and group skills* (6th ed.). Needham Heights, MA: Allyn & Bacon.

Johnson, D. W., & Johnson, F. P. (2000). *Joining together: Group theory and group skills* (7th ed.). Needham Heights, MA: Allyn & Bacon.

Jung, C. G. (1921, 1960). *Psychological types.* Princeton, NJ: Princeton University Press.

Katzenbach, J., & Smith, D. (1993). *The wisdom of teams.* Cambridge, MA: Harvard Business School Press.

Knowles, M., & Knowles, H. (1959). *Introduction on group dynamics.* New York: Association Press.

Kohlberg, L. (1976). Moral stages and moralization: The cognitive-developmental approach. In T. Lickona (Ed.), *Moral development and behavior: Theory, research, and social issues* (pp. 31–53). New York: Holt, Rinehart, and Winston.

Komives, S. R., Lucas, N., & McMahon, T .R. (1998). *Exploring leadership: For college students who want to make a difference.* San Francisco: Jossey-Bass.

Kormanski, C. (1999). *The team: Explorations in group process.* Denver: Love Publishing Company.

Kottler, J. A. (2001). *Learning group leadership: An experiential approach.* Needham Heights, MA: Allyn & Bacon.

Kottler, J. A., & Parr, J. (2001). Stages of development. In J. A. Kottler (Ed.), *Learning group leadership: An experiential approach* (pp. 51–63). Needham Heights, MA: Allyn & Bacon.

Kouzes, J. M., & Posner, B. Z. (1995). *The leadership challenge: How to keep getting extraordinary things done in organizations.* San Francisco: Jossey-Bass.

Kuh, G. (1991). Snapshots of campus community. *Educational Record, 72,* 40–44.

Kuypers, B. C., Davies, D., & Hazewinkel, A. (1986). Developmental patterns in self-analytic groups. *Human Relations, 39* (9), 793–815.

La Coursiere, R. (1980). *The life-cycle of groups: Group development and stage theory.* New York: Human Sciences.

Lewin, K. (1951). *Field theory in social science.* New York: Harper.

Lewin, K., Lippitt, R., & White, R. K. (1993). Patterns of aggressive behavior in experimentally created "social climates." *Journal of Social Psychology*, *10*, 271–299.

Lifton, W. (1967). *Working with groups: Group process and individual growth.* New York: John Wiley & Sons, Inc.

Maslow, A. H. (1954). *Motivation and personality.* New York: Harper.

Mattoon, M. A. (1981). *Jungian psychology in perspective.* New York: The Free Press.

McDonald, W. M., & Associates. (2002). *Creating campus community.* San Francisco: Jossey-Bass.

McGrath, J. E. (1984). *Groups: Interaction and performance.* Englewood Cliffs, NJ: Prentice Hall.

McGregor, D. (1960). *The human side of enterprise.* New York: McGraw-Hill.

Miller, J. (1994). The continuing search for community in higher education. *Vital Speeches*, 334–336.

Mills, T. M. (1984). *The sociology of small groups* (2nd ed.). Englewood Cliffs, NJ: Prentice-Hall.

Moos, R. H. (1979). *Evaluating educational environments.* San Francisco: Jossey-Bass.

Myers, I. B. (1980). *Gifts differing.* Palo Alto, CA: Consulting Psychologists Press.

Napier, R. W., & Gershenfeld, M. K. (2004). *Groups: Theory and practice.* Boston, MA: Houghton Mifflin Co.

Northhouse, P. G. (2001). *Leadership: Theory and practice* (2nd ed.). Thousand Oaks, CA: Sages Publications, Inc.

Peck, M. S. (1987). *The different drum: Community making and peace.* New York: Simon and Schuster.

Pfeiffer, W. J. (1994). *Groups and teams.* San Francisco: Jossey-Bass.

Porterfield, W. D., & Pressprich, S. T., (1988). Carol Gilligan's perspectives and staff supervision: Implications for the practitioner. *NASPA Journal*, *25*, 244–248.

Reilly, A. J., & Jones, J. E. (1974). Team-building. In J. W. Pfeiffer & J. E. Jones (Eds.). *The annual handbook of group facilitators* (pp. 227–237). San Diego, CA: University Associates.

Sampson, K. (1998). Group Development Concepts. In N. W. Dunkel & S.L. Spencer (Eds.), *Advice for advisers: The development of an effective resi-*

dence hall association. Columbus, OH: Association of College and University Housing Officers – International.

Schein, E. H. (1992). *Organizational culture and leadership* (2nd ed.). San Francisco: Jossey-Bass.

Schutz, W. (1958). *FIRO: Three dimensional theory of interpersonal behavior.* New York: Rinehart.

Schutz, W. (1982). *The Schutz measures.* San Diego: Pfeiffer & Co.

Schutz, W. (1992). Beyond FIRO-B. Three new theory-driven measures-Element B: behavior, Element F: feelings, Element S: self. *Psychological Reports, 70,* 915-937.

Shambaugh, P. (1978). The development of small groups. *Human Relations, 31,* 283–295.

Shaw, M. E. (1976). *Group dynamics: The psychology of small group behavior* (3rd ed.). New York: McGraw-Hill.

Sherif, M., & Sherif, C. (1964). *Reference groups: Exploration into conformity and deviation of adolescent.* New York: Harper & Row.

Steiner, I. D. (1976). Task-performing groups. In J. W. Thibaut, J. T. Spence, & R. C. Carson (Eds.), *Contemporary topics in social psychology.* (pp. 393–422). Morristown, NJ: General Learning Press.

Stewart, G. L., Manz, C.C., & Sims, H. R., Jr. (1999). *Team work and group dynamics.* New York, NY: John Wiley & Sons, Inc.

Stogdill, R. (1959). *Individual behavior and group achievements.* New York: Oxford University Press.

Strange, C. C., & Banning, J. H. (2001). *Educating by design.* San Francisco: Jossey-Bass.

Tuckman, B. (1965). Developmental sequence in small groups. *Psychological Bulletin, 63,* 384–399.

Tuckman, B. W., & Jensen, M. A. (1977). Stages of small group development revisited. *Group and Organizational Studies, 2,* 419–427.

Turner, J. C., (1985). Social categorization and the self concept: A social-cognitive theory of group behavior. *Advances in Group Processes, 2,* 77–122.

Vander Kolk, C. J. (1990). *Introduction to group counseling and psychotherapy.* Boston, MA: Merrill.

Von Franz, M. (1971). *Lectures on Jung's typology: The inferior function. Seminar series #4.* Dallas, TX: Spring Publications, Inc.

Wheelan, S. A. (1994). *Group processes: A developmental perspective.* Boston: Allyn & Bacon.

Wheelan, S. A., & Hochberger, J. M. (1996). Validation studies of the group development questionnaire. *Small Group Research, 27* (1), 143–170.

Williams, K. D., & Karau, S. J. (1991). Social loafing and social compensation: The effects of expectations of co-worker performance. *Journal of Personality and Social Psychology, 61*, 570–581.

Yalom, I. D. (1995). *The theory and practice of group psychotherapy* (4ᵗʰ ed.). New York: Basic Books.

Zajonc, R. B. (1965). Social facilitation. *Science, 149*, 269–274.

Discussion Scenarios

1. You have an excellent group of RHA executive officers who have served together for two years. Near the end of the fall semester, your treasurer realizes she will not be returning to school in the spring, and the RHA elects a new treasurer. What can be done to help the new treasurer gain acceptance with the RHA executive board group?

2. In the weekly RHA meetings, one member talks incessantly and has opinions on everything. How would you work with this student?

3. Your hall government council is comprised of one-half veterans and one-half new members. What can be done to facilitate the growth of the group?

4. You serve as adviser to Panhellenic Council. You have become aware that the council is split into two factions—the popular, large sororities and the smaller, less popular sororities. What can be done to build unity among all Panhellenic sororities?

5. You have an RHA group who loved their previous adviser. This adviser remains on campus in another capacity. Members keep going to her for advice and support. How would you handle this situation?

Case Studies

❖ Case Study 1

You recently accepted a new position in the Residence Life Department at Outstanding University. A limited part of your new job duties is to be the first professional staff adviser that the RHA has had in more than seven years. Over several tight budget years, the adviser position was the first to be eliminated. The department is now stable and needs your position for developing academic initiatives and student leadership. You are excited, but a bit nervous.

While on campus for your interview, you picked up a vibe that RHA executive officers and student-leaders perceive that the new adviser will be *theirs*.

You even overheard an RHA executive officer comment, "It is about time they paid some attention to us!" You made your decision to take this position primarily because of the other components of the job— developing academic initiatives and student leadership. However, you feel confident you can handle the adviser role because you worked closely with the hall government in your hall when you were a student leader and a resident assistant.

The semester is beginning. All of the RHA meetings have been scheduled. The first meeting occurs in two weeks. You contact the returning president to see when the first executive board meeting is scheduled. The president immediately takes offense and accuses you of trying to take over the presidential duties and the organization. "We don't need an executive board meeting to set an agenda because I do it all." She then proceeds to tell you what she expects from an adviser—a signature for expenditures, a rubber stamp for the things RHA wants to do, and someone who battles for the students against the administration. Her final expectation is that you are NOT the president of the organization. You are taken back by this outburst and realize you are faced with a challenge. How do your proceed?

Case Study Considerations

- Notify your supervisor of this development and set up an appointment to process this situation.
- Take this as an opportunity to step back and gain some insight into the culture of this organization and student leadership at Outstanding University. Quickly develop a short set of questions that you can casually ask both students and staff about RHA and its leadership.

  o How do students view the organization?
  o How does staff view the organization?
  o What is their purpose?
  o Do they have well-defined goals?
  o What do student-leaders in other organizations think about RHA?

- Your first mission is to understanding what would make this student react in this manner.
- Formulate a rough plan of action based on your interaction with the RHA president and your collection of insight. Then set up a meeting with your supervisor.
- During the meeting with your supervisor, report on the information gained from your data gathering. Clarify what your supervisor and the department expect from your position. Solicit their expertise in working through

conflict situations and process your thoughts for resolution.

- Consider a private meeting with the president to help allay any questions or insecurities this student may have. This meeting may be the opportune time to pass along the expectations the department has for your position and how that impacts RHA. What are RHA member expectations of your time? What are the realities of what they can expect from you?
- Broach the idea of an executive board meeting prior to the first RHA meeting again by explaining the benefits this type of meeting can have on the group—organization, same page work, goal setting, etc.

✤ Case Study 2

You advise a hall council as a part of your new position. One of their favorite end-of-the-semester traditions is hall bowling. Residents play this game by throwing frozen chickens down the hall. You have never seen this bowling, but because it is a tradition, you allow the group to participate in this ritual. After your initial experience, you realize you have made a mistake. The floor is mess and needs to be stripped and re-waxed. The event is a waste of food that could go to better use. You consider halting all future hall bowling events, but are conflicted. While hall bowling is a waste of time, money, and food and is a significant strain on housekeeping staff, it is also a long-standing tradition in the hall. Do you stop the event? If you do, how do you go about making this decision and this change? If you do not stop the event, do you take any action? How do you combat the "that's not that way so-and-so did it" or "our last adviser let us do it, why won't you" mentality?

Case Study Considerations

- Set an appointment to talk with your supervisor about this problem and your thoughts about a resolution.
- Before you meet with your supervisor, collect data about this event. Is it really a long-standing tradition, or something student-leaders told you to get you to go along with it?
- How much money was spent on these chickens and how much time and expense was expended by the housekeeping staff?
- If you decide to cancel this event, what are other ways the group can fulfill the social release of this nature?
- Is there a compromise? Can they continue this event, but pay for clean-up expenses?

- Remember that in most situations, there are options. Explore those options and then choose the best possible outcome.

Student Organization Workshop Using *The Dream Team* (1987)

Movie Synopsis

The Dream Team is a comedy that focuses on four individual mental institution patients: Billy, Henry, Jack, and Albert. Taken out of the institution to a baseball game by their doctor, Dr. Weitzman, an accident ensues when the doctor witnesses a murder and gets beaten up. Soon the four patients find themselves framed for murder and on their own in New York City. To survive, they must go from being four misfits to becoming a working group.

Learning Outcomes

This movie can be used in training to achieve the following goals: 1) to train students on the stages of group of development; 2) to allow students the opportunity to discuss being members of a group, their roles, and have them reflect on their experiences as group members; and 3) to educate students on being capable of working with and communicating concepts related to group dynamics.

Workshop Issues

This movie is perfect for teaching student organizations about the evolution of groups. Members can be placed into small groups for detailed discussion and sharing with the larger group. To incorporate this movie into a training activity, the facilitator needs the following: a copy of the movie; markers and newsprint; and discussion/process questions. The room should be structured with tables and moveable chairs.

Techniques Used

This movie, 113 minutes in length, can be used with half and full day workshops. It is perfect to use on organizational retreats, where the movie can be used for facilitating extensive discussion. Larger groups should be broken down into smaller groups for discussion. In utilizing the movie, two options are applicable. The entire movie can be shown uninterrupted with discussion following the film. This approach works well with a full-day retreat. However, if the workshop has time constraints, pre-selected clips of the movie can by used to illustrate key points.

Regardless of the method used, it might be useful to spend a few minutes talking to participants about group concepts and group dynamics, particularly the evolution of groups and group roles. It is recommended that facilitators use Tuckman's model of forming, storming, norming, performing, and adjourning to frame the workshop. It is helpful to provide workshop participants with process questions before viewing the movie. Distributing questions prior to the movie/clips allows students to view the movie/clips with both educational and entertainment lenses. Once the movie/clips end, small groups can be utilized to determine what stages of development the movie/clips illustrate. Facilitators should spend as much time as they see fit with this discussion. Key to effective discussion is helping participants relate the concepts to thire groups.

Process Questions

1. Identify at least two examples of each of Tuckman's stages of group development from the movie.
2. In what stage of development is our organization currently operating? What evidence exists that we operate in that stage of development?
3. What can group members do to facilitate our group's further development?
4. What do you expect of your adviser as a leader? Do those expectations change at differing stages of development?

12

The Money Management of Residence Hall Associations

Mark Hudson, Jody Stone & Donna Turner-Hudson

Few find money management to be the most exciting part of advising student organizations. It is, however, important not only for the viability of the organization, but because it offers students valuable lessons in ethics, integrity, and practical money management skills.

For many advisers, the main motivation for effectively handling financial management is a desire to avoid the potential for problems if funds are mishandled. Today, institutions expect high degrees of accountability from all student organizations. Advisers need to be skilled, knowledgeable, and vigilant in the tasks of managing money. Despite the challenges, however, advising offers real-life opportunities to help students put organizational values into practice and gain valuable life skills.

When looking at issues such as developing budgets, using technology, identifying funding sources, tracking funds, and more, a valuable tool is the information gleaned through a Fall 2004 national survey of 33 RHAs that represent both public and private institutions. Information on surveys conducted for previously published chapters on this topic can be found in the first and second editions of *Advice for Advisers* (Hudson & Hudson, 1993; Hudson, Hudson & Tattershall, 1998).

Role of Advisers

In the 1980s it was not unusual to find upper-level housing officers attending conferences with RHA representatives. Today the trend is toward professionals with limited experience, such as hall directors or graduate students, serving as RHA delegation advisers. Perhaps there are more senior members of management teams working with groups on home campuses. If not, those new to advising RHA groups may face significant challenges. Over the years, the role of advising has not diminished in scope or importance. In fact, in most cases institutions expect more. An added challenge for RHAs with less experienced advisers may be more frequent turnover in the adviser position. Careful transitioning between outgoing and incoming advisers is critical.

The method by which advisers assist students with managing the financial aspects of organizations is similar in tone and philosophy to the way advisers perform other duties for organizations. Advisers may operate in different ways regarding organization finances. Some serve as *de facto* accountants for organizations, assuming responsibility for alerting the officers to any potential problems and offering well-informed solutions when problems arise. Others believe it is best to play the role of observer, offering timely questions for consideration but generally allowing students to make decisions.

The adviser role may change from one year to the next, as do students and their needs. Depending on the maturity level or organizational experience of groups, advisers may be more or less active in contributing input, making suggestions, or providing reality checks.

How advisers choose to serve may depend on several other factors such as the expectations that institutions have of student organization advisers. Intertwined with institutional expectations is the degree of personal liability to which advisers may be held. As pointed out by Schuh (1998):

> . . . it is important to emphasize that the adviser may very well have a fiduciary responsibility for handling funds, including overseeing the development of a budget and handling funds (Maloney, 1988). Depending on an institution's arrangement for managing student funds, this responsibility could extend to making sure that (a) funds are handled (i.e. deposited and expended) in ways consistent with institutional policies and state law, (b) all funds can be accounted for by an external audit, and most importantly, (c) the trust of the members of the organization is sustained (pp. 126–127).

Effective advisers realize that handling money is a serious responsibility. If advisers co-sign purchase requests or other authorizations to expend funds, they need to be certain that expenditures are consistent with institutional requirements. Simply turning organization funds over to student treasurers and assuming that everything will be fine is myopic at best and, at worst, may subject advisers to legal action. If advisers have limited or no experience working with students who manage organizational accounts, it is advisable to have orientation sessions with institution purchasing agents and comptrollers or their representatives.

Advisers are placed in pivotal roles with respect to organization financial accountability. If problems occur, institutional administrators will turn to advisers for answers regarding financial procedures and rationale for systems in use. Similarly, students will turn to advisers for help and guidance in sorting out and finding remedies for whatever problems may occur.

Many advisers view the financial aspect of the advising position as a necessary evil and consider it less essential to leadership development. However, the adviser's role in assisting with the financial management of RHAs may have an impact on students which lasts beyond the college years. Many students gain initial experiences in managing money through involvement with RHA finances. Advisers who utilize sound financial principles can serve as excellent role models for students who are learning to manage their own money. Likewise, many students involved in organizations as undergraduates will go on to participate in professional or community organizations after graduation. Working with RHA finances can be an ideal training experience for young people who later become community leaders. Lessons gained through the practice of sound business principles and ethical management of organizational finances are some of the most valuable learning opportunities students will have as leaders.

Guiding Principles

Financial management requires a making many decisions. Effective RHA advisers use the financial management process as a teaching tool. Members of RHAs are faced with choices about how they will spend or manage organizational funds. Advisers should encourage them to consider how their decisions measure up to various standards. Basic principles of money management for organizations are found in RHA constitutions and bylaws. These documents offer clear pictures of organizational missions and purposes and serve as anchors for organizations, reminding students why organizations exist and what they offer to campus communities. Advisers should encourage students to use constitutional purpose statements as standards against which proposed financial decisions can be measured. Advisers may also find it useful to use purpose statements as discussion openers that can lead groups through exploration of organizational values and ethics. For example, it is not unusual for RHAs to be approached for contributions by charitable organizations. RHAs may want to discuss this issue before it arises and establish bylaws that outline the organization position on such requests. Failure to set pre-established bylaws makes it very difficult for RHAs to respond to such requests without getting caught up in the emotions that may surround given causes.

Other tools also aid in discussions of organizational ethics. For example, the University of North Carolina-Charlotte offers the 2004-2005 Student Organizations Handbook online, which includes *Put Your Ethics to the Test: Ten Simple Rules to Help You Make Ethical Decisions Day to Day* (Student Organizations Handbook, 2004 – 05, p. 45). Among these rules is "The 'six o'clock news' rule. I will do this knowing that I can go live on the six o'clock news and defend it" and the 'alter ego' rule. When in doubt, I need to discuss this dilemma with someone whose doubts, questions, standards, and perspectives will help me to clarify my own." Advisers can encourage students to develop their own code of ethics, which can serve as guides to financial practices.

Developing Budgets

Budgets can be viewed as blueprints for RHAs. As such, they should reflect the goals and purposes of organizations. RHA members should understand budgets and have the responsibility to adopt and modify them as needed. Any changes to budget documents must meet with the approval of RHA memberships. It is the responsibility of treasurers to keep budgets accurate and up-to-date and make frequent reports to the organization so that members have the confidence to spend funds wisely.

Budgeting organizational funds may be a new experience for many university students. Working budgets can be tangible tools to help students grasp important concepts of fiscal responsibility. Advisers play critical roles in overseeing the budgeting process and working with the organization treasurers and other officers to ensure that the process is handled carefully and that RHAs do not inadvertently overspend funds or underutilize resources.

The most commonly used and simplest budget format is the line item budget. This type of budget reflects all income and expenses through the use of descriptive lines for income and expense items and columns indicating amounts budgeted and spent. For example, the office supply line item would reflect any expenses for pencils, paper, staplers and the like. The amount spent would be recorded on that line next to the budgeted amount, making it easy

Sample Line Item Budget

Residence Hall Association
2005-06 Annual Budget – As of September 25, 2005

	Budgeted Amount	To Date Total	Amount Remaining	Percent Remaining
INCOME:				
Fundraising (Fall)				
Fundraising (Spring)				
Sale of Activity Cards (Fall)				
Sale of Activity Cards (Spring)				
Fee Allocation-Fall				
Fee Allocation-Spring				
TOTAL INCOME				
EXPENSES:				
Telephone Line Charges				
Long Distance Charges				
Office Supplies				
Postage				
Printing				
Capitol Equipment (New Computer)				
Leadership Development				
Fall Retreat				
Spring Retreat				
GLACURH				
Registration				
Transportation				
Duplication of Bids				
Display Materials				
Spirit Items/T-Shirts				
NACURH				
Registration				
Transportation				
Duplication of Bids				
Display Materials				
Spirit Items/T-Shirts				
Programming				
Homecoming				
Haunted House				
Little Siblings Weekend				
RHA Week				
Contingency Fund (5% of income)				
Bad Debt (2% of income)				
TOTAL EXPENSES				
INCOME - EXPENSES				

to determine whether or not expenses are in line with amounts budgeted (see sample line item budget).

When using line item budgets, there are two methods organizations typically use to track expenses and income. One method is incremental budgeting. The amount spent in each line item the previous year serves as a base to which a percentage is added that reflects whatever increases may be necessary. The other method frequently used is zero-based budgeting. Zero-based budgeting requires that the budget developer project expenses based on an actual estimate of what will be spent.

Student organizations often use a combination of incremental and zero-based methods. For example, it may make sense to use incremental budgeting for line items that may vary only slightly from year to year, such as office supplies. However, if organizations take trips to regional conferences held at different sites each year, students would use zero-based budgeting, figuring the mileage to and from destinations and developing transportation line item amounts by calculating the cost of travel expenses per mile.

Uses of Technology for Budgeting

Responses to the Fall 2004 survey indicate that 85% of RHAs use computer programs for developing, tracking, and presenting budgets. It also shows that 15% use paper-only processes such as bank statements for tracking expenses. Of the 85% using software, 65% report using spreadsheet programs such as Microsoft Excel; 12% utilize reports generated by their institutions; 9% use the Quicken program; and 3% use online banking accounting systems. The majority of survey respondents indicate that it is important to develop budgets in formats that are easily understood by members of organizations.

Sources of Funding

One of the most important aspects of managing funds is the initial acquisition of the money. A generalization drawn from RHA advisers responding to the survey is that RHAs with stable bases of funding are consistently successful organizations. One indication of stability is the numbers of dollars organizations have to work with annually. About one-third of survey respondents report annual budgets of $20,000 or less; one-third report budgets of $20,000–$30,000; and one-third report budgets of $30,000–$100,000 annually. All survey respondents indicating that their RHA overall performance could be characterized as "struggling" report annual budgets of $5,000 or less.

Diversity in Funding Sources

Many institutions responding to the survey recognize the wisdom of obtaining funds from diverse sources. Some RHAs combine required fees with monies collected from the sale of services, programs and/or activity cards.

Many RHAs recognize that relying on single resources for all funds can be financially dangerous, depending on the year-to-year stability of the resource. This is particularly true if the sole (or substantial) source of funds is another organization. For example, on some campuses, RHA funds are obtained through the annual allocation process of the institution's student government. Unfortunately, the campus political climate can adversely affect the process and outcome.

Of RHA advisers responding to the survey, 75% report that their organizations also receive in-kind assistance from their housing departments. Typical examples included long distance telephone support, computer and technical support, postage, travel expenses, copying, and office supplies.

Optional Fees or Mandatory Fees

Four out of five survey respondents report that residential students at their institutions are required to pay fees to support the activities and programs of the RHA. (See Table 1.) Alternatively, or in addition to mandatory fees, many institutions rely heavily on predictable revenues generated from service programs. The top four programs reported by survey respondents are sales of welcome or final exam care packages, bed linen sales, loft sales or rentals, and vending proceeds.

Survey respondents reporting less consistent success in meeting organizational goals are those whose income is derived predominantly from optional sources, such as from the sale of activity cards or from collecting or charging fees for events or services in which students may or may not choose to participate.

According to the survey, many advisers advocate the establishment of required RHA fees for the following reasons:

- Required fees can be viewed as endorsements of the value of RHAs by institutions. Because institutions (not student organizations) require that students pay fees, they are not likely to be charged unless institution administrators have faith in student organizations and are committed to maintaining the financial viability of the organizations.
- Having required fees means that organizations are able to budget from year-to-year and project expected funds. This allows organizations to develop and execute programming each year that meets standards of quality that

students can expect. If financial resources vary greatly from year-to-year, maintaining consistent levels of quality programming may not be possible. Having dependable funding sources means that time can be spent on developing services and programs which benefit students (and leaders) rather than on fundraising.

- Despite the advantages of required fees, many RHAs use optional funding systems for a variety of reasons.
- RHAs may not have the option to charge mandatory fees if, for whatever reason, institutions are not supportive of requiring students to pay the fees.
- Optional fees can keep RHAs mindful of accountability to constituents, the students. Residents are likely to choose whether or not they wish to pay fees based on the value they place on services provided by RHAs.
- Because optional fee-charging processes are likely to be localized in nature as opposed to being managed through institutional financial systems, having optional fees may make it easier for RHAs to increase the amount of fees charged from year-to-year as needed rather than if fees were charged by institutions.

Tracking Funds

Accounting for RHA funds in a responsible manner is an important part of the learning process and critical to the success of organizations.

Where Funds are Kept

Looking at the survey, 80% of RHA advisers report that their organizations keep all funds on campus. For many who charge mandatory fees, the use of campus accounts is not a choice of organizations but rather an institutional requirement. Many advisers appreciate the security of institutional accounts and procedures despite the perception that following college or university regulations is often a cumbersome process.

Some RHAs (6% of those responding to the survey) keep all funds in off-campus checking accounts, while another 12% use some combination of off-campus and campus accounts. RHAs using off-campus accounts tend to prefer the ease with which expenditures can be made when there are fewer institutional hoops to jump through. Organizations preferring to keep funds off-campus should consult institution business offices as to whether funds derived from mandatory fees can be kept off-campus, or if only those funds derived from optional sources can be kept in off campus accounts.

Although many institutions require RHAs to keep funds in university accounts, keeping funds in off-campus accounts may put less strain on institutional financial resources. At some institutions, the number of financial trans-actions conducted through campus accounts by RHAs has made it necessary for additional accounts personnel to be hired by the university. Sometimes this expense is charged back to RHAs.

If organizations choose to keep funds in off-campus accounts, members of RHAs, not institutions, are responsible for implementing and maintaining sound business principles. An advantage to this scenario may be that students can benefit from the experience of developing and enforcing their own regula-tions, which can be tailored to fit the organization's particular needs.

Although rules and policies may vary from one institution to another, the following are examples of the steps that may need to be taken when RHAs keep funds in off-campus accounts:

- Organizations may be required by the bank to apply for Federal Employer Identification Numbers. (This is not the same as a tax-exempt status num-ber.)
- Two signatures, one of whom should be the adviser's, should be required on all checks written from organization accounts so that no single indi-vidual can inappropriately withdraw funds.
- Although RHAs keeping accounts off campus may not be able to rely on the services of their institution's auditors, off-campus accounts are not necessarily immune from institutional auditing review.

A number of institutions have experienced problems with off-campus organi-zations that have no institutional affiliation using the institutional name to infer that their enterprise is part of the institution. As a result, some RHAs report that institutional auditors require student organizations who keep their funds off campus to take steps to clarify that they are not institutional entities. Insti-tutions may make this requirement because off-campus funds and financial practices are not subject to institutional control. If RHAs are required to oper-ate as non-institutional entities, they may not be allowed to use institutional letterhead or mailings when fundraising and may be required to collect fees in the name of RHAs and not in the name of institutions. Also, institutional employees may not be allowed to participate in the actual collection of fees.

Good Business Practices

Regardless of where funds are kept, good business practices are recommended to keep organizations out of legal difficulties and to ensure that funds are man-aged responsibly and ethically. Organizations should work with institutional internal auditing departments to develop guidelines for tracking income and expenditures.

Budgeting and Approval of Expenditures

Budgets should be developed and voted on by organizations. (See sample budget.) Treasurers and advisers must make sure that every dollar spent has proper authorization. Thorough and consistent documentation should be in place to show that fund expenditures have been approved in the meeting minutes. Therefore, copies of all minutes with highlighted budget expenditures sections should be kept with all financial records. If broad authorization is given for expenditures after budgets have been approved, the minutes should reflect that fact.

Tracking Income

Money to be deposited, such as from events, should always be counted by two people, one of whom should be the adviser. Counting should be done immediately upon the close of the event; the amount verified by these individuals; and the money placed in a secure location. Money must be deposited as soon as possible, which should never be later than the next business day.

Standardized forms should be used for depositing funds in organization accounts. (See Appendix 1.) These forms should indicate the date and amount of each deposit and where the funds came from. Bank deposit slips should be attached to these forms. Deposit records should indicate how much of the deposit was from cash and how much was from checks.

When money is being collected from individuals, RHAs should provide receipts that indicate time, place, location, and for what purpose the money was collected.

Tracking Expenditures

There are two methods used by most RHAs in making expenditures from organizational accounts. One method involves expending funds directly from the account. Before such expenditures are made, the individual planning to spend the funds should complete a spending authorization form. (See Appendix 2.) Spending authorization forms should indicate all information pertaining to how, where and why the funds are to be spent and should bear two authorized signatures, one of whom should be the adviser's. Some RHAs using campus accounts utilize an institutional credit or purchasing card. Some RHA advisers report that, for accountability reasons, the advisers are required by the institution to accompany organization members in making and signing for purchases when using such cards.

The other method used by RHAs involves reimbursement to organization members for purchases already made on behalf of the organization. Spending authorization forms should be used. (See Appendix 2.) Receipts that show the time, date, and location of purchases should be attached to the reimbursement forms.

Organizations should not reimburse individuals or permit individuals to spend organization funds if receipts are not provided and proper authorization has not been received. Personal purchases made when spending organization funds must be kept separate from organizational purchases.

Auditing/Accountability

Of survey respondents, 70% indicate that their accounts are routinely audited while 36% report that the audit is by institutional auditors, while the remainder indicates that the audit is done by mid- or upper-level housing administrators. Ongoing self-regulation or auditing should be completed and documented, preferably each semester. Financial statements should be used on a monthly basis to ensure all funds are accounted for and are properly recorded. Ramifications should be in place for those individuals who do not comply with organizational fund regulations.

Advisers must ensure that organizations are operating according to good business practices. The Massachusetts Institute of Technology maintains a website (www.web.mit.edu/slp/finances/gbp) offering helpful advice on business practices for student organizations.

RHAs and Taxes

Advisers may be unaware of whether or not their organizations are exempt from paying taxes. It is in the best interest of RHAs to investigate institutional stance with respect to taxes and student organizations. Some institutions choose to distinguish between the financial activities of the institution and those of student organizations. As noted by Tattershall (Hudson, Hudson & Tattershall, 1998):

> Some institutions have made the case that they merely hold the money of student groups in campus accounts but have no control or responsibility for the activity of the student group or its finances. The principal effect of this stance is that the IRS may determine that the financial activities of student groups, specifically RHAs, are not covered under the institution's federal identification number [what is meant is tax exempt status]. Thus,

the university may rightfully claim to be exempt from various federal, state, and local taxes, but student groups may not (p. 138).

Tattershall further advises that each RHA should ascertain whether or not it is eligible to use its institution's tax exempt status. If so, it should keep abreast of any regulatory or policy changes that could alter the RHA's relationship with the institution. If RHA advisers discover that organizations are not eligible to use institutional tax-exempt status, the advice of a local accountant should be sought to determine whether RHAs owe back taxes. As an example, 90% of organizations responding to the survey report they are covered by institutional tax-exempt status.

Another tax-related issue for some RHAs relates to the use of off-campus accounts. A few institutions (five out of 33) report that RHAs keep some funds in interest bearing accounts located in off-campus banks. Some cite using the interest to provide for scholarships. Large amounts of interest income may catch the eye of the Internal Revenue Service. If RHAs are not paying taxes on this income, organizations must make sure they are covered by the institutional tax-exempt status. If RHAs are not covered but wish to continue to generate income in this way, mechanisms must be developed for paying taxes. Given the relatively small return on that type of investment, it may not be worth continuing the practice. Being caught not paying taxes may result in RHAs having to pay back taxes and penalties that could have major impacts on the organizational financial health.

Many RHAs are able to use alumni associations or development offices for scholarship development purposes. This arrangement offers the security of campus accounts and avoids the tax risk. An additional advantage is the enhanced investment potential, as organization funds are pooled with the larger institutional investment portfolio.

Planning for the Unexpected

Good financial management includes planning for unexpected situations in which the organization's finances take a sudden down turn. For example, an RHA plans a large-scale event that is very costly, expecting to make up the expended dollars in ticket sales. But despite careful planning and flawless preparation, the event is a bust and much money is lost.

On some campuses, housing organizations or institutions assume responsibility for underwriting RHAs. It is a good idea to investigate if an institution is prepared to accept responsibility—and to what extent—before the need arises.

If the institution is not willing or able to assist the RHA in time of need, it is best to set up a contingency fund. More than half of the RHAs surveyed report having contingency plans in place.

How much money should be in a contingency fund? This depends, somewhat, on the availability of funds that could be acquired outside the organization to cover losses in time of need. It may be helpful for RHAs to consider setting aside contingency funds that range between five and 25% of the total budget. The percentage is determined by considering the amount of financially risky activities an organization carries out. The amount of necessary contingency should be an item figured into the development of the annual budget. The obvious question is: Would the contingency amount be sufficient to cover the losses of the RHA if a major event completely fails?

Some organizations set aside a fund and let the fund roll over to the next year's budget; however, many feel it is important to spend all the money to the benefit of those who have provided it each year. In this case, the organization could certainly plan a special end-of-the-year event to utilize the unused contingency funds. This would be a great way to recognize the fiscal responsibility that allowed those funds to remain in the account.

More often than not, organizations react to unexpected losses by significantly restructuring their budgets. This is not an inappropriate process but it may result in the inability to fulfill some goals. If a major loss happens near the end of the year, restructuring may not be an option and a contingency fund may be the only way to cover the loss.

Unfortunately, many RHA treasurers and advisers have been taken by surprise near the end of the semester by discovering that smaller account balances exist than had been assumed. It is always wise to check account balances periodically and to double check the organizational records against those that are kept by institution accounting offices or at local banks. Discovering early that less money exists than had been assumed can allow RHAs to reevaluate upcoming activities and reduce the expected outlay of resources.

What About Bad Debt?

Bad debt is incurred when organizations deposit checks as payment for service, but the banks deny checks due to insufficient funds. When checks are returned, that income is lost and the amount must be deducted from organization assets. Organizations are most at risk of this occurrence if they collect fees annually or each semester from individual students and checks are returned for insufficient funds. Organizations may still have opportunities to collect fees from residents if check problems are discovered fairly quickly. However, when institutions collect the fees as part of room and board costs, bad debt is not always realized in a timely fashion, though some part may be recovered if institutions utilize the services of debt collectors

Institutional policies vary, but often institutions do not write off accounts receivable bills for over a year. In the past, many institutions were able to absorb this type of bad debt; however, during this era of shrinking budgets, more of it is getting charged back to organizations. Setting aside small amounts equivalent to the projected amounts of bad debt that institutions typically incur is prudent. For example, if an RHA's budget is $10,000 and the institutional estimate of bad debt is 2%, the RHA should set aside 2%, or $200, for a bad debt fund. This amount should roll over from year-to-year because in all likelihood, bad debt will not be realized in the same year in which it is incurred.

Conclusion

The ability to manage money in a responsible way is not only essential to the life of organizations, but it can provide opportunities for student leaders to build valuable lifelong skills. Acquiring funds through stable sources is essential to successful RHAs. Requiring residence hall students to pay fees to support the activities of RHAs is one way to ensure stable funding. Additionally, the experience of many advisers is that diversity in income sources is the best insurance of stability of funding.

In the development of processes for tracking and expending funds, accountability should be a major goal. It is helpful for advisers to review these processes periodically to make sure they are compatible with current student needs and institutional agendas.

Planning for the unexpected is an important key to financial security. Decisions on how best to do this should be made in consultation with the institution. Managing funds well is an important function within the life of RHAs because it allows organizations to concentrate on the activities that are most important to residence hall students. Putting in sufficient time up front in developing and monitoring processes will ensure that very little time needs to be spent later in managing problems.

References

Hudson, M., Hudson, D.T. (1993). The money management of residence hall associations. In N.W. Dunkel & C.L. Spencer (Eds.), *Advice for Advisers:*

The development of an effective residence hall association (pp. 122–132). Columbus, OH: Association of College and University Housing Officers – International.

Hudson, M., Hudson, D.T., Tattershall, B. (1998). The money management of residence hall associations. In N.W. Dunkel & C.L. Spencer (Eds.), *Advice for Advisers: The development of an effective residence hall association* (pp. 134–143). Columbus, OH: Association of College and University Housing Officers – International.

Schuh, J.H. (1998). *Legal issues*. In N.W. Dunkel & C.L. Spencer (Eds.), *Advice for Advisers: The development of an effective residence hall association* (pp. 120–132). Columbus, OH: Association of College and University Housing Officers – International.

Student Activities Finance Office Handbook (2004), Massachusetts Institute of Technology. *Student activities recommendations for good business practices*. Retrieved December 12, 2004 from http://web.mit.edu/slp/finances/gbp

Student Organizations Handbook (2004–05), University of North Carolina – Charlotte. *Put your ethics to the test, ten simple rules to help you make ethical decisions day to day* (pg. 45). Retrieved December 12, 2004 from http://studentorgs.uncc.edu

Case Studies

✤ Case Study 1

Some students at the University of ABC do not believe they should have to support the RHA through their housing fees. Some have complained to RHA officers about the mandatory fee and say they are unclear as to what benefits they receive in return for the fee. How can the RHA respond to these complaints? What might be the consequences of moving from a mandatory to an optional RHA fee?

✤ Case Study 2

An RHA member comes to a meeting with information from a local bank offering an interest rate on checking accounts that is better than all others in the community. She has checked into the institution's policy for student organizations and has learned that while the institution recommends that funds be kept on campus, organizations are not required to do so. She encourages members of the RHA to vote for removing funds from the institutional account and putting them in the local bank. What should be taken into consideration before this decision is made?

❖ Case Study 3

The RHA has approved a budget that includes funds for an event. The chairperson of the event committee submits several receipts with a request for reimbursement for large expenditures related to the event. Prior to making the expenditures, he did not receive authorization from the RHA to spend the funds. The organization's bylaws make no mention of required pre-authorization before funds can be spent. How should the RHA members respond to the requests for reimbursement?

❖ Case Study 4

The campus-wide student government wants to sponsor an all-campus dance with a popular regional band. The band is expensive, and the student government asks the RHA to share in one-half the cost and to co-sponsor the event. The amount requested would be one-half of the RHA's annual budget. There is some potential for return on ticket sales, but there is no guarantee the RHA would recoup what it has spent. What points should be taken into consideration before responding to this request?

Table 1: Institutional Comparison of Required Fees

	Large Public	Large Private	Small Public	Small Private
Hall Capacity	>1,500	>1,500	<1,500	<1,500
# of Institutions	23	4	3	3
Average Required Fee	$8.50	$9.75	$12.50	$9.00
Range of Required Fee	$1–$39	$4–$16	$1.50–$30	$8–$10

Appendix 1

RHA DEPOSIT REPORT

Source of Revenue: _____

Total Cash: _____ Total Checks: _____ Total Deposit: _____

Total Counted & Verified by: _____ & _____

Account Deposited to:_____ Date Deposited: _____

Attach Deposit Slip to this form and Return to RHA Treasurer for recording.

Appendix 2

RHA SPENDING AUTHORIZATION FORM

Person Requesting Check_____ Date of Request_____

Pay to the Order of:_____

Reason for Request: _____

Amount of Check: _____ Check Number: _____

RHA Treasurer Approval: _____ Date: _____

RHA Adviser Approval: _____ Date: _____

Budget Line: _____ Date Check Cut: _____

Receipts must be attached to this form and returned to RHA Treasurer for processing.

13

Corporate Fundraising

Howie Dumhart

The types of fundraising companies available to the college marketplace are always changing. Still, the basics of residence hall associations (RHAs) and their relationships with fundraising companies has remained constant. RHAs have fiduciary responsibility to provide quality services while protecting the educational and personal environment of students they represent. Meanwhile, the corporations recognize the valuable assets contained within college campuses, primarily the traditional student body and their shopping dollars. Marketers are continually developing programs that enhance the educational and overall experience of college students while creating streams of revenue for company stockholders.

In addition to the changing face of corporate America, many higher education institutions have changed as well. Many institutions now impose service fees or charges in addition to room and board. In some cases, these fees or charges are funneled to RHAs or other student groups to provide budgets for programming efforts. Advisers of groups with funding sources from fees or charges are fortunate and should be mindful of the responsibility to spend monies wisely to benefit all students. For advisers at institutions with less developed programs or where imposing service fees or additional charges is not permitted, working with fundraising companies can be of utmost importance to the development of RHAs. Whether institutions provide RHAs with generous budgets or not, finding ways to work with fundraising companies that provide services for the college marketplace can benefit RHAs and the students they represent.

First and foremost, it should be hoped that the fundraising companies provide services beneficial to students. In addition, it should be hoped that the generated revenues will provide additional educational opportunities for student leaders. It is the responsibility of advisers to guide students through this educational process.

Students must understand what products and services are available, learn how to develop bids, and manage contracts with vendors.

Types of Products and Services

If products or services have mass appeal, and there is an economy of scale, then companies will be available to provide them. Fundraising opportunities exist at many levels on campuses. Intuitive student groups will reap the benefits. Examples of some services include:

- Linens for extra long beds.
- Refrigerator and microwave rentals, or combination type rental products.
- Carpets for residence hall rooms.
- Special fire extinguishers for residence hall rooms that don't use water but are highly effective at putting out small fires.
- Specific needs products like dehumidifiers and air cleaners for residence hall rooms available through local companies.
- Necessities for residence hall rooms available in flea market environments during move-in.
- Welcome to campus kits.
- Working with local or national cellular companies to provide cell phone programs with special benefits to campus and calling areas.
- Discount cards from local businesses that students can use on and/or off campus.
- Contracted laundry service for dry cleaning and regular laundry.
- Wearable clothing that is specific to institutions like "The Dawg Pound" t-shirts for sporting events or t-shirts to highlight a specific event on campus like "I was there for the Sesquicentennial."
- Newspaper sales or readership programs.
- Care packages for final exams.
- Traditional candy sales.
- Holiday packages, flowers or gift for specialty times of the year that have mass student appeal such as Halloween packages, artificial wreaths for door decorations (within fire regulations), birthday surprises, Valentine's Day flowers or candy.

- Flowers for graduation or other gifts.
- Diploma displays for graduating seniors.

The best way to add to the list is to conduct surveys to determine student needs on specific campuses. Attending regional and national conference that offer vendor display areas will afford advisers opportunities to see the latest products and services offered to the college market. Taking the time to read trade magazines or marketing materials sent by companies can keep advisers abreast of what is new and current. Most importantly interacting with colleagues regionally and nationally to find out what is working on their campuses helps advisers learn about what might work on their campuses.

No list of products or services is ever complete or inclusive. There are always new ideas being developed, tested and marketed. The list above highlights the common products and services available in the market today and helps to stimulate ideas about other money generating products and services for student groups.

Contemporary Use of Corporations

Students and educational institutions often feel that they can "do it themselves." This theme is slowly eroding, and more outside consultants or contractors are being hired to provide servies. Examples of outside consultants or contractors on college campuses include, but are not limited to, food services, laundry services, phone services, refrigerator rental services, bookstores, and entertainment services.

These outside corporations can provide valuable resources to support RHA budgets toward successful programs. The question is how RHAs can choose the best corporation as a partner. Vendors constantly develop and offer new products and services to college students. Filtering through this bombardment of services can be time consuming to advisers. The challenge is greater as today's students are sophisticated consumers. They have been marketed to their entire lives and have developed keen senses of recognizing and understanding hype. Even with knowing when they are being marketed to, they are anxious to consume new goods and services. New technology, trends in all types of products, and a constantly changing world feed the thirst for more new technology and services from this generation of students. New products and services can enhance the educational experience of students. However, change for change only, and "things" without purpose and direction will ultimately create environments that are unhealthy and unsupportable. Advisers must assist RHAs in filtering through new products, fads or potential needs.

How to Identify Companies

Several key elements determine if companies have the best interest of institutions, students, and RHAs in mind as they offer products or services to university communities. These elements are:

1. Are products or services necessary to support the educational experience of students? If not, allow students to find services on their own. Advisers are not expected to supply students with all that is needed to improve educational experiences.
2. Will the products or services provide benefits to students not visible at first glance? There are several products that are available through normal channels of distribution. However, when RHAs provide these services through fundraising efforts, they satisfy needs while creating revenue sources. Everyone wins. Providing products for all students many times drives the cost per item down and provides experiences that enhance the common good.
3. Does the company representative understand the essence of the college experience and RHA missions in providing products and services to students? If they are just salespeople attempting to sell products or services without demonstrating support of RHA missions, advisers should beware. Will they be around to support products or services for the long term, or are they just making commissions and moving on? Have they taken the time to do the research necessary to understand the campus, students, and the unique needs of campus residents as compared to the general college population?
4. Does the company understand the entire college experience and give back to the industry as a whole on local, regional, national, or even international levels? If the experience is self-serving without supporting overall higher education, then advisers need to be wary of the quality and integrity of the company. Obviously new or start-up companies have to make sales first before they can give back. The question to ask in that case is: How do they plan to share success as they move forward?
5. Can levels of trust and feelings of respect be established with company representatives and other members of the company with whom advisers and students will interact? This can be the most difficult aspect of the consumer-supplier relationship. Sales representatives are generally nice and trained to develop relationships. Through training in people skills and experience, effective advisers can develop levels of expertise to see through "the pitch" and successfully evaluate the integrity levels of sales representatives.

6. Is the company available when needed? The demands and responsibilities of advisers are numerous and varied. If companies are not flexible and able to meet specific needs or reasonable time demands, then advisers need to question whether to associate with them.

7. Are companies the best at what they do? Time, experience, resources, and commitment are the essence of companies that provide quality services or products. New companies can offer new perspectives; however, established companies with relationships developed over time should adapt and meet the evolving needs of consumers.

8. Are companies current? Even when not pushed by competition, does a company understand the changing market? Are they willing to change to be relevant to today's students?

9. Will the products or services add to the development of RHAs? Projects that take too much work with little return on investment will ultimately drain energy from groups. However programs or projects that require little work or effort on the part of RHAs might provide no value beyond money. A balance can be struck. Finding the right fundraising programs to execute for RHAs needs to include making as much money as possible while providing services that build image and strengthen organizations.

10. Do RHAs want their names associated with the company and its product and services? There are plenty of things students want that companies will sell. However, when projects are complete, will RHAs be proud of their association with that company and their products?

There are no easy answers to finding fundraising companies. Yet advisers who examine potential relationships through reviewing the ten points above will be on the right track to making good decisions and finding the best companies to meet goals.

How to Develop Bids

The first step in the bidding process is to seek expertise on campus through business offices to develop a request for proposal (RFP). However, advisers need to be cautious in allowing business offices to have too much influence on association RFPs and bids to avoid encumbering the flexibility of the group. For example, if a business office forces RHAs to partner with a company just because they were the lowest bidder, they might not necessarily be the best or most qualified company. Business offices on campuses generally have the best interest of students in mind. However their expertise is in creating specifications for specific goods and services common in the market. Most fundraising efforts are fairly unique and generally provide goods and services that are not common and might not be as familiar to the business officer.

If the product or service has been around for a while, standards have been established regarding the quality of the product and service provided. Advisers can create RFPs for desired products or services using established standards based on reasonable economics. It is not feasible to ask companies to provide luxury products at economical prices. However, if the specific quality of products and services is relayed, companies can develop bids that provide the best possible outcome to students.

RFPs need to be specific. Customization is more expensive than generic products. Using school logos on products specific to regions or universities increases costs to suppliers. Essential to the RFP process is seeking bids from companies that can provide the products or services and can meet expectations.

After the bids are developed, they should be reviewed by supervisors or department heads, campus counsel, and/or campus offices responsible for bids to make sure that the bids present no exposure issues for advisers, RHAs, or universities as a whole. Advisers need to monitor the progress of the bid review and not allow campus counsel or others to encumber the process. As agents of their universities, advisers must protect themselves and RHAs by completing this step in the bid review process.

From the viewpoint of companies, the bid development process rarely helps provide higher quality products or services. Many times it just makes everything more complicated for all involved. Advisers need to find quality companies that can be trusted then develop comfortable working relationships with them that ensure students receive the best that RHAs can give them. When products can be readily attained in the market place, the bid process ensures the best financial deal possible from suppliers within the specifications of the bid.

Considerations in Contracts and the Adviser Role

Advisers can be overwhelmed with the aspect of dealing with contracts, but almost every institution has a legal department to assist in the process. Advisers dealing with contracts should make sure the contracts are simple, straight forward, and understandable. If advisers do not understand contracts, they may need to seek more information about the company, products, or services. The contract process, although initially intimidating, is valuable experience for future positions within student development.

Before contracts are written, advisers should develop expectations of the products or services that companies will provide. This information can be developed into working documents that explain the responsibilities of each party and any exchange of monies. In fundraising efforts, RHAs should avoid putting money up front, if possible. Allow the company to bear the economic burden of the success of the program. However, contracts should clearly outline how RHAs will be remunerated for projects.

Advisers should check with supervisors to verify who has contract signature authority. Students should never sign contracts or any type of binding agreements. Advisers may be allowed to sign contracts or binding agreements with the approval of supervisors. Understanding the specifics of contractual relationships with companies is an adviser responsibility. Students generally don't have the experience or the legal right to bind groups or universities to agreements.

Advisers should make sure contracts protect RHAs and institutions as well as the students the services and products are being provided to. Everything should be clearly defined and laid out within contracts, and there should be no questionable areas. Simple contracts are better. Complicated contracts can mean hidden agendas. If advisers don't understand points within contracts, they can ask sales representatives to provide clarifications in writing. Advisers should only sign contracts that protect them and their RHAs. If there are any questions, advisers can request that the specifics of the contractual relationship be drawn up in plainer format then signed as the working agreement between parties. Contracts should be tools for success, not hindrances to processes.

A reality of working within college environments, especially state universities, is that most formal relationships will have to go out to bid. This does add a step to the process, and most advisers would like their RHAs and student leaders to make decisions about programs for students. But it should be recognized that campus business offices, or other offices vested with protecting the integrity of public funds or monies, are often part of the process. Advisers should rely on the professional expertise of business office staff to assist with the contract or bid process. But if RHAs are not going to be obligated to pay money for programs or services to companies, then advisers are encouraged to keep the arrangement as simple as possible. In these situations, it may not be prudent to involve business offices.

Experienced advisers request references from universities that have worked with companies previously and call colleagues to determine the pros and cons of working with those companies. Although it will always be the responsibility of advisers to review programs from the perspective of their institutions, professional associations such as the National Association of College and University Residence Halls (NACURH) and the Association of College and University Housing Officers – International (ACUHO-I), regional associations, and other student development groups provide insight into the quality of companies. Advisers who find companies that provide exceptional services or products should share that information with colleagues regionally and nationally. Sharing information and successes with others is how many RHA groups have grown to provide tremendous student leadership experiences to countless numbers of students.

Conclusion

Fundraising generally revolves around bringing student groups together with companies and converting sweat equity and fun into quality services or products for students. Advisers and RHAs that are willing to put in extra effort to support group fundraising will be successful and reap great benefits.

As a hall director, I prided myself in always having the group with extra money in the treasury. There was no secret to the process. We figured out what we wanted to do, found the way to make the money, and then worked to make it a success. We never fundraised just to raise money but rather had specific purposes in mind that would vest the entire group in the process. Then we created incentives like providing nice shirts, sweatshirts, or other wearable items to individuals that worked the hardest so that they could reap a portion of the success. This helped to make our efforts more successful.

Over time, I found that working with established companies made the process less work intensive and easier to generate good profits. For every need, there are companies—small and large, local and national—that are able to meet the need and related expectations.

14

Legal Issues

Jon Coleman

"A concern for potential litigation, however, should not dominate an innovative
educationally sound residence-hall administration program."
—MILLER & SCHUH

This quote marked the beginning of the legal issues chapter in the first edition
of *Advice for Advisers*. Its advice continues to be relevant to residence hall
association advisers today. As society becomes increasingly litigious, there
is an inclination to eliminate all programs with risk to the institution and the
department. The problem with this approach is that it ignores the fact that
there are educational benefits in risk. There is no way to completely eliminate
risk. Rather it is better to educate student affairs administrators about legal
issues so that they can take reasonable steps to limit risks and educate students
about the risks of involvement.

Residence hall association advisers must understand some of the many
legal issues that they may face in performing advising responsibilities. The
information in this chapter does not replace the need to consult with institutional legal counsel or risk-management offices. The law is constantly
changing and growing to respond to the needs of society. It requires continuous attention to stay aware of the evolution of different areas of the
law. RHA advisers are not able to devote enough time and attention to legal
issues to stay current. However, if they are aware of the existence of the
issues, concerned about the actions of their organizations and members,
and willing to seek out resources when needed, then advisers can limit the
exposure to litigation.

Relationships Between Institutions and Students

The nature of the relationships between students and institutions of higher education often depends on whether the institution is public or private. Many of the rules and regulations that regulate government action also apply to public institutions as courts have interpreted public institutions as being part of the government. In that case, many of the laws and decisions that affect interactions between the government and private citizens apply to colleges and universities. Private institutions are often considered to have relationships with students that are more contractual in nature. While both definitions are broad, neither is complete. Private institutions have been held to public standards and restrictions when they are found to be acting as public entities. In addition, public institutions are not treated exactly like other portions of the state government based on the nature of their work. What this means is that while there is an ability to generalize about the relationships that exist between institutions and students, it is best not to over generalize.

Regardless of the type of institution, it is important that colleges and universities create and follow procedures and guidelines in relationships with students. Courts are willing to look at histories of organization behavior, governing documents, and publications to determine whether institutions have acted appropriately. In *GLSA v. Gohn* (1988), the court examined the student government's procedures for providing funding to groups as well as the history of how it had followed those procedures with other organizations to determine whether a group was being punished for its stance on a controversial issue. The court in *Student Coalition for Gay Rights v. Austin Peay State University* (1972) looked at the student organization's proposed constitution to evaluate its stated goals and objectives to consider its stated purpose and relationship to the mission of the institution. In *Healy v. James* (1972), the court looked at Central Connecticut State College's Statement of Rights, Freedoms, and Responsibilities of Students to determine if college administrators had followed procedures in denying a group the right to organize as a student organization. Handbooks, student organization constitutions and policy books, and even the history of the organization can all be brought into court for judicial review. That is why it is critical to have guidelines and written policies governing organizational operations and policies and to follow them.

Contract Law

Student organizations often have relationships with vendors, outside organizations, and even other student organizations that are governed by contract law. At its most basic, contract law requires the presence of five major elements: promise, offer, acceptance, consideration, and an agreement to contract (Gehring, 2000). While contract law varies from state to state, these elements are standard to the contracting process. A familiarity with them will assist advisers in advising organizations.

To illustrate the different parts of a contract, consider an RHA seeking to arrange transportation to attend a leadership conference. The *promise* part of contracts is when one party offers to perform a task, pay a fee, or refrain from doing something that has value. The promise is the bus company's agreement to transport students to the conference and back on a certain day.

The *offer* is when one party asks if the other is willing to accept the promise. In the example, the offer is the bus company's quote on price and availability to provide transportation for RHA members to the conference.

The *acceptance* is when the other party agrees to the offer and the terms included. In the example, this occurs when the RHA leaders and/or administrators sign the the bus company's contract or the quoted terms are accepted verbally.

Consideration is the other party's exchange for the *promise*. For the trip example, *consideration* is paying the fee for the bus company. A contract cannot exist without this element, so it is impossible to have a contract for one party to perform and the other party not to provide consideration. An example of a contract lacking consideration is if an individual agrees to provide music for a dance while expecting nothing in return except, perhaps, the thanks and appreciation of the RHA. Even if the disc jockey later receives a t-shirt, if the t-shirt was not the original reason for agreeing to the job, it is not consideration, but a gift. Unless there is something of worth given to the disc jockey, the agreement cannot be enforced.

The final element of contracts is the *meeting of the minds*. Though difficult to explain, this element basically means both parties must have meant to enter into a contract with each other. *Meeting of the minds* is most often used in verbal contracts as written contracts and signatures are usually sufficient evidence of intent. For the bus example, calling a bus company to ask for a quote is not a contract, but rather a request for *offers* and this should be clearly expressed that way.

In contract law, there are both verbal and written contracts. It is possible for students or organizations to enter into contracts without the consent or permission of advisers. If organizations have established histories of students entering into agreements with vendors without adviser involvement, then it is not prudent for advisers to suddenly declare that contracts need approval or contracts are invalid because advisers did not know about them. Creating and following standard practices is important for organizations, so planning for problems before they occur is best. Verbal contracts have limitations on the amount of money involved and subject matter. For example, land sales must be in writing. Advisers need to consult state law to know what contracts are required to be in writing. In standard practice, student leaders and representatives need to understand and agree to enter into written contracts only. However, if they do accept a verbal contract within a state that allows verbal contracts in a particular subject matter, the organization may be held to the contract.

Torts

A tort is a legal wrong where a court can provide a remedy to the injured party by finding one party liable for the injury (Gehring, 2000). Under tort law, the most common remedy is financial. However, remedies can include other forms of restitution or actions on the part of the parties including an order to perform some act (e.g. reinstate an officer); cease some behavior (e.g. do not hold the annual street party); or some other judicial order.

The most common form of tort that advisers deal with is *negligence*. Negligence occurs when a person has a duty to another; they fail in performing that duty; and harm results from the failure to perform that duty. An example of negligence is when an RHA hosts a program in the campus swimming pool. There is a duty on the part of the RHA to take care of students attending the program. Is there a lifeguard? Is alcohol permitted? Is student behavior controlled to avoid accident or injury? The duty is to identify foreseeable risks and eliminate or reduce those risks to the best extent possible and to fully educate participants of the risk. There may not be a way to eliminate risk for a skydiving program, but there are steps to take to limit the liability of the organization and its members.

Another area of tort law is *defamation*. Defamation occurs when someone spreads false information either verbally (slander) or written (libel) that harms a person. Harm to a person can include non-physical harm including reputation or opportunity, such as participation in leadership positions. The best defense against a claim of *defamation* is that the information is true; however truth may be difficult to prove depending on the circumstances. While tort law may not directly impact most advisers, it is a good idea for advisers to explore ways to deal with possible claims of *defamation* in election speeches, comments made during meetings or published in newsletters, recommendations, or official correspondence.

Constitutional Law

In the United States, advisers are answerable to both state and federal constitutional law. Because it would be impossible for this chapter to address the 50 individual state constitutions, this discussion focuses on the federal constitution. State constitutions can only expand or broaden the rights granted to citizens by the United States Constitution. They cannot limit rights. So a discussion of federal constitutional law covers the minimum rights allowed in state constitutions.

The First Amendment

The First Amendment grants individuals rights against government action in three major areas: speech, press, and religion (U.S. Constitution, 1791). The courts have been reviewing, interpreting, and changing what the U.S. Constitution means since it was created. This discussion includes some basic concepts including how advisers or organizations may encounter First Amendment issues and what they can do. One cautionary note: This section covers legal issues and implications, not developmental or ethical issues. Just because an organization can legally do something does not mean that it should. That decision is left to advisers and student leaders.

Freedom of Speech. Freedom of Speech is not limited to the ability to speak out. It also includes the ability to listen to speech (Kaplin & Lee, 1997). The ability to regulate speech must not be used to limit student and faculty access to speakers based on the content of their speech. While limitations on speakers who represent clear and present dangers are legitimate, it is a difficult standard to establish. A common reaction on campuses is to create "free speech zones" or other locations where students can express ideas that they have, whether they are popular are not. The courts have returned mixed messages on this issue. The important thing to remember is that students "do not leave their rights at the schoolhouse door" (*Tinker v. Des Moines*, 1969). In *Tinker*, high school students who wore black armbands to protest the Vietnam War were suspended from school. Administrators claimed this act would disrupt the campus. The court found that the students' actions were protected speech and that they retain certain rights even though they were minors in high school.

For advisers at universities, the message from this case is clear: college students retain their civil liberties at universities. *Tinker* is even more important as it involved a high school, a place where courts have traditionally been more supportive of the administration's actions and limits on students' rights. Typically in cases involving universities, the courts give less leeway to administrators based on the age of the students and the expectations of the college environment. *Tinker* did include one important caution. Free speech or expression was not to "substantially interfere with the work of school or the rights of others" (*Tinker v. Des Moines,* 1969). This means that limitations on time, place, and manner (i.e. using sound amplification) can be created as long as they are content neutral (the same for any speech, popular or not) and that the reasons for the rules serve a legitimate educational purpose (Carey v. Brown, 1980).

For instance, creating a free speech zone on the edge of campus from 4:00–5:00 p.m. each day would likely be viewed as unacceptable for reasons of traffic flow, access, and unreasonable time limits. Administrators need to heed the words of Justice Hugo Black who said, "I do not believe that it can be too often repeated that the freedoms of speech, press, petition and assembly guaranteed by the First Amendment must be accorded to the ideas we hate or sooner or later they will be denied to the ideas we cherish" (*Communist Party v. SAC Board,* 1961). While restrictions are necessary, they must be balanced and able to stand up to outside review.

Free Press. Student press, in general, is accorded much of the same rights as the regular press and is subject to the same controls. The institution is not required to pay for the expression of student's views and may exercise certain editorial controls on the newspapers that it produces. Institutions, under the *Hazelwood v. Kuhlmeier* (1988) ruling, can restrict student press when the resulting publication would cause a serious physical disruption of normal school activities. In a recent case, *Dean v. Utica* (2004), a district court judge ruled that the *Hazelwood* guidelines did not apply; distinguished school action by looking at the public versus non-public forum of the paper; and found that where the publication was a legitimate public forum, then control or censorship by institutional authorities face a much more difficult burden to prove that their actions are legitimate. The court also ruled that in the paper's 25-year history, there was no previous involvement in the editorial procedures by the school administration, so involvement now on this one particular story was suspect behavior. Further, the claim by the principal that the article was journalistically lacking was found to have no basis.

While most RHA advisers do not deal with freedom of press issues, these issues are important to consider when students are creating newsletters, Web sites, discussion lists, and other mediums of communicating with organization members and campus residents. Creating clear policies for use and standards are necessary as well as creating policies regarding the level of involvement of advisers in the editorial process. In cases where the students are spending the organization's money and time on these activities, restrictions should be limited and must be fully justified by the department's established policies. Rules need to be based not on content or format but rather on existing standards that apply to both positive and negative expressions. Providing clear distinction between an organization and a Housing Office are necessary and critical if both are able to work together while providing students a forum for expressing displeasure and controversy with the policies and practices of the administration.

Freedom of Religion. For public institutions, this area has two major components. First, the government will not unduly hinder the free exercise of religion and, second, it will not promote a particular religion or religion in general. Advisers must ensure that both components are met in the policies and actions of organizations. For example, policies about using space in halls must be neutral in regards to access. Are there policies addressing non-residence hall groups having meetings in residence halls? If so, for example, the Student Bible Study Group should be treated no differently than the PlayStation© Gamers Association in requests for meeting space access.

Private institutions have greater ability to limit freedom of religion. Since most private institutions are not considered agents of the state, they are not required to give equal time to different religions nor are they required to refrain from supporting a particular religion (Kaplin & Lee, 1997). In many cases, private institutions have a religious heritage that may include a campus chaplain, support for or by a particular denomination, or even mandatory religious services for students. Private institutions are usually allowed to make individual decisions about the free exercise of religion on their campuses. An institution whose religious character prohibits certain behaviors or political views may in fact ban particular organizations, rallies, and [media] materials from their campuses (Student Press Law Center, 2004).

Freedom of Assembly. The right to assemble includes the right to gather for meetings, protests, and other events as well as the right to form organizations for legitimate purposes such as representing issues and socializing. Institutions that create processes for allowing the existence of student organizations must create systems that are fair and equitable to all groups, regardless of the content of the groups' intentions or objectives (Gehring, 1991). In creating systems to recognize student organizations, institutions that seek to deny the benefits of recognition (including access to campus facilities, students, and possible funding) must provide justification that follows standards used for all organizations. Many institutions have adopted policies that provide for the *registration* of organizations rather than the *recognition* of organizations in order to adopt lesser standards for student organizations and to reduce student organization entanglement with institutions (Dunkel & Coleman, 1998). By limiting the degree of connection to the institution, liability for group actions is also limited.

While institutions must provide fair methods for students to organize and create groups, it is not obligated to provide funding, support, or resources to assist students in the exercise of their rights. In *Healy v. James* (1972), a student group attempted to become an official organization at the institution and was prevented from doing so based on their perceived association with a disreputable national organization and perceived potential to engage in disruptive activities. Despite a finding by the dean of student affairs and the student organization committee that the group should be allowed to form, the president refused to allow the group to be recognized. The court found that while institutions do have the ability to regulate student organizations on their campus, including denial for groups advocating violence or planning disruptions, the president's actions in this case were a violation of the students' right to assemble and that student groups must be allowed to organize and have access to facilities in a non-discriminatory basis. Institutions therefore have a responsibility to make sure that any procedures that exist to provide support of any kind is fair and open to all.

GLSA v. Gohn (1988) established that procedures for funding and support must also be fair, and that the exercise of First Amendment rights by groups cannot be used to deny funds. In *GLSA v. Gohn*, the Gay & Lesbian Student Association was cleared for special events funds by the student government budget committee. This clearance historically meant that the group's request would be accepted by the student senate. But in this instance, the student senate refused the group's request based on the senators' personal opposition to homosexuality. The court considered the fact that GLSA was the only organization denied funds that the budget committee had approved and that, in two different years, the GLSA was denied money even when money remained in the budget at the end of the school year. In addition, other student organizations received money that did not qualify for funding under student government regulations where the GLSA had qualified. While the court recognized the difficulty in evaluating the motivations of the individual student senators, and were normally reluctant to intervene in funding discussions by student governments, they recognized the student senators had made public their reasons for voting against the funding: they were against homosexuality in general. The school claimed the case was moot as the year was over and new senators were elected to replace the previous ones who had denied funding. The court found, however, that the student senate had established a clear pattern of discrimination against this organization that did not appear to be changing with the new senators being elected. Because of the length of time from denial of funding to new elections was so short, allowing such an argument would preclude any judicial review or remedy, so the court rejected the school's argument about new senators. In finding for the GLSA, the court clarified that while there is no right to funding, groups cannot be denied available funding based on the content of their speech.

Fourteenth Amendment

The Fourteenth Amendment requires that state governments recognize the rights of citizens guaranteed by the United States Constitution (U.S. Constitution, 1868). This means that state actions, which are represented by the actions of public colleges or universities, must respect all rights granted by the federal government in addition to any rights granted by a state's individual constitution. The Fourteenth Amendment was used in *Dixon v. Alabama* (1961) to require public colleges and universities to recognize the rights of students under the Fifth Amendment, the right of a person to due process of law (U.S. Constitution, 1791). *Dixon* concerned whether a public institution could remove students from the institution for student conduct violations without providing due process of law including some kind of hearing; a right to confront evidence and witnesses; and the ability to present a defense. In this case, students were expelled for practicing freedom of speech and protesting racial segregation in Alabama. The court found that when a state acts in such a way as to injure a citizen, such as removal from an educational institution, it must act in accordance with the due process guarantees of the U.S. Constitution (*Dixon v. Alabama*, 1961).

The Fourteenth Amendment and cases like *Dixon* reinforce that student judicial proceedings need to follow procedures that guarantee students rights as citizens of the United States. Student judicial proceedings should not duplicate the judicial system. The level of due process necessary is dependant upon the level of rights that are in jeopardy. Simple violations resulting in community service, notice, or other sanctions require less formalized requirements as more serious violations where students face possible suspension or expulsion (Gehring, 2000). In general, policies should be in writing to give students more rights and opportunities for review, and staff should err on the side of caution. Courts look at historical decisions made by the institution. If the facts demonstrate that administrators took reasonable efforts to provide students with good judicial systems, they are less likely to find fault.

Federal Laws

The federal government has passed a number of laws that affect higher education institutions and tied compliance to federal funding. Although the federal government is limited in the ability to legislate or exercise control over public or private institutions, it can require institutions that accept federal funds in the form of research monies or financial aid to comply with federal laws. This control allows institutions to decide whether to accept such burdens and restrictions in light of the funding they receive. The laws have been written to apply to the entire institution if any part of the institution receives funding. For example, if an institution's college of pharmacy accepts a grant from the National Institute of Health, the admissions office is bound to federal regulations. Most institutions accept federal money in the form of research or financial aid so must abide by these laws.

Title VI

Title VI of the Civil Rights Act of 1964 requires that no person shall

> ". . . on the ground of race, color, or national origin, be excluded from participation in, be denied the benefits of, or be otherwise subjected to discrimination under any program or activity receiving Federal financial assistance from the Department of Education." (Title VI, Civil Rights Act, 1964)

The federal government interprets "program or activity receiving federal financial assistance" (Title VI, section 100.1, 1964) as the entire college or university. This interpretation requires educational institutions to make sure that policies and practices do not support or promote racial discrimination. No student can be denied the benefits or the ability to participate in any program at any institution that receives federal funding based on race, color, or national origin.

Title IX

Title IX of the Educational Amendments of 1972 addresses the issue of gender equity in much the same manner as Title VI addresses racial and ethnic equity. Title IX requires institutions accepting federal funding to provide access to all programs or services without regard to gender. This law has been used most recently and publicly in promoting gender equity in college sports programs. Through Title IX, additional financial support has been found for more female athletes to participate in sports on the collegiate level. Athletics, however, was not the sole or primary purpose of Title IX. It exists to create opportunities and access for women to achieve and participate fully in all programs offered by colleges. According to Richard Riley, then the United States Secretary of Education, in his comments on the 25th anniversary of Title IX, women have made great strides in education going from lagging behind male students to comprising the majority of both undergraduate students and recipients of Master's degrees (Riley, 1997).

Section 504

Section 504 of the Rehabilitation Act of 1973 provides access to educational programs, services and benefits at institutions receiving federal funding to qualified individuals with disabilities. For specific information about who qualifies for Section 504 discrimination protection, advisers can refer to the Department of Health and Human Services Web site (www.hhs.gov/ocr/504. html). "At the postsecondary educational level, a qualified student with a disability is a student with a disability who meets the academic and technical standards requisite for admission or participation in the institution's educational program or activity" (Department of Education Web site). Once students establish their ability to participate, then reasonable accommodations may be required to assist them in their full participation. For example, a student with a reading disability may require additional time or a "reader" to assist with taking exams.

> What kind of reasonable accommodations are required in college and universities?
>
> At the postsecondary level, the recipient is required to provide students with appropriate academic adjustments and auxiliary aids and services that are necessary to afford an individual with a disability an equal opportunity to participate in a school's program. Recipients are not required to make adjustments or provide aids or services that would result in a fundamental alteration of a recipient's program or impose an undue burden. (Department of Education Web site)

This means that institutions have a duty to provide students with support for their continued involvement including involvement in RHA organizations. Do RHAs provide materials in alternate formats such as BRAILLE or large print? Are hearing impaired signers available where written copies are not? Are programs and services (such as the RHA offices) accessible to students with physical disabilities?

The goal of Section 504 is for students with disabilities to be able to participate in college life, both in and out of classrooms, in such a way as to provide them with essentially similar experiences as other students. Advisers of RHAs should consider how to accomplish this in planning meeting locations, how programs will be organized, or how materials will be presented. It is not required to provide alternatives until notified of their need. Advisers do not need meeting agendas in BRAILLE if there are no visually impaired members, but they should be aware of how to get it done if needed.

FERPA – The Family Educational Rights & Privacy Act

The Family Educational Rights & Privacy Act (FERPA), often called the Buckley Amendment, gives students and families the ability to see student educational records; challenge items contained in records to change them or include alternative explanations with records; and prevent the release of the records to other parties without permission. The restriction does not include directory information like address, phone, and e-mail. However, students should have the opportunity to restrict the release of directory information, usually through the admissions office. For advisers, FERPA will most likely impact access to student academic and disciplinary records, often as they relate to qualifications for involvement in organizations. Administrative staff members are not able to release information without student permission, so explaining the removal of a student from an officer position for a grade point average below the accepted level may prove complicated to advisers who are asked. The answer, "There is a reason, but you must discuss it with the student" is all the answer that should be offered to requests by others.

Currently, there is no right to damages for a violation of FERPA for an individual who sues an institution. In *Gonzaga University v. Doe* (2002) a student sued after a college released information about an alleged case of sexual misconduct to the state teacher certification program, a program that required an "affidavit of good moral character." The student was then denied certification and sued the institution. At trial, the jury found for the student and awarded damages for the FERPA violation. On appeal, the court overturned the jury's award because they said that there was no right for a private person to sue under FERPA, and that the only penalty that exists is that an institution can lose federal funds if the Department of Education determines a pattern of violations has occurred. There has been discussion in Congress to introduce legislation that would allow students to sue institutions that violate FERPA, but no decision has been reached (Student Press Law Center, 2004).

To date, no institutions have lost funding for FERPA violations. It is important to note that there is an exception to FERPA related to legitimate use of student information by institutional personnel. For example, if there is a need for a hall director to know student information, that information can be shared with that staff member, though the staff member, too, is bound by the restrictions of FERPA. The best policy for advisers is not to release personal information about students without the express written permission of students, such as a request for a letter of recommendation or a confirmation of a student's grade point average.

Judicial Impact

How do court systems affect advisers? In the United States, there are 51 court systems that hear trials and appeals: one for each state and a federal system. Each court system has three basic levels: the trial court, the appeals court, and the Supreme Court. The trial court is where evidence is heard and results occur. This has no affect or bearing on other cases that come later. The appeals court is where parties in the trial court go when they do not agree with results from trials. For appeals courts there are geographic areas, called circuits, comprised of a number of trial courts. When an appeals court makes a decision for one case, then that reasoning, or precedent, is to be applied by all of the trial courts in that district. The Supreme Court is comprised of all the appeals courts in the state (or the U.S.). The Supreme Court reviews decisions made by appeals courts. A decision of a Supreme Court is binding on all courts, appeals, and trials in the jurisdiction of that Supreme Court.

Table 1: United States Circuit Courts of Appeals

Circuit	States
First	Maine, Massachusetts, New Hampshire, Puerto Rico, Rhode Island
Second	Connecticut, New York, Vermont
Third	Delaware, New Jersey, Pennsylvania, Virgin Islands
Fourth	Maryland, North Carolina, South Carolina, Virginia, West Virginia
Fifth	Louisiana, Mississippi, Texas
Sixth	Kentucky, Michigan, Ohio, Tennessee
Seventh	Illinois, Indiana, Wisconsin
Eighth	Arkansas, Iowa, Minnesota, Missouri, Nebraska, North Dakota, South Dakota
Ninth	Alaska, Arizona, California, Guam, Hawaii, Idaho, Montana, Nevada, Northern Mariana Islands, Oregon, Washington
Tenth	Colorado, Kansas, New Mexico, Oklahoma, Utah, Wyoming
Eleventh	Alabama, Florida, Georgia
DC	District of Columbia

(U.S. Courts, The Federal Judiciary, 2004)

It is important for advisers to know in which federal district they work because a decision in one circuit (the appeals court for the federal government) does not have the power of precedent in another. A court may look at another circuit, but it is not obligated to follow that appeals court's ruling. In fact, often circuit courts rule differently until the Supreme Court steps in and makes a ruling. This means that just because a case sounds important in another state does not mean that advisers must change policies. Advisers need to review cases and talk to legal counsel, but should not automatically change policies.

The states that comprise the federal circuits are listed in Table 1. As the table illustrates, advisers in Georgia are not in the same circuit as South Carolina. Despite the physical proximity, a case in the Fourth Circuit Courts of Appeals does not have precedent over advisers' actions in Georgia, though the case may generate a great deal of interest and publicity from the public and the university community.

Current Issues

As discussed, RHA advisers must be aware of the legal responsibilities and liabilities that come with their position. The following are areas that may be of particular concern for an adviser.

Travel

Legal concerns pertaining to travel are of special importance to RHA advisers. RHA members often have the opportunity to attend state, regional, and national residence hall conferences and that requires determinations about travel methods. Rather than address specific cases or laws about travel, most legal concerns pertaining to travel involve tort law and negligence. This means advisers need to take basic precautions to ensure the safety of students. Some things advisers should include in travel policies include, but are not limited to: requiring that all travelers wear seat belts while in the vehicles; making sure that drivers are trained or competent to drive vehicles (especially larger vans) which could include driver safety training and clean driving records; having enough drivers so that one person does not drive for too long; and carrying a list of personal information including contact and insurance information for everyone in the vehicle.

Alcohol

Getting involved with sponsoring events in residence halls that involve alcohol is generally not worth the benefits. The value in providing positive role modeling of the appropriate use of alcohol to students at RHA events is not worth the liabilities to institutions and administrators given the litigious nature of society. Some states have enacted laws that provide injured parties the ability to sue for damages from organizations or individuals who supplied someone with alcohol who then caused an injury. These types of laws are often referred to as "dram shop laws." Dram shop laws create the potential for student organizations, advisers, and institutions to be held liable for student behavior (e.g. getting into a car accident or alcohol poisoning) resulting from intoxication. Organizations that provide alcohol to students, even when the students are of age, open themselves to unnecessary financial liability and risk. If alcohol is going to be part of a program, then organizations should limit their involvement as much as possible by not providing funds to purchase alcohol, by ensuring that only legally aged attendees consume alcohol while at events, and by making plans to address any potential issues related to intoxicated participants like violent behavior or driving.

While alcohol use in college and university residence halls as part of sponsored events is rare, it is worth mentioning precautions especially for those situations where all involved students are of legal drinking age. In these rare situations, it is the responsibility of advisers to address the potential issues of the presence of alcohol at events and plan for the appropriate responses for dealing with the possible effects (Tribbensee, 2004). Direct action and plans for dealing with alcohol issues, whether or not the group is providing or sponsoring events with alcohol, must be anticipated and reasonable actions taken. Tribbensee's (2004) warning to faculty members advising student groups alerts all advisers that many of the events sponsored by residence hall groups for college–aged persons have the potential for alcohol abuse, and all advisers need to be aware of this potential and prepare appropriately.

Questions for advisers and organizations considering allowing or providing alcohol for events are: "Do the benefits to having alcohol at the event outweigh the risks?" and "What purpose is the alcohol serving at events that cannot be provided for otherwise?" Being able to provide environments for the responsible consumption of alcohol may be desirable for some organizations and advisers. However, organizations and advisers need to fully realize the risk and potential for harm and liability so that reasonable measures are in place to address any issues that may arise.

Trademark & Fair Use

A popular programming option for students in residence halls is showing movies in student lounges. However, this activity is in violation of copyright laws that prevent public performance of protected works. Simply renting movies from video stores is not sufficient permission to show the movie to groups; a license to publicly display the work is needed. Many institutions have established policies against this practice, including the College of Wooster, the College of Saint Benedict/St. Johns University, and Virginia Polytechnic Institute and State University.

The Motion Picture Licensing Corporation provides information about copyright law on a Web site (www.mplc.com/index2.htm) that explains how displaying movies to even limited groups (such as residence hall populations in floor or hall lounges) is a violation of copyright law. SWANK Motion Pictures, Inc. also provides information for organizations wishing to incorporate movies into programming efforts by providing information for the film chairperson on their Web site (www.swank.com/college/guide.html).

Pay-per-view broadcasts on community cable televison systems are also covered by copyright laws. Costs for these pay-per-view events—including sporting events, movies, and special events like boxing matches—are calculated based upon the expected number of viewers. There is a set fee or residential rate for home viewing, and an awareness that customers may invite friends over to watch with them. However, residence halls are not viewed as homes as it pertains to pay-per-view events or most other additional premium cable services. Rather, they typically must pay commercial or public performance fees to legally receive these programs. Businesses pay different fees to display the event in their premises than homeowners. Part of the difference in pricing is the public performance fee. Problems arise when residence hall communities pay residential rates rather than public performance rates to show movies or events in floor lounges or public areas. Mississippi State University staff discovered this when a hall council paid the residential rate to view a boxing match for a residence hall program, and ended up facing a lawsuit by the fight promoter for failing to pay the public licensing fees (Grandpre, 2000).

Conclusion

Legal issues for RHA advisers are complicated. Most professionals do not have the time to stay current on legal issues in addition to other responsibilities. The best advice to advisers is to take proper precautions and use good judgment about what organizations do and how they relate to organizations. In some cases, advisers may want to consider purchasing insurance as protection for themselves.

Advising places advisers at risk, and they need to ensure that institutions provide proper coverage for advisers acting within their responsibilities. Typically, that means adviser responsibilities need to be listed on job descriptions including travel to and from conferences, attending meetings, programming, and any other related duties to ensure that in the event of accident or legal concern institutions will act to protect advisers. If advising duties are temporary or interim, including assisting with particular events or conference, supervisors should provide formal letters to the personnel files of advisers indicating the additional advising duties and explaining the details of involvement. This action is usually sufficient to offer temporary or interim advisers similar protections. Advisers may still want to investigate the availability and coverage of professional liability insurance offered by organizations such as ACPA and NASPA. This coverage in addition to institution support is recommended when advisers are advising groups that are not part of job descriptions like advising fraternities or sororities.

Finding good legal resources is also a way for advisers to stay informed about legal issues facing higher education and student affairs professions. Kaplan and Lee's (2000) *Law and Higher Education* is a good resource for professionals who want more detailed descriptions of legal issues and concerns in higher education and specifics of the law. A resource for staying current in legal issues is the *Law and Legislative Quarterly* produced by NASPA Region III, Frank H. Julian (Ed.), which provides readers with short summaries of relevant cases and laws affecting the work of student affairs professionals around the country. (www.murraystate.edu/qacd/cbpa/polcrjlst/quarterly/quarterlyhome.htm)

Texas A&M University has integrated risk management planning in all aspects of campus life from student affairs to the classroom. They offer resources and advice for planning for risk including how faculty and staff can address risk in their work. The portal site (www.studentactivities.tamu.edu/risk/facilitator.htm) offers visitors a closer look at some of TAMU's initiatives and structure for dealing with risk management for their staff as well as links to other campus offices and programs that deal with the goal of reducing risk for college students.

Advisers need to prepare for, plan, and anticipate potential trouble. However, no amount of planning or preparation will completely remove all risk to participants or risk of lawsuits to advisers. Advisers should work to limit risks and be aware of when they might need additional information or input from qualified professionals, such as legal counsel, about whether activities or actions have been sufficiently considered. Managing the risk to students and advisers helps reduce the chance of harm and the risk of litigation. It will also provide advisers with a greater sense of security about this aspect of the job so that they can devote the time and energy to the parts of the adviser position that they ultimately find the most rewarding.

References

Barr, M.K. Desler & Associates *Handbook of Student Affairs Administration.* San Francisco: Jossey-Bass.

Dunkel, N. W. & Coleman, J. (1998). *Legal Issues for Advisers.* Presented at NACURH Conference, Lincoln, Nebraska.

Gehring, D. D. (1991). Legal Issues in the administration of student affairs. In T.K. Miller & R.B. Winston, (Eds.) *Administration and Leadership in Student Affairs: Actualizing Student Development in Higher Education.* Muncie, IN: Accelerated Development, Inc.

Gehring, D. D. (2000). Understanding the legal implications of student affairs practice. In M. J.

Grandpre, E. (2000). *Video and fair use.* Presented at SEAHO Conference, Montgomery, AL.

Kaplin, W.A. & Lee, B.A. (1997). A Legal Guide for Student Affairs Professionals. San Francisco: Jossey-Bass.

Miller, T. E. & Schuh, J.H. (1981). Managing the liability risks of residence hall administrators. *Journal of College Student Personnel* 22, pp. 392–395.

Riley, Richard (1997). Title IX: Twenty-Five years of Progress. U.S. Department of Education, retrieved 11/29/2004, http://www.ed.gov/pubs/TitleIX/index.html

Student Press Law Center (2004). Texas university rebukes student paper for supporting gay marriage. Retrieved 11/5/04 from http://www.splc.org/newsflash.asp?id=766&year=2004

Tribbensee, N.E. (2004). Faculty Adviser, Beware: You may be liable. *The Chronicle of Higher Education,* 6/25/2004, p. 11.

U.S. Department of Health and Human Services. Your rights under Section 504 of the Rehabilitation Act. Retrieved 10/5/04 from http://www.hhs.gov/ocr/504.html.

U.S. Department of Education. Office for Civil Rights, Protecting students with disabilities. Retrieved 11/28/2004 from http://www.ed.gov/about/offices/list/ocr/504faq.html.

U.S. Department of Education. Family Educational Rights and Privacy Act (FERPA). Retrieved August 10, 2004 from http://www.ed.gov/policy/gen/guid/fpco/ferpa/index.html.

U.S. Courts. The Federal Judiciary. Retrieved October 2, 2004 from http://www.uscourts.gov/links.html.

Cases Reported

Carey v. Brown, 447 U.S. Supreme Court 455. (1980).

Communist Party v. SAC Board, 367 U.S. Supreme Court 1,137, (1961).

Dean v. Utica, U.S. District Court - Eastern District of Michigan. Reported in the Student Press

Law Center. (2004).

Dixon v. Alabama, 294 F.2d 150. (1961).

Gay and Lesbian Students Association v. Gohn, 850 F.2d 361. (8th Circuit 1988)

Gonzaga University and Roberta S. League v. Doe, 536 U.S. Supreme Court 273. (2002).

Hazelwood v. Kuhlmeier, 484 U.S. Supreme Court 260. (1988).

Healy v. James, 408 U.S. Supreme Court 169. (1972).

Student Coalition for Gay Rights v. Austin Peay State University, 477 F. Supp. 1267 (M.D. TN 1979).

Tinker v. Des Moines, 393 U.S. Supreme Court 503. (1969).

Web sites

Title VI of the Civil Rights Act, 42 U.S.C. § 200d (1964).

Title IX, Education Amendments, 20 U.S.C. § 1681-1688 (1972).

Section 504, Rehabilitation Act, § 504 (1973).

First Amendment, U.S. Constitution (1791).

Fifth Amendment, U.S. Constitution (1791).

Fourteenth Amendment, U.S. Constitution (1868)

Statutes

Title VI of the Civil Rights Act, 42 U.S.C. § 200d (1964).

Title IX, Education Amendments, 20 U.S.C. § 1681-1688 (1972).

Section 504, Rehabilitation Act, § 504 (1973).

First Amendment, U.S. Constitution (1791).

Fifth Amendment, U.S. Constitution (1791).

Fourteenth Amendment, U.S. Constitution (1868).

Case Studies

❖ Case Study 1

You are the adviser of the campus RHA when your executive board tells you that they have a great new idea for elections. They want to have the candidates running for office videotape their speeches and post them on the RHA Web site. Then, over the course of the week, members can post questions to the candidates who will answer them online. In addition, members can post pro/con statements on the election site. No comments or questions will have any names attached to protect the privacy of the process. The candidates would be able to see all of the comments and questions as well and be able to respond.

Then, on election night, the process will only need a short closing question period for each candidate as well as a closing statement from each candidate. The officers are really excited because they feel that this will shorten the typically long election night event, increase questions and participation by members and allow non-members access to the election through the web. There is a great deal of excitement about "bringing RHA elections into the twenty-first century." They tell you that the student Web designer already has everything set up to do this and is ready to go.

- What legal issues do you see as potential areas of concern in this process?
- What is your response to the students when they share their idea with you?

❖ Case Study 2

Your students are planning to attend the regional RHA conference this year. To save money, they have arranged to take university vans to the conference. The trip will take approximately 15 hours each way. To drive university vehicles, including the 15 passenger vans the group is renting, someone only needs to show a driver's license, insurance card, and proof of affiliation with the institution (student, staff, or faculty ID card). The group has reserved two vans to transport students.

The current plan is for students to leave from campus on Friday. Several members live in locations that the group will pass through on the way back to campus and have asked to be dropped off along the way home since the group will be returning on the Sunday before Thanksgiving. The residence halls close the Saturday before Thanksgiving for a week-long break. You are the only adviser to the organization.

- What are your concerns about this event?
- What preparations will you take in planning to travel to the conference?

15

Transportation

Rebecca Loney & Kathleen Loney

There will be times when it is necessary for advisers to arrange transportation for students to conferences, retreats, workshops, or other places of interest. Not only do advisers and groups need to consider time and price, but they need to research a number of other areas prior to leaving for events. No matter what the reason for the trip, proper planning must take place to ensure safe passage.

Travel Considerations

The following are just some of the considerations the RHA adviser must take prior to deciding how groups will travel. When these considerations are addressed and resolved, the travel planning process should be much smoother.

- **Distance.** In planning for group travel, advisers must resolve how far the groups are traveling, whether the groups will need to stay overnight midtrip, and how many days the groups will be gone.
- **Group Size and Special Needs.** The size of groups determines what modes of transportation are best. Also, advisers and groups may be able to join other university groups traveling to the same event in sharing buses, reserving train cars, or even booking group rate airline tickets. Ride-sharing may reduce prices for all involved. If advisers or students with special physical needs travel with groups, special accommodations need to be made with the agencies providing transportation.

- **Available Funds.** Available funds are a determining factor in how long groups may be gone, how many group members may travel, and what modes of transportation are used.
- **Drivers.** If the chosen mode of transportation includes advisers or students driving, advisers need to consider who is authorized to drive, the driving style and experience of drivers, and driving records that include the number (if any) and types of driving violations the student may have committed.
- **Proper Identification.** Depending on the destination, group members may need to provide official picture identification and/or birth certificates and current passports and/or visas. Some of these items take time to request and receive if individuals do not already possess them, so advisers need to allow ample time for group members to secure them. For example, the process to apply for and receive passports can take six to eight weeks.
- **Equipment.** The type of equipment needed to take along may decide the mode of transportation. Trains and airplanes only allow two checked items per traveler and charge more for any excess luggage
- **Transfer of Groups To/From Initial Modes of Transportation.** Advisers may decide modes of transportation based on pre- or post- transfers from original points of travel or final destinations. Advisers need to consider how far away train stations or airports are from final destinations and what other transportation services are available to final destinations.
- **Travel Agencies.** To save planning time, local or university travel agencies may be able to do much of the preplanning and/or research for groups. Advisers can take advantage of this expertise if available.

Possible Modes of Transportation

Different modes of transportation each bring their own list of benefits and concerns that must be weighed before choosing which one best suits a RHA's current needs.

- **Automobiles/Vans.** The most commonly used modes of transportation for group travel are automobiles and vans. For many groups, automobiles and vans are the most cost-effective means of travel. There are several sizes to consider and several ways to rent vehicles.
- **University Vehicles.** Many universities have fleets of vehicles for campus groups to use. When considering the use of university vehicles, advisers should answer the following questions to determine if university vehicles are the best mode of transportation for groups.
  - ✧ Are all group members in university vehicles covered by university

insurance?

❖ Are groups charged by the mile, flat fees, or a combination of both?

❖ Do advisers pay for gasoline then request reimbursement? Are advisers given fleet credit cards, or do advisers or groups absorb full costs?

❖ Do rental fees go by a 24-hour clock?

❖ What shape are vehicles in? Do they have good tires, good brakes, good windshield wipers, and good seat belts? What type of emergency equipment is provided in vehicles (e.g. first-aid kits, survival kits, jumper cables, ice scrapers, shovels, etc.)?

❖ Do universities provide emergency roadside assistance phone numbers?

❖ Who can drive vehicles—staff, graduate students, undergraduate students? What age must drivers be? Do they need special drivers' licenses or any special training to drive larger vehicles like 15-passenger vans?

❖ Can guests from other universities ride in another university's vehicle?

• **Commercially Rented Vehicles.** There are many car rental companies to choose from. Advisers should seek reputable rental companies with acceptable rental prices, and not just go with the least expensive options. Advisers should ask the following questions and make sure they inspect vehicles prior to driving off the rental lot.

❖ What is the minimum age to rent vehicles? What is the minimum age to drive vehicles?

❖ What credit cards are accepted and what is the required minimum available credit? Do credit cards have to be in the name of the persons renting or driving the vehicle? Are other forms of payment accepted?

❖ When traveling with groups, advisers are encouraged to purchase insurance on the vehicle available as apart of the rental. How much is insurance and what does the insurance cover? Some vehicle rental insurance is very expensive and does not necessarily offer better coverage than the lower priced companies. Advisers should verify that the insurance covers the rental of another vehicle if there is an accident and the first rented vehicle needs to be fixed. No group wants to be stranded while a vehicle is fixed!

❖ Are weekly rates available for vehicles, or are daily rates the most cost-effective? Are rentals based on a 24-hour clock? How are extra hours beyond the return time charged? Are they handled by the hour or full day?

❖ Are there additional charges for more than one driver?

♦ Are there additional charges for people driving under the age of 25?

♦ Are there charges per mile or unlimited miles?

♦ If renting vehicles internationally, are rentals paid at the time reserved (prepaid) and do advisers receive vouchers ahead of time stating the prepaid status? Advisers are encouraged to purchase all insurances available on international vehicle rentals.

♦ If renting vehicles internationally, do drivers need international drivers' licenses? If so, where and how can they secure them in that country?

- **Personal Vehicles.** When considering the use of personal vehicles for group trips, advisers should answer the following questions.
  - ♦ Who will drive personal vehicles?
  - ♦ Are personal vehicles covered under university insurance plans?
  - ♦ How will advisers and group members be reimbursed for the use of personal vehicles—by the mile or by gasoline price?
  - ♦ If personal vehicles break down, who is responsible for repair bills?

- **Charter Buses.** Charter buses may be university owned or rented from commercial agencies. When considering charter buses for group trips, advisers should answer the following questions.
  - ♦ How many seats are on each?
  - ♦ Can students from other universities ride on the buses?
  - ♦ Are rental charges by the mile or flat fees per day?
  - ♦ How many drivers need to be hired? What is the length of shift drivers are allowed to drive?
  - ♦ If buses stay with groups for the entire trip, are there charges for bus driver lodging or meals or are those charges included in rental fees?
  - ♦ Are groups expected to pay gratuities to bus drivers? If so, what is the going rate per day, per driver?
  - ♦ What types of insurance are carried on the bus? What types of insurance does the rental company carry on passengers?
  - ♦ If the trip is long distance, will two bus drivers be provided so that no overnight lodging needs to be arranged?
  - ♦ Who plans stops for breaks along the route?

- **Trains.** When considering train travel for group trips, advisers should answer the following questions.
  - ♦ How many group members will be traveling together? If over 10

people are traveling together, advisers need to contact the group department of the train company. A 45-day lead time is suggested when booking train travel.

✧ Advisers should always ask for the best discount rate offered at the time of booking. What payment plan is allowed? What forms of payment are accepted? They also should ask if free tickets for group leaders are available.

✧ Advisers should ask for detailed time schedules for the trip and if there are layovers that might require overnight lodging.

✧ Are any meals included with tickets? If not, what is the price range of the food on the train? Are group members allowed to bring food along and eat while traveling? In other words, do group members have to eat the food on the train?

✧ If it is an overnight train and group members want to sleep, how much are sleeping cars? How many group members can stay in one sleeping car? What meals come with sleeping cars?

✧ How many bags of luggage can be taken? If the group requires other equipment, what is the price per piece of additional items? Are there size or weight limitations?

✧ Is insurance available? How much is it and what does it cover? When does it need to be purchased? At time of ticket purchase or day of travel?

• **Airplanes.** Air travel is a viable option for groups if proper information is gathered. The difficulty with providing specific guidelines or tips for group travel in airplanes is that each airline has its own specifications to abide by. Once groups decide to use air travel, advisers are encouraged to call travel agents or airline group travel specialists for more specifics. Both contacts are able to answer the questions below that are important to know prior to booking flights. Much of this information can be found on airline Web sites when flights are booked.

✧ How many group members will be traveling together?

✧ What city will the group be departing from and what city is the destination?

✧ This information translates into what airport is closest to the departure city and what airport is closest to the destination.

✧ How will group members be transported to and from airports?

✧ What can and cannot be packed in carry-on bags? What can and cannot be packed in checked bags?

✧ How many bags can be carried on? What are the size and weight guidelines for carry-on bags? How many bags can be checked? What are the size and weight guidelines for checked baggage? What type of identification should be placed on each bag?

✧ What type of identification must passengers have with them when boarding a plane? For example, do group members need government issued photo IDs?

✧ Regarding pricing of airline tickets, what size group qualifies for "discounted group tickets?" How much lead-time is needed to book group tickets? What form of payment is acceptable and when is payment required?

✧ When can group members request seats for departure and return flights?

✧ If group members do not have frequent flyer accounts with particular airlines, where and when can they apply for these? When are frequent flyer accounts credited for miles?

Travel Needs

When traveling with groups, advisers should take these items to ensure successful trips.

• **Major Credit Cards.** Advisers should secure university/company credit cards in their names to cover payment for vehicles, payment for meals, last minute purchases or emergencies. Visa and MasterCard are the most acknowledged and accepted credit cards for domestic as well as international travel.

• **ATM Cards.** ATM cards are the best form of immediate cash. Even though users may be required to pay service fees, the fees are typically lower than the expenses of traveler's checks. Advisers are encouraged to carry smaller amounts of cash with them and go to ATMs more often rather than carrying large amounts of cash or traveler's checks to avoid the possibilities of loss or theft. With international travel, there are many ATM machines all over the world, and many times the fee is waived completely. Group members who can assist by standing behind them so that onlookers cannot see codes entered into machines should accompany advisers using ATM machines. Going with groups to ATM machines also provides safety in numbers. Advisers using ATM cards should never walk away from ATM machines alone.

- **Complete Itineraries.** Experienced advisers create day-by-day itineraries for trips. Travel itineraries should be detailed and include location contact information, contact information for the group at locations, and housing addresses and phone numbers for each travel day. Each group member going on trips as well as supervisors and other appropriate staff at home universities should receive copies of itineraries prior to trips. Itineraries help group members make personal travel plans as well as provide contact information to others in case of emergency.
- **Directions.** Advisers are responsible for securing directions to the travel site for all possible means of transportation and points of origination, especially airports, train stations, and all major highways.
- **Emergency Information.** When traveling with groups, advisers must have emergency information for all group members including emergency contacts; medical information like allergies; physical and mental restrictions; lists of daily medications and insurance information. If possible, advisers should encourage group members to bring insurance cards.
- **Passports for International Travel.** When traveling with groups internationally, advisers should have copies of group members' information sheets, passports, and passenger receipts of airline tickets. If advisers are traveling with group members under 18 years old, they need to have permission slips from parents or guardians stating the authority to leave the country with these minors. Permission slips must be notarized and signed by both legal parents, if living, whether or not they are divorced.

Conclusion

Traveling with student groups is an exciting opportunity for advisers. If well planned, trips can go smoothly and safely. Trip planning is simplified by making sure all travel considerations are taken care of before making final decisions. Advisers must balance cost, time, and safety with the benefits and possible limitations of each mode of transportation. At times, costs outweigh the time needed to travel; in other instances, time saved outweighs costs. The most important thing to remember is to plan accordingly, follow the steps described in this chapter, and be able to answer questions provided in each topic area. Traveling with student groups is an enjoyable and safe experience with thoughtful planning.

Case Studies

❖ Case Study 1

You are an adviser taking 20 students to a conference about 450 miles away. The budget is limited, and administrators prefer that students are not asked to pay excessive amounts of money for this trip. You need to be at the conference by 3:00 p.m., so by bus or car, the latest you could leave is 3 a.m. Students can drive vehicles, but only during daylight hours. They must be 20 years old and have clean driving records. Your institution is located near a regional airport hosting one airline and the train station is about 25 miles away. The conference you are going to allows you to stop by two other schools if needed.

Things to consider:

- What is the actual budget?
- What pressure is put on you the adviser and/or the students that will need to drive?
- How many vehicles are needed for this size group?
- What safety precautions need to be taken with each mode of transportation available?

❖ Case Study 2

It is February and four students and an adviser are attending a conference more than 800 miles away. The closest airport that they can fly into is 45 minutes away and requires renting a vehicle to get to the conference site. The only person who may drive a university vehicle is the adviser. Using a university vehicle saves the group money.

Things to consider:

- What is the total cost differential between flying and taking a university vehicle?
- What are some hidden costs with having one driver for an 800-mile trip?
- What is the weather usually like that time of year in the area being driven through?
- What planning needs to occur for each mode of transportation to be successful and safe?

16

Advising Conference Delegations

Cindy Spencer

Conferences are a major focus of the National Association of College and University Residence Halls, Inc. (NACURH). The stated purpose of residence hall student leader conferences has been to share ideas, challenges, and solutions. In article II of NACURH's governing documents, the purpose of the organization is "to design and facilitate programs and informational services to promote the educational goals of residence hall students through discussion groups, seminars, and speakers at the annual conferences and other means of informational exchange throughout the year" (NACURH, 1997, p.2). Among all the services offered to member institutions, conferences continue to be the primary and most utilized NACURH service.

As conferences have expanded through the years, so have the roles and responsibilities of conference delegation advisers. From the first conference with only four member institutions in attendance, to the present day where more than 400 institutions attend, the role of conference adviser continues to be key to the success of conferences.

Advising conference delegations is a rewarding experience. One benefit is the opportunity to work closely with the national communications coordinators (NCCs). During the planning phase, advisers and NCCs make many decisions and plans to prepare for the conference. Other benefits include spending time with and getting to know students in residence hall organizations on a more personal level. Students also have the opportunity to get to know advisers better. Preparing for conferences gives students and advisers more relaxed opportunities for interaction and sharing. In much the same way that advisers develop staff teams, they work with groups of students to bring them together to develop delegations that work like teams.

Preparing for conferences involves numerous details. Most details are handled by NCCs. However, it is important that advisers understand all that is going on and recognize that the ultimate level of responsibility for conference decisions is theirs. The adviser role may change from conference to conference and from year to year. The level of support and advising needed depends on the experience of each NCC as well as the conference experience and maturity level of students in organizations and delegations. Student and adviser experience determines the difference in how active advisers are in contributing to decisions and planning for conference attendance.

Conference Structure, Format and Purpose

As NACURH has grown and leadership development has become more complex, the number of conferences offered has increased to meet those needs. NACURH organizes one annual national conference each spring. The average attendance at annual conferences is approximately 3,000 delegates and advisers. Annual national conferences are usually held in late May, close to Memorial Day weekend, and offer three full days of programming. Students and advisers have opportunities to hear from various guest speakers and attend additional programming sessions. The national conference offers programming on a variety of topics including leadership development, personal development, new programming ideas, gender issues, technology, fundraising, current events, and advising issues. "Track" programming is targeted to specific audiences, such as the National Residence Hall Honorary (NRHH), RHA presidents, NCCs, programming board representatives, and advisers. In addition, many small group discussions or roundtable topic programs allow delegates to have interactive learning experiences. As the student population becomes more sophisticated, programming tracks and topic options have changed to meet their needs. In addition, national conference host staffs provide various programming opportunities specifically for advisers. As most students are not in class during Memorial Day weekend, many national conferences offer "optional day" activities for additional fees. These activities usually involve local activities or historical sites of interest to tourists.

Within NACURH there are eight regions that each hosts regional annual conferences in the fall. Since regional conferences are held during the academic year when classes are in session, they usually begin on Friday evenings and adjourn on Sunday mornings. Regional conferences offer a variety of programming topics similar to those previously mentioned at national annual conferences.

During national and regional annual conferences, NCCs, NRHH representatives, and, in some regions, programming representatives from each institution attend business meetings that may conflict with programming sessions. The advising role at annual conference business meetings can vary greatly. It is helpful for advisers to have conversations with students as well as other advisers at conferences to determine the traditional advising role at annual business meetings for particular conferences.

While the primary focus of annual conferences is programming and leadership development, various social and entertainment options are available as well including movies, dances, karaoke, hypnotists, hospitality lounges with refreshments, and various games. No alcohol is allowed at NACURH-affiliated conferences due to liability and risk management concerns.

In addition to annual fall regional conferences, each region hosts mini-conferences in the spring. Often referred to as "No-Frills" conferences, they are considerably different in format. The primary focus is organized business. They usually do not offer structured programming opportunities and are usually attended by NCCs, NRHH representatives, programming representatives, and/or RHA presidents and advisers. These conferences usually begin on Friday evenings and adjourn on Sunday mornings. No-Frills conference structures vary greatly between the eight regions.

Additionally, various state or sub-regional organizations usually schedule conferences in the spring. Each of these conferences has its own format with different target populations in attendance.

The various conferences can be viewed as a pyramid of leadership experiences. The state or sub-regional conferences serve as bases or foundations of leadership development, followed by the regional conferences and the national conference, all of which build on the leadership developed at the campus level.

At fall regional conferences, students are introduced to NACURH. Attending regional conferences typically motivates new student leaders to initiate programming ideas on their campuses and to set goals based on what they learn from peers. At regional conferences, delegates have opportunities to interact and meet more diverse groups of students from various states or regions than those they met at state and sub-regional conferences. Regional conferences provide good experience for mid-level student leaders prior to attending national conferences. Regional conferences provide the opportunity for students to develop networks of their peers while retaining a sense of familiarity with other student leaders with whom they have attended other conferences and had campus exchanges.

State and sub-regional conferences not only serve as catalysts to spark interest in students seeking leadership roles for the following year but also serve to re-energize "seasoned" leaders. They come at a time, spring semester, when students need to be motivated and excited about what is going on at their campuses. These conferences give them opportunities to share and again learn from peers.

National conferences are designed to meet the needs of experienced leaders and students who have attended past regional, state, or sub-regional conferences. However, advisers may find that for some students, the national conference is their first conference experience. With strong advising and thorough preparation on what can be expected, national conferences can be rewarding experiences for even first-time conference delegates. Students who have significant experience in RHAs, NRHHs, and other campus leadership roles are exposed to ideas from around the nation. Advisers have opportunities to expand their knowledge and experiences through interactions with peers who have a wide variety of years and levels of advising experience from across the country.

Conference Costs

As the number of conferences increases, advisers and student leaders must consider the available financial resources and decide which conferences they will attend based on how the programming meets their specific needs. State and sub-regional conferences usually are the most economical conferences with regards to registration costs, travel costs, and time. Regional conferences currently have registration costs from $125–190 per delegate. No-Frills and mini-conference registration costs currently range from $75–125 per delegate. National conference fees currently range from $175–250 per delegate. Adviser registration fees average $20–50 more than student delegate fees. These additional costs are primarily due to the difference in adviser housing options and special program opportunities offered for advisers. Registration fees include housing and meals.

In addition to registration costs, transportation costs can affect decisions about attendance. Transportation costs can range from $25–100 per delegate for a regional or mini-confernce, depending on the proximity of the conference site to institutions. In some regions, the cost of air travel may need to be considered to attend conferences. National conferences may involve as much as 24 hours of ground travel or the cost of air travel, again depending on the proximity of the institution to the conference site. As the costs of conference fees and transportation increase, more institutions are working together to plan and share economical modes of transportation including charter buses, caravanning in vehicles to utilize all available seats, securing additional authorized drivers, or coordinating travel plans to be eligible for group rates with air travel.

For regional and national NACURH conferences, other optional costs to consider are delegation clothing items (such as t-shirts, sweatshirts, jerseys, and hats), trade items, "spirit packs," and institutional displays and/or banners. These items symbolize delegation spirit and pride that reflect the conference theme or campus traditions. Trade items are brought to the conference and change hands between delegates from different institutions. These items include signs, noise makers, decorated clothes pins, or other "trinkets" that symbolize institutions and organizations or reflect conference themes. For national conferences, many regions ask that each delegate purchase (or institutions purchase for each delegate) a shirt or "spirit pack" to show unity of the region.

Advising NCCs

Advisers need to understand the primary responsibilities of the NCC position. As outlined in the NACURH *NCC Handbook* (NACURH 2004), NCCs are liaisons between NACURH, their regions, and institution residence hall associations. NCCs are responsible for making sure that membership dues are paid and registration forms are taken care of at national conferences or sent to the National Information Center (NIC) by June 1 of each year. NCCs are also responsible for organizing and submitting annual resource reports (NIC report) on some aspect of their institution's residential living environment, government, or programs to the NIC. In order for institutions to vote in any regional or national business meeting or be considered for any regional or national awards, they must be in good standing with NACURH. This means that institution affiliation forms, dues, and NIC reports must be turned in and on file at the NIC. Also, institutions may not have any outstanding debts with any NACURH office or conference staff. Conference delegation advisers need to ensure that NCCs clearly understand their responsibilities and roles prior to and at conferences. These responsibilities include:

- Communicating conference information and marketing the benefits of attending conferences on their campuses to students.
- Serving as chairs of their conference delegations during regional and national conferences.
- Attending any sub-regional pre-conference meetings that are scheduled. These meetings are planned and facilitated by the regional communications coordinator (RCC) and assist in preparing NCCs for business meetings at upcoming conferences.
- Being responsible for all pre-conference materials, arrangements, and

communications. This includes submitting all conference registration materials, submitting any and all award nomination bids for their institutions, and communicating with conference host staff.

- Attending all NCC meetings at regional and national conferences. At regional conferences, these meetings usually begin on the first evening and continue through the next day and typically conflict with program presentations. At national conferences, NCCs need to attend NCC informational meetings and NACURH Corporate Business meetings, and any regional meetings that are scheduled. In addition, at regional and national conferences, NCC training occurs. This training is very beneficial for new NCCs.

- Serving as official voting representatives for their institutions in all business meetings. NCCs need to read all award bids, position bids, legislation, and past business meeting minutes prior to conferences when these items are available.

It is important that NCCs develop clear and consistent lines of communication with conference delegations, advisers, the RCC, and conference host staffs. The roles that advisers and NCCs have in finalizing conference plans may be determined by institutional polices. Advisers and NCCs need to discuss these roles and expectations. Examples are policies concerning reserving institutional vehicles, contracting for buses, purchasing plane tickets, and authorizing checks for conference registration. Advisers need to be aware of institutional and departmental policies and procedures related to travel with students and share these with NCCs.

NCCs work hard to prepare delegations for conferences. As stated in the *NCC Handbook* (NACURH, 2004), encouragement and support are very important when advising and working with NCCs. It is important that delegations realize NCCs are more than just "travel agents." The delegates need to know the responsibilities NCCs have and recognize them for their significant contributions. All delegates must recognize that NCCs are in charge of delegations at conferences.

Bidding for Awards

While the primary focus of conferences is directed at programming and leadership development, another focus is challenging students to take risks and gain recognition. Numerous awards are distributed at different conference levels. These awards include individual as well as institutional recognition. It is important to review award criteria when making decisions about who to nominate. The pin awards, as described below, do not require bids but are initiated by application. Listed below are current awards given at both the national and/or regional level, as defined by the NACURH and NRHH policy books.

NRHH Awards

- **NRHH Outstanding Chapter of the Year.** The NRHH Outstanding Chapter of the Year award is the highest honor an NRHH Chapter can attain. The award recognizes outstanding achievements of an NRHH chapter on the campus, regional, and national levels (NRHH, 2004).
- **NRHH Building Block Chapter of the Year.** The NRHH Building Block Chapter of the Year is given to the Chapter which shows outstanding growth and development during the year of nomination (NRHH, 2004).
- **Outstanding NRHH Member of the Year Award.** The NRHH Member of the Year Award is designed to recognize outstanding service to NRHH and NACURH by an individual who has been directly affiliated with both organizations (NRHH, 2004).

NACURH Individual Awards

- **Distinguished Service Award (DSA).** Purpose: This Distinguished Service Award is designed to recognize distinguished student leadership while serving NACURH, its Affiliates, and member institutions over a several year period (NACURH, 1997).
- **First Year Experience Award (FYE).** This FYE Award recognizes the outstanding contributions of a first year student. This award encourages involved first year students to remain active in leadership positions and to continue improving the residence hall environment on campus (NACURH, 1997).
- **Hallenbeck Service Award.** Named after Dr. Dan Hallenbeck, former NACURH adviser, this award recognizes the outstanding and continuous service to NACURH of a full-time housing or student affairs professional (NACURH, 1997).
- **Student of the Year Award.** The Student of the Year Award recognizes outstanding service to NACURH by an individual who has been directly affiliated with the organization (NACURH, 1997).
- **NCC of the Year Award.** The NCC of the Year Award recognizes outstanding service to NACURH by an individual who has been directly affiliated with the organization (NACURH, 1997).
- **Adviser of the Year Award.** The Adviser of the Year Award recognizes outstanding service by an individual adviser above and beyond the job description while serving in an advising capacity to a residence hall leadership group (NACURH, 1997, 2004).

Pin Awards

- **NACURH Four-Year Service Pin.** The NACURH Four Year Service Pin Award recognizes those students who have spent four years of their collegiate careers living in the residence halls, constantly striving to enhance their residential living environments and NACURH.
- **Gold Pin Award.** The Gold Pin Award is given at the National Chair's discretion. The pin shall be awarded to National Board of Directors (NBD) members and associate directors who have provided leadership and direction in their roles and who have actively participated on the NBD, as evidenced by attending Semi-annual and Annual NBD meetings. The pin also may be awarded to an individual who has received the Silver Pin and who has been recommended in writing to the chair by a regional director or other NBD member. The maximum number of pins that may be given out in a year is equal to the number of regional affiliates in NACURH (NACURH, 1992, 1996).
- **Silver Pin Award.** The Silver Pin Award is a regional award given at the regional director's discretion. The pin shall be awarded to individuals who have provided leadership and direction to the regional affiliate of NACURH. The maximum number of pins that may be given out in a year is equal to the number of regional affiliates in NACURH. (NACURH, 1992).
- **Bronze Pin Award.** The Bronze Pin Award is an institution award given by the RHA or NRHH President. The pin shall be awarded to individuals who have provided leadership and direction to their campus organizations. The maximum number of pins that may be given out in a year is equal to the number of regional affiliates in NACURH

Awards Presented Only In Distinct Situations

- **Stoner Distinguished Service Award.** This award, named after Dr. Ken Stoner past NACURH President and past NACURH Adviser, recognizes distinguished service and dedication to the NACURH organization (NACURH, 1990).
- **The NACURH Service Award.** The purpose of the NACURH Service Award is to recognize leadership within the NACURH Organization.

NACURH Institution Awards

- **NACURH/ACUHO-I Daniel Siler Program of the Year Award (POY).** NACURH recognizes the most outstanding student-implemented program concerning residence halls through the Program of the Year Award.

- **NACURH/ACPA Student Award for Leadership Training (SALT).** The purpose of the Student Award for Leadership Training is to reward student leadership training programs in the residence halls. Co-sponsored by the American College Personnel Association.
- **Commitment to Diversity Award.** The Commitment to Diversity Award is given to an institution that involves a student-directed year-long and campus wide commitment to awareness and education of residential students concerning diversity issues.
- **NACURH National School of the Year.** The NACURH National School of the Year Award is the highest honor a member institution can attain. The award recognizes outstanding achievements on the campus level by a residence hall organization and associated groups, as well as contributions on regional and national levels.
- **NACURH National Building RHA of the Year Award.** The NACURH National Building RHA of the Year Award recognizes those RHAs that have made significant steps in the development of their RHA. The award is designed to honor the RHA that displays tremendous effort and improvement in their residence hall environment from the previous academic year to the present.

Currently, regional award bids are submitted electronically to the Regional Board of Directors (RBD) by NCCs in accordance with established regional timelines. Each region within NACURH has established timelines for bid processes. At the national level, award bids are submitted to the NRHH National Office. Certain bids need to be received at the regional level before being eligible for consideration at NACURH. NCCs should have this information or reference can be made to the NACURH Web site at www.nacurh.org for more detailed information and for the specific regional information. As noted, certain bids are only awarded at the national level.

The role of advisers in regards to bids varies depending on the experience of student leaders. Ideally, advisers provide letters of support where needed for the bids or assist in getting additional letters of support from other offices or administrators on campus. Reading and proofing bids are also roles of advisers. A good learning experience for students is to review bids from previous years. If advisers to not have access to bids from previous years, they can order copies from the National Information Center. Reviewing bids from previous years can assist students and advisers in gaining a better understanding of what is important to include in bids and how to follow the suggested NACURH guidelines and policies.

As with many experiences in working with students, the process of writing bids can be as rewarding as receiving awards. Advisers need to remind students and to role model that the bid writing process is as important as outcomes. While it may sound cliché, being nominated is an honor for individuals. Plus, it is an accomplishment for institutions to implement and accomplish the programs and services described in bids.

Pre-Conference Preparation

A number of important topics and tasks need to be addressed and completed by groups before conferences. Most tasks are completed by NCCs. However, it is important that the advisers work with NCCs to provide the support and knowledge needed. This can be particularly important in reviewing program proposals and arranging travel. Pre-conference tasks include:

- Sharing conference information with residence hall governments, NRHHs, and students in RHAs. In addition to printed information, NCCs can plan information meetings where past conference videos are shown and students who have attended previous conferences talk to groups and share experiences. This process can begin prior to receiving conference registration information. Most conferences provide newsletters, Web pages, and other information a few months prior to the distribution of the actual registration forms and other materials.
- Determining delegation size and make-up following guidelines or delegation caps determined by conference staffs and /or by policies existing within RHAs. A number of dynamics may impact delegation size including campus or organization finances; campus activities such as homecoming or parents' weekend occurring on campus the same dates of conferences; or availability of additional vans or larger buses.
- Developing processes for the selection of delegations and outlining the criteria used to determine who will serve as delegates. As NCCs develop these processes, advisers need to be aware of any delegation slots that might be predetermined by policies existing within RHAs. (A sample questionnaire is provided in Appendix 2.)
- Selecting delegates as soon as possible. It is recommended that a few alternates be selected giving NCCs the option to fill delegate spaces if selected students cancel. Alternates should include both genders, as many conferences require that canceled delegate spaces be filled with same gender students. As conferences approach, students may need assistance from advisers in requesting approval from professors for students to miss classes

or change exams. (See Appendix 3 for an example form.)

- Developing processes for delegates to share what was learned at conferences when they return. Examples include presenting programs for residence halls as well as initiating new programs or fund-raising ventures on campus. Having delegates share handouts from conferences is a good way to begin programming resource files for organizations.

- Discussing delegate accountability with potential delegates early on. This ensures that delegates attend pre-conference delegation meetings; attend program sessions; follow conference and institutional policy; and follow through on any expectations for making presentations to residence hall governments explaining what they learned, new ideas to implement, new resources, etc. (See Appendix 4.)

- Recruiting quality program proposals from delegates to be presented at conferences. The conference program committee relies almost entirely on delegates and advisers to provide programs for conferences. At a minimum, one program proposal should be submitted for every five delegates. Both NCCs and delegation advisers need to review program proposals before they are submitted. Some conference staffs and some residence hall organizations require this step. Advisers are good resources and mentors in assisting students with program ideas. One way to build program presentation confidence in new delegates is to pair them with more seasoned conference delegates to present together. A good resource regarding program presentation at NACURH- affiliated conferences can be found in Appendix 5 and is also located at: www.nacurh.org/resources/Handbooks/ncc/helpful_hints_for_program_presen.php

- Completing and submitting registration information as soon as possible. NCCs receive a variety of mailings, most electronically, through e-mail and on Web sites. Advisers need to make sure that all the various forms required for each individual delegate and each institution are thoroughly and accurately completed. Advisers need to double check deadline dates, registration instructions, and other important information with NCCs to ensure that all administrative necessities are taken care of by deadlines. Conference organizers charge late fees in addition to original registration fees if registrations are submitted after initial deadlines.

- Determining the most effective mode of transportation and making necessary arrangements. A number of factors previously discussed need to be taken into consideration as NCCs and advisers make travel decisions. Recent changes in policies regarding the use of 15 passenger vans within certain states and at individual institutions have significantly impacted conference travel planning.

- Helping students assess personal and organizational needs. While preparing to attend conferences, students should assess how individuals and groups can get the most out of conferences. Preplanning gives students leads on looking for conference programs that can help them with their work on campus. It is good to put these needs or goals in writing so delegations can work as teams to gather critical information and new ideas from programming sessions and networking with students from other campuses.

- Building delegation unity. In order to be strong delegations at conferences, groups need to start by being strong groups on home campuses as they make plans for conferences. Pre-conference meetings with ice breakers and activities that help delegates get to know one another are good starting points. Providing forums for those who have been to other conferences to share experiences and answer new delegate questions is another way to build delegation unity. These meetings also provide opportunities for delegates to work on various conference planning committees. Committees can work on institution banners, institution displays, award bids, spirit and trade items, cheers, fundraising, and clothing. With NCCs being involved in lengthy business meetings at conferences, it is important to decide which students will be "leaders" in their absence. These leaders ensure that delegates have the information they need and facilitate delegation meetings at conferences when NCCs are unavailable. Typically, RHA presidents or any other students who volunteer can serve in this role. NCCs have input into who serves as leaders of delegations in their absence.

- Completing optional institutional conference displays and banners as well as planning roll calls. Though optional, these efforts are opportunities for students to showcase campuses and organizations. Institutional displays can be as simple as poster boards and as complex as displays with moving mechanical parts. Displays usually coordinate with conference themes. Institutional banners vary in much the same way as displays. They can consist of materials like paper, fabric, plastic, or vinyl. Conference staffs establish guidelines for both banners and displays. Roll call expectations and how roll calls are done varies significantly at the regional level. At the national level, each region coordinates roll calls..

- Preparing for spirit as a large part of the conference experience. Cheers are a loud, no cost means of showing institution spirit and pride. Having trade items to share helps delegations feel part of conferences. Trade items can range from computer-generated stickers, buttons, decorated clothespins, and pins to more expensive purchased items. Trade items also can be items leftover from other campus events or programs, including stress balls, cups, and glow sticks. When organizations or delegations bring trade items, they feel more part of the spirit of conferences. Delegation shirts, hats, vests, and painted faces are other examples of spirit that create identity and unity at conferences.

- Creating communication plans including list serves or newsletters to relay information to delegates prior to leaving for conferences. For national conferences, NCCs and advisers need to plan to provide contact information for students, since most stay at locations other than host campuses.
- Compiling delegate insurance information for conference registrations as well as emergency contact information. Having this type of information when traveling to and from conferences is important in case of accidents or health emergencies involving delegates (Self, 1992; Spencer, 1998).

Delegation Meetings at Conferences

Keeping delegations connected at conferences is important but challenging. Scheduling delegation meetings at certain times each day and meeting for meals allows for discussions about what has been learned and how program presentations went. This serves to keep communications flowing and delegates connected. When the NCCs are busy, have delegate leaders facilitate these meetings.

- There are several other ways in which to make delegation meetings as effective as possible. For example, once delegates have checked in and have received program session booklets, they can meet as a group to review program selections and choose which programs each delegate will attend. Program attendance decisions should be based on previously completed group and individual goals assessments. Delegates can maximize their conference dollars by having representation at a variety of workshops. Also, delegates can review the conference schedules as a group and determine times and locations that they will meet to travel to meals, practice and participate in roll calls, and attend keynote speaker sessions and other general sessions.
- Delegations can create delegation rosters including hall/room assignments and phone numbers if phone service is available to use during conferences. With large percentages of students having personal cell phones, cell phone numbers can be included. It is important for the delegates to have NCC and adviser contact information as well.

- Finally, for first time delegates, there may be opportunities to participate in case study experiences. Case studies serve as good learning experiences for student leaders and offer yet another means for delegates to connect at conferences.

After Conference Follow-Up

NCCs and advisers should schedule post conference delegation meetings to have delegates share conference experiences. NCCs and advisers can formalize conference follow-up through written conference evaluations. The information gathered can be used to implement programming ideas gathered at conferences; for planning future conference attendance; and to give NCCs and advisers feedback on how well the delegation was prepared. (See Appendix 6.) Conference attendance can serve as a leadership development milestone as well as a personal and professional milestone for students and advisers.

Building Traditions

Traditions are woven into the campus culture of every higher education institution. Traditions range from freshmen orientation experiences to activities that are connected to particular holidays or calendar events to student organization activities to athletic events.

At many institutions, long-standing traditions connected to conference attendance and residence hall organizations also exist. These traditions include wearing institutional attire to conferences; wearing adaptations of mascots (like tails or ears); or wearing more whimsical items that may not have anything to do with institutions but have traditions for particular delegations at conferences. There is pride in immediate recognition by other delegations. A sense of pride keeps delegates connected, especially if they had a part in developing traditions.

Traditions also can serve as opportunities to acknowledge accomplishments and give praise and encouragement. Examples include gathering conference delegates prior to or after closing banquets; having delegates share experiences and individual or group accomplishments; and then toasting each other with sparkling cider or soft drinks. Whatever format chosen, these kinds of group traditions can be special and memorable events.

Other types of traditions include taking delegation pictures in front of recognizable signs or buildings at each conference sight or having delegations photographed in particular arrangements. Traditions unify delegations and conjure up positive thoughts and feelings when delegates recall conference experiences after they return to campuses or years later when at reunions. Reunions are traditions that can be established. Conference delegation reunions can coincide with other campus activities such as homecomings, alumni weekends, and founder's days.

Technology has assisted in developing and preserving conference traditions and experiences. Photos from pre-conference planning meetings and travel experiences combined with photos from conferences can be compiled to create conference delegation CDs or DVDs. Conference CDs and DVDs can be kept as histories for future students and are guaranteed to add to conversations at reunions in years to come.

NACURH, Inc. is built on long-standing traditions. Sharing in these traditions over the years is one of the many things that keep alumni of NACURH connected to the organization as well as connected to those with whom they shared memories and to new students continuing these traditions today.

Advising gives housing professionals opportunities to impact and touch the lives of many students. Advising also provides unique opportunities to continue to learn and grow from relationships and experiences shared with students. Advising conference delegations and sharing conference experiences with students is an opportunity that every adviser should experience at least once.

References

NACURH, (1997). *National Association of College and University Residence Halls, Inc., articles of incorporation.* Stillwater, OK: Author.

Self, C. (1992, October). Role of a conference delegation adviser. *Intermountain Affiliate of College and University Residence Halls Newsletter.*

NACURH, (2004). *National Association of College and University Residence Halls, Inc., Policy Book.* Stillwater, OK: Author.

Spencer, C. (1998). State, subregional, regional and national conferences. In N.W. Dunkel & C.L. Spencer (Eds.). *Advice for Advisers: The Development of an Effective Residence Hall Association (pp. 208–214).* Columbus, OH: Association of College and University Housing Officers-International.

Appendix 1: Alphabet Soup: A Guide to NACURH Acronyms

NACURH The National Association of College and University Residence Halls. The association has eight regional affiliates: **CAACURH** (Central Atlantic Affiliate of College and University Residence Halls), **GLACURH** (Great Lakes Affiliate of College and University Residence Halls), **IACURH** (Intermountain Affiliate of College and University Residence Halls), **MACURH** (Midwest Affiliate of College and University Residence Halls), **NEACURH** (North East Affiliate of College and University Residence Halls), **PACURH** (Pacific Affiliate of College and University Residence Halls), **SAACURH** (South Atlantic Affiliate of College and University Residence Halls), and **SWACURH** (South West Affiliate of College and University Residence Halls).

NACURH also has two National Offices. NIC (National Information Center) and NRHH (National Residence Hall Honorary)

NACURH has two Corporate Partners. They are OCM (On-Campus Marketing) and USA Today

Some of NACURH's major services include RFI (Resource Files Index) and VTI (Video Tape Index).

Awards are major recognition tools for NACURH member schools:
OTM Of-the-Month Awards
OTY Of-the-Year Awards
POY Program-of-the-Year Award
SALT Student Award for Leadership Training

Officer positions include:
NBD National Board of Directors
RBD Regional Board of Directors
NAA National Associate for Administration
NAF National Associate for Finance
CRC Conference Resource Consultant

Appendix 2: Delegate Application

Name: _____

Campus Address _____

Phone: _____ Email: _____

Please answer the following questions on a separate sheet of paper.

- Are you planning to live on campus next year?

- Why are you interested in attending this year's_____conference on
  ____/____/____?

- What prompted you to apply to be a delegate for ACURH?

- What does team spirit mean to you, and how have you previously   experienced it?

- What, if any, leadership positions do you currently hold in the residence halls? What positions would you like to hold in the future?

- If selected, what do you hope to gain from this experience?

- How would you share what you gained from the conference programs to others on campus?

- Are you available to attend weekly delegation meetings on ___/___/___at
  _____ p.m.?

- Why should you be selected as a delegate to _____ ACURH, and how can you represent (<u>XYZ University</u>) at this conference?

- What skills and experiences would you bring to share with the delegation and others at the conference?

- How would you utilize the information gained at MACURH to strengthen the residence hall experience for others at UND?

Applications are due to <u>(NCC name)</u>, <u>(Location to be returned)</u>, by <u>(deadline date)</u>. You may either e-mail your application to <u>(NCC email)</u>, or send the completed application by intercampus mail. If you have further questions, or need an additional application, please feel free to contact <u>(NCC or Adviser)</u> by email, or by phone at <u>(xxx-xxxx)</u>. Delegates will be chosen and notified by <u>(date)</u>.

Appendix 3: Sample Excuse Form

DATE

To Whom It May Concern:

Each year, the _____ (insert acronym) Affiliate of College and University Residence Halls, hosts a residence hall leadership conference. This conference, held _____/_____/_____ at (host school name and location) will bring together over (number of students registered) from _____ states and the province of _____.

The (school name) Residence Halls Association (RHA) actively participates in the _____ACURH conference. _____(insert number of students attending) student-leaders will be attending the conference, representing the residence halls, (school XYZ), and their respective boards and halls.

I would request that you excuse the following students' class absence on _____/_____/_____ and if at all possible, supply the student with any assignments, tests, or quizzes to do before this date. I appreciate your assistance in allowing students the opportunity to represent the University in attending and presenting programs, and networking with other students, which we believe is an essential part of the learning process.

If you have any questions or concerns about this absence, I would be happy to visit with you further. Please contact me by telephone at _____ _____, or by email at _____. Thank you for your anticipated cooperation in this out of classroom learning opportunity.

Students Attending:

List all students attending

Sincerely,

Appendix 4: Conference Attendance/Accountability Agreement

(This example is where the organization is paying conference and travel fees)

I do hereby accept the invitation extended to me by the Residence Hall Association to attend the _____ conference to be held at _____ on ___/___/___ and agree to the following:

1) To Be Ready! We will meet at the RHA Office at (<u>time</u>) on, (<u>day and date</u>) to travel to (<u>conference location</u>)

2) I will attend a session during each of the program session slots and stay at the conference at all times. I will collect copies of all handout material to be submitted along with a written summary of each session I attended. These reports are due at the RHA meeting to be held on ___/___/___.

3) I agree to attend all delegation teambuilding and work meetings prior to the conference and follow through with any committee expectations.

4) I will represent (<u>school name</u>) and RHA in a respectable and responsible manner. This includes no consumption of alcohol or use of controlled substances.

5) I realize it will be my responsibility to pay for the registration fee if I violate any of the guidelines and am removed from the conference.

6) If not attending, I am responsible for getting a person (of the same sex) to attend the conference from the same board/hall and have them approved by the President of RHA and the NCC. If I am unable to attend and do not have a proxy, I will pay the cost of the registration.

I further realize that failure to follow the above guidelines will result in my paying the registration fee to RHA Policy Board no later than (<u>date</u>). Finally, I accept the responsibility to pay for any expenses I incur; failing to do so will result in these damages being billed to my University account.

Signature _____ Date _____

Address: _____

Position: _____ Phone: _____

Appendix 5: Helpful Hints for Program Presentations

Conference time is drawing near and your NCC or adviser has decided that you are to present a session. Perhaps you were instrumental in a project and have decided to share it at a regional or national conference. You have taken on the responsibility of representing your school by presenting a session to delegates from schools across the region or nation. This is a serious responsibility, so we would like to offer a few suggestions to aid in the preparation of your session.

1. **Research:** Research is an important aspect of your presentation. Knowing how to do a program is easier than teaching others. The more familiar you are with your subject, the more comfortable you will be with presenting it and answering questions.

2. **Integration:** If you spend 10 hours on research, avoid trying to present those 10 hours of information in a 60-90 minute session. Integrate your material with the main points and the goals of your session in mind.

3. **Practice:** Present your session to your residence hall government, your advisers and other interested people; get a feeling for your use of time, clarity and overall effectiveness.

4. **Presentation Style:** There are many different presentation styles to choose from. Here are a few ideas:
   - A straightforward, formal lecture.
   - A lecture/discussion/lecture format.
   - A discussion session.
   - An active/interactive format.
   - Pace yourself so that all important points are given equal time.
   - Use of audio-visual material and structured experiences.
   - When thoughts and important points are clear and simple, they are easier for you and the participants to remember.
   - Giving an "overview" of your session during the first few minutes helps participants know what to expect.

5. **Handouts:** A two-page (2) summary of your presentation is valuable to you and participants. After your research, if you can summarize your thoughts, ideas and main points in two (2) pages, you should have a good working knowledge of your presentation. Participants have the opportunity to take knowledge and information home to be reviewed and studied. All handouts should contain the name of the session, the name of the presenter and the school.

6. **Visual Aids:** Visual aids can add to or detract from your presentation. Think of yourself as a participant when you are preparing your visual aids.
   - Prints need to be clear and large enough for all to see.
   - Colors help.
   - Too much information is distracting.
   - An outline of the presentation is helpful.
   - Become familiar with your audio-visual equipment. Do you have another plan in case something goes wrong with the equipment?

7. **Finally:** It is important to present material that is congruent with the program description submitted for the program schedule. It is quite frustrating when you have limited time at a conference, choose a topic from the many listed, and discover that the session bears no resemblance to the description.

8. **Other comments:**
   - It is hoped that you will find these hints helpful in the preparation of your session.
   - Remember—a conference is only as good as the presenter(s) of its session!!!
   - Thank you for your support of the regional and national conferences!

Appendix 6: Conference Evaluation

1. What was you favorite part of ___ACURH and why?
2. What was your least favorite part of ___ ACURH and why?
3. Please list the programs you attended and give a summary of each, both the good and the bad points. Make sure to note whether this program could be adapted to our own campus and in what way? Did these programs help you in your position?
4. Do you feel going to ___ACURH was a worthwhile time investment? Why or why not?
5. Do you feel that the NCC adequately prepared you for ___ACURH? Why or why not?
6. What do you feel the NCC or adviser could have done differently to better prepare you?
7. Do you feel the expectations set for our group were reasonable? Why or why not?
8. Any other ideas, comments, concerns:

Note: Delegates need to be prepared to answer #3. Cover this expectation in pre-conference meetings.

17

Programming

Greg Block

Programming is a critical component in the mission of housing departments. Student development theories guide housing departments as staff members set goals and objectives for the year. One study states, "Residential living during college is consistently one of the most important determinants of a college student's level of involvement or integration into the various cultural, social, and extracurricular systems of the institution. Compared to their counterparts who live at home or commute to college, resident students have significantly more social interaction with peers and faculty and are more likely to be involved in extracurricular activities and use campus facilities" (Pascarella, Terenzini & Blimling, 1994).

Challenging students through programming is widely accepted as part of what housing departments should and can accomplish. Many studies recommend on-campus, residential experiences as ways to enrich and make college students' education more fulfilling (Kuh, Douglas, Lund, & Ramin-Gyurnek, 1994; Pascarella, Terrenzini & Blimling, 1994; Shuh, 1999; Shuh & Shelley, 2001). Both student staff and student leaders in campus organizations share in the responsibility of creating programs that enrich the life of the students.

As advisers consider their programming options, they should ask themselves what campus groups are doing, and what do advisers want to have happen? Advisers may discover that what they ideally want as end goals is achieved by the programming currently scheduled by student leaders.

Setting Goals

Some campuses may have strong programming committees within residence hall associations (RHAs) and respective hall councils. On other campuses, resident assistant (RA) staff conducts most of the programming, and student leaders have lesser roles in designing or coordinating programs for campus populations. There are a variety of purposes for involving RHAs in campus programming, in residence hall programming, and programming at the floor level. When RHAs are involved in campus programming some potential benefits include: The positive outcomes when students program to students; the bridges that can be created between student leadership and housing departments beyond traditional residence life; developmental tools that give RHAs funding control for programming on campus; and the traditions that develop from RHA and student, leader-based programming models.

Students Programming to Students

Many campuses have multiple groups that program. RHAs often play crucial roles in the programming offered from the department to the residential campus population. One of the primary purposes of RHA programming is to create mechanisms where students program for students. Increased involvement and successful integration into campus life significantly contribute to student retention and development (Ballou, Reavill & Schultz, 1995).

The programs sponsored by RHAs provide educational, recreational, and other benefits. Advisers often focus on the benefits participating students receive from programming. They need also to consider the benefits that the students coordinating the programs receive. The brainstorming and design process causes students to think about a variety of issues. The coordination stage gives students opportunities to learn time management, communication, and presentation skills. There also are benefits that come out of evaluating programs when they conclude. What worked? What did not? What could have been done differently? These are all questions students debate in groups that provide growth through discussion.

With guidance from advisers, programming topics and models assist RHAs in providing programming that meets students' needs. Student leaders, many who may already have lived on campus for a year or more, are part of the process of identifying program needs and coordinating events and activities for fellow students. Students who attend student-planned programs may identify better with the topic, style, or presentation. It stands to reason that those who live with them, and are of the same age and experience, best know the needs and focus of students. Residence halls can provide an informal atmosphere where the combination of student life and the learning process can occur naturally (Schroeder & Mable, 1994).

Designing programs based on such models gives student leaders lifelong training to see the bigger picture. Involvement in residence hall communities has been shown to have a positive effect on learning outcomes (McCluskey-Titus, Oliver, Wilson, Hall, Cawthon, & Crandall, 2002). For example, an RHA wants to offer a dance for a recreational program. This is an opportunity for the adviser to discuss several issues. If problems with discipline tend to occur at certain times of the evening, can the program be steered to this time slot to offer an alternative activity to reduce discipline issues?

There are many other questions that the students must consider when arranging programs. Are they aware of discipline patterns and concerns of the housing administration? Are program locations accessible to all students and do they conform to ADA guidelines? If fees are required to attend programs, are there discounts for those attending as a couple and, if so, how do groups define couples? Is this an opportunity to discuss issues of homophobia that may exist? What this all boils down to is the general question that advisers need to ask themselves: How involved have we allowed student leaders to be in our department?

There are numerous opportunities to assist in student development by having RHA student leaders program for fellow students. The growth organizations see in student leaders is well worth the investment of time from advisers in discussing programming throughout the year.

Student-Led Programming Bridging Campus Communities

Often student-led programming serves as a bridge between housing departments and the university involving maintenance, food service, assignments, and other campus components that the students might not ordinarily give much consideration to.

Advisers should involve student leaders with a variety of staff and administrators within and outside of Housing and challenge RHA student leaders to seek assistance from those whose experience and talent are not historically tapped by students on many campuses. Student leaders enjoy the opportunity to utilize these resources and meet other university staff. For example, there are custodial staff members who have worked on campus in housing departments for years and often have that institutional knowledge of what has worked and what has not. However, the custodial staff is seldom asked for input related to student programming. This is despite the fact they may be able to offer a unique eye on student behavior by what they see and address daily and weekly.

Advisers can challenge student leaders to have meetings with custodians to see what they perceive as student needs.

Student participation also may help build bridges by creating a situation where the custodial staff no longer sees programs for the additional work they require. While students may do an excellent job with post-program clean up, there are instances where custodial staff may still have the burden of additional clean up to get a facility or area to its normal condition. By involving custodians, student leaders may be able to prevent large-scale problems with damage and clean up.

Maintenance staff members are another good programming resource for student leaders. They know buildings well, understand power needs and sources, and can give advice based on this knowledge. One study shows that out-of-classroom experiences assist students in achieving learning outcomes, and that many of these experiences provided real world learning (Kuh, 1995). Involving student leaders in discussions with staff who may be affected by their decisions prepares them for the real world where they will have to think of all angles related to their ideas.

Each semester, advisers can share reports about discipline patterns on campus. Campus judicial officers or representatives from discipline offices are ideal resources for these reports and presentations. Sharing reports about discipline patterns brings information to student leaders so they can assist in correcting negative behavior in the community. Taking this action brings meaning to the meetings and holds various parts of the housing department accountable. Creating and presenting reports every semester to student leaders allows judicial officers to become involved in student life beyond judicial hearings. It also ensures a more global approach in addressing these issues.

Residence life staff often advises RHAs. But have administrators considered advisers from other housing departments or areas of campus to be RHA advisers or co-advisers? Can the campus community create opportunities for other staff to serve as advisers? Most likely, several non-residence life staff people have had experience working with student groups as youth leaders in places of worship, at teen centers in the community, as coaches in recreational leagues, or any number of other situations. Programming committees of RHAs may allow opportunities for non-residence life staff to serve as advisers for specific tasks. For example, food service staff can advise programs where food is being served or shared. Seeking food service staff assistance also ensures that RHAs are aware of all code issues for their community related to the preparation and handling of food. Multicultural affairs staff can be tapped to assist in questions concerning inclusion policies and procedures. Tapping other resources helps to build bridges between RHAs, housing departments, and campus departments.

Funding Programming

There is value in having student leaders take responsibility for the funding of programs. Student fees or housing charges are often the main source of funding for RHAs as well as fundraising on campus. When considering the role of programming for student leadership, it is empowering to look at models where all programs requiring funding of some form must be approved by elected student leadership. The requirement that RAs have to present and explain the need to spend $50 on pizza for a Super Bowl party may lead to events being approved or not approved. What will come from these actions are discussions and opportunities for advisers to truly advise, to supply students with multiple views, and to challenge students to think about what is happening around them.

Campus administrators may not want the additional work or layers of approval that come from student-approved funding models. However, advisers should examine long-term goals for groups to determine if the funding of programming can impact the overall goals for groups.

Being the funding source of programming represents power. Advisers need to examine the power component of campus cultures. Those who control programming funds (such as central office staff, hall directors, RAs, or RHA campus leaders) are often the perceived—and in many cases, the legitimate—sources of power for campus communities. Advisers need to determine end goals and who they wish to have programming funding power and why. Programming funding discussions are challenging and should involve all levels of the organization, both professional staff and student leaders.

Traditions

Traditions are a great part of campus life. Programming by RHAs allows the opportunity for campus traditions to be built. Large scale programs, educational opportunities, and the ability to co-program with other campus groups such as student governments, athletic associations, student unions or campus activities offices may come from these traditional programs.

There is obvious worth in having programs that are handed down from year to year. The ties that are created between various generations of RHA members serve to strengthen groups by providing opportunities for communication between veterans, former members, new members, and leadership.

Challenges

Programming offers many opportunities for student leaders and student learning.

However, there are always challenges in the programming process. Challenges may include determining programming control, programming funding, and the role of RHAs in programming. Advisers need to determine who controls programming on campus. On most campuses, many entities offer programs, and RHA groups are challenged to not offend or encroach on areas others see as their programming territory. Advisers can approach groups that have established programs to build bridges or partnerships.

Another challenge is program funding. Programming is expensive. Advisers need to decide the niche that RHAs play in programming. Is the RHA programming niche floor or community centered? Is it targeted towards buildings, areas or the entire campus population? Determining the programming niche gives direction to funding needs and possible resources. Campus-wide programs can be quite expensive. However, the relative cost for other RHA campus-wide activities, such as clothing drives for local shelters, can be minimal. Advisers need to identify the RHA role in programming to develop budgets and set goals and objectives.

Conclusion

Programming is an instrumental part of living on campus, and RHAs should and can play a large part in developing programming. The ability to provide learning opportunities outside the classroom is generated by these programs. RHA members can learn traditions and have meaningful dialogue with a wide variety of staff from various departments about budgets, funding sources, discipline, menu creation in the cafeteria, and other programming-related topics. Advisers can strengthen their roles by being part of discussions that come from programming within RHAs on campuses. Advisers should constantly be looking for ways to involve RHAs in new and innovative ways within departments and campus communities. This involvement creates opportunities for RHA leaders to be part of every facet of housing organizations.

References

Ballou, R., Reavill, L., & Schultz, B. (1995). Assessing the immediate and residual effects of the residence hall experience: Validating Pace's 1990 analysis of on-campus and off-campus students. *Journal of College and University Student Housing, 25*(1), 16–21.

Kuh, G. (1995). The other curriculum: Out of class experiences associated with student learning and personal development. *Journal of Higher Education, 66*, 125–150.

Kuh, G. D., Douglas, K. B., Lund, J. P., & Ramin-Gyurnek, J. (1994). Student learning outside the classroom: Transcending artificial boundaries. ASHE-ERIC Report No. 4. Washington DC: The George Washington University, School of Education and Development.

McCluskey-Titus, P., Oliver, R. S., Wilson, M. E., Hall, L. M., Cawthon, T. W., & Crandall, P. D. (2002). The relationship between community and academic achievement in residence halls. *The Journal of College and University Student Housing, 30* (2), 11–16.

Pascarella, E.T. Terenzini, P.T., & Blimling, G.S. (1994). The impact of residential life on students. As found in C. Schroeder and P. Mable (eds.), *Realizing the educational potential of residence halls,* (pp. 22–52). San Francisco: Jossey-Bass.

Shuh, J. H. (1999). Student learning in college residence halls: What the research shows. Educational programming and student learning in college and university residence halls. Columbus, OH: Association of College and University Housing Officers-International.

Shuh, J. H., & Shelley, M. C. (2001). External factors affecting room and board rates: How much influence does the housing director have? *Journal of College and University Student Housing, 30* (1), 41–47.

Schroeder, C. C., Mable, P., & Associates. (1994). *Realizing the educational potential of residence halls.* San Francisco: Jossey-Bass.

18

Transitioning of Officers

Ric Baker

Advisers to student groups, particularly residence hall associations (RHAs), have a myriad of opportunities to proactively impact the development of groups as a whole and officers in particular. Some opportunities are spontaneous, such as feedback on programs and meetings. Other opportunities are part of larger, intentional plans. One opportunity that occurs along a more structured timeframe is advising the transition of executive board officers.

Student organizations by nature are dynamic groups whose members are continually joining and exiting. An intentional, year long plan on how to manage and execute the transition of executive board officers lays the foundation for a successful year. This chapter details effective executive board transition interventions, assuming a process that starts at the beginning of the spring semester and carries through the end of the following fall term. If advisers and groups follow alternate academic calendars, some adjustment of the timing of these interventions is warranted.

Transitions

Transitional periods within student groups offer opportunities as well as risks for the future of these groups. Transitions to new environments can cause significant anxiety and may impact the ability of students to persist within positions (Robinson, Burns, & Gaw, 1996). As students make adjustments to new responsibilities, advisers have unique opportunities to guide the experiences. A report from the Center for Mental Health in Schools at The University of

California at Los Angeles (2003) identifies four key intervention tasks that can be initiated by advisers:

- Establish a mechanism for prioritizing development, planning, implementation, and the ongoing evolution of the needed transition programs.
- Develop specific strategies and activities related to each transition program.
- Initiate each transition program.
- Provide ongoing maintenance and creative renewal of all programs designed to support transitions (p. 5).

These tasks serve as the conceptual outline for designing transition strategies within organizations. For the purpose of this discussion, transitional programs are defined as interventions designed by groups and advisers to effectively manage transitions.

Organization models for RHAs vary according to type of institution, mission, and student population. Transition strategies should be designed with each unique organization in mind. Dunkel and Schuh (1998) describe a typical executive board for institutional RHAs as having a president, vice-president, treasurer, secretary, and adviser (p. 26). An RHA organization executive board may also consist of additional officers, such as national communications coordinator (NCC) or other officers that fulfill a specific component of the group's mission. When planning transitional interventions, it is essential advisers design exercises that are general enough to apply to all members yet allow individuals to apply components to their unique positions.

In designing plans to transition officers, advisers need to assume a yearlong process. From initially orienting officers to position descriptions through guiding them through documenting experiences for their successors, the transition process can be effectively stimulated throughout the year. One variable that may shift the timing of interventions with officers is the unexpected officer resignation. A student's ability to participate in leadership organizations is contingent upon many factors, including grade point average, having available time, and of course, being a resident in the halls. Often times these circumstances shift during the academic year and create a situation where a new officer is forced to assimilate into a position. Not only does this change affect the group dynamic, but it also occurs outside the traditional transition time frame. One way to make this change as seamless as possible is through ongoing, accurate record keeping and retention.

Record Keeping

A key tool in the transition and orientation of officers is record keeping. At the University of South Florida, for example, the RHA has developed two functional ways of recording activities. The first of these, a "year in review" document, serves as a polished, scrapbook style report that documents activities, conferences, policy proposals, and other group events. Produced at the end of the year, it provides a historical account of the group activities and collectively shows the group's progress through the years.

The second document is more functional in transitioning officers. This "book of procedures" is updated annually and is a collection of information to assist new officers in what was accomplished last year.

For each office, additional important records are kept including the spreadsheets for the treasurer, important programming contacts for the vice president, and sample minutes for the secretary. Additionally, each officer includes a brief summary of accomplishments during the past year with suggestions on improvement for subsequent officers. This fluid document not only assists the group in historical documentation, it serves as the initial training tool during new officer orientation training that occurs immediately after elections. It also serves as a tool to educate new members on their roles in annual functions sponsored by the organization as well as provides information on non-recurring duties encountered throughout the year.

The adviser role in record retention is important. As it is the advisers who usually remain connected with the RHA from year-to-year, they are the ones in better position to make sure proper records are kept in each officer area. Of particular record keeping importance is money management. Also, accurate minutes and documentation of the group's activities are vital to maintaining group momentum. Advisers need to work with presidents to follow up with officers on record retention on an ongoing basis. Additionally, advisers can address record keeping during one-on-one meetings with officers to provide another check and balance to assist groups in meeting goals.

Position Descriptions

In laying the groundwork for officer transitions, it is essential to start with written position descriptions. Outlining the duties and expectations of each office, position descriptions serve as fundamental tools in orienting new officers to their roles. Additionally, position descriptions illustrate the separation of the functional duties of officers and help reduce role confusion among executive board members.

Many RHAs choose to quantify officer position descriptions within constitutions. This serves a dual purpose. It documents the expectations while maintaining position descriptions within the core charter of the group and minimizes the amount of additions and deletions to position expectations. Changing organization constitutions involves a majority of support that lessens the chances of arbitrary changes due to shifting group dynamics. Position descriptions also serve as guides for disseminating information among the executive board (Chmielewski, 2000, p. 18). Dunkel and Schuh (1998) outline basic position descriptions for key RHA officer positions in Appendix 2. These examples design positions and assess if additional positions are needed given the organizational structure.

To begin the transition process, groups should include position descriptions in application or nomination packets that are distributed to candidates. Communication of this type informs candidates of the responsibilities of positions as well as assists them in preparing for the types of questions they will be asked during the election process. Once elected, advisers should encourage new officers to use position descriptions as the foundation for developing their goals and outcomes for the upcoming year.

Transition Meetings and Training

After elections, a critical juncture in the transitioning of officers takes place. Training new officers is a dynamic, individualized process that differs each year. Students come into RHA leadership positions at various developmental levels with varying rates of ability to complete the new responsibilities outlined within their position descriptions. Returning officers can provide transition assistance. In designing training interventions, advisers should consider the following questions:

- Are there returning officers? If so, are they returning to the same positions or different positions?
- What types of self-assessments did returning officers complete for their previous positions?
- Are any of the returning officers capable of delivering training in certain areas?
- In what areas does the adviser need to lead the training?

One of the most effective ways of training new officers is through transition meetings with existing officers. While existing officers finish out their terms, newly elected officers can shadow their counterparts. This includes sitting with them during final organization meetings as well as setting up individual transition meetings for each new officer. New officer teams together can review resources that outgoing officers accumulated throughout the year such as program evaluations, budget spreadsheets, sample agendas and minutes, and fundraising information. Reviewing the record keeping of previous officers is an important component of acclimating new officers to what has been accomplished in the past as well as provides blueprints for the future. Individual officer transition meetings should occur before more formal officer training late spring semester. Advisers can provide lists for each officer of major topics to cover in transition meetings. Appendix 3 outlines a sample transition list for a typical RHA officer.

The new executive board gathers together for the first time as team to attend the spring training session. This session is an opportunity to begin team building, to assess levels of additional training needed before the end of the academic year, to determine if sufficient leaders are available to lead summer term, and to introduce new board members to housing administrators and liaisons. The functions that are covered during this session are critical if groups are to maintain the momentum of the past year while planning for initial operations in the beginning of the fall term. Advisers should complete brief developmental assessments on each officer to assist in determining what levels of reinforcement training are needed after the transition meeting following fall officer retreats. Based on position expectations, these assessments determine each officer's ability to carry out the duties of the position and identify areas that need attention. A sample self-assessment is included in Appendix 4.

When developing training strategies, advisers should consider several modalities. A portion of the adviser's training time with new officers is spent one-on-one while other topics are best covered as group workshops and retreats. Workshops tend to be topic specific and focused on specific training, while retreats are designed to foster creative thought and develop teams. There are several opportunities for executive boards to attend workshops, such as NACURH-affiliated conferences. However, retreats are typically campus based with topics chosen with a specific group's needs in mind. Depending on the training issues identified by the board and adviser, a balance of these two types of interventions can effectively move organizations along their paths of development.

Retreats serve an integral purpose in the development of boards. Not only do they provide opportunities for groups to develop expectations of each other individually and as teams, but retreats also allow for creativity and sharing not replicated in other settings. As board members grow individually, they also grow as a group. Tuckman (1965) describes a model of group dynamics where students move through stages of getting to know each other, experiencing conflict, adapting to the skills of the group, and capitalizing on individual skills for the team's benefit. Retreats serve as intentional mediums to move groups through stages of development. At educational institutions, retreats are most often scheduled at transition times such as the beginning or end of semesters, or during other break periods. Depending on a group's developmental needs, various themes can be employed.

At the beginning of the academic year, "planning" retreats are most appropriate. Serving to empower new groups, planning retreats helps groups refine annual goals, develop expectations for board members and organizations, and develop the interpersonal bonds that will strengthen each group's ability to perform as a team. Bonstingl (2004) describes seven key elements present in effective retreats:

- Choose a productive environment. Typically, retreats are held outside the normal confines of a group such as a retreat center. If funding is an issue, groups should choose a remote facility on campus.
- Focus on policies and processes, not personalities. Make sure issues and policies that are discussed are done so without personalizing. Avoid the "blame game" and concentrate on ideas and solutions.
- Make relevant data the basis of the group's work. Make use of feedback, evaluations, and suggestions when designing goals and objectives for the new year. Question why certain functions of the organization are strong, while others need improvement.
- Consider every stakeholder group and focus on results. Make sure each member feels valued in expressing his/her views and that each member's portion of the planned outcome is taken into consideration.
- Celebrate and build on strengths. Identify what works well within the group and apply that energy towards working on opportunities for improvement in other areas.
- Provide objective facilitation. This is an excellent task for advisers to assume. Providing an objective voice to keep the group on task and efficient is a critical component often overlooked in retreat planning.
- Provide food, fun, and fellowship. Be sure to plan effectively for healthy meals that meet all dietary needs of the group. To quote NACURH adviser Valerie Averill, "We don't come to retreats to starve" (personal communication, August 2004). Additionally, allow time for unstructured interaction. Spontaneous exchanges often prove to be the highlight of retreats for participants. (pp. 24–25).

Retreats are also effective tools to resolve issues facing groups. Lack of motivation, group discourse, and other issues that organizations struggle with are all excellent motivators for participating in a retreat. Annual retreats are also effective tools in building continuity from year-to-year. Establishing consistent schedules of retreats and workshops perpetuates an environment of learning and transition and builds organization traditions that serve groups and members for years to come.

Evaluating Transition Interventions

A final step in the transition of RHA officers is to evaluate transition interventions. Were the transition interventions effective in moving new officers to desired levels of leadership? Were group mission and history well served by the activities? How did the new officers enjoy the events? Advisers with successful transition programs do not wait until the end of the year to ask such questions. They assess the effectiveness of interventions through the use of benchmarks assessments throughout the year (Morgan & Herzog, 2001). Successful advisers establish benchmarks to evaluate the transition plan and develop timelines throughout the year to mark the progress made. Intentional evaluation of group performance allows advisers do their best work and assists groups in reaching their full potential.

Conclusion

Being intentional in the transition of officers positively impacts students. Utilizing the methods and guidelines discussed within this chapter will assist advisers in developing strong plans to guide their groups through annual changes. Advisers can never assume that each member of an executive board will be able to serve the entire year. Every plan needs to be flexible and adaptable to the ever-changing needs of student groups. Transitions occur, whether on schedule or not, and a key component of advising is assisting students work through transitions.

References

Bonstingl, J.J. (2004). Retreat to greatness. *Leadership, 33,* 24–25.

Center for Mental Health in Schools at UCLA. (2003). *An introductory packet on transitions: turning risks into opportunities for student support.* Los Angeles, CA: Author

Chmielewski, T.R. (2000). Student leadership: A checklist for success. *Principal Leadership,* 1, 2, 18–23.

Dunkel, N.W. & Schuh, J. H. (1998). *Advising student groups and organizations.* San Francisco: Jossey-Bass.

Morgan, P. L. & Hertzog, C. J. (2001). Designing comprehensive transitions. *Principal Leadership, 1, 7,* 10-16.

Robinson, D. G., Burns, C.F., & Gaw, K. F. (1996). Orientation programs: A foundation for student learning and success. *New Directions for Student Services, 75,* 55-68.

Tuckman, B. (1965). Developmental Sequence in Small Groups. *Psychological Bulletin, 63,* 384–399.

Appendix 1: Timetable for Officer Transitions

Spring Semester
- Identify new officer candidates.
- Hold election meeting for candidates – review position descriptions.
- Create election information packets.
- Hold elections.
- Hold transition meetings with new/old officers.
- Facilitate new officer training.

Summer Semester
- Plan officer retreat.

Fall Semester
- Facilitate officer retreat.
- Set goals and expectations.
- Conduct core training follow-up.
- Update book of procedures.
- Identify new officer candidates.
- Prepare for spring elections.

Appendix 2: Sample RHA Job Descriptions

President
- Preside at organization meetings.
- Facilitate executive board meetings.
- Present the organization to the institution.
- Meet weekly with the adviser.
- Be aware of all money matters.
- Assist all executive officers.
- Serve as spokesperson for the executive board and organization.
- Motivate the organization.
- Prepare for all meetings.
- Coordinate campus-wide programs.
- Serve on various committees or task forces.
- Prepare prior to all interviews.
- Be open to all opinions and input.
- Provide follow-up to organizational tasks.
- Inform the executive board of other meeting information.
- Organize executive board retreats.
- Prepare for annual banquet.
- Coordinate the executive board transition.

Vice-President

- Preside at organization meetings in the absence of the president.
- Serve as parliamentarian.
- Direct constitutional updating and revision.
- Facilitate elections.
- Submit term reports.
- Serve as liaison to committees.
- Perform other duties as directed by the president.

Treasurer

- Prepare the organizational budget.
- Serve as chair of the finance committee.
- Prepare purchase orders, requisition forms, or supply requests.
- Audit books twice per term with adviser.
- Maintain financial history of the organization.
- Maintain a working relationship with institutional accounting.
- Inform the executive board of all financial department personnel matters.
- Serve on various committees and task forces.
- Coordinate solicitations.
- Claim all stolen or lost equipment.
- Maintain an inventory of all equipment and its condition.
- Make quarterly reports of all receipts and disbursements.
- Perform other duties as directed by the president.

Secretary

- Record and maintain minutes of all organization meetings.
- Send minutes to all appropriate members and institutional staffs.
- Prepare an agenda with the president for all meetings.
- Keep the organization informed.
- Maintain attendance (roll call) at all meetings.
- Maintain a calendar of events.
- Serve as the organization's recognition coordinator.
- Maintain a phone and email directory of all members.
- Organize an end-of-the-year slide show.
- Reserve meeting rooms for the year.
- Advise on public relations.
- Maintain the office.
- Perform other duties as assigned by the president.

(Dunkel and Schuh, 1999, pp. 53–54)

Appendix 3: Sample Officer Transition Checklist

- Review book of procedures.
- Review strengths and challenges of past year.
- Detail existing commitments that will carry over to next year.
- Inventory supplies utilized by position.
- Locate and inventory computer files for position.
- Determine status of open projects.
- Return office/supply keys to adviser.
- Review institutional contacts utilized by position.

Appendix 4: Sample Self-Assessment of Officer Training Needs

Please respond to the questions regarding your readiness to perform within your position.

1. After the transition meetings with your outgoing officer, in what area of your leadership position do you feel most prepared? In what area of your leadership position do you feel least prepared?
2. Do you know the location of resources identified in your transition packet?
3. Is there any orientation to technology needed to adequately perform your position?
4. Do you feel comfortable on how to access the computer files associated with the position?
5. What is one goal that you have for fulfilling your position?
6. If you could ask your outgoing officer one more question, what would it be?

19

Assessment and Leadership: A Partnership of Intentionality

Dr. Stephen St. Onge, David Rosch & Eric Nestor

Student affairs professionals know that involvement matters. This book is written to support the involvement of student leaders on college and university campuses in ways that improve learning and environments. It is appropriate to include a chapter that incorporates assessment into leadership development programs. By using assessment, student affairs professionals can best understand how to maximize their impact as advisers and how to best impact student environments.

What is Assessment?

Assessment is defined as gathering evidence and information to describe organizational or programmatic effectiveness. Simply put, assessment means gathering data (quantitative or qualitative) to help either understand what is being done or to improve or develop in some area. When dealing with student leadership development, advisers should specifically and intentionally focus on outcomes assessment. Assessing outcomes allows advisers to focus on understanding the relationship between particular interventions and specific learning outcomes. Good leadership development assessment initiatives combine well-crafted learning outcomes with well-designed assessment plans. The first section of this chapter focuses on both issues.

ASSESSMENT TIPS

The following are tips to avoid some of the common pitfalls associated with assessment:

- Don't do a study no one wants. Be sure to share plans, learning outcomes and vision with key constituents.

- Determine who should be involved. Use this as an opportunity to build allies and to tap individual skills related to the assessment project.

- Plan to conduct a study that is valid and usable. Tap faculty resources. They are usually the first critics of flawed data.

- Decide on what the final report will look like before collecting data and make sure information can be provided for that report. Determine the target audience for the report.

- Consider the key data necessary for decision-making. Often this data is contextual based on the personnel and history of an organization or institution.

Figure 1: Assessment Tips (adapted from Upcraft and Schuh, 1996).

Assessment Planning

In preparing an assessment, there are some certain steps that should be followed (St. Onge, 1999). First, plans, learning outcomes, and the study's vision should be shared with key constituents. Second, it needs to be determined who will be involved in the assessment. This is often a good opportunity to build allies and to tap individual skills related to the assessment project. Faculty resources might be called upon. Those preparing the assessment should choose what the final report will look like before collecting data so that the necessary information can be provided for that report. Finally, the report's target audience must be determined and the key data necessary for their decision-making process must be considered. Often this data is contextual based on the personnel and history of an organization or institution.

To produce solid results, assessment planning needs to connect learning outcomes to activities. The first step in assessment planning is to identify the learning outcomes that students are to achieve and then develop a broad set of general questions to address through assessment. Examples of these questions might be, "What should a developed leader be able to do?" or "How does advising contribute to student leadership development?"

It is important to link the mission and vision of a program to learning outcomes and the general assessment questions. For example, if a program is based on a particular model of leadership development (like the Social Change Model), advisers need to ask questions that determine the success of integrating that model and using the model for successful leadership development. It is important to identify the criteria of successful programs as well, a point to be discussed in greater detail later in this chapter. Advisers are encouraged to invite students, faculty and staff to contribute to developing assessment questions. This provides needed input to assessment plans. Advisers look at their work from a particular perspective and set of values. Allowing others to share their thoughts helps to develop well rounded assessment plans. At this point, advisers should clearly identify who they want to provide input.

The next step in developing an assessment plan is to detail available resources. During the beginning of the assessment planning phase, advisers should have a sense of what resources are available for assessment projects. Key questions to ask include:

- What funds are available to support the collection, analysis and reporting of data?
- Does the adviser have the skills to analyze the collected data?
- Does the adviser have the cooperation of those completing assessments? Does the adviser have the support of staff to collect data (hand out surveys)?
- Does the budget support incentives for project participants?
- Is the political climate of the organization supportive of receiving critical feedback?

Perhaps the most important part of assessment planning is the development of a comprehensive assessment model used to guide assessment planning and practice. A model such as the one illustrated in Figure 2 can be used to help staff plan consistent and intentional assessment programs. This model also shows a complete assessment cycle, from generating learning outcomes and strategic goals to communicating assessment results (St. Onge et al., 2001). The elements of the model include:

- **Mission/Values.** Good assessment always starts with a strong foundation. Each organization or program should have an explicit, clear direction.
- **Learning Outcomes/Strategic Objectives.** These elements begin to operationalize the broader mission or vision of an organization. These are broader questions that deal with what specific outcomes advisers hope to achieve.

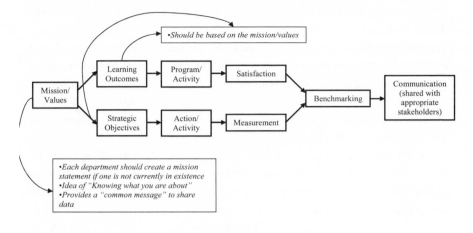

Figure 2

Strategic objectives are quantitative items, like numbers in attendance, and are often more counting-based than learning-based. A strategic goal might be to increase the number of student leaders by 10%.

- **Program Activity/Action.** These elements represent the specific things that advisers do to support the achievement of learning outcomes or strategic objectives. These items might include training activities, events, or interactions.
- **Satisfaction/Measurement.** Often it is a good idea to collect information from participants in program activities or actions to understand how they perceived the events. For example, 20 people may have come to a leadership training program, but did they like it?
- **Benchmarking.** Benchmarking is a comparison of results over time. Advisers may want to compare the number of student leaders over time, their ability to understand the social change model given changes in training sessions over time, etc. Benchmarking is especially useful when trying to assess environmental (climate) change, such as student completion of community service projects over time.
- **Communication.** Communication is sharing what has been learned in order to stimulate conversation as well as program development or program change.

Models such as this are sources of support for staff, especially when assessment is seen as an innovation in the organizational culture, to ensure proper assessment work. The final step, sharing assessment results to stimulate conversation and program development and review, is critical in completing the assessment cycle.

Once basic questions are developed and a model has been identified, one of the final steps is to operationalize the assessment plan by assigning specific tasks and roles such as developing survey/question development, collecting data, analyzing data, and preparing reports/communications. Advisers should also develop a specific timeline for each assessment plan that is consistent with the assessment model used.

The final phase of assessment planning is planning for the reporting of assessment results. Basic guidelines for reports are to communicate information to appropriate users, to address important (real) issues, to ensure timely reports that are easy to read, and to provide full reports preceded by summary report sections. Advisers should define the audiences and determine the level of information to report during assessment planning. This can be achieved by making a preliminary list of primary data users and key decision makers. A reporting plan should also include developing a master chart of all activities related to the assessment project including getting early drafts of reports to stakeholders and a timeline of reporting deadlines and points during the assessment project where key information may be shared. Other format points to consider are to write shorter paragraphs, avoid jargon, and highlight important findings. The following is a suggested outline for writing a formal report:

What is Good Advising?

A key step in assessing leadership development programs is to understand the criteria currently documented on successful programs. Literature on advising student groups provides insight into "best practices" for advising students on college campuses. Komives and Tucker (1998) found that in successful hall councils, the following behaviors were integral parts of the organization:

- Advisers communicate to students that they matter and are central to the mission of the university.
- The institution provided advisers information on how to recruit and retain student volunteers.
- Campus administrations allows for student input in a variety of formats and environments.
- Advisers provide multi-leveled student training and leadership development.
- Student leaders are able to represent and act as a voice of a broad spectrum of student groups and populations.

- Student leaders work to improve the environment within their residence halls and the broader community.

Dunkel and Schuh (1998) further state that the strongest student organizations act as service providers to the campus community and seek a broader vision beyond the confines of campus. Boatman (1988) similarly shares that the most successful student governance systems allow for clear access to advisers and other power brokers within the university system, act within an organizational structure in which all students are properly represented, and feel they can make an impact in the community.

The criteria mentioned above may provide a foundation for advisers to assess their groups and campus support. Advisers also can explore the criteria evident in the leadership development model that is used on their campuses. For example, the social change model of leadership development (Higher Education Research Institute, 1996) is a model used by many campuses. Those who implement the model seek to teach students that "leadership" is not a position a student holds, but rather an action that a student performs. The model further states that leadership takes place in a non-hierarchical and team-oriented environment and is achieved by creating positive change on the campus and in society. By combining these criteria, assessment can focus on some basic questions:

- How would students describe the formal and informal methods of communication on their campus?
- How would students describe their perceptions of their value to the institution?
- How effective are the recruitment and retention efforts for student leaders on campus? What would students suggest are the strengths and weaknesses of the current system?
- How would student leaders rate their impact on campus decision-making? How does the institution include students in key decisions?
- How would students rate the leadership development training currently offered on campus? Does the training reflect the leadership development model used on campus?
- How would student leaders describe their collaboration with other student leaders on campus?
- How would student leaders describe their ability to make change on campus or in the local community?

To address questions related to the social change model, advisers also may want to ask students to respond to the following:

- How would student leaders rate their listening and speaking skills?
- How would student leaders rate their time management?
- How would student leaders rate their integrity and ability to act as a role model for others?
- How would student leaders rate their community impact through service?

Through the development of a set of criteria for a "good advising program," advisers can use the model discussed earlier to assess their effectiveness. The criterion of community service follows for example purposes. One of the elements of a good leadership program is a student group's ability to make an impact on the community through service. The learning outcome phrased as an objective is: "Students will appreciate the value of community service." The adviser can then list the events that the group participated in each semester and create a short survey measuring each student's satisfaction or reflection on the value of community service or what they learned. Over time, the number of projects participated in will increase and the reflections of students on those events will increase. Then the adviser can assess the development of a service oriented student leadership team.

Sharing Instruments: The Syracuse University Example

Since fall 2000, the Office of Residence Life at Syracuse University has continuously assessed various components of residential communities that could be considered aspects of leadership development. These annual assessment projects have provided valuable data on the nature of the student population and behavior in the residence halls. This data has helped advisers to better serve students and laid the foundation for a large-scale leadership program assessment undertaken during the 2003–04 academic year.

Community Survey

One of the Syracuse University staff's primary means of learning about students is through the administering of the annual Community Survey. Since Fall 2000, this survey has been conducted annually in mid-October and is distributed to a 20% random sample of residential students stratified by residence hall, gender, academic year, and ethnicity. The stratification process ensures that the sample is representative of the residential student population in relation to the four identified characteristics. The purpose of the Community Survey is to assess the Office of Residence Life's success in implementing the Community

Action Plan (CAP). The focus is on the outcome of increasing student participation in activities and residence hall meetings.

The survey begins by asking respondents to answer the following statements about their floor community with responses that range from "strongly
disagree" to "strongly agree."

- The people in my floor community care about one another.
- The people in my floor community trust one another.
- The people in my floor community seem to be connected to each other in
  some way.
- The people in my floor community communicate openly with each other.
- The people in my floor community take responsibility for what happens.
- The people in my floor community participate in community events.
- The floor community where I live meets my expectations.
- Study groups have formed in my floor community.
- Residents in my floor community encourage me to succeed academically.
- There is a sense of academic competition amongst floor community members.
- The level of noise in my floor community allows me to study sufficiently.

Next, the survey looks to measure the survey-taker's personal involvement in
the hall community by asking the frequency they:

- Talk with other floor community members.
- Do social things together with floor community members.
- Share personal belongings with other floor community members.
- Confide in another floor community member about personal things
- Study with another floor community member.
- Discuss areas of conflict with floor community members.

Leadership Survey

To better understand the impact of using the social change model for leadership
development on the Syracuse University campus, staff members developed an
instrument focused on questions relevant to the use of that model. The staff
asks students questions about their satisfaction with their leadership experience, about how useful their experiences are for their future learning, and to
understand the sustainability of student involvement (predicted) over time.
The objective is to measure the impact of the training program on individual
perceptions of leadership.

After requesting basic demographic information, some of the specific questions on the survey included:

- What role do you play in your leadership organization (president, executive board, floor president, general body member, etc.)?
- How many semesters have you been involved in leadership organizations?
- How satisfied are you with your experience in your leadership organization?
- How useful to you would you rate your leadership organization experience?
- How dedicated are you to your leadership organization?

On the survey, staff also asked students to state their most important characteristic of a "good leader" and were provided a list of traits. Some responses were clearly skill-based such as time management, while others served to express capacities within the social change model such as dedication to a group and giving back to the community. Staff members also asked students to list characteristics they think represent "leadership." In the inaugural assessment, staff learned that the overwhelming majority of students believe "leadership" means "working to better your community" above all other things.

Students were also asked to rate their skill level along a continuum of skills and capacities staff felt were important to being effective leaders. In an attempt to discover whether experiences in the residence halls made a difference, staff also asked students if their ratings were enhanced by these experiences. Not only did the students rank themselves highly, but they also felt that their experiences in the residence halls contributed to their ability to be effective leaders.

Good assessment never ends with the initial data collection process. Only through benchmarking in subsequent years does the information really shed light on the experiences of Syracuse University students. Fortunately, staff plan on using several questions from the initial assessment in future data collections, while adding additional questions to collect new information.

Conclusion

This chapter supports the development of intentional student leadership development programs on college and university campuses. The first step toward establishing these programs is to understand the elements of successful assessment planning and practice. Advisers are encouraged to adopt or adapt the model in this chapter for use on their campuses. The literature cited provides a set of basic criteria for leadership programs, and is a good starting point for advisers. Advisers' understanding of the institutional context and what they have already learned about leadership on their campuses should enhance these criteria. These criteria also serve as a beginning point from which to develop assessment questions. The authors have shared some proven instruments and encourage readers to seek other instruments to use. Advisers also are encouraged to share what they have learned and document their progress.

References

Boatman, S. (1988). *Strong student governments . . . and their advisement.* Campus Activities Programming, 20(9), 58–63.

Dunkel, N.W., and Schuh, J.H. (1998). *Advising student groups and organizations.* San Francisco: Jossey-Bass.

Higher Education Research Institute (1996). *A social change model of leadership development, Version III.* Los Angeles: UCLA Press.

Komives, S. and Tucker, G. (1998). Successful residence hall government: Themes from a national study of select hall government structures. *Advice for Advisers: The Development of a Residence Hall Association.* Columbus, OH: Association of College and University Housing Officers – International.

St. Onge, S., Cahill, M., Nestor, E., Tyler, J., & Wetter, N. (2001). Assessment Report, Syracuse University Strategic Plan. Syracuse, NY.

St. Onge, S. (1999). Developing a strategic plan for assessment in student affairs. *Assessment Update* 11 (4), 10–11.

Upcraft, M. L., & Schuh, J. (1996). *Assessment in student affairs.* San Francisco: Jossey-Bass.

20

Relationships with Other Campus Organizations

Jeff Novak & Carolyn Miller

"Alone we can do so little; together we can do so much!"
—Helen Keller

The purpose of this chapter is to illustrate why it is essential for residence hall associations (RHAs) to cultivate positive and mutually beneficial relationships with a myriad of university constituents. Creating partnerships takes effort, time, and occasionally the willingness to lose some of the organization's individual identity. It means seeing and desiring a broader perspective and giving up some turf to achieve it. The synergy and the ability to do more through collaboration are evident and powerful with long-lasting effects. RHAs represent the entire campus population, serving as natural conduits to a variety of people including faculty, staff, and other student organizations. Often, RHAs create programs, actively participate in policy formation, address pertinent issues, and provide input in monetary decisions that effect resident students (Verry, 1993). Since RHAs can be identified as a form of learning communities, four essential principles that characterize learning communities are discussed and practical applications are shared. Another area that RHAs emphasize is service. Since leadership and service learning are intertwined, the roles RHAs play are emphasized. Finally, the relationships within RHAs as well as the ones between RHAs and other campus constituents are examined.

Review of Background Literature

The American College Personnel Association's Student Learning Imperative addresses many issues, needs, and reasons why student groups such as RHAs

342

are practical avenues for student development. The hallmarks of a college-educated person include: practical competence skills and a coherent integrated sense of identity; self-esteem; confidence; integrity; aesthetic sensibilities; and civic responsibilities (Astin, 1996). Skills such as decision-making and the ability to resolve issues with others occur within the RHA setting. Furthermore, the concepts of "learning," "personal development," and "student development" are inextricably intertwined and inseparable (The Student Learning Imperative, 1996). Higher education has traditionally organized its activities into "academic affairs" and "student affairs." However, many are now convinced that enhancing student learning is a campus-wide initiative with benefits for all. No longer does academic affairs take care of the intellectual aspects of students' lives and leave student affairs just to guide the out-of-classroom experience. Collaboratively enhancing student learning is the essence of university partnerships (Ballard & Long, 2004).

It is widely accepted that approximately 75% of college student learning occurs outside of the classroom (Astin, 1996; Chickering 1974; Blimling, 1999). This is why resident communities and RHAs are excellent platforms for student learning. The impact of "academic" programs is mediated by what happens outside of the classroom. Living in campus housing maximizes opportunities for educational, social, cultural, and extracurricular involvement. Peer group relations, for example, appear to influence both affective and cognitive development (Astin, 1996). If residents are involved with student organizations or volunteer opportunities, they apply classroom knowledge within these environments. These practical applications substantiate and enhance students' knowledge base and skills development.

Membership in RHAs as well as other purposeful organizations increases student learning. Exposure to governance, mission statements, and working with others increases student attention toward civic responsibilities. Certain conditions promote learning more than others. For example, learning and personal development are enhanced when students participate in groups organized around common curricular interests (Astin, 1996; Schroeder, Mable, and Associates, 1994).

While attending to conditions that support learning and personal development, synergy results when students and institutional agents interact in ways that foster student interest and feelings of belonging. The goal is to create environments where all students have opportunities to participate in, contribute something to, as well as take something from, an experience (Kuh, Schuh, Whitt & Associates, 1991). Residential communities are structured to promote the examination of individual values, cultural understanding and appreciation, and many other outcomes associated with effective undergraduate education (Fenske, 1989). RHAs can model this for universities by actively creating and recruiting others in order to make cultures student-centered.

RHAs Focus on Learning Communities

In *Realizing the Educational Potential of Residence Halls,* Charles Schroeder (Schroeder et al., 1994) expands on his earlier work by outlining the four I's: involvement, investment, influence, and identity which are "principles essential to the development, implementation, and maintenance of learning communities" (p. 176). Schroeder further states that, "the principles are both sequential and cyclical—that is, increased student involvement leads to increased investment, which in turn, leads to greater influence and eventual identity with the unit" (p. 175). These four I's provide a theoretical foundation for a discussion of practical suggestions aimed at building solid relationships within RHAs and between RHAs, residence life offices, and other campus groups.

The emphasis on and experience with partnering also help students in their future careers. Many companies now emphasize strategic partnering with clients rather than working solely for clients. Those who work to actively develop other leaders have always been a sought after commodity in all types of professions.

Involvement

Since RHAs represent students living in campus housing, they should be organizations that are convenient to join, welcoming, and non-threatening. They should want members to become actively involved. The improvement of residential community living is a common task that brings students together and promotes ongoing interaction. Most RHAs begin the year with leadership training that focuses on members getting to know one another and on basic skills. Members assist with goal setting and begin to feel that they belong and matter to organizations. Many members become friends and provide ongoing support as well as healthy challenges to one another. These interactions are positive and needed, especially on campuses where there is a strong emphasis on the use of technology and limited face-to-face interaction.

Once personal relationships are established, work on projects, policies, and programs can begin. It is natural for these organizations to work closely and continuously with the housing or residence life offices. In order for these relationships to be supportive, contact must be regular and reciprocated. RHA advisers serve as liaisons between students and staff. One way to create ongoing and open communication is to include and allow RHA presidents to report during weekly professional staff meetings. It is beneficial for RHA members to get to know directors of residence life or chief housing officers (CHOs). By cultivating these key relationships, CHOs will realize that ongoing student input and feedback is critical. This enables RHAs to feel they are partners in the operation of departments.

Another important way for residence life offices to help involve RHAs is by assisting members with their personal, social, and career growth. Pascarella & Terenzini (1991) state that extracurricular involvement, particularly in leadership positions, has at least modest implications on student career paths. This may stem from the fact that such involvements enhance self-confidence along with interpersonal and leadership skills. Additionally, research indicates students are more likely to take advantage of educationally purposeful out-of-class learning opportunities when both the institution and students devote time, effort, and resources toward this end (Chickering, 1974; Kuh et al., 1991).

Investment

Investment is a reflection of psychological ownership. It flows naturally from involvement. Investment is also a consequence of the ethic of care. Students clearly care about one another and their group (Schroeder et al., 1994).

Students become more comfortable with their roles and want to become more involved as they feel vested with other RHA members as well as in organization goals. Motivated by organizational pride, members want to utilize their leadership skills to move groups forward. Members' expectations are clearly defined and officers' responsibilities are clarified in RHA constitutions.

Many times, RHAs institute recognition programs closely with National Residence Hall Honoraries (NRHHs) in order to thank members for their time and contributions. RHAs are comprised of volunteer members who are not paid employees. Therefore, residence life offices need to find ways other than monetary compensation to show investment in RHAs. One of the main ways is by helping RHAs obtain funding to realize their goals. It is highly advisable that a certain amount of money per residence hall student be allocated to RHA budgets. Residence life offices also can support RHA fundraising efforts. Additionally, residence life offices should help investigate and be receptive to additional avenues of monetary support.

Depending on philosophy and availability, some residence life offices invest in the goals of RHAs by providing executive board members with honorariums. This benefit can range from account credits to reduced room/ meal costs to cash stipends. Others offer priority departmental employment consideration.

Providing RHA offices is another way residence life offices can invest in groups. Many successful RHAs have office space which they use to conduct meetings, store belongings, and hold office hours. Ideally offices should be located in places that are central to campus and should promote awareness and accessibility.

Residence life offices also can assist RHAs by providing access to copy machines, telephones, fax machines, and computers. Assisting groups in connecting with other campus resources such as food services and conference offices may help them form fruitful partnerships and receive additional benefits from institutions.

Influence

Influence is essentially a consequence of an ethic of responsibility, where control is vested in the group members and students exert maximum influence over their physical and social environments. This principle— influence—is the cornerstone of student governance and a major characteristic of learning communities (Schroeder et al., 1994). RHA members come from individual residential communities and together serve as the voice of all residents. Each hall must be adequately and appropriately represented in order to promote the total welfare of the residence hall population. Since RHA members help establish expectations for one another and have the ability to change the constitution, they feel invested and therefore assist with holding others accountable.

Students need to understand that they are members of an educational community and that their actions influence how much they and others will benefit from the residence hall as well as the total student experience (Chickering & Reissner, 1993). When students become involved and are willing to work with others, they can make a difference and promote change.

One of the most critical relationships to develop is the one between RHAs and student government associations (SGAs) on each campus. Since SGAs represent all students and RHAs represent the residents, these groups overlap representation and serve as official student voices within institutions. Many times, SGAs institute more formal meeting atmospheres and have more detailed and sophisticated constitutions. These partnerships provide groups with other points of view. Groups can support one another even when issues fall more to another group's realm. One way to ensure that these partnerships are developed and maintained is to include communication with or representation from other groups within the framework of constitutions. Some institutions utilize an ex-officio approach and some authorize one another to serve as voting members of each other's organizations.

RHAs and SGAs also can reach out to other student organizations and promote active cultures of collaboration. Through the pooling of resources, finances, and office space, all can more effectively meet the needs of diverse student populations. Utilizing a cooperative approach to leadership training allows all student leaders to network, share perspectives, and make better use of session presenters. By training collectively, the brainstorming of ideas will lead to broader perspectives and improve chances for the implementation of ideas.

Through the front end promotion of these relationships, the foundations are in place for the future. If tragedies occur, all can work together to address them rather than coming together for the first time. Also, when major campus issues that impact all students (such as safety, dining, transportation, funding, and parking) need to be addressed, cohesive student organizations represent student needs in a unified, rather than disjointed, manner.

Students must be full participants in any effort to modify their residential environments, for they will ultimately determine the meaning and impact of any institutional policy (Kuh et al., 1991). As such, RHA members should be consulted on a continual basis regarding procedural changes and policy modifications recommended by staff. For example, many colleges and universities will not allow residence hall handbooks to be changed without RHA approval. Additionally, if students want a policy implemented or changed, a resolution can be brought to the RHA, discussed and voted on by the members, and, if approved, forwarded to the appropriate administrators.

Depending upon policies and procedures within each institution, the involvement of the RHA can be integrated into the housing system. One example of student leader input in decision-making is having an RHA member serve on the board that makes recommendations regarding students who appeal to break their residence hall contracts. RHA members also gain a sense of involvement by serving on departmental committees, programming task forces, and staff search committees.

A critical time of the year for collaboration between RHAs and the residence life offices is during the development of the office budget. It is important to involve RHA members in this process from beginning to end. In addition, the process of resource allocation provides many teachable moments if students have access to forums in which the trade-offs, conflicts, politics, and compromises that are part of institutional resource allocation are discussed (Kuh et al., 1991). They will gain valuable knowledge regarding budget development within the department and the overall budget situation at the institution. This will enable RHA members who participate in the process to help the residence life professional present and explain the budget to the whole RHA, hall governments, and individual students. It will also make members aware of departmental and divisional priorities and set the stage for identifying others to partner with to ensure these are supported.

Identity

True leadership is accrued through skill attainment and the learning that occurs during different experiences. Leadership does not just occur. It must be cultivated, planned for, and actively pursued. If students are comfortable within their organizations and know where they are going, then they can focus on more global perspectives and work as team members at a level that deals with campus issues.

A vital aspect of serving as leaders is communication. It is essential to communicate within organizations so that members operate with the same understanding. It also is critical for organizations to communicate with other organizations about activities so that others can benefit from the information, join in the activities, improve the activities, or to avoid duplicating the same efforts. Positive and ongoing communication leads to stronger teamwork.

RHA missions include providing residence hall students with the best possible community experiences. This includes making resolutions for policy recommendations and facilities improvements as well as initiating fun social, educational, and service opportunities and activities. Most of the students within RHAs focus on improving the quality of the overall community through addressing student needs. This type of common focus is characteristic of a learning community. If RHAs are active team members of university communities, students are more inclined to take interest in campus initiatives and get involved on a broader level. Ballou, Reavil, and Schultz (1995) found that students residing in campus housing demonstrate a greater amount of scope and quality of effort in using resources and opportunities on their campuses. This type of climate, when fostered by RHAs, leads to cultures where students focus more on commonalities rather than differences. This enables students to take things to the next level rather than become complacent and maintain during their time as a college student.

Students who are RHA members can illustrate their identity by wearing RHA apparel. This occurs on home campuses as well as during local, state, regional and national conferences. Some RHAs also denote members by placing name signs on their room doors. This actually serves to identify RHA representatives within their communities and also to recognize RHA representatives on an ongoing basis. RHAs promote awareness at the beginning of the school year so that students know they are there to represent them. It is ideal to have welcome letters waiting in each student room upon their arrival. This is a positive first impression and may result in recruiting new members to join RHAs. It also is beneficial for RHAs to be visible and present during residence hall check-in, student organization fairs, and campus events.

Residential communities that promote student learning and development are characterized by a high degree of student participation and involvement, student control of environment, common interests and purposes, high degrees of social interaction and social stability, transcendent values, and student influence. In effective learning communities, students know that their participation and involvement are central to their day-to-day experience (Schroeder et al., 1994).

Service Learning and RHAs

Since the 1990s, the concept of service learning has emerged as a powerful, valuable, and promising trend in American higher education (Shapiro & Levine, 1999). Students today are entering colleges and universities with much more experience and involvement in community service than in previous years due to community service graduation requirements at some high school as well as heightened senses of civic responsibility. Often, as students enter institutions, their time spent toward volunteerism does not carry forward from high school. Perhaps this is due to the inability to find vehicles for engagement, a lack of time, or interests pursued in other areas. Service learning in higher education can help prepare students to become more well-rounded, caring and responsible citizens.

RHAs, as umbrella organizations for students residing on campus, should encourage, support, and role model the spirit of volunteerism. RHAs should partner with residence life offices and other campus constituents to develop programs and service activities aimed at engaging residents in service (Scheuermann, 1996). As mentioned previously, influence is an integral component of a RHA. The RHAs ability for collaboration among residents through peer influence serves as an excellent avenue to promote service.

At its core, service learning is about collaboration between faculty and students to positively impact others. Service learning provides exemplary, ongoing opportunities for collaborative activities between academic affairs and student affairs in which both parties can make significant contributions to the educational process (McHugh-Engstrom & Tinto, 1997). Service learning principles include a community voice, orientation and training, meaningful action, reflection, and evaluation (Mintz & Hessner, 1996). Many institutions are structured with faculty interaction programs that provide opportunities for teaching staff and residents to learn more about one another. Some colleges and universities have first-year experience programs and residential colleges supporting this initiative. RHAs can aid in these enterprises by collaboratively partnering and providing guidance to resident students while promoting philanthropic ventures. RHAs should be involved in determining critical needs that their involvement would benefit from. RHAs can work with other campus departments to assess both campus and external community needs in order to obtain knowledge to make informed decisions and structured initiatives (Komives, Woodard, & Associates, 2003). RHAs can partner with other organizations to help provide orientation and training and opportunities, reflection time, and evaluation.

Service learning includes a shared vision with those in collaboration working side by side to develop and ultimately implement a quality program (McHugh-Engstrom, 2003). A growing number of colleges and universities now require a set number of service hours to be completed prior to graduation. In addition, there are faculty members who have expectations for student coursework that include service. Participation in service learning encourages students to make meaningful connections between what is learned in the classroom to real-world experiences, increasing students' levels of civic responsibility and concern for social justice. Therefore, it is imperative that both faculty and students connect and work together.

RHAs have long supported philanthropic interests. Many assist with crisis situations and tragedies when they occur on campus, along with participating as regular volunteers for a myriad of service agencies within the community. Students are more likely to take advantage of educationally purposeful out-of-class learning opportunities when both the institution and students devote time, effort, and resources toward this end (Kuh et al., 1991). It is clear that students who are more involved in their living community ultimately find greater satisfaction in their living environment and demonstrate increased collaboration both academically and socially with peers and others in the campus community (Arboleda, Wang, Shelley, and Whalen, 2003). RHA members are in key leadership positions that can really set the pace for an entire campus.

RHA Role in Campus Leadership

Partnerships don't just happen. They need to be intentionally sought out, planned for, and maintained. They need to be cultivated and nurtured. RHA leaders should review their mission statements and goals and decide who they can work with in order to build partnerships. RHAs need to be innovative and willing to take risks by branching out to new partners. In addition to housing offices, RHAs should consider other student life departments, faculty, and other organizations such as SGAs, activities boards, campus diversity committees, faculty and staff senates, the parent councils, and the alumni associations.

Some partnering on campus already occurs, such as when committees comprised of faculty, staff, alumni, and students come together to plan for major events such as Homecoming and Founder's Day. Instead of making partnering limited to key events, why not utilize this approach on other important matters such as promoting student and faculty interaction and establishing safe campus communities throughout the year? At the state, national, or international levels, RHAs have worked with other RHAs and organizations to assist colleges and universities coping with the effects of natural disasters or tragedies and to voice opinions on legislation affecting students and higher education.

Advisers who understand the tenets of involvement, investment, influence, identity, and the importance of service learning can help RHAs build solid foundations of skills and knowledge that will enable them to form connections with others. Critical to advising RHAs is the ability to help guide members to reach out to other campus constituents and form meaningful partnerships.

Conclusion

It is imperative that advisers keep in mind the principle that actions speak louder than words. Partnering, to some degree, starts with advisers. If advisers actively seek out new opportunities to partner with others within the campus community and they foster the development and maintenance of positive relations with others, students will see this. Then, they will be more inclined to follow the lead and try to incorporate this type of action into their own lives and missions. Additionally, by having these relationships in place, advisers can then assist students with getting linked to the correct people while paving the way for them. This will then enable them to utilize partnerships to accomplish their goals, widen their perspectives, and more thoroughly and efficiently serve the students whom they are representing. Partnering is powerful; it is the true synergy that maximizes the development and impact which groups of dedicated leaders can have.

References

Arboleda, A., Wang, Y., Shelley, M. C., & Whalen, D. F. (2003). Predictors of residence hall involvement. *Journal of College Student Development, 44* (4), 517–531.

Astin, A., W. (1996). Involvement in learning revisited. Journal of College Student Development, 37(2), 123–134.

Ballard, S., & Long, P. (2004 November-December). Profiles in partnership: Finding strength in collaborative leadership. About Campus, 16–22.

Ballou, R. A., Reavil, L. K., & Schultz, B. L. (1995). Assessing the immediate and residual effects of the residence hall experience: Validating Pace's 1990 analysis of on-campus and off-campus students. Journal of College and University Housing, 25, 16–-21.

Blimling, G. S. (1999). A meta-analysis of the influence of college residence halls on academic performance. Journal of College Student Development, 40, 551–561.

Chickering, A. W. (1974). Commuting versus resident students. San Francisco, CA: Jossey-Bass.

Chickering, A. W. & Reissner, L. (1993). Education and identity (2nd ed.). San Francisco, CA: Jossey-Bass.

Fenske, R. H. (1989). Historical foundations in student services. In Delworth, U., Hanson, G. R. & Associates (Eds.), Student services: A handbook for the profession. San Francisco, CA: Jossey-Bass.

Komives, S. R., Woodard, D. B., & Associates (2003). Student services: A handbook for the profession. San Francisco, CA: Jossey-Bass.

Kuh, G. D., Schuh, J. H., Whitt, E. J., & Associates. (1991). Involving colleges. San Francisco, CA: Jossey-Bass.

McHugh-Engstrom, C. (2003). Developing collaborative student affairs-academic affairs partnerships for service learning. In Jacoby, B., & Associates (Eds.), Building partnerships for service learning: San Francisco, CA: Jossey-Bass.

McHugh-Engstrom, C., & Tinto, V. (1997 July–August). Working together for service learning. About Campus, 10–15.

Mintz, S. D., & Hessner G. W. (1996). Principles of good practice in service learning. In Shapiro, N. S., & Levine, J. H. (1999). Creating learning communities: A practical guide to winning support, organizing for change, and implementing programs. San Francisco, CA: Jossey-Bass.

Pascarella, E. T. & Terenzini, P. T. (1991). How college affects students. San Francisco, CA: Jossey-Bass.

Scheuermann, C. D. (1996). Ongoing co-curricular service learning. In Jacoby, B. & Associates, (Eds.), Service learning in higher education: Concepts and practices: San Francisco, CA: Jossey-Bass.

Schroeder, C. C., Mable, P., & Associates. (1994). Realizing the educational potential of residence halls. San Francisco, CA: Jossey-Bass.

Shapiro, N. S., & Levine, J. H. (1999). Creating learning communities: A prac-

tical guide to winning support, organizing for change, and implementing programs. San Francisco, CA: Jossey-Bass.

Verry, B. (1993). The organizational structure of RHAs. In Dunkel, N. D., & Schuh, J. H. (1998). *Advising student groups and organizations.* San Francisco, CA: Jossey-Bass.

Case Studies

❖ Case Study 1

You are the adviser at a large public institution with a Division 1A football program. The marching band, which has always practiced next to the football team practice field, has had their space taken away by the athletics department at the request of the football coach who said the music was disruptive to his practice. An alternative site for the band has been suggested on one of the intramural sports fields. The intramural sports program and the fields are paid for by monies generated through activity and service fees and funded by the student government association (SGA). All the intramural sports fields (a total of seven) are used between the hours of 3:30–6:30 p.m. on a daily basis. Time cannot be extended due to darkness. There are current concerns, even with lighting, about going later in the evening, as it will further harm the already overused fields.

The marching band is not willing to change times thus creating a conflict with the athletics, recreation, and sport clubs departments. The board of trustee 's chairman decides it is important to have a good band and decides to move the band to the southeast of campus and take one of the currently used fields. Now the student-run Outdoor Adventure program is concerned that its recently built Challenge Course will become an unsafe venue due to the noise. Student sport clubs are losing one of the fields to the band. Lastly, the field happens to be located near a residence hall. Students in that hall are concerned the noise will disrupt their living environment.

- What role should the RHA take in this situation?
- As the adviser to the RHA, what role would you take in directing the organization to work with other campus groups to bring concerns to the administration?
- Who would you notify that the RHA is considering taking a stance on this issue?

- Knowing that the directive came from the board of trustee's chairman, how do you balance student needs with your role as staff member of the institution?

❖ Case Study 2

You are the RHA adviser. Your colleague is the NRHH adviser. The RHA is currently an umbrella organization over the NRHH chapter. The RHA budget was drastically cut, which has resulted in fewer students being able to attend leadership conferences, less money for programming, and less money for the end-of-the-year recognition banquet. The NRHH had planned to receive as much money as they had in years prior from RHA. Despite the RHA budget being cut, NRHH is still requesting their money. How do you work with your executive board, your colleague, and your colleague's executive board to resolve this matter?

21

Advising in an Information Age: Technology and Advising

Mark Miller & Christy Melton

Technology is constantly evolving and staying on top of the latest technologies is important for many fields, including advising. Properly applied, computer technologies can enhance RHA functions, helping student leaders to both share with and gather information from their advisers, student bodies, and each other.

Technologies in Current Use

Although advisers do not need to be technology experts in order to be effective, it is important to have a basic understanding of the established and emerging technologies students are using. Among these tools and programs are:

E-mail

E-mail needs little explanation as it has become "perhaps the most popular and familiar channel for communicating through the Internet" (Wood & Smith, 2001, p. 9). As such, checking and writing e-mail messages are daily activities for most student affairs professionals (Winston, Creamer, Miller, Brown, Carpenter, & Cooper et al., 2001) and students (Smith, 2001). Despite the usefulness and ubiquity of e-mail usage, it may create or exacerbate conflict if used carelessly or improperly. Advisers should consider the following guidelines for e-mail usage:

- Balance e-mail and other electronic communications with telephone and face-to-face discussions. Although e-mail can enhance adviser to student relationships and communication, it is rarely sufficient to build them.
- E-mail messages can be misunderstood or unintentionally come across as rude more easily than verbal or face-to-face conversations. Be extra careful with wording and politeness when communicating via e-mail and encourage students to do the same. Typing in all capital letters implies shouting.
- Do not allow students to rely on e-mail to address problems. Although e-mail can occasionally help students resolve issues by expressing feelings they aren't comfortable discussing in person, it more often exacerbates the problem. Handle mediations and sticky situations in person. If e-mail messages are received that anger receivers, encourage them to wait before replying rather than immediately firing off responses.
- Teach and demonstrate to students how to e-mail appropriately. While chat acronyms, smileys, and typing in all lowercase letters without punctuation might be fine for sending a note to a friend on RHA, they are not appropriate for formal RHA communications or contacting members of the upper administration. Today's students learn to e-mail informally from an early age. Hall government provides a teachable moment where advisers can introduce the e-mail skills necessary for communicating in a professional environment (Netlingo: http://www.netlingo.com/inframes.cfm).

Listservs

Automated e-mail mailing lists are called several names, most often "Listservs" after the program of that name created by L-Soft International. They all work in similar ways. E-mail messages are sent to a central address where they are automatically distributed to everyone on the list. This functionality is often incorporated into Internet groups. Both student and professional associations use Listservs to keep in touch, disseminate information, and gather and share ideas. Lists of several student affairs Listservs, and directions on how how to subscribe to them, are available at www.studentaffairs.com/lists.

Instant Messenger (IM) Programs

Instant messenger programs allow Internet users to identify and chat online with others via text messages in real time. Users compile lists of their online friends and are alerted when their friends are online and trying to contact them. Instant messenger is commonly used among college students as a quick and easy way to communicate with peers. Real time texting tends to be even more informal and conversational than e-mail. Users often abbreviate using a large number of acronyms and express emotions through the use of graphical or character-based faces called "smileys" or "emoticons." Extensive lists of commonly used acronyms and smileys are available at www.netlingo.com/e-mailsh.cfm and www.netlingo.com/smiley.cfm respectively.

Commonly used instant messenger programs include ICQ (www.icq.com), Microsoft MSN (www.msn.com), Yahoo Messenger (www.yahoo.com), and AOL Instant Messenger, also known as AIM (www.aim.com). Each messenger program has similarities, but the features they offer may vary. Basic versions of all of the major IM programs are available as free downloads. Users create, or are issued screen names or other identifiers that serve as their online identities that others use to contact them. Users then create buddy lists that are comprised of all other users that they choose to track. AOL Instant Messenger seems to be the IM most used by RHA-affiliated groups, and AIM screen names are included in the NACURH school directory. AIM features include member profiles, search features, easy to create chatrooms, and the ability to link multiple screen names to share buddy lists. Users can post away messages which inform buddies when they are not at the computer, they can become "invisible" so that other users will be unable to see if they are online, and they can check to see how long their buddies have been "idle" or away from the computer. Buddy list windows can also include stock tickers, advertisements, and news. Other IM programs, such as Trillian, are also available. They allow users to combine several IM services into one master list, preventing the user from having to run multiple services at the same time (www.trillian.cc).

Today's college students routinely use IM programs to communicate with each other and to keep track of friends or buddies. Use of IM programs has become so common that students often expect or assume that advisers and supervisors use them as well. Many may want to contact advisers using these programs. However, some schools have policies dictating the use of IM programs on office computers. This means advisers considering using instant messenger programs need to review institution policies. If advisers elect to use this method of communication with students, they may need to address boundaries and expectations regarding the use of instant messenger programs from the beginning. For instance, advisers may want to discuss with students when they can contact them using IM; when they will be online; any situations where they would rather be contacted by more traditional communications method; and what they consider appropriate conversation. Some advisers who commonly use instant messaging for personal or other purposes create second public screen names to use for communication with students. Furthermore, if students would like advisers to communicate with them using instant mes-senger programs, advisers may want to remind them they have access to the information students choose to post in profiles or away messages. This may help to deter awkward situations where students may post information or mes-sages that may be inappropriate.

Internet Telephony and Video Conferencing

For years, scientists to science fiction writers have imagined a future where humans are able to see and speak to each other while separated by long distanc-es. Though this has been possible for some time, these technologies are begin-ning to mature. Voice and video communication over the Internet is becoming simpler, cheaper, and more reliable. Most Internet telephones currently avail-able use hard wired boxes that plug into broadband Internet sources. Boxes such as these are provided by industry leader Vonage as well as cable and tradi-tional phone companies that have entered the Internet phone market. These ser-vices have monthly fees, usually for unlimited domestic use. Regular phones are plugged into the designated boxes and operate like traditional phones.

On college campuses, administrators are more likely to see services such as Skype, a program that uses peer-to-peer technology similar to that used for file sharing to provide free computer-to-computer voice calls. Instead of using tra-ditional phones, headsets with earphones and microphones are plugged directly into computers. Calls to other computer users are free. Calls to land or cellular phones are also possible, but these calls are charged small, per minute fees. Skype is similar to an instant messenger service in which users speak instead of typing to chat in real time. It is used as a way to meet others found through searching online profiles, and it can be used to share or exchange files and data. Multiple user conference calls also can be held (www.skype.com). Similar free services that also include real-time video also are available, but are gener-ally jerky and of poor quality. Their use will likely increase as the technology evolves. Internet voice and video communications have obvious and immedi-ate application for students scattered among different schools, such as state or regional boards. However, it is likely that these technologies will increasingly be used to communicate locally, just as e-mail and instant messenger began as ways to communicate over distance and now are commonly used to communi-cate with others in the same building.

Web Pages

The Internet itself is a global network of interconnected servers and other com-puters. One of the most accessed and well-known aspects of the Internet is the

World Wide Web. The Web is, according to the NetLingo dictionary (2005), "a collection of graphical pages on the Internet that can be read and interacted with by computer." The term "Web page" itself once referred to the amount of content that would fit on one screen or piece of paper, but now is most commonly used to refer to one file written in Hypertext Markup Language (html) that may be accessed through the Internet. It is also used to refer to a group of connected and related Web files (i.e. "Does your RHA have a Web page?" "Yes, it includes a homepage and a page about each hall council.") A group of Web pages is more properly called a Web site, which is also correctly written as "Web site" (http://www.netlingo.com/inframes.cfm).

Although individual members may spend much more time using e-mail and instant messenger, Web sites are the technology most commonly employed by RHA groups. It is becoming increasingly common to have elected or appointed members whose primary or sole responsibility is the creation or improvement of organizational Web sites. Due to the potential importance of Web pages and their widespread use by RHAs, Web sites are discussed in detail later in this chapter.

Blogs

Blogs can best be described as online journals that individual users can create and update as often as they like. Occasionally they may provide links to other Web sites, news stories, or anything else on the Internet that catches the authors' interest. Meanwhile, readers may have the opportunity to make comments on the different entries. They are generally easy to use and have user-friendly templates that users can customize. Blogging is popular among college students as an easy way to post their thoughts and get feedback from others, in addition to reading about their friends or contacts. There are many blogging and online journals that are commonly used among students, including LiveJournal (www.livejournal.com), Xanga (www.xanga.com), and Blogger (www.blogger.com). Like instant messenger services, each of these has different features that are specific to that service. LiveJournal is one of the most popular services. Users register, create user names, and then customize the appearance of their individual journals. Each registered user is provided with a profile page, where the user can include an e-mail address, instant messenger contact information, birthday, interests, and location. Users then can update the journal as often as they like. They can then create lists of friends and easily access all posts by those friends. Users can also add groups or feeds to their friends lists, which allows the users to get constant up-to-date information and posts that concern their interests. Their friends and other users can post comments to entries and start discussion threads concerning the topics. Any user may search for other users that share their interests. Students may often create groups for their friends or organizations and allow others to join them and access group member entries (www.livejournal.com).

It is important for RHA advisers and other student affairs professionals to be aware of blogs, especially if students with whom they have contact are regular users and readers of each other's blogs. Although blogs can provide insight and a form of community, this method of communication can occasionally turn into a passive aggressive way for students to express frustrations with each other and the organizations with which they work, leading to individual or group-wide conflicts. Advisers should remain aware of this technology as it continues to develop and increase in popularity among college students.

Discussion Boards or Forums

Electronic discussion boards (often referred to simply as "boards") and forums are in some ways similar to Listservs in that users write e-mail messages or other messages to be shared with large groups. They both tend to include "threads" of conversation as users reply to previous notes. However, with boards and forums all messages and responses are posted to a central site (usually Web-based) that all users can view. They are usually organized in outline form where each main message or "post" is followed by all of the responses discussing that topic. The terms "board" and "forum" are used interchangeably, but boards tend to be open for anyone to use while forums generally require users to register or join a "community" to participate.

RHAs use boards and forums to solicit feedback, discuss issues, and share ideas. Boards and forums take a bit more effort to use than Listservs, as users must actively and regularly check them instead of having messages appear in their e-mail in-boxes. However, the advantage to boards and forums is that those who join later or who routinely delete e-mail messages can go back to read or search through previous posts and topics. NACURH has created forums covering a variety of topics including answers to various questions, regional discussion areas, and reports from national executives. Forums are available at http://www.nacurh.org/forum. Anyone may read the information posted, but to write or respond to a post, a user must register. Registering involves a brief online process where users create user names and provide demographic information and preferences.

Groups

Another form of online community is referred to simply as a "group." Groups are communities that are created by "owners" or group moderators, usually around specific topics. They commonly include several of the functions listed previously. For example, "Yahoo! Groups" each include a forum, listserv, and instant messaging capabilities. They also allow members to share files including data and pictures, contact information, and links. Users may also conduct polls online and post events to online calendars. Most groups are open for anyone to join, but individuals moderate them and have the ability to restrict membership and posts (www.yahoo.com).

Several regions and RHAs use groups to communicate and share information. They offer a wide range of free services but contain and distribute third-party advertisements. One note of caution: it is important that multiple student leaders, including advisers, have the passwords and authorization to fully access and moderate groups formed by RHA organizations. This is necessary to avoid the possibility of one key person leaving without passing on the ability to change or modify the group.

Online Communities

Online communities are virtual communities that exist on distributed computer networks such as the Internet. They often focus on particular topics such as gaming, newsgroups, or some common interest among participants. The members of online communities generally communicate through message boards or forums. Online communities offer some of the same functionality of groups, but typically options and communication tools are more robust and there is a greater focus on online social interactions among members. Online communities have existed locally on campuses for some time.

Online communities are becoming more universal, primarily with the recent introduction of global online communities like The Facebook.com. The Facebook is an online community designed specifically for college students, which includes participation at over 300 colleges and universities. More than one million students have registered to join this community (Copeland, 2004). Once students register for this service, they have access to a wealth of information about fellow students who have also registered. Students can list the classes they are taking, their interests, contact information (phone, address, and instant messenger name), major, birthday, high school, relationship status, and organizations in which they are involved. Users join groups of interest, add friends to their contact lists, and search for other users of the service using any criterion that is listed. The site even lets a searcher know the last location from which another user has logged in. Users may also send messages to one another and post messages on other users' "walls."

File Sharing

Those involved in file sharing run computer programs or "clients" which provide interfaces for finding and downloading files on other computers, usually while sharing files located within certain directories of their hard drives. Modern file sharing networks generally leave files on users' individual computers rather than relying on central servers. Although file sharing has been most closely associated with downloading music, the technology can be used for any type of file including programs, movies, and pictures. File sharing can create problems for colleges and universities. Sharing or downloading large files can use large portions of Internet bandwidth. There are also legal and ethical issues involved when copyrighted files are shared. Advisers need to be alert for the presence of file sharing clients or illegally downloaded music, programs, or other files on RHA-owned computers.

Advising Students Who Use Technology

It is becoming very common for local and regional RHA organizations to create elected or appointed positions whose sole responsibilities are to manage technology and Web pages. Often the students holding these positions have programming or other Internet-related experience, whether self-taught or learned through coursework. This often puts student life professionals who know little about computer programming in the potentially uncomfortable position of advising students who are experts in the field. While it is important for advisers to have a basic understanding of the technology and terminology involved, they don't need a great deal of technical knowledge to be effective advisers. In fact, advisers should ask the same questions of student Webmasters or technology coordinators that they would ask of leaders in more traditional RHA roles, such as planning events and programs.

Project Participants

Most projects that utilize the types of computer technology discussed here require students to set them up and to maintain them. That means it is important to identify committed groups of students and to be sure they each know exactly what their responsibilities involve. It is extremely important that at least two (and preferably more) students within an organization have access to Web pages and other information systems and know how to maintain and operate them. Of course, good records and training should always accompany officer transitions, but it is important not take a chance on major Web pages, forums or voting systems becoming unusable due to the resignation or graduation of an individual.

Project Costs Measured in Time as well as Money

Event planning is usually thought of in financial terms. While certain software packages or equipment purchases may be costly, in general the cost of new Web pages or other technology improvements is measured in time. Before students get started, advisers should ask them to develop reasonable estimates of how much time it will take to create and maintain projects. The amount of time to create and maintain projects should then be compared to the anticipated benefits and amount of time volunteers have to devote to the projects to be sure they are feasible and offer good returns on the time invested. The "under construction" links and pages found so often on RHA-related Web sites (often for months or more) are a testament to how many ambitious projects take longer than anticipated or stall altogether. Even with considerable forethought, projects may take longer than anticipated. Planning ahead can avoid many pitfalls.

Project Timelines

Once students have considered the scope of projects and decided they are realistic and worthwhile endeavors, it is critical for them to create timelines and deadlines. Action plans should include identifying various milestones to be met, designating those who are responsible for completing those milestones, and then communicating the project progress to others in the group. These progress reports could occur during weekly RHA or officer meetings, or they could consist of formal or informal updates to the president or another officer. Technical projects are often long-term, and creating a system of accountability from the beginning helps students stay on task and avoid problems down the road.

Advertising

Students often consider the advertising possibilities created by technology. However, technical projects also require advertisement. The greatest online forms, voting systems, Web pages, or other online resources are only valuable if others know about and utilize them.

Policies, Legalities, and Ethics

Advisers should be familiar with technology policies and guidelines at their institutions and have the responsibility to make sure organizations are operating within these policies and guidelines. Advisers need to check to be sure that students are not using copyrighted images or text without permission and are abiding by campus standards for Web pages and bulk e-mailing. All software that is installed or used, especially on RHA or campus-owned machines, must be fully licensed for that machine. Downloading pirated or "cracked" programs where the copyright protection has been broken is obviously illegal, and it also is illegal to install software on more than one machine without permission. Software programs come with policies on when and how they may be installed and used.

Project Goals

One key to using technology effectively is to always keep the end purpose in mind. Technology should be a tool to help RHA groups achieve goals, not a goal in and of itself. For example, many groups decide to build Web pages without ever discussing why these pages are needed or what the group hopes to accomplish through having them. Starting with goals in mind can help direct and focus efforts. Needs assessment is just as important when developing technology initiatives as it is for planning programs. Advisers need to help students be intentional in their use of technology. Once a project is completed, it is equally important to assess its success. Advisers should encourage students to review original goals for Web pages or technical projects and measure how well the end results achieve the objectives. Students can use this process both to fine-tune or follow up on efforts and to generate future goals.

By asking the right questions, even the least tech-savvy advisers can greatly enhance the effectiveness of their organizations' utilization of technology. In addition to fulfilling advising duties, taking an active role in this area creates great opportunities for advisers to stay familiar with the latest technologies used by students.

Web Pages

The World Wide Web provides an almost unlimited volume of information. Web sites from individual institutions, professional associations, NACURH-affiliated regions and affiliate groups, and other sources can provide valuable ideas and resources. In addition to using the Web as an information source, the creation of an organizational Web page is one of the most common ways RHAs utilize technology.

When seeking to design or improve a Web site, simplicity and usefulness are the current buzzwords. Google (www.google.com), a company that is nearly synonymous with Internet search, is one of the most successful sites on the Internet (Vogelstein, 2004). It also is famous for being one of the most simple and functional. While RHA Web sites do not need to go to that extreme, options and

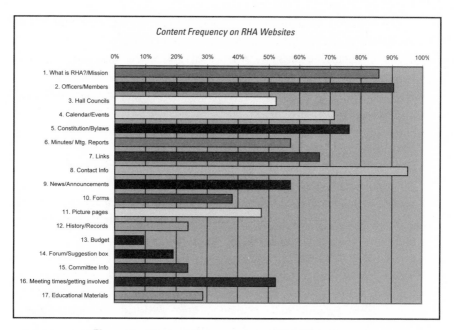

Figure 1: Content Frequency on RHA Web sites

navigational tools (buttons, links, drop-down boxes, etc.) should be clear and limited to a manageable number. The page as a whole should be uncluttered and easy to read. Users being able to find the information they are looking for quickly is of supreme importance. Simplicity is a good place to start, but a worthwhile Web site also must include the right content in order to be useful.

RHA Web Page Content

RHA Web sites have hundreds of different designs and formats, but they feature similar content. A 2005 survey of RHA Web sites (Miller, 2005) identifies 17 types of content that frequently appear on RHA Web pages. Figure 1 lists the percentage of sites surveyed that include each type of content.

Key to Figure 1

1. **What is RHA?/Mission.** Descriptions or explanations of organizations and/ or prominent displays of mission statements.
2. **Officers/Members.** Names (and usually contact information) for officers or the entire membership.
3. **Hall Councils.** Sections on the hall councils or area governments.
4. **Calendar/Events.** Upcoming events and programs, either in list or calenda-format.

5. Constitution/Bylaws. Organization constitutions or other governing documents.

6. Minutes/Meeting Reports. Summaries of events and decisions at recent meetings, usually in the form of formal meeting minutes.

7. Links. Three or more links to organizations or resources other than local hall governments. The most common sites receiving links were NACURH national and regional sites. Some also linked to their university housing offices and/or other student organizations or resources.

8. Contact Info. Information on how to contact or communicate with RHAs. Office phone numbers and organizational e-mail addresses were provided most often, but some also included additional contact numbers, postal addresses, and/or the physical locations and operating hours of RHA offices.

9. News/Announcements. Sections, usually main or front pages, devoted to recent and current events, awards, and news, intended to be frequently refreshed. Most items were short blurbs or headline links to a separate page. Although programs and events were occasionally referenced, items were not limited to events and seemed directed at informing rather than encouraging or helping students plan to attend events.

10. Forms. Forms of various types, either to be completed online or downloaded and printed.

11. Picture Pages. Pages or online albums devoted primarily to photos of recent events, programs and conferences.

12. History/Records. Organizational histories (longer than one paragraph) or archives containing minutes, bids, goals, or other documents from previous years.

13. Budget. Information on RHA budgets or finances and how monies were spent or allocated.

14. Forum/Suggestion Box. Online mechanisms intended primarily as ways that resident students can provide suggestions, input, or feedback to RHAs.

15. Committee Info. Current RHA committees, often with lists of chairs or members. Committee sections also sometimes included committee goals, purpose, or reports of activities.

16. Meeting Times/Getting Involved. Information on how to join or become involved with RHAs, usually in the form of invitations to attend meetings and announcements of meeting times and locations.

17. Educational Materials. Handbooks, advice, or other information and training materials directed at residence hall student leaders serving on RHA or Hall Councils.

All 17 functional areas can be included on RHA Web sites. Including all 17 functional areas will result in comprehensive sites; however, this approach requires much time and effort and may result in Web sites with more information on them than students really need or can easily access. A more productive approach is to refer student leaders back to the goals for the site and how the goals fit into larger missions of the organizations. When designing, revising or evaluating a Web site, the Web Style Guide (Lynch & Horton, 2001) suggests that the process begin by answering the following questions:

- What is the mission of your organization?
- How will this Web site support your mission?
- What are your two or three most important goals for the site?
- Who is the primary audience for the Web site?
- What do you want the audience to think or do after having visited your site?
- What Web-related strategies will you use to achieve those goals?
- How will you measure the success of your site?
- How will you adequately maintain the finished site?

Once student leaders determine the goals and audience for the site, it should become clearer which types of content should be featured. For example, if the primary audience for a site is internal (such as members of a RHA or hall council), student leaders may want to feature training materials, downloadable forms, links to Web resources, history, and records. It would be extremely important in this case to make the site as useful and functional as possible without wasting time or cluttering the interface with elaborate multimedia content or designs. To encourage site use, it is helpful not only to mention the existence of the site, but also to demonstrate or otherwise incorporate the site into member training and orientation. Students will return to the site if they feel that it provides worthwhile content or can help them be more effective in their positions.

If primary audiences for RHA Web sites are external (i.e. the residential student body), content such as the purpose or mission of RHA, recent news, upcoming programs, forums, and contact information should be featured prominently. Although pictures, layout, and design become more important when trying to appeal to a mass audience, simplicity and usability are still the most important factors.

No matter how great the design and content of Web pages, having them doesn't accomplish anything unless the intended audiences view them. Promoting Web pages is absolutely critical if RHAs want them to be viewed by student bodies. It is equally important to be sure the content on Web sites makes users want to come back. Polls, interactive content, and fun or clever features may help, but fresh content and valuable information are better long-term draws. While often requiring advertisement themselves, either online or otherwise, Web pages also may serve as key components of overall advertising strategy by enhancing (but not replacing) other efforts.

Advertising

Many campuses may have unique opportunities for advertising through technology, including traditional and new media sources. Most campuses have radio stations that are student run on which student organizations can advertise, often for free. A growing number of campuses also offer campus television channels. Many include message boards on which student organizations can post advertisements or messages. Traditional advertising venues, such as newspapers, often also offer online options.

There are other ways that institutions may provide opportunities for student groups to advertise. Many institutions run campus-wide, online event calendars to which any student organization may submit events for advertisement and listing. Students can then check these calendars for upcoming events. Student union buildings may have screens or televisions which constantly alternate advertisements. RHAs should investigate the options and services that their campuses offer and take full advantage of them. For example, Louisiana State University offers a "PSA Program." This program allows university departments or student organizations to create public service announcements to promote university-related events. Approved PSAs appear on the screensavers of all university public access computers (Louisiana State University, 2004). Other schools may have similar technology available to campus groups. In the absence of programs like this, RHAs or other campus groups may consider creating screensavers to use for advertising in computer labs in residence halls.

RHAs may be able to tap campus resources not available to other student organizations. For example, data pulled from student information or housing management systems may be used to create mass personalized e-mail messages. Each of these systems can export reports (usually in Excel or database format) containing names, e-mail addresses, and other demographic data. The mail merge function of Microsoft Word (2003) or other similar programs can then be used to target and e-mail specific groups of students, such as all residents of the third floor of a certain building or everyone on campus with birthdays for a particular month. By linking other data collected (such as lists of all hall council members or everyone who expressed interest in a certain program) to that pulled from the housing information system, the options for personalization and communication are nearly limitless. As with all technologies, there are important factors that must be considered when sending personalized mass e-mail messages. Like all forms of advertisement, e-mail messages, whether generic or personalized, become less effective if overused. Restraint should be shown in order to avoid alienating those that RHAs are trying to reach. Potentially more seriously there are obvious privacy concerns and potential for abuse involved with sharing housing data with students. Reports pulled for these purposes must be filtered to exclude individuals who have requested that information remain confidential under the federal Family Educational Rights and Privacy Act (FERPA, 1974). Although demographic data may be released under the law, best practice dictates that advisers or other professional personnel confidentially retain the actual report or student data source pulled from information systems. Students may create and submit Word documents with merge fields already inserted. Advisers or technical staff can then simply select the appropriate data source and complete the merge, choosing electronic mail for the output. (One tip – if advisers are sending RHA merged e-mail from their accounts, they need to be sure to temporarily change the "reply-to" address to direct responses to the main RHA e-mail address or appropriate students in order to avoid being swamped with responses.) Setting up personalized e-mailing systems can involve a steep learning curve and require some technical assistance to get them working, but doing so can produce very significant rewards and opportunities. RHAs should work closely and cooperatively with other organizations and housing department to dovetail efforts and utilize all possible advertising resources.

Technology also offers attractive third-party advertising opportunities. Historically it has been difficult to target very specific local populations with Web-based advertising. However, this is changing. For example, users can elect to advertise on The Facebook for a fee of $15 per day using targeted ads only viewable by students on their campus. The administrators of the site claim the ads will be displayed approximately 40,000 times per day, though this will vary based on factors such as the number of campus users (www.thefacebook. com). In the future, fee-based, online advertising may prove both affordable and effective as compared to traditional methods such as posters.

Providing Additional or Improved Services for Residential Students

Advertising, information sharing, and communicating are major functions of information technology. However, technology also offers ways to enhance other RHA functions.

Meetings

RHA meetings are valuable not only as ways of conducting business, but also as ways for individual members to connect and recharge. Although technologies exist to have "virtual meetings" and to otherwise conduct business over computers, they should be used only when meeting in person is impractical, such as when advising groups from a distance. However, other technologies can make meetings more effective or efficient without negatively impacting opportunities for interpersonal interaction. It is becoming common for RHA administrative officers with access to laptop computers to bring them to meetings to take minutes. Although minutes taken "on the fly" should always be reviewed and formatted before distribution, getting even rough drafts of meetings as they occur saves time and also improves the level of accuracy and detail. To further increase the quality of minutes, student leaders can consider attaching data projectors so that entire groups may view first drafts as they are created. It is more likely that mistakes will be caught at the time minutes are taken rather than during the "approval of minutes" on agendas the next week. Projecting minutes also can help members follow discussions and see the way that parliamentary or other meeting procedures operate. Once the meeting minutes are in electronic format, student leaders can consider making them widely available by posting them on Web sites, e-mailing them to Listservs that any residential student or administrator may join, or a combination of those or other means. Publicly posting or distributing minutes keeps members informed and aware of organizations and activities and also makes groups more accountable to constituents.

Assessment and Feedback

Many RHA mission statements mention representing or otherwise serving residential students. In order to serve and advocate for students, it is important to know and understand their needs and opinions. Online tools can gather feedback in a number of ways. Online suggestion forms can gather feedback anonymously from students. Forums and bulletin boards that require registration are less anonymous, but topics can be introduced and discussed lending much greater depth to the feedback or suggestions. Finally, online surveys or polls can provide focused data to guide or support efforts to change campus policies or direct programming efforts. Tools for all of these functions are available, and many are without cost. Students or campus programmers also may be able to create custom applications. RHAs should carefully evaluate specific needs before selecting the best options for them and their students.

Some criteria to take into consideration include cost; flexibility; availability of either online or live support in case of problems; security and verification of users; goals of organizations as they relate to gathering feedback; and ease of use, maintenance, and implementation.

When conducting polls or surveys, analyzing the data properly is a necessary step. Professors or other research experts should review the design and wording of any important surveys prior to administration. Modern statistical packages are user-friendly enough that nearly anyone can run basic statistical analysis. Correctly designing surveys and running stats on the data collected not only gives organizations a clearer idea of what the information collected actually means, it can also add great weight to any presentation to administrators regarding student opinion.

Elections

Conducting open elections with high voter turnout adds legitimacy to representative student organizations. This is often not easy to achieve. Overall participation in student elections declined severely over recent decades from an average range of 26–30% in 1977 to only 11–15% in 1997 (Levine & Cureton, 1998). Elections also present other challenges. Staffing and operating polling places can be time-consuming. Election processes may also be vulnerable to fraud or error. Some institutions have successfully addressed these concerns by moving to online elections. Most election systems begin by sending personalized e-mail messages to each eligible voter with instructions and addresses or links for secure voting Web sites. At secure voting Web sites, students log in using user names and passwords. A list of candidates appears, usually with accompanying biographical data or platforms for each candidate. The results of votes go into secure databases viewable only by those running the election. Results are usually available immediately after the election ends.

Proponents of e-voting claim that "online voting is consistently doubling and tripling voter turnout" when implemented on college campuses (www. collegevote.com/benefits.php). Many institutions use third-party services such as "CollegeVote.com" and "e-lection.com" to run elections. Others write their own code. At Centenary College of Louisiana, the RHA and Student Government Association officers worked together with the campus Webmaster to develop an online voting system usable by both groups. Third-party solutions promise high levels of security and ease of implementation, but involve considerable ongoing costs. Proprietary systems require skilled personnel and more effort upfront, but may be tailored to the specific needs of organizations and may be considerably cheaper over the long term. Either way, RHAs should consider working cooperatively with student governments and other organizations on campus to create benefits of scale and share costs.

Programming

Technologically oriented programs, from "how-to" educational programs to video game tournaments, are very popular among students. As video games are constantly being updated created, and marketed, students are investing a great deal of time and money in this technology. This is indicative of an important trend. Some analysts estimate that the global market for interactive video game software is already as large as the global box office receipts total and is growing faster than other major entertainment industries (Game Developers Association of Australia, 2003). By regularly communicating with students, advisers and RHA members can keep up-to-date with and take advantage of current trends in video gaming on campus. Facilitating community-building programs centered on gaming can have impressive attendance and participation. It may be worthwhile to invest in resources that student leaders can use to provide these programs. Purchasing gaming systems and making these available to student leaders to check out and use for programming can be quite beneficial. Other resources that may be valuable to purchase for student leaders to check out are karaoke machines, audio equipment, and data projectors. Additionally, RHAs may elect to buy the rights to movies from national vendors such as Swank Motion Pictures, Inc. (2005) to create libraries that they can use for both educational and community building programs.

Technology can also be used to enhance existing programs. For example, student leaders may take photos at events to post online or make available for all students to purchase through a number of online vendors. Additionally, providing online resources for finding additional information is quite useful for adding an additional component to an existing educational program. Microsoft PowerPoint (2003) slide shows or other visual aids are easy to create and useful for adding to presentations. Computerized program evaluations administered during events or later online or via e-mail can improve response rates and make compiling assessment data much easier.

Potential Issues Resulting from Computer Use

While technology and the Internet can open up new worlds and opportunities to individuals and organizations, it also can prove harmful if not used appropriately. RHA advisers should keep abreast of potential difficulties that could arise concerning technology. Some have even postulated an "Internet-dependency" that can affect college students and others. While the average person spends 15 minutes per day on the Internet, the average college student spends 100 minutes per day online. According to one study, 9.8% of college students fit the criteria for Internet dependency. These students may spend around 400 minutes per day online, have difficulty interacting with others in person, and allow the Internet to interfere with sleep and academics (Smith, 2001). It is important for advisers to identify and help students address unhealthy behaviors if they begin to interfere with their academic, social, or extracurricular lives.

Generally, RHAs have at least one computer available for members to use. This creates challenges if not managed appropriately. One common problem is the installation or downloading of illegal software and/or music on RHA computers. As most college campuses provide fast and easily accessible Internet access, it is easy to download programs and music. This is often illegal when dealing with copyrighted materials. As machines in RHA offices are generally available to multiple users, it can be nearly impossible to track illegal downloads and software to one person. Therefore, organizations can be liable for illegal materials found on organization computers.

Additionally, security issues can arise in many forms. Most organizations will make their machines accessible by password. There also may be passwords for other technology functions of the organization, such as e-mail, Web site editing, and instant messenger programs. Although there may be guidelines about which students may have access to the passwords, it is difficult to prevent students from sharing passwords with other members or students. For this reason, passwords should be changed often and distributed only to authorized members of the group.

Furthermore, as these machines are not the students' personal computers, they may be more lax with the precautions they take to safeguard computers from various maladies. Viruses are often problematic and can be devastating to organization computers, files, and archives. Advisers should ensure that organization computers have up-to-date virus protection software, in addition to making sure that this software is run regularly and frequently. Universities may often have anti-virus programs available for free to students, faculty, staff, and student organizations. Advisers can check with campus technical staff to see if these services are available to them.

Spyware and adware also can be problems for computers, as many Web sites that students visit can and do install these programs on these machines. Spyware collects and distributes personal information about users or computers while users surf the Web. These programs may render Internet usage extremely slow and frustrating. Adware also tracks Internet usage and uses that information to show ads on computer screens, generally in the form of "pop-ups" (www.netlingo.com/inframes.cfm). Many anti-spyware and anti-adware programs are available that can be downloaded for free. These programs should be run frequently to eliminate all these malicious programs from computers. Examples include Spybot Search and Destroy (www.safer-networking.org/en/index.htm) and Ad-aware (www.safer-networking.org/en/index.htm)

The easiest way to reduce the occurrences of these problems is to develop detailed and thorough guidelines and policies governing the use of organization computers. RHA advisers should work closely with organization leaders to develop these guidelines. Close attention should be paid to passwords, downloads, who checks e-mail, if instant messenger programs are allowed, and who is allowed to use computers. If organizations own laptop computers, policies are necessary that state who is allowed to use laptop computers; if the laptop computers can be checked out; who gets priority for checking out or using the laptop computers; and what constitutes appropriate use.

Recognition

Although traditional methods of recognition are essential tools for advisers, technology provides simple yet effective ways to recognize student leaders. One easy way to do online recognition is through organization Web sites. Posting the names of award winners or others who have done exemplary work on the front pages of high traffic Web sites is a morale booster that brings quick, easy, widespread recognition. Another simple method of recognition is including names of outstanding students in weekly information e-mail messages or other e-mail messages.

Of the Month awards (OTMs) is an award program run by the National Residence Hall Honorary, an affiliate branch of NACURH. OTMs are monthly awards given to students and staff in a variety of categories ranging from RA or executive board member to programs from a number of categories. Students may write up short descriptions of nominees and submit them to each institution's respective NACURH region for consideration. NACURH itself has introduced tools for submitting these award nominations electronically (http://otms.nrhh.org). Many schools also have competitions on the campus level for OTM winners, with student leaders across campus submitting nominations for winners to be selected by campus committee. The campus winners are generally submitted for regional (and state, if applicable) consideration. With the recent developments in OTM submission technology in NACURH, schools can use the national OTM database to collect electronic submissions for their respective schools. Alternatively, some schools have developed online systems that students can use to make OTM nominations. For instance, Virginia Polytechnic Institute and State University's chapter of NRHH allows students to register to write OTMs and submit them online into a database. The selection committee then downloads these submissions to determine the campus winners (http://www.rhf.vt.edu/nrhh). Online submission systems work well because students can easily access systems at any time and can submit award nominations at their own pace. It also allows processes to be paperless, which is usually more convenient for nominators and selection committees.

NACURH also sponsors many awards throughout the year. Member schools may submit bids to have individuals, programs, or organizations considered for these awards. In addition, if students wish to run for positions on regional or national boards in NACURH, they generally must submit bids for consideration in their pursuit of the position of interest. Some RHAs and local NRHH chapters may also require bids of those who wish to run for positions at their respective schools or for award nominations. A bid may consist of, but is not limited to, some combination of the following: a description why the nominee is deserving; letters of intention or recommendation; resumes; pictures and budgets or other supporting documentation. Many NACURH regions have moved to online bidding in an effort to make bids more accessible to member schools and promote a paperless process. This process varies by year and region, but generally requires institutions to submit PDF versions of the completed bid to a member of the regional board by a deadline. The regional board member then posts these bids online so that all schools can access them for review prior to the conference.

These electronic processes provide a number of advantages. They can reduce paper use, provide opportunities to review the information in advance of the conference or meeting, and allow for easier archiving of resources. Electronic bidding also greatly reduces printing costs, which saves money for bidding schools and also levels the playing field so that organizations with access to binding machines, color copiers, and other such equipment do not have an advantage over schools with more limited resources.

Other Resources for Advisers and Students

This chapter gives an overview of the technologies commonly used by RHAs in an effort to coach advisers on ways to help students use technology effectively and to offer some practical suggestions for ways RHAs can more fully utilize information technologies. It is in no way exhaustive, and will certainly become outdated over time. Many resources are available online for advisers and student leaders to gather additional information.

Listservs

Multiple Listservs are available for professionals and students. Each region in NACURH and many state RHA organizations host Listservs to which anyone may subscribe. Additionally, many regions also offer RHA adviser Listservs to keep advisers up-to-date on issues and information about the regions. Many state and regional professional organizations also have Listservs that may be beneficial to advisers or other professionals that work in Residence Life. As lists vary by region, the best way to get connected is to contact the regional or state advisers to determine what listserv opportunities are available to advisers regionally. A quick Web search using a site such as Google (http://www. google.com) or a visit to a portal site such as StudentAffairs.com (http://www. studentaffairs.com/lists) can turn up additional possibilities.

Official NACURH and NRHH Web sites

The NACURH Web site contains information about services offered, history, and other resources. Several valuable tools are linked from the main site.

On the Web site (www.racurh.org), the NACURH forums provide venues to have questions answered and to share ideas with others. Also, the Resources page contains documents such as handbooks and national policy books. It also contains one of the most valuable links on the site. The "School Directory/ Affiliation" link indicates the status of a particular school's affiliation and also provides contact information for schools, advisers, and students from other NACURH-affiliated institutions.

Links to each regional Web site can be found on the NACURH Web site. It is worth reviewing pages associated with other regions. Many of these provide not only region specific information but also a full range of features, links, and information materials. Many regional Web sites will also link to state RHA associations, if applicable.

The Resource File Index (RFI) is a service offered to all NACURH member schools. Annually, each RHA must submit a report to the RFI that describes a program, project, policy implementation, conference, or some other major event that has happened in that respective organization. The reports are then added to the RFI and are catalogued. Any member school can search through these archives online and order reports, taking advantage of the thousands of documents available on nearly any topic related to residence halls. The National Information Center is beginning to make the full text of documents available online, which will allow students immediate access to information and greatly increase the value of this already valuable resource.

National NRHH Web site: NRHH maintains a site separate from NACURH, but it is accessible from a link on the NACURH navigation bar. The NRHH site (www.brhh.org) provides information and documentation concerning all aspects of NRHH. It also includes a link to one of the most useful sites on the Web, the OTM Web site (www.otms.nrhh.org). This site can be used to submit OTMs, but also contains the full text of all the OTMs that have been submitted online. Using the advanced search form, it only takes moments to pull all of the award-winning programs of the past year or more. These reports contain hundreds of ideas examples in all categories. The reports also include contact information for the student leaders or planners involved, so they can be used to network or ask for advice and suggestions.

RHA Web sites

RHA Web sites can provide ideas not only for technological and online initia-tives, but also often include information on programs, organizational structure, meetings, and other related topics (Miller, 2005). When looking for the Web site of an individual institution, an online search engine is usually the fastest way to find it.

Conclusion

Information available through the Internet is broad in scope and continuously changing and being updated. As information technology evolves and changes, advisers need to continue to gather new information, evolve advising methods, and be flexible enough to change with the times. At the same time, the same tried-and-true active listening skills, thought-provoking questions, and sincere interest in student activities that worked before personal computers and the Internet arrived on campuses are still effective even when applied in relation to modern technologies.

References

Ad-Aware. Retrieved January 28, 2005, from http://www.safer-networking. org/en/index.htm

AOL Instant Messenger. Retrieved January 28, 2005 from http://www.aim.com

Blogger. Retrieved January 28, 2005, from http://www.blogger.com

CollegeVote.com. Retrieved January 26, 2005, from http://www.collegevote. com/benefits.php

Copeland, L. (2004, December 28). Click clique: Facebooks's Online College Community [Electronic version]. The Washington Post, p. C01.

E-lection.com. Retrieved January 26, 2005 from http://www.e-lection.com

Facebook, The. Retrieved January 28, 2005 from http://www.thefacebook.com

Family Educational Rights and Privacy Act of 1974 20 U.S.C. § 1232 et seq (1974).

Game Developers Association of Australia. (2003). Game industry fact sheet. Accessed January 25, from http://gdaa.com.au/teachers-forum/Documents/industryfactsheet.pdf

Google. Retrieved January 30, 2005 from http://www.google.com

ICQ. Retrieved January 28, 2005 from http://www.icq.com

Levine, A & Cureton, J.S. (1998). When hope and fear collide: A portrait of today's college student. San Francisco: Jossey-Bass.

LiveJournal. Retrieved January 28, 2005 from http://www.livejournal.com

Louisiana State University. (2004). Public access computer lab PSA program. Retrieved January 19, 2004 from http://appl003.lsu.edu/ocsWeb/palhome.nsf/$Content/PSA%20Program%20Policy

Lynch, P.J. & Horton, S. (2001). Web style guide (Rev. ed.). New Haven, CT: Yale University.

Microsoft MSN. Retrieved January 28, 2005 from http://www.msn.com

Microsoft Corporation. (2003). Microsoft Powerpoint 2003. [Computer software].

Microsoft Corporation. (2003). Microsoft Word 2003. [Computer software].

Miller, M. R. (2005) [Content frequency on RHA Web sites]. Unpublished raw data.

National Association of College and University Residence Halls Web site. Retrieved January 2005, from http://www.nacurh.org/form.

National Residence Hall Honorary OTM Web site. Retrieved January 28, 2005, from http://otms.nrhh.org

Netlingo.com Dictionary of Internet Terms. Retrieved January 15, 2005, from http://www.netlingo.com/inframes.cfm

Skype. Retrieved January 28, 2005, from http://www.skype.com/

Smith, D. (2001, May). One tenth of college students are dependent on internet, research finds. Monitor on psychology, 32 (5). Retrieved January 28, 2005, from http://www.apa.org/monitor/may01/internetdep.html

Spybot Search and Destroy. Retrieved January 28, 2005, from http://www.safer-networking.org/en/index.htm

StudentAffairs.com. Retrieved January16, from http://www.studentaffairs.com

Swank Motion Pictures, Inc. Retrieved January 28, 2005, from http://www.swank.com

Trillian. Retrieved on January 28, 2005 from http://www.trillian.cc

Winston, R.B., Jr., Creamer, D.G., Miller, T.K., Brown, S.J., Carpenter, D.S., Cooper, D.L., et al. (2001). The professional student affairs administrator: Educator, leader, and manager. New York: Brunner-Routledge.

Virginia Polytechnic Institute and State University. National Residence Hall Honorary. Retrieved January 20, 2005, from http://www.rhf.vt.edu/nrhh

Vogelstein, F. (2004, November 29). Are these guys for real? [Electronic version]. Fortune, 150 (11).

Wood, A.F. & Smith, M.J. (2001). Online communication: Linking technology, identity, and culture. Mahwah, NJ: Lawrence Erlbaum Associates, Inc.

Xanga. Retrieved January 28, 2005 from http://www.xanga.com

Yahoo Messenger. Retrieved January 28, 2005 from http://www.yahoo.com

22

Professional Development for RHA Advisers

Valerie S. Averill

The support of the adviser is one of five components critical for a successful and effective residence hall association (Wyatt & Stoner, 1987). "Without a doubt, the most effective means of administrative support is the leadership and commitment provided by the professional staff member serving in the role of adviser to the RHA" (Wyatt & Stoner, 1984, p. 4). The role of the adviser was also one of five areas identified as key to RHA effectiveness in a study by Komives and Tucker (1998). Advisers of student groups owe it to their students and institutions to be current and proficient in the theories and practices which maximize the potential of RHAs and each student member.

Professional development is an ongoing, lifelong process with stages similar to Erickson's stages of human development. "The professional development of student affairs practitioners might be a subset of general human development, related to age as much as to a particular field of employment" (Young, 1987, p. 21).

Professional development is "a planned experience designed to change behavior and result in professional and/or personal growth and improved organizational effectiveness" (Merkle & Artman, 1983, p. 55). Averill and Bradley (1998) define it as "the learning process one pursues in an effort to develop, refine, and master skills and knowledge that will enhance one's job performance," in this case the advising role.

A Review of the Literature

Higher education literature contains many articles on student development, the importance of student involvement in the residential academic community, and the training of successful academic advisers. The literature on student personnel and higher education gives little insight, however, into the collective knowledge and skills necessary to be effective and successful RHA advisers. Also, the literature does not provide direction for the professional development of student group advisers.

Professional organizations have identified standards of practice and professional competence for student housing departments and their staff. The American College Personnel Association (ACPA, 1993), the Association of College and University Housing Officers-International (ACUHO-I, 1991), and the Council for the Advancement of Standards for Student Services/Development Programs (CAS, 1986) have all published standards and guidelines. These documents provide valuable information against which to evaluate departmental activities, functions, and quality of service. They also provide information on the types and levels of education and experience recommended for various staff positions. For example, ACUHO-I Standards (1991) include a functional area called Education/Programming, which states "the residential learning community provides educational opportunities for students and other members of the campus community. Staff involvement in educational opportunities ensures that learning experiences are oriented toward promoting maturity and are grounded in human/student development theory and research" (p. 7). The subsections of Educational Opportunities and Staff Activities include examples of the types of activities and experiences that should be available to students and the activities and functions expected of staff.

Chief housing officers were surveyed to rank order lists of competencies gleaned from the literature that they believe to be important in young professionals (Dunkel & Schreiber, 1992; Ostroth, 1981). These surveys provide a valuable inventory of skills upon which to focus training efforts, including interpersonal communication and leadership; the ability to work cooperatively and effectively with a wide range of individuals; and the ability to assess student needs and interests. Although 78.2% of the respondents in Ostroth's (1981) survey ranked the ability to advise groups as an important competency, a prescription for the training and development of RHA advisers is nowhere to be found.

The Role of the Adviser

"The role of the adviser can be an integral element in the success of the student organization and in ensuring that the educational potential of the extra-curriculum is realized" (McKaig & Policello, 1984, p. 45). Adviser roles are addressed by several authors (Averill, 1993; Boersig & Wallington, 1998) and generally fall into the categories of educator/trainer; historian/source of continuity; fiscal agent; group development facilitator/conflict mediator; liaison and resource person; and counselor and confidant. Komives and Tucker (1993) write that successful advisers are professional educators; understand how to work with volunteers; are flexible and have high tolerance for ambiguity; are highly engaged; develop talent; and possess multiple skills, beliefs, and values. Mentors, supervisors, teachers, leaders, and followers are roles assigned to today's advisers, according to Dunkel and Schuh (1997).

Dunkel and Porter (1998) report that RHA advisers and presidents agree that the five most important adviser responsibilities are meeting with the executive board, interpreting policy, attending meetings, serving as an information resource person, and motivating students. In addition, Cuyjet (1996) asserts that "as advisers to student organizations, their members, and their leaders, student affairs educators need to be competent programmers, and they need to be able to effectively transfer these abilities to students who come to them for advice and mentoring" (p. 387).

Certainly many of the skills identified by professional associations and affirmed by the studies of Dunkel and Schreiber (1992) and Ostroth (1981) are important to the successful fulfillment of the above-mentioned advising roles and responsibilities. In addition, Cuyjet (1996) believes that "it is critical to focus on the development of the relationship between advisers and groups in order to maximize their effective interaction.... Formal training for advisers is an excellent medium for building these relationships. Such a program provides an opportunity for the campus activities office or the dean of student's office to provide tangible support for organizational well-being" (p. 408). To successfully fill these diverse responsibilities, ongoing professional development and training for the adviser is essential.

Purposeful and Intentional Development

Dunkel and Schreiber (1992) suggest a formal plan of professional development be created. Despite the attempt to formalize this concept, for many student personnel professionals, the plan is usually hit or miss. Little thought goes into decisions concerning how much money to spend and where to focus attention. Many young professionals rely primarily on training given during their orientations or through departmental staff development sessions.

The first step in designing a formal adviser professional development plan is self-assessment to determine strengths and weaknesses. How current is the adviser's knowledge of student and group development? Is the adviser aware of legal issues that affect student groups and advisers? Whether an adviser is in the first year of advising or the tenth, a critical self-review of knowledge and skills is necessary in order to create an appropriate and effective professional development plan.

DeCoster and Brown (1991) suggest that the "potential curriculum for student affairs staff development" consists of facilitating interaction with colleagues and associates, developing functional skills and specific competencies, promoting self-understanding and self-actualization, exposure to innovative programs, providing opportunities for professional renewal, and conveying theoretical and philosophical knowledge (p. 568). Dannells (1994) categorizes professional development into conventional and non-conventional activities. Conventional activities include taking and/or teaching graduate courses, reading scholarly publications and conducting research, joining professional associations and association involvement, and attending state, regional and national conferences.

Professional Associations

Four key objectives of professional associations are "to advance understanding, recognition, and knowledge in the field; to develop and promulgate standards for a professional practice; to serve the public interest; and to provide professionals with a peer group that promotes a sense of unity" (Nuss, 1993, p. 365). Many housing and residential life professionals rely on involvement in one or more professional organizations to meet ongoing professional development needs. According to a 1993 study, 354 of the 905 respondents (39.12%) cite professional growth opportunities as the single most important factor that causes them to affiliate with ACUHO-I (Moser, 1993). This study also reports that 342 of 926 respondents (36.93%) identify the opportunity for professional networking as the leading reason for continued affiliation with ACUHO-I (Moser, 1993).

Several organizations cater to the needs of higher education professionals. A brief description of four major organizations related to housing and residence life is provided in Appendix 3. In addition, Bradley (1993) identifies five other organizations which serve certain groups or interests in higher education, including the National Association for Campus Activities (NACA); BACCHUS (Boost Alcohol Consciousness Concerning the Health of the University Students); GAMMA (Greeks Advocating the Mature Management of Alcohol) Peer Education Network; the National Association for Equal Opportunity (NAFEO); and the National Association for Women in Education (NAWE).

Student Associations

Advisers have attended state, regional, and national RHA conferences for decades. Typically, RHAs or housing departments pay for advisers to accompany students to conferences. Some used to joke that this was chauffer duty or delegated the conference to other staff persons to "share the experience." Times have changed, and serious adviser development programs are now on student conference program agendas! Now advisers can serve their RHAs and themselves by attending these conferences.

The National Association of College and University Residence Halls, Inc., (NACURH) and its regional affiliates recognize the essential nature of RHA advisers and have taken steps to provide adviser training and development at conferences. ART curriculum is presented annually at NACURH national conferences and at many regional affiliate conferences. The NACURH annual national conference provides an adviser program track featuring professional staff facilitators from across the country. The adviser program track is specifically designed to foster communication on advising issues, current topics related to advising, and professional development. The NACURH national conference periodically hires professional consultants to provide additional adviser training and development. In 2004, "The Adviser Is In" clinic debuted, inviting advisers to drop in and have informal chats on advising challenges and experiences.

Creative Strategies for Professional Development

It is easy for advisers to chart a professional development course when money is not an obstacle. The ability to attend conferences sponsored by the above-mentioned associations and to order the latest scholarly books at will would go a long way toward fulfilling adviser professional development. However, many advisers find themselves challenged when the need or desire to pursue professional development conflicts with the financial resources available. Housing and residence life departments take a variety of different approaches to the ongoing training and development of staff. Financial restraints often limit the number of staff members who attend conferences as well as whether those conferences are national, regional, or statewide gatherings. Some departments create their own series of training workshops, either using their own staff or hiring consultants, in order to provide information on topics they deem important to their entire department. Other departments make sure in-house libraries contain the latest scholarly works on the profession so that staff may be current in the knowledge and use of various theories and practices.

In addition to, or regardless of, the number and types of professional development opportunities provided by departments, meaningful development is limited only by creativity and time. With the growth of the Internet, access to information is only a click away. The following list of activities, though not exhaustive, is offered as a springboard for developing professional development ideas:

1. Subscribe to a NACURH regional RHA adviser listserv or one of the many listservs that facilitate communication with colleagues around the country.
2. Take an online course through ACUHO-I.
3. Spend a day in the RHA office. Encourage members to ask you "why" more often.
4. Surf the Internet for online journal articles on advising and current student trends.
5. Research one aspect of the advising role and write an article for publication.
6. Become ART certified. If already certified, offer to be an ART presenter. Even if not yet certified, if you have mastered one or two session topics, offer to present a topic to a neighboring institution as an in-service for their staff.
7. Offer to present an article or book review at each staff meeting. One learns best what one teaches, and everyone benefits from this type of professional development!
8. Offer to be a guest speaker for student organizations on campus. Offer to present on topics on which you are an expert as well as those which cause you to acquire new knowledge and skills.
9. Acquire syllabi from student personnel graduate courses and read the assigned books and articles.
10. Attend free teleconferences.
11. If other departments on campus subscribe to publications that carry articles related to advising, make arrangements to read them. (NACA's The Programmer is an excellent example.) Mutually share materials from your department in exchange!
12. Volunteer to teach a class on campus and become a student of student behavior.
13. Create a support network and learning group by having a regularly scheduled "brown bag" lunches with colleagues who also advise student groups in your department and/or on your campus.

14. Offer to present a professional development session on advising student groups to the residence life department or student affairs division.
15. Work with your RHA and NRHH to plan a leadership development retreat.
16. If no-cost course hours are part of your benefits package, enroll in a student personnel graduate class. If that program is not offered, choose a related class in the Leadership or Business curriculum or another class of interest.
17. Create a file of advising articles and resources. Soon you'll create a personal library of helpful information to use and to share.

Conclusion

Areas for professional development and training were identified based on the key roles and responsibilities of advisers as well as skills and competencies identified as important for housing professionals. Many of the advising skills mentioned in this chapter are taught in graduate programs, but not usually in the context of advising student organizations. For advisers who graduated even a few years ago, a whole new body of research and knowledge is being taught today.

By attending national and regional conferences and/or being involved in professional associations, RHA advisers can learn from and network with advising colleagues and professionals on the cutting edge. While conference attendance costs money, meaningful involvement can sometimes be acquired only through the cost of membership. Regardless of the opportunities to attend conferences, investment in professional development should not end there. Just as a successful recipe requires multiple ingredients, a meaningful plan of professional development incorporates many strategies including the effective yet low cost or free ideas for development listed above.

Advisers must take responsibility for their own training and development. Before advisers can make good use of these resources, they should self-assess their advising skills and strengths to determine areas in need of attention. The Adviser Inventory and Professional Development Plan at the end of the chapter are designed to help advisers self-identify training needs. Advisers owe planning for professional development to themselves, to the profession, and to the students.

References

American College Personnel Association. (1993). *Statement of ethical prin-*

ciples and standards. Washington, DC: Author.

American College Personnel Association. (1996). *Members resource directory.* Washington, DC: Author.

Association of College and University Housing Officers-International. (1991). *Ethical principles and standards for college and university student housing professionals.* Columbus, OH: Author.

Averill, V., & Bradley, P. (1998). Professional development for RHA advisers. In N.W. Dunkel & C.L. Spencer (Eds.), *Advice for advisers: The development of an effective residence hall association* (pp. 216–225). Columbus, OH: ACUHO-I.

Averill, V. (1993). Responsibilities of an RHA adviser. In N.W. Dunkel & C.L. Spencer (Eds.), *Advice for advisers: The development of an effective residence hall association* (pp. 20–26). Columbus, OH: ACUHO-I.

Boersig, P., & Wallington, E. (1998). The first advising position. In N.W. Dunkel & C.L. Spencer (Eds.), *Advice for advisers: The development of an effective residence association* (pp. 10–23). Columbus, OH: ACUHO-I.

Bradley, P. (1993). Professional development for advisers. In N.W. Dunkel & C.L. Spencer (Eds.), *Advice for advisers: The development of an effective residence association* (pp. 198–207). Columbus, OH: ACUHO-I.

Council for the Advancement of Standards for Student Services/Development Programs. (1986). *CAS standards and guidelines for student services/development programs.* Washington, DC: Author.

Cuyjet, M. J. (1996). Program development and group advising. In S.R. Komives & D.B. Woodard, Jr. (Eds.), *Student services: a handbook for the profession* (3rd ed., pp. 397–414). San Francisco: Jossey-Bass.

Dannells, M. (1994, October). Professional development: *Taking the initiative to improve our practice.* Speech to the Kansas Student Personnel Conference, McPherson, KS.

DeCoster, D. A., & Brown, S. S. (1991). Staff development: personal and professional education. In T.K. Miller, R. B. Winston and Associates (Eds.), *Administration and leadership in student affairs: Actualizing student development in higher education* (2nd edition, pp 563–613). Muncie, IN: Accelerated Development, Inc.

Dunkel, N.W., & Porter, D. (1998). Residence hall association adviser responsibilities. *The Journal of College and University Student Housing, 27*(2), 15–19.

Dunkel, N.W., & Schreiber, P.J. (1992). Competency development of housing professionals. *Journal of College and University Student Housing, 22*(2), 19–23.

Dunkel, N.W., & Schuh, J.H. (1998). *Advising student groups and organizations.* San Francisco: Jossey-Bass.

Komives, S., & Tucker, G. (1998). Successful residence hall government: Themes from a national study of select hall government structures. In N.W. Dunkel & C.L. Spencer (Eds.), *Advice for advisers: The development of an effective residence hall association* (pp. 35–50). Columbus, OH: ACUHO-I.

McKaig, R., & Policello, S. (1984). Group advising – defined, described, and examined. In J. H. Schuh (Ed.), *A handbook for student group advisors* (pp.45–70). Alexandria, VA: American College Personnel Association.

Merkle, H.B., & Artman, R.B. (1983). Staff development: A systematic process for student affairs leaders. *NASPA Journal.* 21(1), 55–63.

Moser, R. (1993). *ACUHO-I member satisfaction and needs assessment.* Columbus, OH: ACUHO-I Members Needs and Services Tasks Force.

National Association of Student Personnel Administrators. (1998). *Member handbook.* Washington, DC: Author.

Nuss, E. M. (1993). The role of professional association. In M. J. Barr (Ed.), *The handbook of student affairs administration* (pp. 364–377). San Francisco: Jossey-Bass.

Ostroth, D. D. (1981). Selecting competent residence hall staff. In G. S. Blimling & J. H. Schuh (Eds.), *Increasing the educational role of residence halls* (pp. 65–80). New Directions for Student Services, No. 13. San Francisco: Jossey-Bass.

Wyatt, K., & Stoner, K. (1987). A model of professional education. In L.V. Moore & R. B. Young (Eds.), *Expanding opportunities for professional education* (pp. 19–25). New Directions for Student Services, No. 37. San Francisco: Jossey-Bass.

Young, R. B. (1987). A model of professional education. In L. V. Moore & R. B. Young (eds.), *Expanding opportunities for professional education* (pp. 19–25). New Directions for Student Services, No. 37. San Francisco: Jossey-Bass.

Appendix 1: Adviser Inventory and Professional Development Plan

Successful professional development is the result of an intentional plan. Advisers are encouraged to take this opportunity to reflect on their strengths and areas in need of improvement regarding advising responsibilities and to make a plan to expand and enhance their knowledge and skills.

Experience Assessment and Reflection

1) I have been a student group adviser for: _____ (years and/or months).

2) I have served as adviser for the following types of groups:

3) I enjoy these aspects of being an advising:

4) I am challenged by these aspects of advising:

Skills Assessment

5) I know the following skills, theories, and concepts are important to successful advisers:

6) I believe I am proficient in the following areas, and I know this because:

7) I need to improve my skills and knowledge in these areas:

Development Plan

A. Development Area:
   Strategies for Improvement:
   Time Frame and Evaluation:

B. Development Area::
   Strategies for Improvement:
   Time Frame and Evaluation:

C. Development Area:
   Strategies for Improvement:
   Time Frame and Evaluation:

D. Development Area:
   Strategies for Improvement:
   Time Frame and Evaluation:

Appendix 2: Bibliography

Advising

Dunkel, N.W., & Schuh, J. H. (1998). *Advising student groups and organizations.* San Francisco: Jossey-Bass.

Dunkel, N.W., & Spencer, C. L. (1998). *Advice for advisers: The development of an effective residence hall association.* Columbus, OH: ACUHO-I.

Schuh, J. H. (Ed). (1987). *A handbook for student group advisers.* Alexandria, VA: ACPA.

Housing Operations

Schroeder, C. C., & Mable, P., (Eds.). (1994). *Realizing the educational potential of residence halls.* San Francisco: Jossey-Bass.

Winston, R.B., Jr., & Anchors, S., (Eds.). (1993). *Student housing and resident life.* San Francisco: Jossey-Bass.

Student Personnel and Higher Education

Astin, A. W. (1993). *What matters in college: Four critical years revisited.* San Francisco: Jossey-Bass.

Barr, M. J. (Ed.). (1988). *Student services and the law.* San Francisco: Jossey-Bass.

Chickering, A.W., & Reisser, L. (1993). *Education and identity.* San Francisco: Jossey-Bass.

Komives, S. R., & Woodard, D.B., Jr. (Eds.). (1996). *Student services: A handbook for the profession* (3rd ed.). San Francisco: Jossey-Bass.

Pascarella, E.T. & Terenzini, P.T. (1991). *How college affects students.* San Francisco: Jossey-Bass.

Appendix 3: Professional Organizations Affiliated with Housing

- **American College Personnel Association (ACPA)**
  Mission: To provide professional programs and services for educators who are committed to the overall development of students in post-secondary education (ACPA, 1996).

  Contact: American College Personnel Association
  E-Mail: info@acpa.nche.edu   Web Site: http://www.acpa.nche.edu

- **Association of College and University Housing Officers-International (ACUHO-I)**

  Mission: The Association of College and University Housing Officers-Internation (ACUHO-I) is the preeminent professional association dedicated to suporting and promoting the collegiate residential experience by:
  - Creating value through services, information, and collegial relationships that are indispensable to its members; and
  - Continually changing and adapting in ways that assist members in meeting the needs of dynamic campus environments.

  We do this with the constant purpose of making a postive difference in the lives of memeners and those they serve.

  Contact: ACUHO-I   Web Site: http://www.acuho-i.org

- **National Association of College and University Residence Halls, Inc.**

  (NACURH). NACURH is the largest student-run, tax exempt organization in the country.

  Vision: The National Association of College and University Residence Halls, Incorporated, recognizes living on campus as an integral part of the college experience, and therefore strives to be the organization of choice for residence hall leaders by providing comprehensive resources for college and university students seeking to create the ultimate residence hall environment and experience.

  Mission: NACURH is the leading national organization advocating for the interests and welfare of residence hall students, while also providing opportunities for their personal growth and development. It is an organization of students committed to developing leadership, honoring diversity, recognizing achievement, stimulating engagement and involvement among students who reside in college and university residence halls. Through its regional and national programs and services, it provides leadership opportunities for students, shares resources about residence hall programs and best practices, and coordinates its activities with appropriate professional associations and commercial partners.

  NACURH National Board of Directors are students, and most terms of office expire each May; therefore inquires should be made to the National Adviser.

  Contact: Valerie S. Averill   E-Mail: averill@reserv.usf.edu
  Web Site: http://www.nacurh.org

- **National Association of Student Personnel Administrators (NASPA)**

  Mission: To serve student affairs administrators who bring an institution perspective to work with students in higher education (NASPA, 1998).

  Contact: NASPA

  E-Mail: office@naspa.org   Website: http://naspa.org

About the Authors

About the Editors

NORBERT W. DUNKEL is the Director of Housing and Residence Education at the University of Florida in Gainesville. He has held various administrative positions at the University of Florida, South Dakota State University, and the University of Northern Iowa. He cofounded the Association of College and University Housing Officers – International (ACUHO-I) National Housing Training Institute and served as its codirector from 1990 – 2000. Norb currently serves on the ACUHO-I Executive Board as Vice President.

Norb has authored over 40 articles and chapters, and served as an associate editor for The College Student Affairs Journal and as editor of The Journal of College and University Student Housing.

Norb has edited or authored nine books and monographs including co-editing with Beth McCuskey the book, Foundations: Strategies for the Future of Collegiate Housing, in 2006, and co-authoring with Jon Coleman in 2004 the book, 50 Years of Residence Hall Leadership: NACURH, Inc. Norb also co-edited a monograph in 2003 with Jim Grimm, Campus Housing Construction.

Norb received the ACUHO-I Presidential Service Award in 2005. In 2004, he received the NACURH Ken Stoner Distinguished Service Award and the 2004 James C. Grimm ACUHO-I Leadership and Service Award.

CINDY SPENCER is the Director of Residence Life and Education at the University of North Dakota. She has worked in housing and residence life positions at the University of Texas- San Antonio, the University of Nebraska-Kearney, Ball State University, the University of Tennessee, the University of Georgia, and Western Kentucky University. Cindy has served as Chair of the ACUHO-I Internship Committee. She served on the GLACUHO and SWACUHO Executive Boards and on a wide range of committees within ACUHO-I, GLACUHO, SEAHO, and SACSA. She served as co-editor on the first and second editions of Advice for Advisers: The Development of an Effective Residence Hall Association.

Cindy has served as an adviser to student organizations for the past 22years. She currently serves as the adviser to the Association of Residence Policy Board at the University of North Dakota. She served as the founding adviser for the Tennessee Association of College and University Residence Halls (TACURH). Cindy has advised the NRHH National office and two conference staffs. Cindy was inducted into the SAACURH Adviser Hall of Fame in 1992. As an adviser, she was the SAACURH recipient in 1993 of the Daniel Hallenbeck Award for Career Service. Cindy was inducted into the Association of Alumni and Friends of NACURH in 1996. She received the Indiana Residence Hall Association Advisor of the year award in 1997. Cindy served as the NACURH Conference Resource Consultant from 1995-2001. She received the Stoner Distinguished Service Award from NACURH in 2001. In 2005, Cindy was the MACURH recipient of the Daniel Hallenbeck Award for Career Service.

Chapter 1: First-Year Advising Challenges

KEVIN "KD" LINKOUS is the assistant director for academic and developmental services as well as residence hall association adviser for the department of residential life at Louisiana State University. He has been advising residence-hall governments for nine years at various institutions in the southeast (Radford University, Western Carolina University, and Appalachian State University). He researched and created the concept of the Master ART series of adviser training while helping to coordinate the Adviser Recognition and Training (ART) Institute for the SAACURH region from 2000-2004, and continues to coordinate ART Institute programs for the annual NACURH conferences. He is pursuing a doctoral degree in higher education with a concentration in student affairs at Louisiana State University and is planning to focus on the various aspects of student leadership and effective advising methods.

Chapter 2: The Responsibilities of Advising

ALLAN BLATTNER is the associate director of staff and student development at the University of North Carolina – Charlotte department of housing. He received a Masters degree in higher education and student affairs at the University of Vermont. He has served as an RHA advisor on four campuses and as the co-adviser to the 2002 NCARH Host Committee. He is a member of the Association of Alumni and Friends of NACURH and served as NACURH national chairperson in 1989.

CASEY TULLOS is assistant director of staff and student programs at the University of North Carolina - Charlotte department of housing. She received a Masters degree in education from the University of Georgia in 1997. While working as a residence coordinator, she volunteered to co-advise the Resident Students Association and has been working with the organization for the past eight years.

Chapter 3: Training Advisers

JULIE MCMAHON is the assistant director of housing for residence education at the University of Florida. Her undergraduate degree is in health fitness and promotion from Central Michigan University. She earned a master's degree in counseling, guidance, and educational leadership from Murray State University (KY). She has been a certified ARTist since 1999 and a Master ARTist since 2004. McMahon was awarded the NACURH Hallenbeck award in 2005, and is a member of the A.A.F.N.

SEAN J. PIERCE is assistant director of housing and residential life for the Harriet L. Wilkes Honors College of Florida Atlantic University. His undergraduate degree is in mass communications with concentrations in writing and production for television and film. His master's degree is in interdisciplinary studies with concentrations in curriculum development and psychology. Both degrees were earned at Frostburg State University (MD). Pierce has been a certified ARTist since 2002 and a Master ARTist since 2004. He is currently serving as the SAACURH regional advosor (2006).

Chapter 4: Choosing An Advising Style

MATHEW R. CHETNIK is associate director of residence life at Salem State College in Salem, Massachusetts. He has a Masters degree in student development with developmental emphasis from Appalachian State University in North Carolina and has served as the NEACURH Regional Adviser since 1997.

KATHLEEN M. NEVILLE is director of residence life at Salem State College in Salem, Massachusetts. She has a Masters degree in student development and higher education from the University of Maine and served as the NACURH Conference Resource Consultant from 2001-2004.

Chapter 5: Residence Government Effectiveness

GARDINER TUCKER is director of residential life life at the University of Colorado at Boulder. He received a doctorate of philosophy degree from the University of Maryland and has previously worked as a faculty member in the Higher Education and Student Affairs Leadership doctoral program at the University of Northern Colorado.

Chapter 6: Traditional and Alternative Organizational Models for RHAs

PHYLLIS MCCLUSKEY-TITUS is associate professor and coordinator of the college student personnel administration Master's degree program at Illinois State University. Prior to joining the faculty, she held positions in housing and residence life at Florida State University, Indiana University of Pennsylvania, Syracuse University, and Western Illinois University. She holds an Ed.D. in higher education administration from Florida State University, an M.S. degree in college student personnel from Western Illinois University, and a B.A. in history from Western Illinois University.

JANET W. PATERSON is Dean of Students at Illinois State University. Previously she was associate director of student life at Illinois State University; assistant director of student activities, adjunct assistant professor of educational administration, training specialist in human resources, and student activities adviser at Texas A & M University; Central Office Manager of the Association for Student Judicial Affairs; and resident director and conference coordinator at the University of Denver. She holds a Ph.D. in education administration from Texas A & M, an M.S. degree in college student personnel administration from Indiana University, and a B.A. in psychology and sociology from Millikin University (IL).

Chapter 7: Advising Student Organizations in Residential Learning Communities

DIANE "DP" PORTER is the assistant director of housing for academic initiatives at the University of Florida. She has advised students in residence hall associations on the hall, campus, and state levels, and is the director of the Adviser Recognition and Training (ART) certification program. She holds a Ph.D. in higher education administration from the University of Florida, an Ed.S. degree in curriculum and instruction, an M.A. degree in K–12 reading, and a B.S. degree in middle school education, all from Appalachian State University (NC).

She would like to thank the following people for their collaboration and for contributing time and materials to this chapter: Terra Peckskamp, Syracuse University; Denise Gowin and the Office of Residential Programs and Services, Indiana University-Bloomington; John Purdie and Heather Kind-Keppel, University of Missouri-Columbia.

Chapter 8: Motivating and Recognizing Student Leaders and Student Organizations

JACQUE BOLLINGER is assistant director of residence life - staffing at the University of Wisconsin Oshkosh. She has worked professionally in residence life and housing for 20 years. Some of her accomplishments include former GLACURH

Regional Adviser, past president of the Wisconsin College Personnel Association (WCPA), and proud graduate of the National Housing Training Institute (NHTI).

Chapter 9: Understanding Today's Students

GARY KIMBLE is associate director of residence life at The University of Southern Mississippi. He has been active in housing and residence life for 27 years. During that time he has served as adviser to hall governments, residence hall associations and campus organizations.

LAKECIA A. JOHNSON-HARRIS is assistant director of residence life at The University of Southern Mississippi. Currently, she serves as adviser for the Rho Eta Alpha chapter of NRHH and as adviser for Alpha Kappa Alpha Sorority, Inc.

Chapter 10: Current Issues

PAULA BLAND is assistant director for residence life at the University of Colorado at Boulder. She has extensive experience working with residence hall student leaders and has advised many student organizations. She serves as the conference resource consultant on the National Board for the National Association of College and University Residence Halls, Inc.

Chapter 11: Group Dynamics, Theory, and Evolution

TONY W. CAWTHON is professor of counselor education and student affairs at Clemson University. He has authored more than thirty publications, served as co-editor of *New Directions for Student Services* #108, and has been actively involved in SACSA, ACPA, and ACUHO-I. He is currently editor of *The Journal of College and University Student Housing*.

D'AUN GREEN is associate director of residence life at Texas Tech University. She has worked in university housing for almost twenty years. She has been actively involved in ACUHO-I and served as conference program chair for the 2004 Annual ACUHO-I Conference.

Chapter 12: The Money Management of Residence Hall Associations

MARK HUDSON is director of university housing and dining services at Eastern Illinois University. He is currently an adviser to EIU's residence hall association and has extensive advising experience with local RHAs, NRHH chapters, and NACURH regionally affiliated groups and conferences as well as NACURH national conferences and offices. Hudson has been recognized for his commitment to developing student leaders with numerous awards including NACURH's Kenneth Stoner Lifetime Achievement Award.

JODY STONE is assistant director of housing for residence life at Eastern Illinois University. He began his advising experience with student organizations in 1993. He has advised the Illinois Residence Hall Association and National Residence Hall Honorary and currently serves as adviser to Eastern Illinois University's Residence Hall Association. Stone received his Adviser Recognition Training Certification (ART) in 2003 and was recognized with GLACURH's Hallenbeck Adviser of the Year Award in 2003.

DONNA TURNER HUDSON is a mediator, trainer, and consultant in the field of conflict management. Previously, she worked with student leaders in both residence life and student organizations positions. She continues to offer training and conflict management services to organizations and agencies, including university housing departments. She was inducted as an honorary member of the National Residence Hall Honorary at the University of North Dakota.

The authors would like to express appreciation to Eastern Illinois University graduate student Tony Zucca for his invaluable assistance in the compilation of the data from the survey that proved to be a significant resource for this chapter.

Chapter 13: Corporate Fundraising

HOWIE DUMHART began his career in student development as a Community Adviser, (CA commonly RA) at Trenton State College (TSC) in 1975 where he graduated with a history education degree in 1977. He returned to TSC for a graduate degree in Counseling and Higher Education leaving the campus after 1980 to form the first of his companies to serve the higher education market. In 1981, Campus Fund Raisers (CFR) was created to provide fundraising programs to RHA groups. Howie was co-owner of this company until 2000 when CFR merged with On Campus Marketing to form OCME where he served as partial owner and a board member. Student Advantage acquired OCME in 2001. Student Advantage sold the company to Alloy, Inc. in 2003 and continues serves the college market as OCM. Howie left the company in October 2004 to pursue more family time and to determine new directions. He is married to Edye Hartmann Dumhart and has two children, Justin and Danelle. The Dumharts reside in Pennington, New Jersey, which is located 10 minutes from his collegiate educational and business roots at TSC, now The College of New Jersey.

Chapter 14: Legal Issues

JON COLEMAN is a doctoral student at the University of Georgia studying student affairs administration. He received a Bachelor of Arts degree and Juris Doctorate (Law) from the University of Florida and a Master's of Science in education from Southern Illinois University in Carbondale. He has advised residence hall organizations for more than eight years and has been involved with both NACURH and the Adviser Recognition and Training Institute (ART).

Chapter 15: Transportation

REBECCA LONEY is the Assistant Direcor for Leadership and Community Development at North Dakota State University. Previously, she was a hall coordinator at the University of Northern Iowa and through her roles, served as a conference bid teamleader, THA and NRHH Adviser. She received her B.S. in Athletic Training from the University of North Dakota and her M.S. in College Student Personnel from Western Illinois University.

KATHLEEN LONEY is the director of Youth Ministry for the Diocese of Fargo and continues to help groups large and small in their travel planning. She has worked with student groups for more than twenty years and spent twelve of those years as a travel agent specializing in group travel.

Chapter 16: Advising Conference Delegations

CINDY SPENCER is director of residence life and education at the University of North Dakota. She has worked in housing for more than 20 years. She has advised campus RHA and NRRH chapters, served as regional adviser, and served as the NACURH Conference Resource Consultant for seven years. She was co-editor of the past two editions of *Advice for Advisers*. Cindy has been actively involved in SEAHO, GLACUHO, UMR, and ACUHO-I throughout her housing career.

Chapter 17: Programming

GREGORY S. BLOCK is associate director of housing and residential life at New Mexico State University. He is a member of the ACUHO-I *Journal* Board, serves on the Publications Committee for ACUHO-I, and recently served on the executive board for the Association of Inter-Mountain Housing Officers. Block has attended a large number of national and regional student leadership conferences. He is completing his doctoral studies at NMSU.

Chapter 18: Transitioning of Officers

RIC BAKER is coordinator of residence education at the University of South Florida as well as a doctoral student pursuing an Ed.D. in educational leadership. He earned a Bachelor of Arts in American history from the University at Albany and a Master of Science in student personnel administration from Buffalo State College. He has advised residence hall associations for six years in both the PACURH and SAACURH regions.

Chapter 19: Assessment and Leadership: A Partnership of Intentionality

STEPHEN ST. ONGE is vice president for student services at Clinton Community College in Plattsburgh, New York. He worked at Syracuse University in residence life while earning a doctorate in higher education administration. He received his Master's degree in college student personnel from Bowling Green State University in Ohio and his Bachelors of Science from the University of Vermont. He serves as associate editor of the *Journal of College and University Student Housing* and as an adjunct faculty member in the Department of Counselor Education at Plattsburgh State University, and has served at the Department of HIgher Education at Syracuse University.

DAVID ROSCH serves as assistant director for leadership in the office of residence life at Syracuse University. He has advised various leadership organizations within residence life for eight years and is enrolled in the higher education doctoral program at Syracuse University.

ERIC M. NESTOR is coordinator for assessment, operations, and technology in the office of residence life at Syracuse University in New York and is currently a doctoral student in Syracuse University's School of Education. Eric received his master's degree in counseling and college student personnel and his bachelor's degree in history from Shippensburg University of Pennsylvania.

Chapter 20: Relationships with Other Campus Organizations

JEFF NOVAK is associate director of housing and residence life at the University of Central Florida. He is active in ACUHO-I, SEAHO, and Florida Housing Officers. Previously, he worked at East Carolina University. He is currently pursuing his doctorate in Educational Leadership and earned hios Masters and Bachelors degrees at teh University of Central Florida.

CAROLYN "WAZ" MILLER is director of residence life and assistant vice chancellor at East Carolina University. She is involved with the ACUHO-I STARS College and served as program chair for the ACUHO-I annual conference in 2000. She also served as a regional adviser for two different regions within NACURH.

Chapter 21: Advising in an Information Age: Technology and Advising

As part of his responsibilities directing the Duke MBA - Global Executive program, MARK MILLER uses technology to advise elected students located on five continents. Prior to coming to Duke University in 2004, Miller served as assistant dean of student life and director of residence life at Centenary College of Louisiana. During his six-year tenure, Centenary attended its first regional conference, founded a NRHH chapter, had two students elected to the NACURH National Board of Directors, and received five national annual awards from NACURH including "School of the Year." He has been recognized by NRHH as national Adviser of the Month and is the 2003 recipient of the national Dan Hallenback Service Award.

CHRISTY MELTON is the assistant director of residence life at Wofford College. Previously, she was a graduate hall director and the graduate adviser to the Virginia Tech Residence Hall Federation and has co-advised various multicultural organizations. While completing her undergraduate degree at Centenary College of Louisiana, she held executive board positions in the campus residence hall association and NRHH and served as regional director of SWACURH as well as founding president of the Louisiana Residence Hall Association. In 2004, Melton was recognized as the Virginia Tech General Adviser of the Year and the Virginia Association of College and University Residence Halls Adviser of the Year.

Chapter 22: Professional Development for RHA Advisers

VALERIE S. AVERILL is assistant director of residence life at the University of South Florida. She is currently the NACURH Inc. national adviser. She earned her Ph.D. from Kansas State University in 1999. Her dissertation is titled *Leadership Practices of RHA Advisers as Indicators of Effective Advising*.